AUTHOR

TITLE   Verbal learning and memory.

SUBJECT No.   153.133 | Pos

Penguin Education

Verbal Learning and Memory

Penguin Modern Psychology Readings

General Editor
B. M. Foss

Advisory Board
P. C. Dodwell
Marie Jahoda
S. G. Lee
W. M. O'Neil
R. L. Reid
Roger Russell
P. E. Vernon
George Westby

Verbal Learning and Memory
Selected Readings

Edited by Leo Postman and Geoffrey Keppel

Penguin Books

Penguin Books Ltd, Harmondsworth
Middlesex, England
Penguin Books Inc, 7110 Ambassador Road
Baltimore, Md. 21207, U. S. A.
Penguin Books Australia Ltd, Ringwood
Victoria, Australia

First published by Penguin Books Ltd. 1969
First published by Penguin Books Inc 1970
Copyright © Leo Postman and Geoffrey Keppel, 1969

Printed in the United States of America by
Kingsport Press, Inc.
Set in Monotype Times

Contents

Part Two Organization in Recall

Part Three Transfer

Introduction

The period since the Second World War, and in particular the last decade, has witnessed a major expansion of research in the field of verbal learning and memory. This rise in activity has been reflected in a steady growth in the volume of research publications. More important, there has been not only a rapid accumulation of factual information but also a drastic re-evaluation of traditional theoretical assumptions, conventional experimental procedures, and methods of analysis. If the field of verbal learning is not undergoing a revolution, it is certainly in a phase of accelerated evolution.

Historically, research on verbal learning and memory is deeply rooted in the tradition of associationism. This tradition can be traced directly to the first systematic experiments on rote learning by Hermann Ebbinghaus which placed central emphasis on the acquisition and retention of serial asociations. The experimental procedures and methods of analysis introduced by Ebbinghaus laid down the basic guide-lines for the subsequent course of the discipline: the systematic investigation of the conditions governing the establishment of associative linkages between discrete verbal units remained the primary concern of his successors. As psychology adopted the methodology and language of behaviourism, the study of verbal learning was integrated into the mainstream of stimulus–response associationism. In contrast to developments in the field of animal learning, however, the main interest of students of verbal learning was in the establishment of empirical laws rather than in the construction of formal theories. It is true that there were important attempts to extend to verbal learning basic principles of behaviour theory, notably those derived from classical conditioning, but the prevailing orientation remained empirical and pragmatic.

The research carried out within this tradition produced a standard methodology of laboratory experimentation, an armamentarium of measures of performance, and a basic framework for the description of the phenomena of learning and retention. The emphasis remained throughout on the systematic exploration of functional relations. Experimental tasks were ordered along dimensions defined by the requirements placed on the subject; performance in these tasks was studied as a function of the characteristics of the learning materials, the conditions of practice and subject variables. It is clearly impossible to provide even the sketchiest summary of the experimental findings and empirical generalizations which were accumulated in the sixty years or so following the appearance of Ebbinghaus' classical treatise. Some flavour of the organization of the field which emerged out of this research may be conveyed by a brief glance at the table of contents of the textbook by J. A. McGeoch and A. L. Irion which provided a definitive summary of the work on verbal learning and memory as of 1952 (*The Psychology of Human Learning*, Longmans, Green, 1952). The chapter headings which reflect most directly the continuing substantive concerns in the field are the following – intraserial phenomena, the distribution of practice and reminiscence, the role of frequency, transfer of training, retention and forgetting, learning as a function of the material learned and of certain modes of practice and presentation, individual differences and learning. The chapter headings reflect clearly the bent towards the systematic exploration of functional relations and the delimitation of problem areas in terms of classes of experimental observations. There is, to be sure, a considerable amount of theoretical discussion in the book, but much if not most of the work that is reported remains within the definite boundaries laid down by the classical conception of associative learning.

This picture has been changing rapidly. It is difficult to pinpoint with confidence the converging trends which are responsible for the changing complexion of the field. There are certain developments, however, which stand out clearly. One of these has been the impact of advances in psycholinguistic and linguistic theory. Much of the current work focuses on the role of language habits in learning and retention. The influence of associative hierarchies established through linguistic usage on the mastery of new verbal tasks is being explored extensively. A more drastic departure from the tradition is the growing body of work concerned with the influence of grammar on learning.

The adoption by several influential investigators of the language and concepts of information-processing theory is clearly reflected in the current literature. Apart from the introduction of useful new methods of quantitative analysis, this influence is apparent in the types of experimental questions which are being asked and the explanatory principles which are brought to bear on the interpretation of the results. Interest has centred on the conditions limiting the individual's capacity for processing information, the mechanisms by which incoming information is coded and decoded, the characteristics of memory storage systems and the process of retrieval. In some cases, to be sure, there is only a translation of old problems into a new terminology, but in many others the change in conceptual framework has shaped the direction of the research. These influences are most clearly in evidence in research on short-term memory and on free-recall learning.

There has been a continuing trend towards the construction of mathematical models for the description of behavioural data. A substantial proportion of this work has been concerned with the analysis of phenomena of verbal learning and memory. Regardless of the ultimate validity of the various models, very useful products of this approach have been the insistence on precise quantitative formulations of theoretical assumptions and experimental hypotheses, and the development of analytic methods which permit a careful description of the fine grain of the learning process.

There are other trends which are perhaps less tangible but of considerable importance for the development of the discipline. First, investigators of verbal learning and memory have freed themselves increasingly from the constraints imposed by standardized experimental procedures and methods of analysis. For many years the conventional tasks of serial and paired-associate learning by the anticipation method, administered in an essentially uniform fashion, accounted for the large majority of laboratory experiments. These procedures are still in wide use today, but they are used critically and in a far from uniform manner. The experimental arrangements are changed freely in order to obtain data relevant to a particular substantive question; the characteristics of the tasks themselves, and the interplay between procedural variations and performance, are the frequent object of

11

experimental scrutiny. New methods are being added constantly, and today there would be little point in cataloguing a set of standard tasks and procedures. The same is true of the learning materials used in experimental investigations. Nonsense syllables have long since lost their status as the standard verbal units used as a matter of course in the study of a wide variety of problems. It is widely recognized that they should be used only when their special properties are directly relevant to the experimental question, for example, when the interest is in the acquisition of novel response units or in differentiation of items composed of overlapping elements. The use of common English words in the construction of the learning tasks eliminates or minimizes the influence of such factors and permits the analysis to focus directly on associative processes. The emphasis on the role of language habits has, of course, led to the increasing use of sequentially organized materials, including sentences, as well as of lists of discrete verbal units. Thus, the choice of both materials and of experimental procedures has tended to become increasingly specific to the substantive problem under investigation.

Second, there has been a continuing trend away from descriptive and parametric studies to analytic experimentation. There has been a decline of interest in the exploration of task variables for their own sake and increasing concern with the analysis of the gross phenomena of learning and retention into component processes and the testing of hypotheses about the conditions and characteristics of such processes. As a consequence, studies of verbal learning and memory have come to play an important role in the examination of general principles of learning theory. Last but not least, the boundaries between research on verbal learning and on other higher mental processes, such as concept formation, thinking, and decision-making, have become increasingly blurred. The free interchange of theoretical ideas and methods is serving to enhance the scope of all these areas of specialization and holds out the promise of their eventual integration.

An emphasis on the currents of change should not be allowed to obscure the basic continuity of the developments in research on verbal learning and memory. The classical methods and analyses have provided a solid foundation for much if not most of the contemporary work. An attempt has been made to reflect in the selection of readings for this volume both the historical continuity and the thrust of innovation and change. While the articles are grouped under such traditional headings as acquisition, transfer, and retention, it is hoped that the common developments in the experimental analysis of these processes will become apparent.

Part One **Acquisition**

This section samples some of the major variables which have been considered in experimental analyses of the process of acquisition. To put these topics into perspective, it is useful to take as a point of departure the classical conception of an association as a connexion between a stimulus and a response built up gradually through practice. The effective stimulus is specified by the experimental operations, and the response is defined by the performance requirements imposed on the subject. Associative connexions are assumed to vary in strength. Each contiguous occurrence of the stimulus and response adds an increment to the strength of the association, and such increments are reflected in the probability of the correct response.

The articles included in this section make it clear that this classical conception of association no longer provides a common theoretical framework for investigations of verbal learning. Quite on the contrary, much of the recent research on the conditions and mechanisms of acquisition has been motivated by dissatisfaction with the classical view, or at least represents drastic departures from it. There appears to be wide agreement that verbal learning represents a far more complex process than the strengthening of one-step associative connexions. Experimental and analytic methods have advanced sufficiently to permit us to set aside this gross model of habit formation and to focus on the fine grain of the acquisition process. The work on stimulus selection and the analysis of associative learning into component stages are cases in point. There is less agreement on the fundamental assumption that the acquisition of verbal habits represents a process of incremental growth, even when the reference is to complex chains and networks of associations rather than to one-step

15

associative bonds. The conflict between the incremental and the all-or-none conceptions of association makes it apparent that debate about the basic mechanisms of acquisition is likely to continue for a long time.

Traditional views of the major functional relations in acquisition also continue to come under experimental scrutiny. The application of improved experimental methods and analytic procedures has in some cases led to the revision of widely accepted empirical generalizations, and in others helped to bring into focus the mechanisms responsible for the observed functional relations. In the present section examples of such developments may be found under several headings: temporal factors, meaningfulness, perceptual factors, intentional *v.* incidental learning.

We shall now comment briefly on each of the topics considered in the articles in this section.

Stimulus Selection

In any analysis of association the specification of the units that are linked through practice is an essential first step. Historically stimulus–response theorists proceeded from the assumption that the stimulus defined and manipulated by the experimenter was also the functionally effective one. Thus, Hull (1943, p. 112) asserted that 'under most circumstances there is a close approximation to a one-to-one correspondence, parallelism or constancy' between the physical and the functional stimulus. The same assumption was made, explicitly or implicitly, by most investigators of verbal learning and memory. To be sure, the potential importance of contextual stimuli was recognized early – responses can become associated to background events as well as to the stimuli which determine the response contingencies and are identified in the instructions to the learner. Changes in context were shown to produce decrements in performance (e.g. Dulsky, 1935; Pan, 1926). The interpretation of such findings emphasized the conclusion that the effective stimulating conditions include elements additional to those manipulated in the experiment; removal of these elements reduces the probability that the learned response will be elicited (McGeoch, 1942, p. 501). If the stimuli to which the subject is instructed to respond are designated as nominal, then the effective stimuli represent compounds of nominal and contextual elements. From this point of view the drops in performance resulting from changes in context may be viewed as continuous with the generalization decrements observed in conditioning situations.

When the functional stimulus is a compound, the question arises as to the relative effectiveness of the components in eliciting the prescribed response. If the contextual features are variable, the nominal elements will be preponderant since they provide the only basis for the establishment of stable response contingencies. However, when nominal and contextual elements are perfectly correlated, the distinction between them becomes arbitrary; under these circumstances the response may become more strongly associated to the context than to the nominal stimulus. An important study by Weiss and Margolius (1954) provided an example of precisely this state of affairs. In their experiment the learning material was a list of paired associates in which the nominal stimulus terms were nonsense syllables and the responses were English words. During acquisition each of the syllables was presented against a distinctive, coloured background. The strength of association between the response and each of the stimulus components was assessed in a subsequent test of recall. Different groups were tested with (a) the syllables alone, (b) the colours alone and (c) the original compounds. Performance was best when the original compound remained intact; when only a single component was presented, recall was far higher to the colours than to the syllables. Clearly the associations were stronger to the contextual than to the nominal elements.

The findings of Weiss and Margolius showed that subjects exposed to a stimulus composed of redundant elements may respond selectively to one of these elements. The designation of one of the elements or of the total compound as the appropriate stimulus will not prevent selection as long as the components are perfectly redundant. Thus, depending on the subject's selection biases, the degree of discrepancy between the nominal and the functional stimulus may vary. These considerations shift the emphasis away from the summative effects of stimulus components to a process of stimulus selection by the subject. The two approaches to the identification of the functional stimulus are not mutually exclusive. The addition of contextual elements may make the functional stimulus more extensive than the nominal one; stimulus selection may make it more restricted.

The implications of the mechanism of stimulus selection for verbal learning were discussed by Underwood (1963) in a chapter which provided the point of departure for much of the current research on this problem. On the basis of the available evidence he concluded that in a paired-associate situation (a) the subject will select as the functional stimulus the minimally necessary differentiating component, (b) selection will favour the component with the highest meaningfulness, and (c) more than one component may become functional when the compounds comprise two or more distinct classes of elements, but configurations of elements are not likely to be the functional stimuli (p. 47).

The study by Underwood, Ham and Ekstrand (Reading 1) presents clear evidence for meaningfulness as a determinant of selection. It also illustrates the transfer design which is used to identify the functional stimuli after the end of acquisition. The basic characteristics of the procedure, which involves tests with single components as well as with the original compound, have already been indicated in the summary of the study by Weiss and Margolius. Several subsequent experiments on paired-associate learning in which the stimuli were compounds composed of distinctive units (verbal units and colours or two separate verbal units) have confirmed the existence of a strong and dependable bias towards the selection of components of high meaningfulness (Cohen and Musgrave, 1964; Houston, 1967; James and Greeno, 1967; Spear, Ekstrand and Underwood, 1964). Components which form a set of low inter-item similarity will be favoured (Cohen and Musgrave, 1966) as will be elements to which the subjects have had previous exposure in the experimental situation (Houston, 1967).

Stimulus selection is not confined to choices between distinctive units within a compound. When the nominal stimulus is a single verbal unit, such as a trigram, there can still be selection of elements from within the unit, i.e. single letters. Any element which is unique to a given unit and hence defines a stable response contingency can be selected (Jenkins, 1963). The study by Postman and Greenbloom (Reading 2), shows that such single-letter cue selection is much more likely when the nominal stimulus is poorly integrated than when it is a readily pronounceable unit. The latter type of unit is not usually fractionated even when the elements are completely redundant. Thus, regardless of whether the stimulus is a compound or nominally a single unit, it is always perceptibly discrete elements that are selected. The results also make it clear that pre-experimental habits of processing information decisively influence the choice of functional elements, for example the first element in a sequence is heavily favoured. Finally, attention is called to the difficulty of establishing unequivocal criteria for inferring the occurrence of stimulus selection from the results of transfer tests. The basic point here is that a transfer test makes it possible to determine what has been learned but does not necessarily permit firm conclusions about the course of acquisition. Thus, a transfer test administered after the attainment of a high criterion will not be sensitive to stimulus selection that had its locus early in learning. Since high criteria of mastery have typically been used, it is possible that the existing experimental findings systematically underestimate the amount of stimulus selection which occurs in the course of acquisition.

All-or-None versus Incremental Learning

The question of whether associative strength grows incrementally or changes from zero to a maximum in an all-or-none fashion represents an issue of long standing in the theory of discrimination learning. The debate between these opposing views became known as the continuity–noncontinuity controversy (Kimble, 1961, pp. 128–34). The same issue came to a head, perhaps rather belatedly, in the area of verbal learning with the appearance of the article by Rock (Reading 3) which is reproduced below. Rock addressed himself to the question of whether in paired-associate learning associations are formed on a single trial or gain strength gradually as a function of repetition. To answer this question Rock introduced what became known as the drop-out method – items which were missed on a given test trial were removed from the list and new ones substituted for them. Under these conditions the occurrence of the first correct response cannot be attributed to the accumulation of associative strength through repetition; rather the association must necessarily be formed on a single trial. The number of trials to mastery of the list was no greater under the drop-out procedure than in the control condition in which the items remained unchanged throughout learning. The results appeared to give support, therefore, to the hypothesis of one-trial learning. Rock used both paired nonsense syllables and letter-number pairs in his experiments. The results obtained with nonsense syllables are complicated by the factor of response learning. Since the theoretical issue concerns exclusively the principles governing the development of associations, it is clearly desirable to minimize the role of response learning in experimental tests of the all-or-none hypothesis. In the discussion which follows, only experiments meeting this requirement will be considered. Most of the studies which bear critically on Rock's analysis fall into this category.

Rock's results aroused great interest among investigators of verbal learning and stimulated a considerable amount of empirical work and theoretical discussion. The main outcome can be summarized briefly. First, the main finding that speed of learning to a criterion of mastery is comparable under the drop-out and the conventional procedure is repeatable, although at least slight differences in favour of the control condition are often found (Clark, Lansford and Dallenbach, 1960; Underwood, Rehula and Keppel, 1962). Second, it has been demonstrated conclusively that results obtained by the drop-out method are subject to a potentially serious bias because of the high probability of item selection entailed by the procedure. All the pairs missed on a given trial are removed from the list, i.e. the items which are eliminated are selected for difficulty. It becomes likely, therefore, that the substitute pairs introduced into the list are easier than those they replace. The more the items in the initial list (which remains unchanged under the control treatment) vary in difficulty, the more serious the bias in favour of the drop-out condition becomes. The fact of item selection is demonstrated directly when it can be shown that the final lists of the drop-out groups are easier to learn than the initial lists (Underwood, Rehula and Keppel, 1962). The bias produced by item selection inevitably renders the results obtained by the drop-out procedure ambiguous and precludes a decision between the one-trial and the incremental interpretations based on such data.

It is not accidental that the drop-out procedure, which appeared to be peculiarly well suited for an evaluation of the one-trial hypothesis, is vitiated by item selection. The critical empirical question entailed by the hypothesis is whether any associative strength accrues to an item prior to the occurrence of the first correct response. Thus, the items whose state must be evaluated are those which have produced one or more failures. Such items necessarily represent a relatively difficult subset within the general pool from which they are drawn. Whenever they are compared with the average item in the pool or with that subset of items which does not produce failures, the problem of selection for difficulty is bound to arise. However, as the article by Taylor and Irion (Reading 4) shows, the probable effects of the bias and the consequent difficulties of interpretation depend on the experimental paradigm. Moreover, differences which are obtained in the teeth of the bias carry considerable force of conviction. The experiment of Taylor and Irion takes its point of departure from the implication of the all-or-none hypothesis that there should be no transfer to subsequent tasks from learning trials which fail to yield a correct response. This prediction follows, of course, from the assumption that associative strength remains at zero prior to the occurrence of the first correct response. The results of the experiment provide clear evidence contrary to this prediction. Special attention is called to the discussion section of the paper in which the interpretative problems posed by item selection are assessed. Other studies using comparable transfer designs and yielding results consistent with those of Taylor and Irion have been reported by Underwood and Keppel (1962) and by Schwartz (1963).

Rock's approach to the problem of one-trial learning was clearly influenced by Gestalt theory, which has traditionally viewed association as a special case of organization in accordance with the laws of perceptual grouping (Kohler, 1941). Note the parallel he draws between the successful use of mnemonic devices and insightful learning. Insight refers, of course, to a sudden perceptual change which leads to an immediate and complete solution of a problem. If the formation of associations depends on the perception of relations between the terms which are to be linked, it may be expected to occur in an all-or-none fashion. The issues raised by Rock are thus directly related to the classical continuity–noncontinuity controversy.

It is of some historical interest that a short time after the appearance of Rock's study a theorist with a drastically different theoretical orientation became an advocate of the all-or-none hypothesis. A well known article by Estes (1960) signalled a major revision in the author's influential theory of stimulus sampling. The theory had previously assumed that a given nominal stimulus is composed of a set of elements and that each element is conditioned to the response in an all-or-none fashion. For a stimulus composed of multiple elements the resulting changes in response probability are incremental. The critical change introduced by Estes is the treatment of a complex stimulus, such as a nonsense syllable or a word, as a single patterned element (see also Estes, 1961). Since the postulate of all-or-none conditioning is retained, it follows that the probability of the response at any given point in practice must be either 0 or 1. That is, an association is either not present or it is at maximal strength.

For purposes of evaluating this version of the all-or-none hypothesis Estes introduced an experimental procedure which became known as the RTT design – a reinforcement (presentation) trial followed by successive tests (Estes, Hopkins and Crothers, 1960). This experimental arrangement was chosen to provide an answer to the question of whether any associative strength is built up prior to the occurrence of the first correct response. Given a distribution of correct and incorrect responses on the first test, the critical measures are the conditional probabilities of the two classes of responses on the second test. According to the all-or-none position a correct response on the first trial reflects an association of maximal strength, and an incorrect response one of zero strength. Hence the conditional probability $C_2 : C_1$ (correct on test 2, given a correct response on test 1) should be $1 \cdot 0$, and $N_2 : C_1$ (incorrect on test 2, given a correct response on test 1) should be zero. However, if there is forgetting between test trials, $C_2 : C_1$ will fall below unity and $N_2 : C_1$ will show a corresponding increase. The expected value of $C_2 : N_1$ is zero since items failed on the final test are assumed to have no associative strength; by the same token $N_2 : N_1$ should be $1 \cdot 0$. The predictions attributed to incremental theory are generated on the assumption that all items benefit equally from a reinforcement and that the successes and failures on the first test trial represent fluctuations around a threshold of recall. It follows that $C_2 : N_1$ should equal $C_2 : C_1$.

The results obtained by Estes in his experiments on paired-associate learning conformed to the prediction of all-or-none theory. In particular, the values of $C_2 : N_1$ appeared not to exceed the level expected on the basis of chance guessing whereas $C_2 : C$ was quite high, although far enough below unity to indicate some forgetting between test trials. It is readily apparent, however, that the evaluation of the conditional probabilities is rendered uncertain by the bias of item selection discussed above. The expectation that $C_2 : C_1 = C_2 : N_1$ can be maintained only on the assumption that the reinforcement has raised the associative strength of all items to the same level. This assumption is clearly not tenable since the items failed on the first test (N_1) can be supposed to be a subset selected for difficulty. $C_2 : N_1$ should, therefore, be less than $C_2 : C_1$, as it invariably is. The value of $C_2 : N_1$ will depend on the proportion of failed items whose associative strength is near the threshold of recall, with zero as the limiting case. However, if the value is in fact greater than zero, a critical prediction derived from the all-or-none hypothesis is disconfirmed.

Like Rock's studies, Estes' 'miniature experiments' became the focus of a sustained controversy. The paper by Jones (Reading 5) was an early reply to Estes. The logic of the analysis of conditional probabilities is examined critically. Jones's own experiments show that the distributions of responses obtained in an extended series of successive tests – R T T T T – yield results inconsistent with the all-or-none hypothesis. The main finding of interest is that responses which are first given correctly on the second trial ($C_2 : N_1$) are thereafter repeated much more frequently than they should be if they were merely successful guesses. The larger the number of test trials on which an initially failed item has been given correctly the more likely it is to remain correct on the next test. These findings indicate that the items failed on the initial test trial represent a distribution of associative strengths, with at least some values sufficiently close to the threshold of recall to permit correct performance on subsequent test trials. This conclusion receives additional support from the results of a study by Postman (1963) which shows that the conditional probability $C_2 : N_1$ increase reliably with the number of reinforcements preceding the first test trial. If each reinforcement produces increments in associative strength, the proportion of items approaching or exceeding the threshold should be a direct function of the number of presentation trials. The experimental findings fully bore out this expectation.

Neither Rock's nor Estes' procedure permits a clear-cut decision between the all-or-none and the incremental interpretations. The bias of item selection entailed by both types of experimental design constitutes a major methodological obstacle which so far has remained intractable. Data which are apparently all-or-none can be readily handled by incremental theories with the aid of appropriate assumptions about the distributions of item strengths relative to a threshold of recall. Moreover, widely disparate positions, such as those of Rock and Estes, converge on the prediction of all-or-none learning, so that the theoretical implications of the hypothesis remain far from clear. The existing state of affairs was well summarized in a review by Restle: 'Since several different association theories, and several different cognitive theories, all have the capacity to explain all-or-none learning, the simple fact of all-or-none learning is not appropriate for the decisive confrontation of major theoretical approaches' (1965, p. 323).

Two-Stage Analysis of Associative Learning

In the analysis of associative learning it has proved useful to conceive of the process of acquisition as being divided into two successive stages, viz. a response-learning and an associative stage (Underwood and Schulz, 1960). During the first of these stages the required responses become available units in the subject's current repertoire. If the responses are not in his pre-experimental vocabulary, they must be integrated into available and reproducible units (see Mandler, 1954); if the responses are already integrated and familiar, the subject must learn to restrict himself to the set of items included in the task. Depending on the characteristics of the prescribed units, therefore, the first stage may involve both response integration and response recall, or only the latter. During the second stage each response term is associated with the appropriate stimulus. It is recognized that the two stages may proceed concurrently. For certain analytic purposes, however, it is convenient to think of them as successive, i.e. to assume that responses must be available before they can enter into new associations.

Historically the distinction between the two components of acquisition was slow to receive systematic attention. The reasons for the long neglect of response processes can probably be traced to the classical work of Ebbinghaus which profoundly influenced the subsequent development of research in verbal learning and memory. Ebbinghaus' approach was rooted in the tradition of philosophical associationism, and an overriding emphasis on associative processes has characterized the main stream of theoretical analysis of verbal learning ever since. This emphasis was, of course, strongly reinforced by the later application of the concepts and principles of conditioning to verbal learning. Moreover, serial learning, which Ebbinghaus adopted as his standard task and which was used widely by his successors, did not permit of a ready separation between stimulus and response functions.

Nevertheless the first explicit statement of the two-stage conception of acquisition appeared in the context of an investigation of serial learning (Hovland and Kurtz, 1952). This study presented evidence for the importance of the factor of response availability – prior familiarization with a pool of nonsense syllables from which the experimental lists were drawn significantly increased the speed of acquisition. However, the conclusion that prior response learning was responsible for the observed improvement does not strictly follow since in a serial list most items presumably function as both stimuli and responses. An experimental isolation of the response-learning phase becomes possible only in the paired-associate situation in which stimulus and response variables can be manipulated independently. Reading 6 by Underwood, Runquist, and Schulz illustrates the use of the two-stage conception of paired-associate learning as an analytic device. Again prior response familiarization is used to manipulate the factor of response learning. As predicted, subsequent paired-associate learning is significantly facilitated. Furthermore, application of the two-stage analysis helps to provide an explanation of the finding that stimulus similarity has a more detrimental effect on paired-associate learning than does response similarity (e.g. Underwood, 1953). This asymmetry becomes understandable on the assumption that inter-item similarity has a positive effect on response recall which serves to offset the negative effect of associative interference; there is no comparable factor to mitigate the associative interference produced by stimulus similarity. The present study shows that inter-item similarity does, in fact, facilitate the response-learning stage and thus lends at least indirect support to this explanation. Subsequent research has given strong additional support to this analysis of the effects of intralist similarity (Underwood, Ekstrand and Keppel, 1965).

It will be useful at this point to make explicit some of the methodological problems which constrain the analytic use of the two-stage conception of associative learning. A distinction must first of all be made between the manipulation of variables which are assumed to influence the two stages on the one hand, and the direct measurement of the stages on the other. Prior familiarization of the response terms can be used to reduce or to eliminate the response-learning stage. If such training facilitates subsequent paired-associate learning, there is presumptive evidence for the response-learning component of acquisition. It is possible, of course, that response familiarization influences the associative stage as well. However, if greater effects on acquisition are obtained by familiarization of the responses than of the stimuli, the inference that there is a significant response-learning component is strengthened. Such asymmetrical results of familiarization are, in fact, typically observed (Underwood and Schulz, 1960). Even so, alternative interpretations of the effects of familiarization remain possible. For example, Saltz (1961) has argued that response familiarization has a positive influence on acquisition because it enhances inter-item differentiation.

Direct measurement of the stages of acquisition calls for the use of tests which are differentially sensitive to the two components. Tests of free recall have conventionally been used to determine response availability *per se*. Such tests were given after different amounts of paired-associate practice in the experiment of Underwood, Runquist, and Schulz in order to assess the progress of response learning. As expected, response recall was found to increase more rapidly than overall performance on the paired-associate task and reflected the positive effects of inter-item similarity. To chart the course of associative learning, matching procedures have been used in which the subject is presented with both the stimulus and the response terms and is required to identify the correct pairings (Horowitz and Larsen, 1963; Jung, 1965). The results have in general been consistent with the two-stage conception. It is useful to recognize, however, that the results obtained by such probing techniques are subject to an important limitation, viz. they require a mode of responding which is drastically different from that during the preceding acquisition trials. This limitation is likely to characterize any method designed to measure separately the components of a complex learning process.

Meaningfulness

One of the major determinants of the speed of acquisition of a verbal list is the meaningfulness (m) of the units included in the task. The systematic investigation of this task variable, and in particular the demonstration of important differences between stimulus m and response m, has given strong support to the two-stage conception of associative learning.

In the context of experiments on verbal learning, m refers to an aggregate of properties each of which is defined in terms of a distinct measuring operation. The scales generated by the different measuring operations are correlated with each other and in combination they serve to define m as a composite of characteristics (Underwood, 1966). Relevant scale values are based on (a) the proportion of individuals reporting an association to a given item within a limited period of time (Archer, 1960; Glaze, 1928); (b) the number of different associates given to an item per unit of time (Noble, 1952); (c) ratings of the number of associates evoked by an item (Noble, Stockwell and Pryer, 1957); (d) ratings of familiarity (Noble, 1953); (e) ratings of pronunciability (Underwood and Schulz, 1960).

Reading 7 by Cieutat, Stockwell and Noble uses two of these scales, viz. those based on the number of associates elicited by an item (m) and on ratings of the number of associates (m'). Both experiments reported in this study agree in showing significant

27

positive effects of both stimulus and response m on learning, but a far greater influence of the latter than of the former. This pronounced asymmetry is a highly dependable finding and has been confirmed in numerous investigations of the relation between m and learning. It is clear that m exerts a more important influence on the response-learning than on the associative stage.

A comprehensive series of experiments investigating the relation between m and learning was subsequently published by Underwood and Schulz (1960). Again the effects of response m were found to be consistently greater than those of stimulus m. To account for the powerful influence of m on the response-learning stage, Underwood and Schulz formulated the 'spew hypothesis' which asserts that 'the more frequently a verbal unit has been experienced, the more quickly this will become a response in a new associative connection' (p. 86). Measures of m are highly correlated with frequency of occurrence in the language. Thus, the spew hypothesis asserts that the higher the m of an item the more readily it will become available as a recallable response which can enter into new associations. Within a given learning situation the spew principle must, however, be modified in an important way. Once a subject has been exposed to the list which he is to learn, he rapidly comes to restrict his responses to items within that list. What Underwood and Schulz call a 'selector mechanism' comes into play and serves to limit the learner's responses to the appropriate ensemble of items. The spew principle operates within the bounds imposed by the selector mechanism, i.e. for the responses included in the list, the order of availability is directly related to frequency (m).

It is important to emphasize that the spew hypothesis applies to the response-learning stage only; it does not entail any prediction about the speed with which associations will be formed once the responses have become available. The relatively weak relation between stimulus m and speed of learning continues to pose a troublesome interpretative problem. At the present time there is no well-supported theoretical formulation of the mechanisms by which stimulus m exerts its influence on the establishment of associations.

It is apparent that the response-learning stage occupies a substantial proportion of the total learning time when integration of unfamiliar units is required. When the units are familiar, the response-recall stage is relatively short but by no means negligible. When it is desired to chart the course of associative learning *per se*, a method of practice must be used which may be assumed to eliminate the requirement of response availability. Reference has already been made to the use of tests of associative matching for this purpose. Multiple-choice tests, in which the subject must choose the correct associate from a set of alternatives all of which are items from within the list, have likewise been used with a view to eliminating the factor of response availability (e.g. Schulz, Weaver and Ginsberg, 1965). Even in such cases, however, response familiarity may exert subtle effects on performance since the search time required to locate a particular item is inversely related to the meaningfulness of the units (Lovelace and Schulz, 1966).

The study of verbal discrimination learning by Runquist and Freeman (Reading 8), provides a further example of biases attributable to response processes in a situation which on *a priori* grounds may be expected to be free of such influences. The experimental findings indicate that the sheer ease of enunciating the correct alternative may have a significant effect on the speed with which a discrimination task is mastered. Here the characteristics of the overt responses – what Cieutat, Stockwell and Noble refer to as 'motor patterning' – becomes a significant source of variance. The possibility of such biases should not, however, be allowed to obscure the general value of the verbal discrimination procedure, especially when familiar English words are used as the learning materials. The procedure has been employed with considerable success in the investigation of the conditions determining the establishment of discriminations between correct and incorrect alternatives. Recent experiments using this procedure give strong support to the conclusion that the critical cue for discrimination is the difference in frequency of occurrence in the experimental situation between the correct and the incorrect alternatives (Ekstrand, Wallace and Underwood, 1966).

Perceptual Factors: Isolation

While the mainstream of the theoretical analysis of verbal learning has been in the tradition of associationism, an important alternative has been posed by the Gestalt position, which holds that learning and memory are governed by the same principles of organization as are manifested in the laws of perceptual grouping. As already noted, Gestalt theory regards association as a special case of organization: the relation between the items to be linked is critical and determines the readiness with which they can be grouped into a coherent organization (Kohler, 1941). Once an organization has been formed, it is preserved in the nervous system as a memory trace. Memory traces are subject to change over time, but these changes are again governed by the same principles of organization as the primary experiences of perception (Koffka, 1935).

One of the major empirical facts advanced in support of the Gestalt position was the 'isolation effect' described by von Restorff (1933) and subsequently named after her, the von Restorff effect. The basic finding of von Restorff's experiments was that an isolated item presented against an homogenous background was favoured in recall. For example, if a single nonsense syllable was introduced into a series of numbers (or vice versa) the unique or isolated item was recalled far better than the average homogeneous or 'crowded' item. Von Restorff attributed this result to autonomous changes in the memory traces laid down by the exposure to the experimental series. Specifically, the traces are assumed to form aggregates in which the representations of similar items are assimilated to each other and lose their distinctiveness. The trace of the unique or isolated item, however, does not become absorbed into the aggregate; rather it retains its distinctive identity and thus stands out like a figure against an homogeneous background.

This interpretation of the von Restorff phenomenon did not, however, remain unchallenged by association theorists. The most influential alternative explanation was offered by Gibson (1940, 1942), who argued that the isolation phenomenon could be derived from the principles of intra-serial generalization and differentiation. According to Gibson, generalization tendencies among the items in a list retard the course of acquisition. The task cannot be mastered until the items have been differentiated from each other and the generalization tendencies reduced accordingly. The isolated item by virtue of its dissimilarity from the other units in the list enjoys a high degree of differentiation from the outset and thus is subject to less interference and has an advantage in acquisition. In the context of Gibson's analysis differentiation refers to the stimulus function of the isolated item, but the argument can be readily extended to encompass response generalization and differentiation as well.

The explanation of the von Restorff effect and its many subsequent elaborations and modifications has remained a matter of theoretical controversy. The voluminous literature on this subject has been reviewed by Wallace (1965) and will not be considered further. Reading 9, Erickson, is included here as an example of a methodologically sophisticated attempt to evaluate the explanation of the phenomenon in terms of differential associative interference. While Erickson finds that the traditional hypothesis cannot account for his results, he introduces certain additional assumptions about differential mediators elicited by the stimuli of the isolated pairs which make it possible to accommodate his findings within the framework of a stimulus–response analysis. Apart from its intrinsic interest, the history of the von Restorff phenomenon provides a good illustration of the fact that crucial experiments which permit a clear-cut decision between alternative theoretical interpretations are a rare occurrence indeed.

Distribution of Practice

The topic of distribution of practice introduces the problem of temporal variables in acquisition. The first systematic investigation of rote learning and memory by Ebbinghaus (1885) brought to light the fact that interpolation of rest intervals between successive periods of practice increases the efficiency of learning. On the face of it, the facilitative influence of distribution of practice represents a paradox: one might expect time intervals interpolated between one practice period and the next to produce forgetting and hence to retard acquisition, but the observed effect is in the opposite direction. It appears that the rest intervals allow positive factors to come into play which outweigh the normal decline in performance over time.

Experimental evidence on the effects of distribution has been accumulating steadily since the original discovery of the phenomenon. For purposes of experimental manipulation, distributed practice is defined in relative terms and typically contrasted with massed practice. For example, a condition in which there are 2-minute intervals between successive trials may be compared with one in which the inter-trial intervals are zero or quite short, for example 6 seconds. Degree of distribution can be varied over a wide range; intervals of one day have been used in the acquisition of verbal lists (e.g. Keppel, 1964). An alternative design holds the time between successive learning periods constant but varies the amount of practice during each period. The latter procedure is, however, less common than the spacing of learning trials. The inter-trial intervals are considered rest periods in the sense of being free from formal practice on the experimental task. Rest periods which occur in the laboratory are, however, usually filled with some activity designed to prevent rehearsal. The available evidence indicates that the nature of the interpolated activity is a variable of some importance. Thus, a rapid rate of responding established by a task performed during the inter-trial interval may carry over to the subsequent learning trials (Underwood, 1952).

Both perceptual-motor and verbal tasks have been used in investigations of distributed practice. There is no question but that motor learning is greatly facilitated by distribution. The situation is quite different in verbal learning. There is, to be sure, a large number of studies in the literature which report some degree of facilitation in the acquisition of verbal lists. Among the classical experiments are those of Hovland (1938, 1940, and Reading 10), which demonstrated distribution effects in the learning of serial lists of nonsense syllables and showed the magnitude of these effects to be a function of such variables as rate of presentation and length of list. The most thorough and definitive investigation of the influences of distributed practice on verbal learning has been carried out by Underwood in an extended series of experiments. One paper from this series is Reading 11 by Underwood and Richardson, and this illustrates the procedures and methods of analysis used in this research. The major conclusion from these studies is that facilitation by distributed practice in verbal learning 'occurs only under a highly specific set of conditions, and the magnitude of the effect when it does occur is relatively small'

(Underwood, 1961, p. 230). Underwood goes on to point out that, in view of this state of affairs, learning by distributed practice is very inefficient. When the total time to learn including the rest intervals is considered, massed practice is clearly superior.

The most recent data (Underwood and Ekstrand, 1967) suggest that distribution is most likely to have a facilitative effect when the materials consist of non-word units and interference is produced by formal inter-item similarity. Such interference may inhibit the development of associative strength. To the extent that the interpolation of rest intervals permits the inhibition to dissipate, speed of acquisition is increased. At the present time the properties of the inhibitory process are not understood. There has been little support for the hypothesis that the effective inhibition is a matter of work decrement or fatigue; the evidence suggests that the critical source of inhibition is associative interference. In any event, dissipation of the inhibition appears to have relatively minor effects on the course of acquisition. It should be noted, however, that proactive inhibition at recall is substantially reduced when either the interfering list or the test list is learned under conditions of distributed practice (Keppel, 1964; Underwood and Ekstrand, 1966). The mechanisms responsible for this reduction in interference are probably quite different from those which produce whatever small effects are observed in acquisition.

The Total-Time Hypothesis

In the investigation of temporal variables such as distribution of practice (length of interval between successive trials) and rate of presentation, it has been conventional to measure speed of acquisition in terms of the number of trials to mastery. Alternatively, the number of correct responses per trial is related to the temporal variable. A trial is, of course, an arbitrary unit of work since its duration can be varied at will. However, a trial of a given duration can be translated into a measure of learning time. The time measure specifies the amount of practice in standard terms which are comparable from one situation to another. At a given rate of presentation there is a one-to-one relation between the number of trials and total learning time. When the rate of presentation is varied, an evaluation of the effect of this variable in terms of a trial measure becomes equivocal, since the learning time per trial varies inversely with the rate of presentation. The usual finding has been that the number of trials to mastery increases directly with the rate of presentation (e.g. Hovland, 1938). But since manipulations of rate produce concomitant changes in the duration of trials, the critical question is whether total learning time varies significantly as a function of rate. This argument is developed by Bugelski in Reading 12. His study of paired-associate learning presents striking evidence for invariance of total learning time over a wide range of variation in presentation time per item on successive trials. In a subsequent experiment Bugelski and Rickwood (1963) allowed their subjects to control the lengths of the presentation intervals. The average learning time fell well within the range of values obtained in the earlier study. These results point to an important principle of invariance – the total learning time to mastery remains constant regardless of how that time is distributed over trials. Bugelski's findings received strong support in a number of subsequent studies. Parallel results have been obtained in studies of serial learning, although that evidence is not as consistent as in the paired-associate experiments. (For a recent review of the relevant literature see Cooper and Pantle, 1967.)

The total-time hypothesis has a direct bearing on the classical problem of whole v. part learning. The question has been whether it is more efficient to practice a given task as a whole from the outset or to divide the material into parts; under the latter procedure the parts are mastered separately and combined in the end. The early studies investigating this problem yielded inconsistent results (e.g. G. O. McGeoch, 1931). In a recent re-examination of the problem by Postman and Goggin (1964, 1966), the findings were in general in accord with the total-time hypothesis. Regardless of the difficulty of the materials, the difference in total learning time between the whole and part conditions remained invariant at or near zero for paired-associate learning; the part method had only a slight and task-specific advantage in serial learning.

Important support for the principle of total-time invariance has come from studies of free recall. In fact, the principle was first formulated explicitly by Murdock (1960) on the basis of the results of experiments in which free recall was measured after a single presentation of a list of words. It was found, first of all, that the number of words recalled increased both with the length of the list and the presentation time per item. However, a change in one of these variables could be compensated by a corresponding change in the other, i.e. recall remained the same as long as the total presentation time was kept constant. Thus the following combinations of list lengths and presentation times per item yielded essentially equal recall scores: 20–3 (a 20-word list presented at a rate of 3 seconds per item), 30–2, 40–1·5, 60–1.

Subsequent experiments by Waugh (1962, 1963, 1967) have demonstrated the generality of the total-time principle in free recall. These studies show that the amount of recall remains invariant with total presentation time regardless of how that time is distributed over individual items. Thus if an item appears more than once in a list, its probability of recall increases as a linear function of the aggregate study time devoted to it. This invariance holds for lists of a given duration; however, as the number of items presented at a constant rate, and hence list duration, is increased, the amount recalled grows at a negatively accelerated rate. Waugh has suggested that such diminishing returns of study time reflect increasing difficulties of retrieval as the total ensemble of items is enlarged.

In discussing the psychological basis of the total-time phenomena which have been observed, Cooper and Pantle (1967) introduce a distinction between nominal and effective study time which parallels that between the nominal and the effective (functional) stimulus in studies of stimulus selection. Exposure duration as measured by a clock constitutes the nominal study time; the period actually utilized for rehearsal is the effective study time. These authors suggest that the total-time principle may be expected to hold if the effective time is linearly related to nominal time, and provided that the requirements of the learning task can be met by simple rehearsal (repeated evocation of representational responses). The latter restriction is indicated because the total-time hypothesis implies that each increase in exposure duration makes a constant addition to the amount of effective practice.

Incidental Learning

In experiments on human learning, instructions are normally sufficient to motivate the subject to perform the experimental task. The materials to be mastered and the nature of the required responses are specified. The subject who follows instructions is an intentional learner. In many other situations learning is incidental in the sense that it occurs in the absence of instructions and presumably without intent. The question arises, therefore, to what extent and in what ways intent to learn influences acquisition. In experiments directed at this problem, the administration of instructions to learn defines the intentional condition, and the omission of such instructions, the incidental condition. It is apparent that these operations do not ensure a sharp discontinuity between the two conditions of learning. Given the subject's past history and the laboratory setting, more or less transitory sets to learn may develop under the incidental treatment. Nevertheless, the comparison between the two conditions is of systematic interest because it permits an evaluation of the effects of learning instructions on performance. The extent to which instructions prepare a subject for a subsequent test of recall may be expected to influence the results obtained on such a test, even if there is no discontinuity between intentional and incidental learning.

In the absence of instructions to learn, some procedure must be used to ensure that incidental subjects are exposed to the learning materials. The procedure used for that purpose constitutes the orienting task. For example, the subject may be asked to rate the materials on such characteristics as familiarity or pleasantness, to give associations to each of the stimulus words, and so on. In many early studies, incidental learners performing an orienting task were compared with intentional subjects who were simply instructed to learn the stimulus materials. Typically performance on a test of retention was substantially higher under the intentional than under the incidental condition. Such findings are ambiguous, however, since it remains uncertain whether the difference in performance is a function of the instructions or attributable to the distracting influence of the orienting task on the incidental subjects. In order to isolate the effect of the instructional variable, it is necessary to require intentional as well as incidental subjects to carry out the orienting task. The addition of an orienting task usually lowers the amount of intentional learning, so that the difference between the intentional and the incidental treatment is correspondingly reduced when the appropriate comparisons are made. (For a review of the experimental literature on incidental learning see Postman, 1964.)

The responses to the stimulus materials which are required by the orienting task may be more or less similar to those which normally come into play when a subject is instructed to learn. The greater the similarity the smaller should be the difference in performance between intentional and incidental learners. The experiment by Mechanic (Reading 13) provides strong support for this hypothesis. In the acquisition of items of low meaningfulness, the difference between intentional and incidental subjects is eliminated altogether when the orienting task forces the repeated pronouncing of the prescribed units and thus promotes the process of response integration. By contrast, the intentional learners have a substantial advantage when the orienting task calls for responses (number guessing) which are clearly irrelevant to the integration of the verbal units.

Findings such as these lead to the conclusion that intent *per se* has little or no influence on the amount learned under given conditions of exposure. The intent to learn induced by instructions is typically found to be a positive factor because it serves to activate responses to the materials which are favourable to acquisition. If the same responses can be aroused in an incidental learner by means of an appropriate orienting task, there is no evidence for a residual effect of intent. This conclusion is strengthened by an examination of the functional relations in intentional and incidental learning. Major task variables, such as meaningfulness and interitem similarity, have parallel effects under the two conditions of practice. Whatever systematic differences are found may be reasonably attributed to the differential responses made to the stimulus materials (Postman, 1964). Thus, the available evidence suggests that there is no discontinuity between intentional and incidental learning, but that instructions represent a highly effective method of activating those responses to the stimulus materials which are essential for acquisition.

Acquisition

References

ARCHER, E. J. (1960), 'Re-evaluation of the meaningfulness of all possible CVC trigrams', *Psychological Monographs*, vol. 74, no. 10.

BUGELSKI, B. R., and RICKWOOD, J. (1963), 'Presentation time, total time, and mediation in paired-associate learning: Self-pacing', *Journal of Experimental Psychology*, vol. 65, pp. 616–17.

CLARK, L. L., LANSFORD, T. G., and DALLENBACH, K. M. (1960), 'Repetition and associative learning', *American Journal of Psychology*, vol. 73, pp. 22–40.

COHEN, J. C., and MUSGRAVE, B. S. (1964), 'Effect of meaningfulness on cue selection in verbal paired-associate learning', *Journal of Experimental Psychology*, vol. 68, pp. 284–91.

COHEN, J. C., and MUSGRAVE, B. S. (1966), 'Effects of formal similarity on cue selection in verbal paired-associate learning', *Journal of Experimental Psychology*, vol. 71, pp. 829–38.

COOPER, E. H., and PANTLE, A. J. (1967), 'The total-time hypothesis in verbal learning', *Psychological Bulletin*, vol. 68, pp. 221–34.

DULSKY, S. G. (1935), 'The effect of change of background on recall and relearning', *Journal of Experimental Psychology*, vol. 18, pp. 725–40.

EBBINGHAUS, H. (1885), *Über das Gedächtnis: Untersuchungen zur experimentellen Psychologie*, Duncker and Humblot. (Translated by H. A. Ruger and C. E. Bussenius as *Memory: A Contribution to Experimental Psychology*, Teachers College, Columbia University, 1913.)

EKSTRAND, B. R., WALLACE, W. P., and UNDERWOOD, B. J. (1966), 'A frequency theory of verbal discrimination learning', *Psychological Review*, vol. 73, pp. 566–78.

ESTES, W. K. (1960), 'Learning theory and the new "mental chemistry"', *Psychological Review*, vol. 67, pp. 207–22.

ESTES, W. K. (1961), 'New developments in statistical behavior theory: differential tests of axioms for associative learning', *Psychometrika*, vol. 26, pp. 73–84.

ESTES, W. K., HOPKINS, B. L., and CROTHERS, E. J. (1960), 'All-or-none and conservation effects in the learning and retention of paired-associates', *Journal of Experimental Psychology*, vol. 60, pp. 329–39.

GIBSON, E. J. (1940), 'A systematic application of the concepts of generalization and differentiation to verbal learning', *Psychological Review*, vol. 47, pp. 196–229.

GIBSON, E. J. (1942), 'Intra-list generalization as a factor in verbal learning', *Journal of Experimental Psychology*, vol. 30, pp. 185–200.

GLAZE, J. A. (1928), 'The association value of non-sense syllables', *Journal of Genetic Psychology*, vol. 35, pp. 255–69.

HOROWITZ, L. M., and LARSEN, S. R. (1963), 'Response interference in paired-associate learning', *Journal of Experimental Psychology*, vol. 65, pp. 225–32.

HOUSTON, J. P. (1967), 'Stimulus selection as influenced by degrees of learning, attention, prior associations, and experience with the stimulus components', *Journal of Experimental Psychology*, vol. 73, pp. 509–16.

HOVLAND, C. I. (1938), 'Experimental studies in rote-learning theory. III. Distribution of practice with varying speeds of syllable presentation', *Journal of Experimental Psychology*, vol. 23, pp. 172–90.

HOVLAND, C. I. (1940), 'Experimental studies in rote-learning theory. VII. Distribution of practice with varying lengths of list', *Journal of Experimental Psychology*, vol. 27, pp. 271–84.

HOVLAND, C. I., and KURTZ, K. H. (1952), 'Experimental studies in rote-learning theory: X. Pre-learning, syllable familiarization and the length-difficulty relationship', *Journal of Experimental Psychology*, vol. 44, pp. 31–9.

HULL, C. L. (1943), *Principles of Behavior*, Appleton-Century-Crofts.

JAMES, C. T., and GREENO, J. G. (1967), 'Stimulus selection at different stages of paired-associate learning', *Journal of Experimental Psychology*, vol. 74, pp. 75–83.

JENKINS, J. J. (1963), 'Stimulus "fractionation" in paired-associate learning', *Psychological Reports*, vol. 13, pp. 409–10.

JUNG, J. (1965), 'Two stages of paired-associate learning as a function of intralist-response similarity (IRS) and response meaningfulness (M)', *Journal of Experimental Psychology*, vol. 70, pp. 371–8.

KEPPEL, G. (1964), 'Facilitation in short- and long-term retention of paired associates following distributed practice in learning', *Journal of Verbal Learning and Verbal Behavior*, vol. 3, pp. 91–111.

KIMBLE, G. A. (1961), *Hilgard and Marquis' Conditioning and Learning*, Appleton-Century-Crofts.

KOFFKA, K. (1935), *Principles of Gestalt Psychology*, Harcourt, Brace.

KÖHLER, W. (1941), 'On the nature of associations', *Proceedings of the American Philosophical Society*, vol. 84, pp. 489–502.

LOVELACE, E. A., and SCHULZ, R. W. (1966), 'Comments on Martin, Cox, and Boersma', *Psychonomic Science*, vol. 5, p. 72.

McGEOCH, G. O. (1931), 'Whole-part problem', *Psychological Bulletin*, vol. 28, pp. 713–39.

McGEOCH, J. A. (1942), *The Psychology of Human Learning*, Longmans, Green.

MANDLER, G. (1954), 'Response factors in human learning', *Psychological Review*, vol. 61, pp. 235–44.

MURDOCK, B. B., Jr. (1960), 'The immediate retention of unrelated words', *Journal of Experimental Psychology*, vol. 60, pp. 222–34.

NOBLE, C. E. (1952), 'An analysis of meaning', *Psychological Review*, vol. 59, pp. 421–30.

NOBLE, C. E. (1953), 'The meaning-familiarity relationship', *Psychological Review*, vol. 60, pp. 89–98.

NOBLE, C. E., STOCKWELL, F. E., and PRYER, M. W. (1957), 'Meaningfulness (m') and association value (a) in paired-associate syllable learning', *Psychological Reports*, vol. 3, pp. 441–52.

Acquisition

PAN, S. (1926), 'The influence of context upon learning and recall', *Journal of Experimental Psychology*, vol. 9, pp. 468–91.

POSTMAN, L. (1963), 'One-trial learning', in C. N. Cofer and B. S. Musgrave, eds., *Verbal Behavior and Learning: Problems and Processes*, McGraw-Hill.

POSTMAN, L. (1964), 'Short-term memory and incidental learning', in A. W. Melton, ed., *Categories of Human Learning*, Academic Press.

POSTMAN, L., and GOGGIN, J. (1964), 'Whole versus part learning of serial lists as a function of meaningfulness and intralist similarity', *Journal of Experimental Psychology*, vol. 68, pp. 140–50.

POSTMAN, L., and GOGGIN, J. (1966), 'Whole versus part learning of paired-associate lists', *Journal of Experimental Psychology*, vol. 71, pp. 867–77.

RESTLE, F. (1965), 'Significance of all-or-none learning', *Psychological Bulletin*, vol. 64, pp. 313–25.

SALTZ, E. (1961), 'Response pretraining: differentiation or availability?', *Journal of Experimental Psychology*, vol. 62, pp. 583–7.

SCHULZ, R. W., WEAVER, G. E., and GINSBERG, S. (1965), 'Mediation with pseudomediation controlled: chaining is not an artifact', *Psychonomic Science*, vol. 2, pp. 169–70.

SCHWARTZ, M. (1963), 'Transfer from failed pairs as a test of one-trial versus incremental learning', *American Journal of Psychology*, vol. 76, pp. 266–73.

SPEAR, N. E., EKSTRAND, B. R., and UNDERWOOD, B. J. (1964), 'Association by contiguity', *Journal of Experimental Psychology*, vol. 67, pp. 151–61.

UNDERWOOD, B. J. (1952), 'Studies of distributed practice: VI. The influence of rest-interval activity in serial learning', *Journal of Experimental Psychology*, vol. 43, pp. 329–40.

UNDERWOOD, B. J. (1953), 'Studies of distributed practice: IX. Learning and retention of paired adjectives as a function of intralist similarity', *Journal of Experimental Psychology*, vol. 45, pp. 143–9.

UNDERWOOD, B. J. (1961), 'Ten years of massed practice on distributed practice', *Psychological Review*, vol. 68, pp. 229–47.

UNDERWOOD, B. J. (1963), 'Stimulus selection in verbal learning', in C. N. Cofer and B. S. Musgrave, eds., *Verbal Behavior and Learning: Problems and Processes*, McGraw-Hill.

UNDERWOOD, B. J. (1966), *Experimental Psychology*, Appleton-Century-Crofts, 2nd edn.

UNDERWOOD, B. J., and EKSTRAND, B. R. (1966), 'An analysis of some shortcomings in the interference theory of forgetting', *Psychological Review*, vol. 73, pp. 540–9.

UNDERWOOD, B. J., and EKSTRAND, B. R. (1967), 'Effect of distributed practice on paired-associate learning', *Journal of Experimental Psychology, Monograph Supplement*, vol. 73, no. 4, part 2.

UNDERWOOD, B. J., EKSTRAND, B. R., and KEPPEL, G. (1965), 'An analysis of intralist similarity in verbal learning with experiments on conceptual similarity', *Journal of Verbal Learning and Verbal Behavior*, vol. 4, pp. 447–62.

UNDERWOOD, B. J., and KEPPEL, G. (1962), 'One-trial learning?' *Journal of Verbal Learning and Verbal Behavior*, vol. 1, pp. 1–13.

UNDERWOOD, B. J., REHULA, R., and KEPPEL, G. (1962), 'Item selection in paired-associate learning', *American Journal of Psychology*, vol. 75, pp. 353–71.

UNDERWOOD, B. J., and SCHULZ, R. W. (1960), *Meaningfulness and Verbal Learning*, Lippincott.

VON RESTORFF, H. (1933), 'Über die Wirkung von Bereichsbildungen im Spurenfeld', *Psychologische Forschung*, vol. 18, pp. 299–342.

WALLACE, W. P. (1965), 'Review of the historical, empirical, and theoretical status of the von Restorff phenomenon', *Psychological Bulletin*, vol. 63, pp. 410–24.

WAUGH, N. C. (1962), 'The effect of intralist repetition on free recall', *Journal of Verbal Learning and Verbal Behaviour*, vol. 1, pp. 95–9.

WAUGH, N. C. (1963), 'Immediate memory as a function of repetition', *Journal of Verbal Learning and Verbal Behaviour*, vol. 2, pp. 107–12.

WAUGH, N. C. (1967), 'Presentation time and free recall', *Journal of Experimental Psychology*, vol. 73, pp. 39–44.

WEISS, W., and MARGOLIUS, G. (1954), 'The effect of context stimuli on learning and retention', *Journal of Experimental Psychology*, vol. 48, pp. 318–22.

1 B. J. Underwood, M. Ham and B. Ekstrand

Cue Selection in Paired-Associate Learning

B. J. Underwood, M. Ham and B. Ekstrand, 'Cue selection in paired-associate learning', *Journal of Experimental Psychology*, vol. 64 (1962), pp. 405–9.

Consider a paired-associate list in which the stimulus term for each response consists of two distinct components, A and B. Both components are consistently present on each learning trial. Assuming that learning occurs in this situation, there are many possible interpretations which may be given as to what the effective stimulus or cue is for each response. It might be said that the effective cue is a configuration formed by A and B. Or, it might be said that each component is independently a cue for the response; that one or the other component is the effective cue, but not both, and so on.

The present study is predicated on the notion that when a complex stimulus is presented to *S* a selection process may occur so that the effective cue for the response is some component of the complex stimulus that is actually presented. Thus, the assumption is that there may be a discrepancy between the nominal stimulus (the stimulus actually presented *S*) and the functional stimulus (the component of the nominal stimulus which becomes the effective cue for response elicitation). That such discrepancies may exist is suggested by the reports of *S*s that they have used only a single letter of a three-letter stimulus as the effective cue (Underwood and Schulz, 1960). Such discrepancies might also be inferred from the so-called context experiments (e.g. Weiss and Margolius, 1954) in which the removal of a component of a compound nominal stimulus produces a decrement in recall, although such studies offer other interpretative possibilities, e.g. the functional stimulus is a configuration and the removal of any component reduces the effective associative strength.

If cue selection occurs – if only a part of a compound stimulus becomes the functional stimulus – certain variables should influence the selection. The hypothesis tested in the present experiment is that given two components of different classes as the nominal stimulus, the more meaningful component will become the functional stimulus. This hypothesis seems very close to the notion of differences in discriminability as a variable determining stimulus selection, a notion suggested by Sundland and Wickens (1962), and for which some experimental support was obtained.

The particular predictions for the present study may now be specified. Two lists for original learning were constructed. The stimulus compound for one list consisted of colors and low-meaningful trigrams; for the other list the compound consisted of colors and common three-letter words. For the first list it was assumed that the colors were more meaningful than the trigrams; therefore, the functional stimuli should be the colors. In the case of the word–color compound it was assumed that the words were more meaningful than the colors, hence, the functional stimuli should be the words. (It would have been more precise to have used two sets of verbal units of known meaningfulness for the compounds, but the use of colors was recommended by the desire to keep the experiment continuous with the context experiments.) Given the above assumptions, it was predicted that following the learning of the list with the trigram–color compounds, very little decrement would be observed if the trigrams were removed on a transfer test, but that a great loss would appear if the colors were removed from the compound. Contrariwise, in the case of the word–color compounds, removal of the words on a transfer test would result in a large loss but removal of the colors would have little effect on transfer performance.

Method

The general procedure required that half the Ss learn an original list with trigram–color compound stimuli, and half learn a list with word–color stimuli. To test for each component separately on a transfer list required four groups. However, to determine precisely the amount of decrement occurring required two control groups for which the stimuli on the transfer test were the same as on original learning. Thus, the design called for six groups. Let W stand for words, T for trigrams, and C for colors, and the symbols before a hyphen designate the stimulus during original learning, those after the hyphen the stimulus on the transfer test. The six groups are, therefore: WC–WC and TC–TC (the two control groups); WC–C and TC–C (only color stimuli on transfer test); WC–W and TC–T (the verbal units appear alone as the stimuli on the transfer test).

Table 1

Stimulus Components Used in the Lists

Words	Trigrams	Colors
GAS	GWS	Red
DAY	DWK	Brown
NEW	NXQ	Yellow
DIE	DHX	Blue
BAD	BWD	Orange
GOT	GVS	Black
BED	BXD	Green

Lists

The materials for the lists are shown in Table 1. Each list consisted of seven pairs. The three-letter words all have AA ratings in the Thorndike–Lorge (1944) list except the word GAS, which is rated A. The trigrams have quite low associative connections between letters as based on the Underwood–Schulz (1960) tables. It should also be noted that the trigrams have relatively high formal similarity as indexed by repeated letters. The purpose of this was to minimize the possibility that a single letter (such as the first letter) might become the functional stimulus. The frequency of repeated letters in the word list is about the same as for the trigrams and the repetitions are in the same positions. Both lists have the same initial letters.

The color components were made of construction paper and pasted on the vellum tape. Rectangular frames of color completely surrounded the verbal unit, the width of the frame being approximately $\frac{1}{4}$ in. When the color was the only component on the transfer test the frame appeared exactly as it had during original learning, the verbal unit having been removed. The par-

Acquisition

ticular colors paired with particular verbal units appear in the same row in Table 1. The response terms were the single digit numbers 2 through 8.

On both learning and transfer trials the rate of presentation was 2 sec for the stimulus alone, and 2 sec for the stimulus and response together. Four different orders of the pairs were used. Anticipation learning was used throughout.

Procedure

The original learning was carried until the S achieved one perfect recitation of the list. The transfer tests were carried for ten trials with S instructed to give as many correct responses as possible on the first transfer trial. The usual paired-associate instructions were given prior to original learning. In addition, S was told that both the word (or trigram) and color would appear consistently together from trial to trial. The intent of these instructions was to inform S of the nature of the stimulus compound without, at the same time, biasing him toward 'using' one or the other components. Prior to the transfer trials S again was fully informed as to the nature of the stimulus which would be present on these trials. Approximately 45 sec elapsed between original learning and the first transfer trial.

Each of the six groups contained twenty Ss. Twenty blocks were made up such that each condition occurred once within each block, with the order of the six conditions within a block being randomly determined. The Ss were then assigned to the schedule in terms of their appearance at the laboratory. No S was lost for failure to learn.

Results

The mean numbers of trials to attain the criterion on original learning are shown in the left portion of Table 2. Differences among the three WC groups and among the three TC groups represent random variation, the F being less than 1 in each case. For the 60 WC Ss the mean is $8 \cdot 67 \pm 0 \cdot 63$, and for the 60 TC Ss, $10 \cdot 52 \pm 0 \cdot 65$. The difference ($1 \cdot 85 \pm 0 \cdot 90$) gives a t of $2 \cdot 06$, which is just past the 5 per cent significance level.

The mean performance on each transfer trial is shown in

Figure 1. The upper section refers to the T C groups, the lower section to the W C groups. For the T C groups it can be seen that when the colors alone were used as stimuli, transfer was virtually complete; the performance of this group is only slightly below the control (TC–TC), thus indicating that the colors alone were

Table 2

Mean Number of Trials to Criterion on Original Learning and Mean Number of Items Lost on First Transfer Trial

Cond.	Original learning		Transfer	
	Mean	σ_m	Mean	σ_m
WC–WC	8·80	0·97	—	—
WC–W	8·00	1·18	1·20	0·44
WC–C	9·20	1·14	2·50	0·47
TC–TC	11·55	0·95	—	—
TC–T	10·00	1·20	2·85	0·36
TC–C	10·00	1·21	0·05	0·37

completely effective functional stimuli. If *only* the color component was the functional stimulus, performance of group T C–T should start at zero. It does not. For at least some Ss the trigrams were also functional stimuli for at least a few responses.

The lower section of Figure 1 shows that for the W C groups neither the words nor the colors developed complete effectiveness. The colors are less effective than the words, but the words alone show some loss as compared with the control.

The clearest inferences concerning the functional stimuli in original learning can be made from the performance on the first transfer trial. Since group T C–T C showed a larger criterion drop than did group W C–W C, loss scores have been calculated. To do this, each S's score on the first trial was subtracted from the mean score of the appropriate control group. These loss scores are shown in the right section of Table 2. A 2 × 2 analysis of variance was performed on these scores, using as one classification variable T C and W C as identified in original learning, and as the

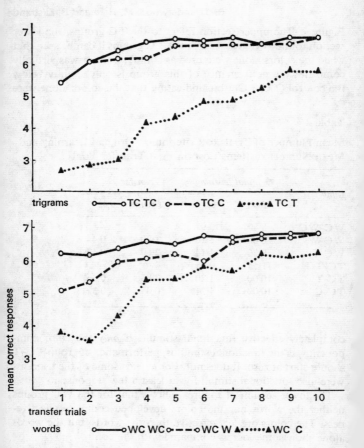

Figure 1 Acquisition curves on the ten transfer trials

other, colors and verbal units on transfer. Only the interaction F was significant, being 25·31; with 1 and 76 df, the F needed for the 1 per cent significance level is approximately 7·00. Thus, the predictions that for the TC lists the colors would become the functional stimuli and that for the WC lists the words would become the functional stimuli, are given some support.

Discussion

The transfer tests for the TC compounds showed that color alone was a completely effective functional stimulus. This fact precludes an interpretation of the functional stimulus as being a configuration. However, it was noted that the trigram stimuli were not completely ineffective on the first transfer trial. There are at least two possible interpretations of this finding. First, it may mean that some trigrams, quite independently of the color component, become associated directly with the response term. Secondly, it may mean that some associative connection may have developed between the color and trigram components of the stimulus compounds. Thus, when the trigram is presented, the correct anticipation is mediated by associations running from the trigram to the color to the response term. The present data do not allow a choice between these two alternative interpretations.

The transfer data following learning of the WC lists raise three interpretative problems. First, it was noted that transfer was greater when the words became stimuli than when the colors became stimuli. Two circumstances could lead to this finding. (a) Most Ss in original learning used words as stimuli for *all* associations but a few Ss used colors as stimuli for all associations. (b) All Ss used words as stimuli for *most* associations during original learning but used color as stimuli for a few associations. Given a large number of Ss a choice between these two alternatives could be made by examining the distributions of scores on the first transfer trial. If the first of the two possible explanations is appropriate, the distributions should be bimodal when words alone or when colors alone are stimuli on the first transfer trial. If the second alternative is appropriate, each distribution should be continuous. Actually, bimodality is suggested in the present distributions but with only twenty cases in each this may be quite fortuitous.

The second interpretative problem is the same as that posed for the TC compounds where the data show that for some associations for some Ss both the trigram and the color elicited the response. Such dual functionality may also be deduced from the data for the WC compounds. On the first transfer trial a mean of approximately 5·0 correct responses occurred when the words were presented alone and 3·8 when the colors were presented alone. These two values sum to 8·8, which is appreciably higher than the mean of 6·3 shown by the control Ss on the first transfer trial. Clearly, dual functionality of the two components obtained for at least some Ss. However, just as in the case of the TC compounds, this apparent duality may result from direct associations between the components and the response term or it may result from mediation between the stimulus components.

The third interpretative problem presented by the results of the WC compounds is the fact that the words showed greater transfer than did the colors. As stated in the procedure section, it was believed that the words would be more meaningful than the colors. We have no independent evidence for this and it may not be valid. The Ss, being much more practiced in dealing with word stimuli than with patches of color as stimuli, may be biased toward the selection of the verbal stimuli. The data are quite in harmony with such a notion. However, a somewhat different approach may be taken to the problem. An empirical test can be made to determine which stimulus compound leads to most rapid learning when this learning is not preceded by learning in which the compound is present. To determine this three new groups of fifteen Ss each were run. One group learned the trigram–number pairs, a second the word–number pairs, and the third the color–number pairs. The mean total correct responses in 10 trials were $38·80 \pm 3·61$, $51·20 \pm 3·52$, and $50·40 \pm 2·19$, respectively. While the F is significant far beyond the 1 per cent level it is clear that most of the variance is produced by the trigram–number pairs. The words and colors do not differ appreciably in their effectiveness as stimuli. The small difference in favor of the words occurred primarily on the first three trials. Thus, it seems quite reasonable to conclude that when S is given a compound consisting of common words and colors, he is likely to select the words as functional stimuli, not necessarily because they are more meaningful, but because he is more accustomed to dealing with such stimuli.

Finally, it may be stated that the results of the present experiment, taken in conjunction with the study by Sundland and Wickens (1962), would seem to indicate that it may be more fruitful to view the so-called context experiments as experiments investigating the variables determining cue selection.

Summary

This experiment was based on the assumption that when S is presented a compound stimulus in a verbal-learning experiment, cue selection may occur. Word–color or trigram–color compound stimuli were used in learning original paired-associate lists with numbers as responses, followed by a transfer test in which one or the other components alone was presented as the stimulus. Control groups were also used, these groups being given further trials with the original compound stimuli.

The results show:

1. For the trigram–color compounds, color was a completely effective stimulus on the transfer test. The trigrams, however, also produced a small positive transfer effect. The selection of the color component as the primary functional stimulus was assumed to be due to its higher meaningfulness.

2. For the word–color compounds, transfer was higher when the words appeared alone than when the colors appeared alone. This may be due to a bias Ss have toward dealing with verbal material (as compared with the color patches used) rather than to higher meaningfulness of the words.

It was concluded that experiments dealing with the effects of context changes on retention may be viewed as representing cases of cue selection.

References

SUNDLAND, D. M., and WICKENS, D. D. (1962), 'Context factors in paired-associate learning and recall', *Journal of Experimental Psychology*, vol. 63, pp. 302–6.

THORNDIKE, E. L., and LORGE, I. (1944), *The Teacher's Word Book of 30,000 Words*. Teachers College, Columbia University.

UNDERWOOD, B. J., and SCHULZ, R. W. (1960), *Meaningfulness and Verbal Learning*, Lippincott.

WEISS, W., and MARGOLIUS, G. (1954), 'The effect of context stimuli on learning and retention', *Journal of Experimental Psychology*, vol. 48, pp. 318–22.

2 L. Postman and R. Greenbloom

Conditions of Cue Selection in the Acquisition of
Paired-Associate Lists

L. Postman and R. Greenbloom, 'Conditions of cue selection in the
acquisition of paired-associate lists', *Journal of Experimental Psychology*,
vol. 73 (1967), pp. 91–100.

The amount and positional distribution of letter-cue selection in paired-
associate learning were investigated. Two types of list composed of
trigram-digit pairs were used. The stimulus terms were easy to pronounce (EP) in one, and hard to pronounce (HP) in the other. After
learning to criterion, different groups were tested for digit recall with 1
of 4 classes of cues: 1st letter of trigram, 2nd letter, 3rd letter, whole
trigram. Those tested with single letters were also required to reproduce
the missing stimulus letters. When S failed to reproduce additional
letters but recalled the digit, single-letter selection was inferred. The
level of stimulus-letter reproduction was considerably higher for EP
than HP items. There was little selection in Cond. EP but a substantial
amount in Cond. HP which was largely limited to 1st letters.

When a stimulus in a paired-associate list consists of a number of
elements, any fraction of these elements which is not duplicated
in other stimulus terms may serve as an effective cue in learning.
To the extent that such cue selection occurs, the functional
stimulus differs from the nominal stimulus (cf. Underwood, 1963;
Underwood, Ham and Ekstrand, 1962). If the stimuli are trigrams, and there is no duplication of letters in the list, any one of
the three letters in a trigram may in principle become the functional stimulus. The Ss report that they do, in fact, attempt to
learn responses to single letters (Underwood and Schulz, 1960,
pp. 298 ff.). Evidence on the amount of selection and on the positional distribution of single-letter cues was presented in a recent
study by Jenkins (1963). The learning materials were paired
associates, with trigrams as stimuli and single digits as responses.
After acquisition of the list the stimulus letters, divided into three
groups according to position in the trigram, were presented to Ss
one at a time with instructions to recall the appropriate digits.

Correct responses to letters from each of the three positions were above chance. The amount of recall was highest to the first letter, lowest to the middle letter, and intermediate to the final letter. However, the sum of recalls to single letters fell short of 100 per cent when allowance was made for chance successes. The results were, therefore, interpreted as indicating considerable, but less than perfect, selection of single-letter cues.

While the findings reported by Jenkins are consistent with the assumption that single letters at each of the three positions in a trigram are selected as functional cues, they do not constitute conclusive support for this interpretation. It is not known how frequently responses to a single letter were mediated by recall of either one or both of the remaining letters. To the extent that mediation occurs, correct recalls do not in fact reflect associations to single letters. Given the possibility of mediation, the distribution of correct responses to the individual letters of a trigram does not necessarily permit clear conclusions about the amount of selection. It is true that if the correct response is given to more than one letter, failure to select a single element is indicated. However, if there is correct recall to only one of the letters, it does not follow that this particular letter was in fact selected during learning since mediation cannot be ruled out. If the functional stimulus in learning includes more than one element, success in the reproduction of the total set of elements may vary with the position of the cue presented on the test of recall. Thus, only one of the three letters may be effective in reinstating the functional stimulus, and recall to that letter could still be mediated. In light of these considerations it appears that selection of a single letter can be inferred unequivocally only if (a) that letter elicits the correct associate, and (b) S is unable to reproduce the remaining letters of the trigram at the time of recall.

The present study had two purposes: first, to determine the amount and positional distribution of single-letter cue selection that remain in evidence when the contribution of mediated recall is taken into account; and second, to investigate the effect on cue selection of the pronunciability of the stimulus terms. The more pronounceable the trigrams, the more likely Ss are to respond to them as units, i.e. pronunciability may be taken as an index of the degree of pre-experimental integration of the stimulus terms.

Acquisition

Hence single-letter cue selection should decrease as the stimuli become more pronounceable.

Method

Design

Under all conditions of the experiment *S*s learned a list of paired associates with trigrams as stimuli and digits as responses. Attainment of the criterion of acquisition was followed by a test of recall. The variables manipulated were (a) the pronunciability of the stimulus terms, and (b) the nature of the cues presented on the test of recall. The stimulus terms were either hard or easy to pronounce (HP *v*. EP). One of the following sets of cues was presented on the test of recall: first letters of trigrams, second letters, third letters, the whole trigrams. Each of these sets of cues was used with a different group. With two levels of pronunciability and four types of recall cues, there were eight independent groups which will be designated as HP–1, HP–2, HP–3, HP–W, and EP–1, EP–2, EP–3, and EP–W, respectively.

Each type of cue was given to a separate group because successive tests of the same *S*s are not independent of each other. This consideration applies especially to the reproduction of stimulus letters since each condition of testing involves presentation of a set of letters as recall cues. However, for purposes of subsidiary comparisons all groups tested with single-letter cues were given two additional recall trials in which the two remaining sets of such cues were presented in succession. The order in which the remaining sets were administered was counter-balanced. Thus, half the *S*s in groups HP–1 and EP–1 were exposed to the second letters on the second recall trial, and to the third letters on the third recall trial. The order of presentation was similarly balanced for the other groups tested on single letters.

Lists

The learning materials were lists of six paired associates. The stimulus terms were trigrams, with no repeated letters within a list. The HP and EP lists of stimuli were selected on the basis of the pronunciability ratings of Underwood and Schulz (1960,

appendix E). Two different lists were used at each level of pronunciability. In Cond. HP the mean pronunciability ratings of
the two lists were 7·6 and 7·8; in Cond. EP the mean rating was
3·0 for both lists. There were only minor variations in the m value
of the letters in the three positions of the trigrams of any of the
lists according to Anderson's (1965) norms. The responses in all
lists were the digits from 2 through 7.

Procedure

The paired-associate list was presented at a 2:2-sec rate, with a
4-sec intertrial interval. There were four different orders of presentation. Learning was to a criterion of one perfect recitation.
There was an interval of 2·5 min between the end of paired-
associate learning and the beginning of the test of recall. During
that interval Ss were instructed in the recall procedure.

For the test of recall, the appropriate stimulus cues were presented on cards; a separate card was used for each item. When a
single-letter cue was presented, the positions of the missing letters
were indicated by dashes. For example, when group HP–1 was
tested for recall of the trigram CKB, the recall cue had the form
C – –. The Ss were instructed to call out the missing letters and
the digit that had been paired with the stimulus in the list. When
the whole trigram was the cue, Ss were simply instructed to give
the appropriate digit to each item. A digit response was required
to each stimulus cue, i.e. Ss were asked to guess if they thought
they could not recall the appropriate digit. All Ss were reminded
of the fact that there were no repeated letters in the trigram stimuli
and that the responses were the digits from 2 through 7. The deck
of stimulus cards was handed to S who was allowed to pace himself, calling out his responses which were recorded by E. After the
test of recall Ss filled out a questionnaire in which they were
asked to state whether they had paid equal attention to all three
letters of the stimulus trigrams, and if not, which of the letters
they had singled out.

Subjects

There were eighteen Ss in each of the eight groups. The Ss were
undergraduate students who were not necessarily naïve to rote-
learning experiments. Assignment to conditions was in blocks of

Acquisition

eight, with one *S* from each condition per block. The running order within blocks was determined by means of a table of random numbers.

Results

Trials to criterion

There were no significant differences among the groups learning a given type of list. The mean number of trials to criterion was 8·1 for Cond. HP, and 6·2 for Cond. EP. The difference between the two types of list is significant, t (142) = 3·80, $p < 0.01$. The pronunciability of the stimulus terms has a relatively small but reliable effect on speed of acquisition.

Reproduction of stimulus letters

Table 1 presents the mean numbers of additional letters reproduced by *S*s tested with single-letter cues (row of total scores). The maximum possible score is 12 since there were two letters to

Table 1

Mean Numbers of Stimulus Letters Reproduced

Letter reproduced	Position of cue					
	EP–1	EP–2	EP–3	HP–1	HP–2	HP–3
First	—	5·06	4·83	—	3·28	2·94
Second	5·33	—	4·78	2·72	—	2·17
Third	5·22	4·83	—	2·89	2·50	—
Total	10·55	9·89	9·61	5·61	5·78	5·11

Note: MS_w for total scores = 7·84.

be reproduced for each of six trigrams. The amount of stimulus recall in Cond. EP is high, being of the order of 80 per cent. The values for Cond. HP are considerably lower, averaging about 45 per cent. The difference between the two levels of pronunciability is highly significant, F (1, 102) = 70·40, $p < 0.001$. Cue position is not a significant source of variance and does not interact with type of list, $F < 1$ in both cases.

56

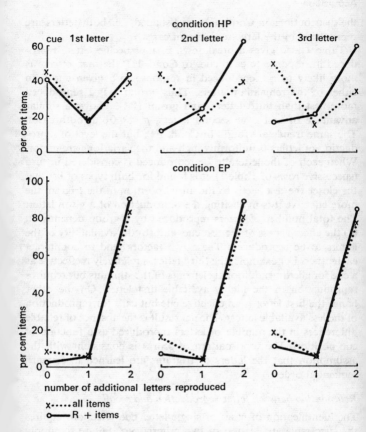

Figure 1 Distributions of stimulus–letter reproductions and recalls.
(Dotted line shows percentages of all items for which zero, one, and
two letters were reproduced. Solid line shows percentages of all recalls
coinciding with different levels of letter reproduction)

For any given trigram S could reproduce either zero, one, or
two of the missing letters. Figure 1 (dotted lines) shows the percentages of occurrence of the three scores for each of the groups.
The distributions in Cond. HP are V-shaped, i.e. scores of 0 and
2 are considerably more common than a score of 1. By contrast,

the distributions in Cond. EP are J-shaped, i.e. both letters are reproduced in the large majority of cases.

Table 1 also gives a breakdown of the specific letters reproduced in response to each cue. In Cond. HP the first letter was more likely to be reproduced in response to a given cue than either of the remaining letters. Thus, group HP–2 reproduced more first than third letters, and group HP–3 shows a similar advantage of first over second letters, $p < 0.01$ in both cases. The same trends are found in Cond. EP, but the level of reproduction of letters is uniformly high and the variations are minor. When each of the letters to be reproduced is considered in turn (successive rows of Table 1), it is found for both types of list that the closer the test cue is to the initial position in the trigram the more effective it is in eliciting the reproduction of a given letter. The total number of letters reproduced by a group depends on (a) the effectiveness of the test cue, and (b) the availability of the letters to be reproduced. These two factors tend to counteract each other. For example, the third letter is relatively ineffective as a cue for eliciting additional elements of the stimulus but requires reproduction of the highly available first letter. On the other hand, the first letter is an effective cue but calls for reproduction of the less available letters. The net result is the absence of reliable differences in the number of letters reproduced as a function of cue position. The total pattern of scores is consistent with the assumption that the letters of trigrams are learned in forward sequential order.

Relationship between letter reproduction and recall

The identification of cases of single-letter cue selection requires the successive application of two criteria, viz. failure to supply additional letters and correct recall of the response. Stimulus-letter reproduction in Cond. EP was uniformly high, and this fact in itself indicates that there is little cue selection when the stimulus terms are easy to pronounce. In Cond. HP, however, no additional letters were reproduced in close to half of the cases, and the conclusions to be drawn about selection depend critically on the relationship between stimulus reproduction and recall. For purposes of assessing this relationship, correct recalls (R+) were divided into three categories according to the number of stimulus letters reproduced along with the response digit: S_0R+, S_1R+, S_2R+. The subscript indicates the number of letters reproduced. The percentages of all recalls that fall into each of these three categories are plotted in Figure 1 (solid line) along with the percentages of letter-reproduction scores. If the level of stimulus-letter reproduction has no differential effect on recall, then the percentages of cases in categories S_0R+, S_1R+,

Table 2

Conditional Probabilities or Recall, Given Different Numbers of Letters Reproduced

| No. letters reproduced | Group | | | | | | | | | | | |
| | EP–1 | | EP–2 | | EP–3 | | HP–1 | | HP–2 | | HP–3 | |
	N	p	N	p	N	p	N	p	N	p	N	p
0	9	0·33	17	0·35	19	0·53	48	0·71	46	0·15	53	0·19
1	8	0·75	4	1·00	5	1·00	19	0·74	20	0·75	17	0·76
2	91	0·98	87	0·91	84	1·00	41	0·88	42	0·88	38	0·92

Note: N = number of cases in which a given number of letters was reproduced; p = conditional probability.

and S_2R+ should be determined entirely by the relative frequencies of S_0, S_1, and S_2, i.e. the two distributions of percentages should coincide. Divergence of the distributions indicates a shift in the probability of recall as a function of the number of letters reproduced. In each case the percentage of recalls falls below the expected value at S_0, and above the expected value at S_2. The divergence of the two distributions is more pronounced for groups HP–2 and HP–3 than for group HP–1; there are no comparable differences among the three groups in Cond. EP. The probability of recall increases with the level of stimulus reproduction but not at the same rate for all groups.

The degrees of association between stimulus reproduction and recall are summarized in terms of the conditional probabilities shown in Table 2. The values shown are the probabilities of recall, given zero, one, and two correct letter reproductions – $R+ : S_0$, $R+ : S_1$, and $R+ : S_2$. The frequencies of cases of S_0, S_1, and S_2 are also shown. The value of $R+ : S_0$ is substantially higher for group HP–1 than for any of the remaining groups. Consequently, while all the groups show increases in the conditional probabilities as a function of the number of letters reproduced, the gradient is least steep for group HP–1. It should be noted that in Cond. EP the absolute frequencies of cases in categories S_0 and S_1 are small; nevertheless S_0 yields the lowest conditional probability in each case. The trends shown in Figure 1 and Table 1 indicate that a substantial number of cases satisfying both criteria of single-letter cue selection is obtained only for group HP–1. There are also moderate amounts of two-letter selection for each of the three groups in Cond. HP. These conclusions are borne out by the statistical analyses of the recall scores which are presented in the next section.

Recall scores

Table 3 shows for the single-letter groups the mean frequency per S of the three categories of recall scores, viz. S_0R+, S_1R+, and S_2R+. Each of these measures represents, for a given S category, the mean of the products of the number of cases and the conditional probability of recall (Table 2). The relative magnitudes of the scores correspond, of course, to the recall distributions in Figure 1.

For purposes of statistical analysis the three scores of each S were corrected separately for guessing. The correction was based on the assumption that one response on the recall test would be correct by chance. This chance correction was then divided among the three categories of scores in accordance with the distribution of stimulus-letter reproductions. Thus, if the letter reproductions of a given S yielded three scores of 0, one score of 1, and two scores of 2, the chance correction was 0·50 for category S_0R+, 0·17 for S_1R+, and 0·33 for S_2R+. Analysis of variance shows that Recall Category is a highly significant source of variance, $F(2, 204) = 200\cdot44$, $p < 0\cdot001$.[1] Over-all S_2R+ is by far the most frequent category; there are approximately equal numbers of occurrences of S_0R+ and S_1R+. However, Recall Category interacts significantly with Pronunciability, F (2,

1. Heterogeneity of variance could not be eliminated. However, the results of the analysis were considered acceptable in view of the high levels of significance obtained.

$204) = 54 \cdot 18$, $p < 0 \cdot 001$. This interaction reflects primarily the fact that the peak in category S_2R+ is sharper for EP than for HP. The higher-order interaction, Recall Category × Pronunciability × Cue Position, is also significant, $F(4, 204) = 3 \cdot 32$, $p < 0 \cdot 01$. Further analysis shows that Recall Category interacts significantly with Cue Position in Cond. HP ($p < 0 \cdot 02$) but not in Cond. EP ($F < 1$). These tests confirm the conclusion that the distribution of the recall scores of group HP–1 differs from those of groups HP–2 and HP–3, and that the distributions of the three groups in Cond. EP are essentially parallel.

The total recall scores of the single-letter groups will now be evaluated and compared with those of the groups tested with whole trigrams. The total scores of all groups are shown in Table 3. In Cond. EP the amount recalled is generally high. The scores

Table 3

Mean Numbers of Responses Recalled

Group	Recall category			
	S_0R+	S_1R+	S_2R+	total
EP–1	0·17	0·33	4·94	5·44
EP–2	0·33	0·22	4·39	4·94
EP–3	0·56	0·28	4·67	5·51
EP–W	—	—	—	5·61
HP–1	1·89	0·78	2·00	4·67
HP–2	0·39	0·83	2·06	3·28
HP–3	0·56	0·72	1·94	3·22
HP–W	—	—	—	5·72

Note: MS_w for total recall scores $= 1 \cdot 82$.

of group EP–W and of the single-letter groups are comparable; among the latter group EP–2 shows some disadvantage. By contrast, group HP–W is clearly superior to the single-letter groups in Cond. HP. Group HP–1 surpasses groups HP–2 and HP–3, with the latter two yielding closely similar scores. Comparison of the corresponding groups in Cond. HP and EP shows that the amounts recalled to the whole trigram (groups W) are virtually identical but that the total scores of the single-letter groups are higher in Cond. EP. The difference between the single-letter groups is greater for the second- and third- than for the first-position cues. The main effects of Pronunciability and Type of Test are highly significant, $F (1, 136) = 26·29$ and $F (3, 136) = 9·78$, respectively; $p < 0·001$ in both cases. The interaction of these variables is also significant, $F (3, 136) = 5·57$, $p < 0·001$. A breakdown of the interaction by means of orthogonal comparisons shows that (a) the difference between the amounts recalled to whole trigrams and to single letters is greater in Cond. HP than EP ($p < 0·01$), and (b) the variation among single-letter groups is likewise greater in Cond. HP ($p < 0·05$).

The recall scores of groups EP–W and HP–W indicate that the postcriterial drop is equal for the two types of list. The total scores of the single-letter groups in the two conditions diverge because in Cond. EP the large majority of recalls are successfully mediated by reproduction of the total trigram, whereas in Cond. HP there are frequent failures of mediation and a substantial amount of single-letter selection occurs only for group HP–1.

Individual differences

The gradients of conditional probabilities shown in Table 2 imply that there should be a substantial positive correlation between the number of stimulus letters reproduced and the amount recalled by individual Ss in all groups except HP–1. The product-moment correlations between the two measures are $-0·05$, $0·71$, and $0·72$ for groups HP–1, HP–2, and HP–3, respectively. The corresponding values in Cond. EP are $0·80$, $0·55$, and $0·76$. A coefficient of $0·47$ is significant at the $0·05$ level, and one of $0·60$ at the $0·01$ level. Thus, HP–1 is the only group which fails to show a reliable positive relationship between stimulus reproduction and recall. This lack of correlation reflects the high conditional probability $R + : S_0$ which distinguishes group HP–1 from the other groups and which is attributable to single-letter cue selection.

The next question to be considered is whether the amount o single-letter selection manifest at the time of recall is related to speed of acquisition. The assessment of this relationship wa limited to group HP–1 since a substantial amount of selection was found only for that group. The percentage that categor

S_0R+ was of all correct recalls was used as a measure of S's disposition to select the first letters as the functional stimulus. The product-moment correlation between this index and the number of trials to criterion was $0 \cdot 60$ ($p = 0 \cdot 01$). Thus, the slower the acquisition of the list the greater was the relative amount of single-letter selection. The implications of this rather unexpected finding will be discussed below.

Postexperimental inquiry

The Ss' responses to the postexperimental questionnaire are fully consistent with the conclusions based on the distributions of stimulus reproductions and recalls. Of the 72 Ss in Cond. HP, 67 gave interpretable answers to the questions about stimulus selection. Thirty-five Ss stated that they tended to select one letter as a cue; 32 out of 35 Ss named the first letter as the one selected. Ten Ss named two letters; the first, second, and third letters were named eight, six, and six times, respectively. In Cond. EP the responses of 68 Ss could be used. Twelve Ss stated that they favored a single letter; in 11 out of 12 cases the first letter was named. Several of the responses were, however, qualified by indications that the amount of selection was slight or not deliberate. Three Ss listed two letters, the frequencies of the successive positions being 3, 2, and 1. It is clear that single-letter selection is reported much less frequently in Cond. EP than in Cond. HP. When selection is reported, the first letter is chosen in all but a few scattered cases.

Comparison of independent and repeated measures

The results of the second and third tests of the single-letter groups have not been considered thus far because of the inherent limitations of successive recall measurements. As expected, the distributions of stimulus-letter reproductions show upward shifts on the second and third tests due to prior exposure to the relevant letters. As a consequence, there was some reduction (from $1 \cdot 89$ to $\cdot 30$) in the mean number of cases in category S_0R+ for HP–1. Other changes in recall scores were minor, and the conclusions concerning selection remain essentially unchanged when repeated rather than independent measures are used.

The question remains of whether successive tests with single letters produce amounts of recall which are equal to those obtained with whole trigrams. A comparison was made between the number of *different* responses recalled correctly on the three successive tests of the single-letter groups and the scores of the groups tested with the whole trigrams. The mean recall score of group EP–W is 5·61; whereas the mean number of different responses recalled by the single-letter groups in the same condition is 5·78. A conservative conclusion is that recall to whole trigrams is at least as high as repeated recalls to single letters since the latter provide more opportunities for chance success. The mean number of correct recalls for group HP–W is 5·72, and 5·17 for the single-letter groups in that condition. This difference is significant, $F(1, 68) = 4·34, p < 0·05$. The comparison is again conservative in view of the probable bias in favor of the single-letter groups. The superiority of group HP–W is in accord with the conditional probabilities shown in Table 2. Except in apparent cases of single-letter selection the probability of recall increases markedly with the number of stimulus letters reproduced. The Ss' ability to reproduce both the missing letters is far from perfect, even if there are three opportunities to do so. Thus, the presentation of the whole trigram maximizes the number of cases which have the highest conditional probability of recall.

Discussion

The results of the experiment show that (a) there is little evidence for single-letter cue selection when the stimulus terms are easy to pronounce, and (b) such selection is largely limited to letters in the initial position when the stimulus terms are hard to pronounce. Selection may be expected to occur only among functionally discrete units. The EP trigrams are well-integrated sequences of letters to which Ss are likely to respond as single units. Hence selection, which would involve the breaking up of functional units, occurs only sporadically in Cond. EP. By contrast, in Cond. HP the trigrams are not integrated units, and it is reasonable to suppose that Ss initially respond to the letters as discrete elements. The conditions are, therefore, favorable to selection. The most economical procedure which is then open to Ss is selection of the first letter. Use of the first letter minimizes the amount of time spent in scanning elements other than the selected one and thus effectively lengthens the anticipation interval. It is clear both from the recall distributions and the postexperimental reports that Ss do indeed heavily favor the first letter when they select a single element. Thus, while the results provide supporting evidence for stimulus selection, they also serve to delimit the conditions under which selection is likely to occur and the choices of cues which may be expected to be made.

The present findings call attention to several methodological and interpretative problems which arise in the analysis of stimulus selection. First, it is apparent that correct responses to single elements on a test of recall do not by themselves constitute evidence for stimulus selection since such responses may be mediated by reproduction of additional letters. For this reason the dual criterion used in the present study was introduced, and only those cases in which S failed to reproduce additional letters and also gave the correct response were classified as instances of single-letter selection. This dual criterion must be recognized as conservative. It is quite possible that some Ss practiced single-letter selection early in acquisition and then proceeded to respond to the remaining elements as well, or perhaps learned additional letters incidentally. At least some of the cases classified as two-letter selection may reflect this course of events. Thus, the amount of selection which occurred at some time during the acquisition is probably underestimated. However, the possibility cannot be ruled out that in some instances Ss began by responding to more than one letter and narrowed the effective cue down to a single letter later in learning. These considerations bring to the fore the fact that a test of transfer or recall cannot yield full information about how a task was acquired; instead, it permits the assessment of what has been acquired. In the present case the application of the dual criterion provides an estimate of the numbers of responses which were associated with only a single element at the point at which criterion was reached. While indexes based on tests of transfer and recall may underestimate the amount of selection which occurs in the course of learning, there is no reason to suppose that the comparisons among experimental treatments are systematically biased by the inherent limitation of such measures.

Second, it is useful to recognize that criteria of selection must be established without reference to S's intentions. This point requires explicit attention because of the possibility mentioned earlier that additional letters are learned incidentally while S is deliberately trying to associate a response to a single letter only. Whatever S's deliberate mode of attack, once additional letters are acquired, they can, and probably do, serve as functional cues. For this reason the reproduction of additional elements constitutes evidence against single-letter cue selection, regardless of whether these elements were acquired intentionally or incidentally.

It is possible at this point to speculate about the reasons for the inverse correlation between speed of learning and relative amount of single-letter selection in Group HP–1. This relationship was unexpected because associations should be established more rapidly to a single letter than to two letters or the whole HP trigram. The latter prediction is made on the assumption that (a) even under conditions of low formal similarity the discriminability of stimuli decreases with the number of elements and (b) single letters elicit a larger number of associations which can serve as mediators than do unfamiliar trigrams. Thus, the larger the number of single-letter cues used by S, the faster the list should be acquired. However, fast Ss may practice selection on the early trials and then add further elements either intentionally or incidentally. The latter alternative is quite likely since speeds of intentional and of incidental learning are correlated (Plenderleith and Postman, 1956). Group HP–1 does, in fact, show a negative correlation between trials to criterion and the number of stimulus letters reproduced, $r = -0.51$, $p < 0.05$. Thus, there are fewer cases meeting the dual criterion of single-letter selection for fast than for slow Ss. An alternative interpretation is that in spite of the inherent difficulties of the task, fast Ss are efficient in developing associations to the whole trigram and hence are less likely than slow Ss to have recourse to selection.

A third methodological point concerns the relative precision of analyses of selection based on the scores of independent groups and on repeated measurements of the same Ss. If the dual criterion of selection is to be applied, it becomes necessary to use independent groups since successive tests inflate the level of stimulus-letter reproduction. The fact that the two kinds of analysis yield congruent conclusions in the present case points to the stability of the effects of the experimental treatments. Nevertheless, some bias introduced by the upward shifts in the distributions of letter reproductions was noted. Such biases may, of course, become critical in the context of other analyses.

References

ANDERSON, N. S. (1965), 'Word associations to individual letters', *Journal of Verbal Learning and Verbal Behavior*, vol. 4, pp. 541–5.

JENKINS, J. J. (1963), 'Stimulus "fractionation" in paired-associate learning', *Psychological Report*, vol. 13, pp. 409–10.

PLENDERLEITH, M., and POSTMAN, L. (1956), 'Discriminative and verbal habits in incidental learning', *American Journal of Psychology*, vol. 69, pp. 236–43.

UNDERWOOD, B. J. (1963), 'Stimulus selection in verbal learning', in C. N. Cofer and B. S. Musgrave, eds., *Verbal Behavior and Learning: Problems and Processes*, McGraw-Hill, pp. 33–48.

UNDERWOOD, B. J., HAM, M., and EKSTRAND, B. (1962), 'Cue selection in paired-associate learning', *Journal of Experimental Psychology*, vol. 64, pp. 405–9.

UNDERWOOD, B. J., and SCHULZ, R. W. (1960), *Meaningfulness and Verbal Learning*, Lippincott.

3 I. Rock

The Role of Repetition in Associative Learning

I. Rock, 'The role of repetition in associative learning', *American Journal of Psychology*, vol. 70 (1957), pp. 186–93.

Although repetition has long been regarded as essential in associative learning, there is some doubt as to how it achieves its beneficial effects. One possibility is that, in learning a list of items, the strength of association between each pair develops gradually, with each repetition adding an increment to the bond, until it is so strong that the first item produces recall of the second. According to this interpretation, repetition is a factor in the *formation* of associations. Another possibility is that repetition is essential because only a limited number of associations can be formed on any one trial. On each new encounter with a list of items we learn new ones, until finally we have learned them all. From this point of view, associations are formed in one trial, and improvement with repetition is only an artifact of work with long lists of items. Typical behavior in experiments on rote learning and in examples from everyday life indicate that some associations are formed in one trial, but such evidence does not prove conclusively that associations are not ordinarily formed by a process of gradual strengthening.

If associations are formed by a process of gradual strengthening based on repetition, it should be easier to form an association between items which have already been presented together on one or more previous trials, but which S has not yet been able to get right, than between items presented together for the first time. There are several ways of testing this assumption, but the method used in the experiments to be reported here seems most direct. A control group is given the task of learning a list of paired associates to a criterion of one errorless trial. An experimental group is handicapped by removing all pairs which S fails to get right after every trial and substituting new pairs for them. The new pairs are randomly selected from a pool of pairs prepared in advance and from which the initial lists for the two groups also are randomly selected. This means that the experimental group always has the same number of pairs to learn on any given trial – the same number as has the control group – but only some of them will have been seen previously (those already learned) and some will never have been seen previously. Training of the experimental group also is continued to a criterion of one errorless trial.

For the experimental group, then, a pair is either learned the first time it is seen, or it is removed, and S does not, therefore, have what might be presumed to be the benefit of repetition in *forming* associations. If a pair is learned on that first occasion, it will remain in the list as long as S continues to get it right. Thus pairs successfully mastered on one trial are repeated, but the repetition does not affect the formation of associations, although S gains whatever benefit may accrue from repetition *after* associations are formed. This critical distinction between the role of repetition in forming associations and the role in fixing or reinforcing associations already formed will be discussed later. For the present, it suffices to say that the experimental group has to form associations without benefit of repetition.

Experiment I

Method

Two groups, of twenty-five college students each, were required to learn a list of twelve letter–number pairs, which were printed on 3×5 in cards. The left-hand member of each pair was either a letter of the alphabet or a double-letter. The right-hand member was a number from 1 to 50, since fifty such card-pairs were prepared corresponding to the twenty-five letters and double-letters, excluding the letter I. (The reason for using this type of pair will be discussed below.) The numbers were assigned to the letters by means of a table of random numbers, and the twelve pairs to be used for each S were randomly selected by shuffling. In the case of Ss in the experimental group, the remaining thirty-eight cards were available as a pool from which new ones could be selected to replace unlearned pairs after each trial. It was thought unlikely that there would be a need for more than thirty-eight substitute-pairs.

A metronome was used to time a 3-sec exposure of each card and a 5-sec interval between successive cards. S was instructed to associate the letter or letters on each card with the number, and that the serial order of cards would be randomly changed from trial to trial. In view of the procedure used with the experimental group (to eliminate a sense of surprise and lack of understanding of the task which might otherwise be expected), S was told in advance that new pairs might be shown from trial to trial, although the total number would remain the same, and that it was his task to try to learn all those shown at any time.

A recall-test for paired associates was used after every trial. On the back of every card was printed only the first item of the letter-number pair. The twelve cards used in that learning trial were therefore reversed, shuffled, and presented at the rate of one every 5 sec, S's task being to respond with the correct number. In the case of the experimental group, the cards were sorted in two piles as S responded, depending upon whether he was right or wrong. New cards were then substituted for the wrong ones, and these were shuffled together with the right ones in preparation for the next trial. There was a 30-sec interval between each test-trial and the subsequent learning trial.

After about three-fourths of the Ss had been tested, it was noted that the average first-trial performance of the experimental group was higher than that of the control group. To correct for this sampling error, the remaining Ss were not assigned to a group until they had completed the first trial. Those doing relatively well (four or more pairs correct) were then assigned to the control group and those doing relatively poorly (three or fewer correct) were assigned to the experimental group. Since the procedure is the same for both groups for the first trial, this was a perfectly good way of equating the groups. The result was that the two groups as finally constituted had virtually identical scores on the first trial.

Results

It turned out that the number of extra pairs available for substitution in the lists of the experimental group was not sufficien in every case. For five Ss, the experiment had to be discontinued because there were insufficient new cards to substitute for un-learned pairs on the last trial given. These Ss were scored 10+ which means that they would have required at least ten trials to reach the criterion. Similarly, there were three Ss in the control group who did so badly that work with them was discontinued before the criterion was reached, and they too were scored 10+. The median number of trials to reach the criterion for the two groups was exactly the same; namely, 4·75. The semi-interquartile range also was identical for the two groups; namely, 1·45. If the cases scored as 10+ are excluded, the mean of the control group is 4·55 and the SD is 1·9, while the corresponding values for the experimental group are 4·35 and 1·2. As can be seen by inspection, the mean difference falls far short of statistical significance ($t = 0·41$). The mean number of errors (no response *plus* wrong answers) to criterion was 17·9 for the control group ($SD = 9·9$) and 17·2 for the experimental group ($SD = 8·6$), and this difference too lacked statistical significance ($t = 0·24$). A plot of the mean number of correct responses per trial yields highly similar curves for the two groups. There was thus no advantage for the control group.

The reason for using letter–number pairs instead of other material, e.g. nonsense-syllable pairs, in the first experiment was as follows. It was thought that, if nonsense-material were used, the control group might have an advantage unrelated to the hypothesis under investigation. Repetition for this group would certainly have had the effect of making each individual item familiar, and there was reason to suppose that it would be easier to form associations between familiar items than between un-familiar ones, even though the familiar items had never in the past been associated with each other. Since one does not have to learn the items as such if they are familiar, one can concentrate on the associations to be formed. If nothing else, it ought to be easier to *recall* a familiar item than an unfamiliar one. By using pairs of letters and numbers which were already familiar, an attempt was made to eliminate this factor. Of course, even here one might argue that the control group had an advantage because of the additional familiarization in successive trials with the material used. Nevertheless, the use of familiar material would minimize this factor, and the results suggest that, even if there were such an advantage, its effect was negligible. In using familiar items, however, the problem arises of finding material in sufficient quantity and in other respects suitable for this type of experiment. By using letters and double-letters with numbers, fifty pairs were obtained but, as noted above, even this number turned out to be insufficient. Primarily to overcome this short-coming, and in spite of the objection mentioned above, it was decided to repeat the experiment with pairs of nonsense syllables. There is also something to be said for using this more traditional material because of the greater possibility afforded for comparison with previous work.

Experiment II

Method

The procedure followed that of Experiment I, except that pairs of three-letter nonsense syllables were used. They were taken from Glaze's list of syllables of 47 per cent and 53 per cent association value (Glaze, 1928; Hilgard, 1951). Eighty pairs were made up, from which eight were randomly selected as the starting list for Ss of both groups, and there remained a pool of seventy-two pairs from which pairs could be randomly drawn as needed to substitute for unlearned pairs in the case of the experimental group. A response was scored correct if S pronounced the syllable correctly, and partially correct responses were scored as wrong. It was not necessary in this experiment to assign Ss to one or the other group after determining their scores for the first trial, because it turned out that performance on this trial was not significantly different for the groups as they were randomly con-stituted. There were fifteen adults of both sexes, mostly college students, in each group.

Results

In addition to the thirty Ss, there were eight Ss who did not succeed in learning the list to the criterion, three in the control group and five in the experimental group. In all these cases, E discontinued the experiment because it was obvious that there was little likelihood that S would master the task in the time available. Several of these Ss were evening-session students tested at night, after work, when they were tired. In a few cases, the students had to return to a class, and therefore could not continue to the criterion, and two were somewhat older people. The pool of seventy-two pairs turned out to be more than adequate and had nothing to do with the discontinuation of the experiment for the Ss of the experimental group.

Considering first the results for the fifteen Ss of each group who did learn, the mean number of trials to reach the criterion turned out to be identical, namely, 8·1. The SD was 3·0 for the control group and 2·4 for the experimental group. The mean number of errors to criterion was 26·7 for the control group ($SD = 11·4$) and 29·2 for the experimental group ($SD = 12·6$). The difference is not statistically significant ($t = 0·55$). If the eight Ss who failed to reach the criterion are included, scoring them as 15+, the median number of trials also is identical for the two groups; namely, 8·5. The semi-interquartile range is 3·2 for the control group and 4·2 for the experimental group. The learning curves for the two groups are again similar.

Discussion

There were reasons for expecting superior performance in the control groups of these experiments, entirely apart from the question of repetition. The possible advantage of familiarity, which applies particularly to Experiment II, has been mentioned. A second reason is that a recall test rather than a matching test of recognition was used. In a matching test, S must recognize which item belongs with which, but he does not have the additional task of recalling the second item. He need only recognize it. It is, therefore, an easier task, and it is reasonable to suppose that the strength of an association must be greater for recall than for matching. If so, there must have been many instances in which the Ss of both groups were scored wrong but would have succeeded in a matching test. In fact, the many cases where S gave a partially correct response (almost the right number in Experiment I or two of the three letters correct in Experiment II), but was scored wrong, point in this direction. No doubt in such cases

73

as well, S would have been correct if he had the advantage of a matching test. This would mean that an association did in fact exist, and the Ss of the experimental groups were penalized by having such pairs eliminated. A matching test was not used because it entailed certain technical difficulties in the case of the experimental groups in view of the unpredictable change of items from trial to trial. That the control groups were not superior despite this possible advantage, however, makes the case against the incremental theory all the stronger.

Another reason that one might have expected superior performance of the control groups relates to the fact that wrong pairs were removed from the list for the experimental groups even if they had been correct on one or more previous trials, although that happened only occasionally (primarily during the first few trials). Since it may be assumed that an association has been formed once S gets a pair correct, it was not necessary to remove these pairs to test the hypothesis under consideration. Doing so consequently constituted something of a very strict procedure for the experimental groups. When the same thing happened to an S in the control group, he had what is no doubt the advantage of being presented with the same pair again. If the association continued to exist – and failure on the previous trial was a matter of momentary forgetting – he would not really have to learn the pair. The S in the experimental group, however, had to learn a new pair to take its place. Why the control groups do not learn more rapidly in view of these reasons is not clear, except that apparently they do not add up to an advantage of strength sufficient to reveal itself under the conditions employed.

There is one other difference between the conditions of the two groups which, however, might be said to favor the experimental group. It may be argued that for every S there are certain pairs which are easier to learn than others. That being the case, the easy pairs may be the ones which are learned on any given trial, while the difficult ones are eliminated by a process of 'natural selection'. The new pairs substituted are not necessarily easy, but the reconstituted list on the whole is not as difficult as that with which the control group is faced on a corresponding trial. It is not easy to deal with this objection experimentally if difficulty is defined idiosyncratically, because the only way of finding ou about a pair is to present it to that S for learning. Work on this problem is now in progress. Even if it should turn out, however, that the difficulty factor does work to the advantage of the experimental group, the meaning of such an advantage must be seen in the proper perspective. As things now stand, there are the several factors, mentioned above, which tend to favour the control group, and which ought to counterbalance any such advantage, but even if control of difficulty were to impair the performance of the experimental group to some extent, the question of interpreting the magnitude of the superiority of the control group would remain. One might still be struck by the level of performance achieved by the experimental group without benefit of repetition.

The present results seem to support the thesis that, in the classical multiple-item learning situation, associations are formed in one trial. Informal observations and introspective reports support this finding. Most Ss succeed in learning only a few pairs per trial, and many do so with the aid of some mnemonic device. The theoretical significance of the widespread use of such devices in rote learning experiments has not been sufficiently emphasized in the past. The successful use of such devices may mean that an idea suddenly occurs to S which enables him to link two items then and there; it has, to some extent, the character of insightful learning. Some Ss concentrate on one or two pairs and hardly even attend to the rest; other Ss do try to learn them all. With or without the use of devices, the difficulty in getting more than a few pairs correct in any one trial has to do with the presence of so many other pairs.

It follows from the argument that repetition is important only for the learning of *additional* associations that in situations with few associations to be formed, repetition would not be required at all. This deduction can easily be tested by presenting Ss with only one pair of items (under conditions of incidental learning which eliminate the possibility of 'silent' repetition).[1]

Why, in multiple-item learning situations, it is not possible as a rule to learn more than a few associations on any one trial, remains to be investigated, but the following point must be

1. Preliminary results reported by F. B. Springfield (1955) indicate that almost all Ss do succeed in establishing an association in one trial.

considered: If, a few seconds after any given pair is exposed during learning, and before the next pair is shown, E were to test for retention, there is little doubt that most Ss would give the correct response. Would this result not mean that an association was in fact formed, and that the failure to get all items right on a test following the entire series is a matter of forgetting of already formed associations? In that event, one could regard forgetting due to the presence of many items as an instance of retroactive inhibition. According to this conception, repetition would not be required to *form* associations, even in the case of long lists of items, but only to strengthen them sufficiently to resist interference. The present experiments rule out this type of explanation, since Ss do as well with substituted new pairs as with the original ones. It is as if pairs which are not retained by the time of the test leave nothing in the nervous system of any value for future use. The Ss frequently comment spontaneously that they do not recognize the items of a pair which they have seen several times before.

The question is really one of deciding on a criterion for the existence of a formed association. It probably makes more sense – in terms of what we usually mean by associative learning – not to define success by the easy test of immediate memory, but rather by the traditional delayed test. At any rate, it may be said that repetition is required in rote learning, as defined by this latter criterion (the traditional one), because for some as yet unknown reason or reasons the existence of many items interferes with the formation of more than a few associative connections of a nature which is of any value beyond immediate memory. The hypothesis of von Restorff concerning loss of individuality of traces under conditions of crowding is relevant here, but leaves many questions unanswered (von Restorff, 1933).

It seems clear that repetition plays another role in rote learning; namely, that of strengthening, or reinforcing associations once they are formed. There is little question that, in everyday life, we have strong associations between items which have been experienced contiguously very often. Experiments on over-learning clearly demonstrate this point, but they do not distinguish between the role of repetition before associations are formed and after they are formed, the impression being tha repetition serves continuously to build up the strength of the association from zero-value to a value far in excess of that required for initial recall on the test following the learning trial. The present results show that this is not the case; repetition does not seem to be of value in forming associations. Hence, it must be concluded that, in overlearning, only the repetition *after* the association is formed is effective in strengthening it.

The present findings are certainly compatible with the thesis that an association is essentially the after-effect of an organization of the items during the initial experience (Köhler, 1941). Interestingly enough, however, the exponents of this point of view have never denied the importance of repetition in associative learning, tending to believe that, in the case of nonsense material in monotonous series (as contrasted with meaningful material), repetition is needed to consolidate what would otherwise be very unstable or weak trace-interrelationships (Koffka, 1935). Thus, in the case of rote learning it was implicitly taken for granted that associations are formed by a process of gradual strengthening. On the other hand, the present findings are incompatible with incremental theories, including those which stress the law of effect.

Summary

In two experiments, the learning of paired associates was studied. In each case, the traditional procedure was used for a control group, while for the experimental group unlearned pairs were removed and new ones submitted after each trial. No significant differences in rate of learning were found. This result suggests that repetition plays no role in the formation (as distinct from the strengthening) of associations, other than that of providing the occasion for new ones to be formed, each on a single trial.

References

GLAZE, J. A. (1928), 'The associative value of nonsense syllables', *Journal of Genetic Psychology*, vol. 35, pp. 255–67.

HILGARD, E. H. (1951), 'Methods and procedures in the study of learning', in S. S. Stevens, ed., *Handbook of Experimental Psychology*, pp. 541–4.

Acquisition

KOFFKA, K. (1935), *Principles of Gestalt Psychology*, Harcourt, Brace, pp. 556–71.

KÖHLER, W. (1941), 'On the nature of associations', *Proceedings of the American Philosophical Society*, vol. 84, pp. 489–502.

SPRINGFIELD, F. B. (1955), *The Learning and Retention of a Single Pair of Associates*, B.A. thesis, New School for Social Research.

VON RESTORFF, H. (1933), 'Ueber die Wirkung von Bereichsbildung im Spurenfeld', *Psychologische Forschung*, vol. 18, pp. 299–342.

4 A. B. Taylor and A. L. Irion

Continuity Hypothesis and Transfer of Training in
Paired-Associate Learning

A. B. Taylor and A. L. Irion, 'Continuity hypothesis and transfer of
training in paired-associate learning', *Journal of Experimental Psychology*,
vol. 68 (1964), pp. 573–7.

Rock's experiments on one-trial learning were recast in the context of a
transfer of training experiment. *S*s learned a first list of paired-associate
adjectives to a partial criterion and then learned a second list that was
derived from the items to which *S* had never responded correctly during
practice on list 1. Four conditions, allowing for a range of possible
transfer effects from positive transfer to negative transfer, were employed. The differences among the groups in their performances on list
2 support a multitrial, continuity interpretation of learning.

A conventional approach to the study of verbal learning assumes
that such learning proceeds by the gradual accretion of the
strengths of the appropriate S–R connections over a number of
trials. Recently, this view has been challenged by the experiments
and theoretical formulations of Rock and his associates (Rock,
1957, 1958; Rock and Heimer, 1959) who support an all-or-none
interpretation of associative bonds. Rock's view has been supported by results obtained in a novel experimental situation
wherein incorrectly anticipated items are removed from lists of
paired associates and replaced by new pairs following each presentation of the list. Results obtained under such a substitution
condition are compared with results obtained under the more
usual condition in which no substitutions are made. Some of the
findings in this situation have indicated that learning proceeds at
approximately the same pace whether or not the substitutions are
made. Rock has interpreted these findings as demonstrating that
learning is a discontinuous process either taking place on a
particular trial or not at all. It is further held that, until an *S*
makes a correct anticipation of a particular item, he had learned
nothing with respect to it.[1]

1. A number of investigators have questioned the validity of Rock's
experimental results on the grounds that, since the most difficult items are

Acquisition

Rock's experiments, and those which his findings have stimulated, have the general characteristics of transfer of training experiments although they have not usually been considered in this way. If they are examined from this point of view, it will be seen that what Rock is maintaining is that zero transfer should be obtained in both his substitution and nonsubstitution conditions. Two studies, one by Schwartz (1963) and the other by Underwood and Keppel (1962), have had the specific orientation of transfer experiments. Both experiments obtained results that failed to support Rock's hypothesis. However, neither experiment studied the full range of possible transfer effects, and it is from this standpoint that the present experiment was designed. In it, separate conditions were arranged for the substitution of items that should produce high positive, zero, and high negative transfer. According to a noncontinuity view, no differences in subsequent learning should result, providing only that S had not responded correctly to the original items. Under a conventional interpretation, it would be expected that subsequent learning would proceed most rapidly under the positive transfer condition and least rapidly under the negative transfer condition.

Method

Subjects

Eighty female undergraduate students in Newcomb College of Tulane University served as Ss in the experiment. All of the Ss were students in introductory psychology sections and had previously served in a verbal-learning experiment, but none of the Ss had participated in a verbal-learning experiment in which paired-associate learning was used. The Ss were divided, at random, into four groups of twenty Ss each.

---

less likely to be correctly anticipated, the substituted items are, on the whole, easier to learn than the ones they replace and that, hence, Rock' findings may be artifactual. However, since these considerations are per: pheral to the thesis of the present study, we shall not deal with this portio of the relevant literature.

Procedure

The same general procedure was followed under all four experimental conditions. Following instruction in the task, *S* was given practice on a list of twenty paired-associate adjectives until she had correctly anticipated not fewer than six nor more than twelve different response words. Thus, eight to fourteen items remained to which *S* had never made a correct response. The *S* was then given an immediate test on this first list which was done by presenting the stimulus items alone and asking *S* to give as many correct associations as possible. The test was given in order to pick up any new associations that *S* might have formed on the last trial of practice, but to which she had not had an opportunity to respond correctly. Following this test, a 2-min rest intervened during which time *E* constructed the final list which *S* was to learn. The second and final list consisted of eight pairs of paired-associate adjectives and was learned to a criterion of one perfect repetition. The learning of both lists was by the 'flash-card' method. The stimulus word was typed on one side of a 3 × 5 card and the response word was typed on the reverse side. The *S* was exposed to the stimulus item for 3 sec, then the response item for 3 sec, and so on through the list. Between trials, there was a 15-sec rest during which *E* shuffled the cards.

There were four basic lists of twenty paired-associate adjectives each. These lists were related to each other in various ways, and these relationships constituted the independent variable of the experiment. The lists were:

1. The A B list (Examples: ready–thrifty; total–vital; heated–level)
2. The A C list (Examples: ready–formal; total–implied; heated–exact)
3. The D C list (Examples: oblong–formal; zigzag–implied; western–exact)
4. The A Br list (Examples: ready–vital; total–level; heated–thrifty)

The second list to be learned always consisted of eight pairs taken or derived from the A B list. It will be noted that the A B and A C lists have the same stimuli, but different responses; the A B and

D C lists have no words in common; and the A B and A Br lists are composed of the same words, but the response words in the A Br list are paired with different stimulus words than in the A B list. From what is known about transfer of training, it would be expected that, if Ss practiced the A B list first and then learned the A B list (relearning of the same list), high positive transfer should result. On the other hand, if Ss practiced the A C list first and then the A B list, high negative transfer should occur. Practicing on the D C list and then the A B list should produce little or no transfer of training. Finally, on the basis of results reported by Porter and Duncan (1953), Ss who practiced the A B list first and then learned the A Br list should show the greatest amount of negative transfer. The procedures outlined above were followed in the present experiment except that the second list was always composed of items to which S had not responded correctly during the first-list training or on the test. Let us examine the conditions in detail:

Condition I (positive transfer; A B–A B). The S was given practice on the A B list until she had responded correctly to at least six different items. She was then given a test (stimulus items only presented) on list A B. From the items to which she had not responded correctly at any time during the practice or on the test, a second, eight-item list was constructed. The actual eight pairs used in the second list were selected at random from the pairs to which S had never responded correctly. The S then learned this eight-item list to criterion.

Condition II (zero transfer; D C–A B). The S was given practice on the D C list until she had responded correctly to at least six different items. She was then given a test (stimulus items only) on list D C. Finally, she learned a list of eight pairs of items taken at random from the A B list. This second list was learned to criterion.

Condition III (negative transfer; A C–A B). The S was given practice on the A C list until she had responded correctly to at least six different items. She was then given a test on the A C list. From the items on the A C list to which she had never responded correctly, eight items were selected at random. The corresponding items (those with the same stimulus words) were taken from the A B list and used to construct the second list which was then learned to criterion.

Condition IV (*maximum negative transfer; A B–A Br*). The *S* was given practice on the A B list until she had responded correctly to at least six different items and then was given a test on the A B list. From the items on the A B list to which she had never responded correctly, eight items were selected at random. The response words within these eight pairs were re-paired with the stimulus words and these eight re-paired items made up the second list which was then learned to criterion.

One final item of procedure should be noted. When practicing on the first list, *S* was stopped at the end of the trial on which she had made her sixth correct anticipation. It should be noted that *S* need not have made six correct anticipations on that trial. If she responded correctly to an item at any time during practice on list 1, this correct response was counted as one of her correct anticipations, and practice on list 1 was discontinued after she had responded correctly to six different items. It is evident that *E* had no control over the actual number of correct responses that *S* would make on any given trial. A particular *S* might skip from five correct anticipations to nine correct anticipations within the lapse of a single trial. For this reason, a certain amount of leeway was created in the design of the experiment. It was required that *S* respond correctly to at least six different items. On the other hand, if *S*, during practice on list 1 and on the subsequent test, responded correctly to more than twelve different items, she had to be dropped from the experiment since not enough items remained to make up list 2. In all, thirteen *S*s were discarded because they exceeded this 12/20 criterion. In each case, the discarded *S* was replaced by the next *S* reporting to the experiment.

Results

For all four conditions, the three forms of list 1 appeared to be of comparable difficulty, and the 6/20 criterion was met with relative ease. Because the original learning data, as well as all of the other data, fitted Poisson distributions, all scores were transformed by use of the square root transformation, $S = \sqrt{X + 0.5}$. Trials to reach the 6/20 criterion on list 1 were subjected to an analysis of variance and the resulting *F* was not significant, $F(3, 76) = 1.14$.

Acquisition

Because the Ss learned list 2 to a performance criterion and, hence, n decreased as practice progressed, the data for the learning of list 2 are presented in modified Vincent curve form in Figure 1. It will be seen that, if group II (DC–AB) is considered

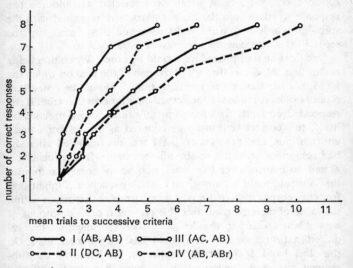

Figure 1 Trials to reach successive criteria on list 2 as a function of the relationship between list 1 and list 2

to represent the control condition which exhibits approximately zero transfer, then Cond. I (AB–AB) exhibits positive transfer while Cond. III (AC–AB) and IV (AB–ABr) show negative transfer.

An analysis of variance was conducted with respect to the numbers of correct anticipations on trial 2 of list 2 for the four conditions. This analysis resulted in an F ratio that was significant at the 0·05 level, $F(3, 76) = 16·13$. In terms of t tests between pairs of conditions, all comparisons are significant except for the difference between the two negative transfer conditions, III and IV.

The numbers of trials required to reach the criterion of one errorless trial on list 2 were also analysed. Again, a significant F

was obtained, $F(3, 76) = 19·80$. When t tests are used to compare pairs of conditions in terms of trials-to-criterion scores, only the comparisons of Cond. I with III and IV and Cond. II with III and IV are significant. Condition I did not differ significantly from Cond. II and the two negative transfer conditions (III and IV) did not differ between themselves.

Discussion

One problem that seems to be impossible to overcome in experiments of the type we are considering is the selection of second-list items according to their difficulty. As we have noted, above, such selection has been the basis for a considerable proportion of the criticisms that have been directed against Rock's findings. While it cannot be claimed that selection of items on the basis of their difficulty was avoided in the present study, it can be pointed out that this form of selection probably served to minimize rather than to maximize the differences obtained between conditions. In specific terms, in Cond. I (AB–AB), selection according to difficulty had the highest probability of occurring. In Cond. II (DC–AB), there was no possibility of the occurrence of selection since the list 2 items were drawn at random from the complete pool of AB items. Under Cond. III (AC–AB), selection may have occurred with respect to the stimulus segments of the pairs and, on the assumption that difficulty of the stimulus segment contributes to the difficulty of the whole item, the list 2 items may have been systematically too difficult. However, it should be noted that, unless one assumes that the difficulty of a pair is entirely determined by the difficulty of the stimulus segment of the pair, there should have been less selection under Cond. III than under Cond. I. In the same way, selection may have occurred under Cond. IV (AB–ABr) in terms of the difficulty of the stimulus segments and the response segments, but not in terms of their specific association. The net effect of these selections should have been to make list 2 under Cond. I, III, and IV more difficult than under Cond. II. Thus, the difference between Cond. I and II is probably systematically too small and the differences between Cond. II on the one hand, and Cond. III and IV on the other, probably are systematically inflated. However, the finding that the learning of list 2 under Cond. I (which should have been maximally difficult on the basis of item selection) was more rapid than the learning of list 2 under Cond. III and IV, lends support to the general validity of the present findings.

For group I (AB–AB), list 2 was derived from missed or incorrectly anticipated items in list 1. For group II (DC–AB), list 2 consisted of completely new items. Even between these two conditions of our experiment, there was evidence to support the continuity point of view, and this evidence is considerably strengthened when the negative transfer conditions (AC–AB and AB–ABr) are also considered. In the light of these findings, it would appear that Rock's findings may have resulted, in part, from the fact that his conditions were arranged in such a way as to produce only a limited range of transfer effects (from positive transfer to zero transfer rather than from positive transfer to negative transfer). When the negative transfer groups are added, a clear picture supporting a continuity point of view emerges.

References

PORTER, L. W., and DUNCAN, C. P. (1953), 'Negative transfer in verbal learning', *Journal of Experimental Psychology*, vol. 46, pp. 61–4.

ROCK, I. (1957), 'The role of repetition in associative learning', *American Journal of Psychology*, vol. 70, pp. 186–93.

ROCK, I. (1958), 'Repetition and learning', *Scientific American*, vol. 199, pp. 68–72.

ROCK, I., and HEIMER, W. (1959), 'Evidence of one trial associative learning', *American Journal of Psychology*, vol. 72, pp. 1–16.

SCHWARTZ, M. (1963), 'Transfer from failed pairs to a test of one-trial vs. incremental learning', *American Journal of Psychology*, vol. 76, pp. 266–73.

UNDERWOOD, B. J., and KEPPEL, G. (1962), 'One-trial learning?', *Journal of Verbal Learning and Verbal Behavior*, vol. 1, pp. 1–13.

5 J. E. Jones

All-or-None versus Incremental Learning

J. E. Jones, 'All-or-none versus incremental learning', *Psychological Review*, vol. 69 (1962), pp. 156–60.

The process of learning may be conceived of as the gradual strengthening of connections between events or, alternatively, as the establishment of such connections in an all-or-none fashion. Estes (1960) presented results which suggest that evidence for the all-or-none position tends to be obscured by the traditional techniques of grouping data. In one of a number of miniature experiments cited by Estes (1960, pp. 213–15) paired associates were recalled on successive test trials (T_1, T_2) after a single reinforced presentation (R_1). The sequence was R_1, T_1, rest, T_2. Estes argued that, if an incremental theory is tenable, the probability of a correct response appearing on T_2 should be independent of recall on T_1. An all-or-none theory suggests that correct responses on T_2 should occur only by chance unless a correct response was given on T_1 (see Figure 1). A close relationship was found between recall on T_1 and T_2, i.e. of the 49 per cent of cases correct on T_1 75 per cent were correct on T_2 (C–C cases) and of the 51 per cent of cases incorrect on T_1 91 per cent were incorrect on T_2 (N–N cases).

Estes' statement of incremental theory forces upon it the assumptions that a reinforced presentation results in equal increments in associative strength for all items in all subjects and that the strength of competing responses is equal in all cases. His deductions concerning the probability of a correct response on T_2 do not necessarily follow if these assumptions are not made. Estes contends that he has disposed of the point of item difficulty and individual differences by demonstrating that for his subjects and with his items a second reinforcement (R_2) interpolated between T_1 and T_2 yields approximately the same percentage of newly correct responses on T_2 (46 per cent) as occurred on T_1

following R_1 (40 per cent) (Estes, 1960, pp. 215–16). However, any prediction of the relative percentages of newly correct responses following one reinforced presentation and following two, involves making assumptions about the distributions of item difficulty and learning ability. The character of those distributions for such a limited number of items and subjects can be known only empirically. Although the approximate equivalence of the obtained percentages is consistent with an all-or-none interpretation, the demonstration does not at all preclude the possibility that R_1 results in unequal increments for different cases.

According to the latter view, the associations have achieved unequal strengths after R_1, hence they do not have equal probabilities of appearance. Subclassifying the cases into those which do (C) and those which do not (N) appear on T_1 biases the probabilities of appearance on T_2 without further reinforcement in favor of the C cases. Assuming that there is no forgetting between T_1 and T_2, the C–N and N–C cases represent approximately half of those in which the associations are at about threshold strength and the number of cases in each should be approximately equal. (The proportions will be equal in the special case where the C/N split on T_1 is 50/50.) Forgetting is reflected in an increase in the number of C–N cases and a decrease in the number of N–C cases. That is, incremental theory does not have to predict the frequency of N–C cases. However, it can predict trends in the N–C and C–N categories when the conditions of the experiment produce greater or lesser degrees of forgetting. According to the all-or-none theory, forgetting will be reflected in an increase of cases in the C–N category but the frequency of cases in the N–C category will be unaffected unless subjects are guessing intelligently, in which case it will decrease.

Another problem which precludes uncritical acceptance of Estes' interpretation is the indeterminate theoretical chance level. According to an all-or-none theory the number of N–C cases should be no greater than that expected on the basis of sheer guessing. The chance value depends on the population of responses among which the subject is guessing, which might be a number less than, equal to, or greater than eight, the number of items presented, and cannot be specified other than empirically. The alternative forms of guessing might be referred to as 'in telligent', 'unintelligent', and 'stupid' guessing. Further information is necessary in order to evaluate whether the N–C cases which do occur, whatever their number, are sheer guesses or possible true recalls. This information is not available in the data as collected by Estes but an extension of his procedure may clarify why N–C cases do occur and also indicate whether associations have been established by R_1, though not revealed on T_1.

Three experiments are reported here. The first is a replication of Estes' experiment with the trial sequence R_1, T_1, 'rest', T_2, confirming his result. The second is a variation and extension of Estes' procedure, the trial sequence being R_1, T_1, T_2, T_3, T_4. The third is a repetition of Experiment II using a double-blind technique.

Experiment I

Twenty-seven housewives acted as subjects in Experiment I. Each of eight associate-pairs, a consonant as stimulus and a number as response, were shown on separate 3 in $\times$ $2\frac{1}{2}$ in cards. The responses were the numbers 1 through 8. The experimenter sat at a table opposite the subject and presented the cards manually after shuffling. On R_1 the cards were each held while the subject read aloud the consonant and the number. On test trials cards bearing only the consonant stimulus were shuffled and then presented. The test cards were held until the subject responded with the number she thought correct or with a guess. No omissions were allowed. T_2 followed T_1 after approximately minutes during which time the subject took part in another experiment which involved sorting cards bearing lines of different lengths and orientations. There was no warning that a second test would be made.

Experiment I was not an exact replication of Estes'. Apart from the usual differences of experimenter, subject, time, and place the present experiment differed from Estes' in four respects: (a) In the present experiment consonants rather than three-consonant syllables were used as stimuli. (b) Because the cards were shown manually the presentation and between-presentation duration were variable whereas Estes timed both of these intervals.

Acquisition

(c) No omissions were allowed whereas Estes was forced to accept some omissions because of the restricted intertrial interval. (d) The 'rest' period between T_1 and T_2 was longer than that allowed by Estes and occupied with a different activity. From Estes' full report of his experiment (Estes, Hopkins, and

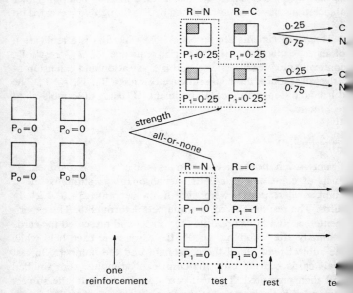

Figure 1 Schema representing effects of a single reinforcement accordin to incremental (upper branch) v. all-or-none (lower branch) theories. (Squares represent subjects with the proportion of darkened area in eac indicating the probability of the correct response, C, for the given individual.) (From Estes, 1960, p. 214)

Crothers, 1960) it appears that the 'rest' interval was br (estimated at $1\frac{1}{2}$ minutes) and was used for a reinforced presen tion of other items from the list. The probable unimportance these procedural differences can be assessed from the results Experiment I which are essentially the same as those obtained Estes. Of the 53 per cent of cases correct on T_1 75 per cent w correct on T_2 (C–C) and of the 47 per cent not correct on T_1 81 per cent were not correct on T_2 (N–N).

Experiment II

The subjects for Experiment II were the same twenty-seven women who served in Experiment I. Both experiments were conducted in the same session, Experiment II first, and were separated by approximately 7 minutes during which time the subject took part in the card-sorting experiment. The procedure was as described for Experiment I except that the test cards were reshuffled and represented immediately until four test trials were completed. The experimenter gave no indication beforehand that more than one test would be made. The stimuli were consonants, none of which appeared in Experiment I. The responses were again the numbers 1 through 8.

The probability of recall on T_{2-4} largely depends on whether the correct response is given on T_1 (see Figure 2), again confirming Estes' findings. However, features of the results are difficult to reconcile with an all-or-none theory.

Although the percentage of N–C cases (29 per cent) is well within the range of chance variation, it is necessary to explain the tendency to repeat those guesses on T_3 and T_4, i.e. N–C–C and N–C–C–C cases. One would expect all-or-none theory to require the N–C–C and N–C–C–C values to approximate 0·29, i.e. the guessing rate established on T_2. The incremental interpretation demands that those values approximate 0·50, these cases being at threshold strength. The obtained values of 0·61 and 0·77 are too high for either of these interpretations. These cases cannot be fully accounted for as part of a general tendency to repeat earlier calls on later trials. Of those who change their call on T_2, having been wrong on T_1, 61 per cent of those correct repeat the second call once and 36 per cent twice while of those again incorrect only 37 per cent repeat the second call once and 14 per cent twice. If the N–C cases are regarded as guesses it is necessary to explain why those calls are repeated with a much higher probability than incorrect responses. If they are regarded as true calls the expected N–C–C and N–C–C–C values are 0·50, or less (if forgetting occurs), but in fact the values increase.

The implication is that there is some kind of feedback which distinguishes past responses as correct or incorrect. One possible source of such information under the conditions of Experiment II

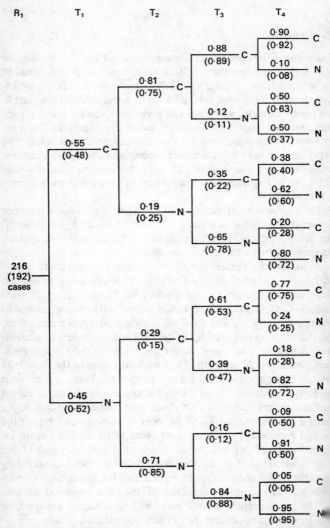

Figure 2 Results of Experiment II and Experiment III (in parentheses). (Empirical values are proportions of instances in which correct, C, and incorrect, N, responses on a given test trial were followed by C and N responses on the following test trial)

is the experimenter, who knows whether the response is correct or not. Experiment III was conducted to check this possibility. A new group of twenty-four subjects drawn from the same population learned the items used in Experiment II. One experimenter presented the paired-associates on R_1 and a second experimenter, who was unaware of the correct associations, presented the test cards on T_1 to T_4. The results of Experiment III appear in brackets in Figure 2. Again a high proportion of calls correct for the first time on T_2 were repeated on T_3 and T_4 – a proportion considerably in excess of repetitions of incorrect calls. Of those correct on T_2 53 per cent repeat the response once and 40 per cent twice, while of those incorrect only 32 per cent repeat the call once and 12 per cent twice.

If the feedback does not originate from an unwitting experimenter then it must be somehow induced by the response itself. Bearing in mind that the associations in question are assumed to be at threshold strength and also the fact that recognition is easier than recall, it seems not unreasonable to suggest that in some cases the subject may recognize that the response she has just given as a guess was actually correct. Such an interpretation renders quite conceivable the notion that learning can occur on test trials. Estes *et al.* (1960) in fact noted such a phenomenon. However, the interpretation suggested does require that an association of liminal strength be set up on R_1 and is therefore consistent with an all-or-none interpretation.

Further, comparison of the results of Estes' experiment with those of Experiments II and III shows an effect which is also handled more readily by an incremental theory. If the total number of correct responses is taken as an index of retention then it is apparent that forgetting between T_1 and T_2 is greatest in Estes' experiment and least in Experiment III (see Table 1). The trend is consistent with the fact that Estes' subjects learned other associations between trials while the subjects in Experiment II sorted cards and in Experiment III there was no interpolated activity. From Table 1 it is also seen that as forgetting increases so the proportion of cases in the C–N category increases, as predicted by both theoretical approaches, but also that the proportion in the N–C category decreases. A χ^2 test based on the frequencies in the N–C categories showed the latter effect to be significant at the 0·001 level of confidence. The effect cannot be accounted for in terms of an increase in the population of responses among which the subject is guessing. The expected

Table 1

Trends in C–N and N–C Cases as a Function of Forgetting and a Comparison of N–C Values with Those Expected on the Basis of Intelligent Guessing (g)

Experiment	Percentage correct		Retention index T_2/T_1	C–N	N–C	g
	T_1	T_2				
III	0·55	0·57	1·04	0·19	0·29	0·2
II	0·53	0·48	0·91	0·25	0·19	0·2
Estes	0·49	0·39	0·80	0·29	0·09	0·2

N–C values for intelligent guessing were calculated as follows. I C is the proportion correct on T_1, c the probability that an ite will be learned on R_1, and g the probability that the corre response will be guessed, then the equation for C (Estes et a 1960) is:

$$C = c + (1 - c)g$$

Substituting the obtained value of C and an arbitrary value of (with the limitation that $g < C$) into the equation, solve for c. new estimate of g is obtained from:

$$g = \frac{1}{n(1 - c)}$$

where n is the number of items in the list. The new estimate o is then substituted into the equation and the procedure reiterat until a stable value of g is obtained. The g values obtained af three iterations are shown in Table 1. A χ^2 test of the obtain N–C values against the frequencies predicted for intellig guessing yielded a p of 0·001. That is, the drop in the N–C f quencies as a function of forgetting exceeds that expected sim as a decline in the chance level.

The data of Experiment II strongly suggest that subclassify

the cases according to their history on successive trials does no more than sort them in order of difficulty, each case being one item for one subject. The probability of appearance of a correct response on T_4 is: for cases formerly correct on all three trials (C–C–C cases), 0·90; for cases formerly correct on two of three occasions (C–C–N, C–N–C, and N–C–C), 0·50, 0·38, and 0·77 respectively; correct on one of three occasions (C–N–N, N–C–N, and N–N–C), 0·20, 0·18, and 0·09 respectively; for those never before correct (N–N–N), 0·05. A similar ordering can be observed in the data of Experiment III. According to the all-or-none position the T_4 probabilities should be the same for all categories with the exception of C–C–C.

The writer appreciates Estes' statement that he does not mean to offer the experiment he reports as crucial tests of incremental versus all-or-one theory and agrees with his thesis that theorists should examine closely the extent to which their concepts are artifacts of experimental procedures. But insofar as the miniature experiments are used as demonstrations, they are taken to create difficulties for incremental theory. Considered in the context of additional information from the experiments reported in this paper these same data raise difficulties for all-or-none theory. The criticism directed at the miniature experiments is not that they are too simple but that they are incomplete.

References

ESTES, W. K. (1960), 'Learning theory and the new "mental chemistry"', *Psychological Review*, vol. 67, pp. 207–23.

ESTES, W. K., HOPKINS, B. L., and CROTHERS, E. J. (1960), 'All-or-none and conservation effects in the learning and retention of paired associates', *Journal of Experimental Psychology*, vol. 60, pp. 329–39.

6 B. J. Underwood, W. N. Runquist and R. W. Schulz

Response Learning in Paired-Associate Lists as a Function of Intralist Similarity

B. J. Underwood, W. N. Runquist and R. W. Schulz, 'Response learning in paired-associate lists as a function of intralist similarity', *Journal of Experimental Psychology*, vol. 58 (1959), pp. 70–78.

Paired-associate learning of verbal lists can be divided logically into two phases. These two phases will be called the response-recall or response-learning phase, and the associative phase. The response-learning phase is conceived of as the learning required to make the responses readily recallable. This first phase must necessarily precede the second phase, the associative phase, since the response must be available before it can be associatively connected (second phase) to a specific stimulus in the paired-associate list. It is possible, of course, that certain components of the response (e.g. the first letter) may develop associative strength to the stimulus before the entire response is available.

This division of rote learning into two phases is not new (e.g. Hovland and Kurtz, 1952), but so far as is known it has not been used systematically as an analytical device. Certain considerations suggest that variables which are known to affect the overall rate of learning operate differentially during the two phases. For example, the fact that meaningfulness of responses in paired-associate learning influences the rate of learning to a greater extent than does stimulus meaningfulness (Sheffield, 1946) could be interpreted to indicate that as response meaningfulness increases both the response–recall phase and the associative phase are enhanced, whereas, when stimulus meaningfulness increases through a corresponding range only the associative phase is facilitated.

The present studies are concerned with intralist response similarity and its role in the two phases of learning as outlined above. The general hypothesis to be tested is that the higher the intralist response similarity the greater the facilitation of the respon learning phase. Since it is known (Feldman and Underwood, 1957) that with the type of lists to be used high intralist response similarity impedes over-all paired-associate learning (as compared with low intralist response similarity), it must follow from the hypothesis that the negative or interference component of high response similarity occurs primarily in the associative phase.

That the response-recall phase would be enhanced by high intralist response, similarity could be expected on at least two somewhat independent bases. First, it is known that high inter-item similarity (at least meaningful similarity) and associative connection are almost perfectly correlated (Haagen, 1949). Thus, if S recalls one response, the recall of other similar responses should be facilitated. The clustering effect of items of high similarity shown by Bousfield and Cohen (1955) suggests the operation of this principle. A second way of viewing the situation would suggest simply that if all responses in a paired-associate list are similar, S merely has to remember a single concept and then give instances of that concept in the response-recall phase. If all responses are dissimilar, however, as many different 'concepts' as there are responses must be learned. Either way of viewing the situation suggests that the response-recall phase will take place more rapidly with items of high similarity than with items of low similarity.

In the major conditions of the present studies two 10-item paired-associate lists are used. In one list the ten responses are dissimilar adjectives, and in the other they are adjectives all of which have a more or less common meaning. In one set of conditions, Ss are taught the ten responses *before* they become responses in a standard paired-associate list. Teaching S the responses may be thought of as isolating the response-learning phase. The hypothesis stated above leads to two predictions about the results of these procedures. First, when Ss are taught the responses before they become a part of a paired-associate list, it must be predicted that acquisition of the ten similar responses will take place more rapidly than the acquisition of the ten dissimilar responses. Secondly, having taught S the responses before they become a part of a paired-associate list, it must be predicted that when they do become responses in this paired-associate list the initial learning process will occur more rapidly than will learning in control conditions where the initial learning of the responses has not taken place. This prediction must be limited to the early trials corresponding to the period during which response learning is believed to occur. While it might appear that if response learning is facilitated the associative phase would 'get started sooner' and that over-all learning would thereby be facilitated, there is nothing in the hypothesis which asserts this. Teaching S the responses before these responses become a part of a paired-associate list is assumed merely to remove the bulk of the response-learning phase in paired-associate learning.

In another set of conditions standard paired-associate learning is used but Ss are stopped at various points in learning and are asked to give all the response items they can remember. The prediction is that more responses will be given from the high-similarity list than from the low- (at least early in learning), even though the over-all rate of learning is slower for the high-similarity list.

Experiment I

Method

Materials. For the basic learning task two lists of ten pairs wer used in which the stimulus items were nonsense syllables and th response items were two-syllable adjectives. The stimuli wer taken from a previous study (Underwood, 1953a) and were (from 46–53 per cent association value (Glaze, 1928) and of lo intralist similarity. The responses were also taken from a previou study (Underwood and Goad, 1951). In one list all responses wer more or less synonymous in meaning (cheerful, sunny, carefre pleasant, gleeful, laughing, happy, genial, jolly, smiling). In th other list the responses were unrelated in meaning (spicy, rounde hairy, equal, modern, tiresome, fiery, faithful, plastic, guilty On the average both sets of responses have about the sar Thorndike–Lorge (1944) frequency. In pairing a syllable and adjective an attempt was made to avoid any apparent conne tions between the two.

General design. Three basic conditions each involved pair associate learning of the high-similarity list and the low-similar list, with separate groups learning each list in each condition. In one condition of response learning (Cond. RL), *S* learned the responses alone before learning the paired-associate list. In this RL procedure the responses were presented in varying order from trial to trial for five trials with a recall test being given after each trial. One group learned the high-similarity responses and another the low-similarity responses before proceeding to their respective paired-associate lists. A control condition (Cond. C) involved no pretraining. A comparison of learning the paired-associate lists for RL and C conditions should indicate the effectiveness of learning the responses prior to paired-associate learning. The third condition (Cond. PA–RL) was designed to determine the extent of response learning (RL) during paired-associate learning (PA). Various groups were stopped at different points during paired-associate learning and given a single free recall of the responses. This response learning was tapped at six points, namely, after 1, 2, 3, 5, 8 and 13 exposures of the paired-associate lists. Since each *S* was stopped only *once* during learning, the PA–RL conditions involved twelve groups, six for each of the paired-associate lists.

Subjects and procedure. A total of 320 *S*s served in the experiment, twenty in each of the sixteen groups. Condition RL involved two groups; Cond. C, 2 groups; and Cond. PA–RL, twelve groups. The *S*s were assigned to one of the sixteen groups randomly with the restriction that one *S* was assigned to each group before there were any replications. All *S*s were naïve to verbal learning experiments.

In the standard paired-associate learning fifteen anticipation trials were given under all conditions. Lists were presented on a memory drum at a 2/2-sec rate, with a 4-sec intertrial interval. Five different orders of the pairs were used to minimize serial learning with an equal number of *S*s being started on each order. For the response-learning phase of the two RL groups, the set of responses was presented in five alternate learning and recall trials. The *S* was clearly instructed that he was not to learn the adjectives in order since they would be in a different order on each trial. The recall period after each learning trial was 1·5 min. The *S* simply wrote down on a sheet of paper as many responses as he could remember. Since there were five trials and five orders, an equal number of Ss was started on each order to avoid any possible serial position bias. None of these orders was the same as subsequently used in paired-associate learning. For the paired-associate learning for these RL groups the S was provided with a card on which all the responses were listed. The intent of this was that if any of the responses were forgotten of those just learned, or if learning had been incomplete on five trials, the responses would still be available. However, few Ss appeared to use the information on these cards; the majority reported that they simply did not have time to make use of the information during paired-associate learning.

In the PA–RL conditions, S was stopped after the appropriate number of trials on the paired-associate list, read the instructions for response recall, and then given 1·5 min to write down all the responses he could remember. The S did not know beforehand that such a recall would be asked for. The instructions made it clear to S that he was to write down all the adjectives he could remember without regard to order. After the recall period he was informed that he would not be interrupted again and the standard learning of the paired-associate list continued until fifteen anticipation trials were completed.

Results

Response learning. The mean number of correct responses on each of the five response-recall trials for the RL groups is shown in Figure 1. Initially the similar responses are recalled better than the dissimilar responses, although by trial 4 performance is approximately equal on both lists and asymptotic for a majority of Ss in both groups. The t on the total correct responses over the five trials for the two groups was 3·09 ($p < 0·001$). The relatively pure response learning occurs more rapidly for responses of high similarity than for those of low similarity.

The results from the response recall trials for the PA–RL groups are plotted in Figure 2. A comparison of Figure 1 and Figure 2 shows that response learning is much higher when occurring independently (Figure 1) than when measured as a component of standard paired-associate learning (Figure 2). Nevertheless, the same general relationship between the recall

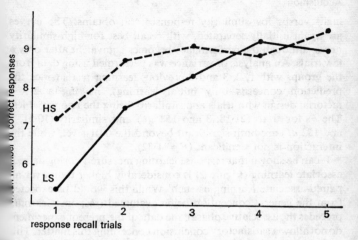

Figure 1 Mean correct responses on each response–recall trial as a function of high similarity (HS) and low similarity (LS)

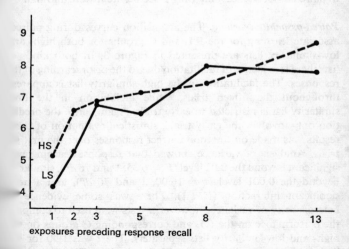

Figure 2 Mean correct responses on response recall during paired-associate learning as a function of similarity (HS v. LS) and number of exposures preceding response recall

high- versus low-similarity responses still obtains. The curves are again initially separated, with recall best for high-similarity items, although the performance becomes equivalent after only a few trials. An analysis of variance was performed using data from the groups with 1, 2, 3 and 5 previous learning trials (since the prediction concerns only initial learning), making a 2×4 factorial design with trials and similarity being the two variables. The Fs for trials (21·18, 3 and 152 df) and similarity (10·51, 1 and 152 df) are both significant beyond the 0·01 level, while the interaction is not significant ($F = 1·32$).

It can be shown that response learning measured during paired-associate learning (Figure 2) is considerably higher than over-al paired-associate learning as such. While this would be expecte from the general conception being evaluated (response learnin precedes the associative phase), the data of the present experimen do not allow a satisfactory conclusion concerning this matter. Thi is because in the measurement of response recall during paired associate learning essentially unlimited recall time was given, whil in paired-associate learning only 2-sec per item were allowed.

Paired-associate learning. The acquisition curves during paire associate learning for the R L and C groups for both high- an low-similarity lists are presented in Figure 3. In both kinds lists there is evidence of facilitation due to the prior learning of tl responses. The facilitation in the high-similarity list is appare throughout the fifteen trials, while facilitation in the lo similarity list is restricted to early trials. Again, since the predi tion only involves the early trials, statistical evaluation of the results was made on the total correct responses over the first trials. Analysis of variance showed that response learning w significant beyond the 0·02 level ($F = 6·35$, 1 and 76 df), similar beyond the 0·001 level ($F = 16·00$, 1 and 76 df), and a no significant interaction ($F < 1$). There was some evidence heterogeneity of variance; however, t tests were used to comp: the performance on the R L and corresponding C groups on high- and low-similarity lists separately. The t was 1·90 for high-similarity condition and 1·77 for the low. These are b significant beyond the 0·05 level if one assumes a single-tai alternative.

Other evidence on response learning. From the above comparisons it may be inferred that response learning of similar items occurs more rapidly than response learning of dissimilar items. Thus, early in learning a paired-associate list, *S* should have more responses available if the responses have high similarity than if

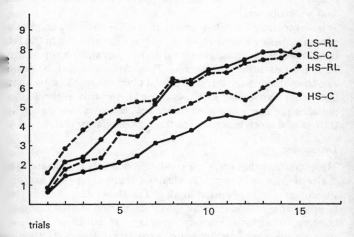

gure 3 Paired-associate learning in Experiment I as a function of response learning (RL *v.* C) and intralist response similarity (HS *v.* LS)

y have low similarity. If this is true, evidence for it might be nd in actual paired-associate learning. The point at which h evidence would be least contaminated by the associative ase would be the first anticipation trial. The *S* would be ex-ted to give more *different* responses on this trial if the re-nses have high similarity than if they have low similarity. Such analysis ignores the question of whether the response was ropriately paired with its stimulus; rather, a simple count is le of the number of different responses occurring. Five such parisons are available from the PA–RL conditions; that is, e are five conditions in which a low-similarity list was taken ugh at least one anticipation trial by standard procedures and comparable conditions for high-similarity lists. There is an tional comparison which can be made using the C groups, and one further comparison from a second experiment to be presented shortly. The comparisons were between the mean number of different responses given on the first anticipation trial of the high-similarity and low-similarity lists. In six of the seven comparisons, the mean was larger for the high-similarity lists. The over-all mean was 2·31 for the high-similarity lists and 1·76 for the low-similarity lists.

In contrast to the above expectations, if S has been taught the responses before paired-associate learning (as was true in the RL conditions) the high-similarity list should not show a superiority in number of different responses. Two tests of this can be made one from the present RL groups and another from two comparable groups appearing in Experiment II. In both of these comparisons the mean number of different responses was higher for the low-similarity lists than for the high-similarity lists.

Discussion

The prediction that response recall will be initially greater when the responses are similar in meaning than when they are dissimilar is clearly supported in all of the above data. This is true whether the response recall is taken during paired-associate learning, whether a response-learning procedure is used, whether the responses in paired-associate learning as such examined. The prediction that the initial performance during the learning of a paired-associate list will be facilitated by the prior learning of the responses is not supported as clearly. The differences, while small, are in the predicted direction and closely approach statistical significance. However, it is possible to attribute this small facilitation to some kind of warm-up or learning-to-learn (or both) produced by response learning and which independent of the particular responses which were learned. Therefore, Experiment II was run which duplicated the RL and C conditions with the exception that the C groups in this second study were given irrelevant response learning prior to paired-associate learning. Thus, if relevant response learning facilitated paired-associate learning over and above that produced irrelevant response learning, the differences found in Experiment I cannot reasonably be attributed to warm-up and practice effects.

Experiment II

Method

The RL conditions of the previous experiment were replicated exactly, with both the high- and low-similarity lists being used. The C groups in Experiment II, however, were given five response learning and recall trials on irrelevant lists before being given the paired-associate lists. The lists were irrelevant in the sense that none of the items appeared in the paired-associate list. Such irrelevant learning should produce the same warm-up and practice which the RL groups might get in learning a relevant list. The irrelevant responses learned in the response-learning phase for the group subsequently learning the paired-associate list with high similarity among responses were: shifty, crafty, expert, cunning, cagey, wily, foxy, clever, skillful, and tricky. For the group learning the paired-associate list with low similarity among responses the items for the irrelevant response learning were: hybrid, crumbling, vulgar, fiscal, worldly, inform, warlike, neuter, sterile, and flashy.

A total of sixty Ss served in the experiment, fifteen in each group. All Ss were naïve to verbal learning experiments. All procedures were exactly the same as those in Experiment I, except as noted above, and except for the fact that during paired-associate learning the RL groups were not provided the card on which the correct responses were written.

Results

The response-recall data showed essentially the same results as did Experiment I. The difference between high and low similarity was somewhat less than in Experiment I, but still significant statistically on the first recall trial.

As may be seen in Figure 4, the results of the learning of the paired-associate list duplicate almost exactly those of the first study. For both high- and low-similarity lists the RL group exhibits better performance than the C group. The only clear difference between the results for the two studies is that in the present results the RL group is facilitated throughout all fifteen trials on the low-similarity list; this was not true in the first study. Direct comparisons between the results of the two studies are not

Acquisition

justified since the *S*s in Experiment II, as a group, were faster learners than those in Experiment I.

Analysis of variance of the total correct responses on the first six trials gave significant *F*s for both similarity (7·53) and relevance of response learning (9·81). With 1 and 56 *df*, the *F* at the

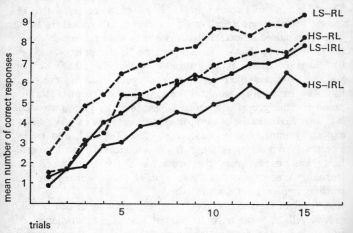

Figure 4 Paired-associate learning in Experiment II as a function of preresponse learning (RL *v.* IRL) and intralist response similarity (HS *v.* LS)

0·01 level is 7·12. Separate *t* tests between the R L and C group gave values of 2·32 for high similarity and 2·23 for low similarity both of which are significant at the 0·05 level with 28 *df*. Th conclusion seems justified that prior learning of the response facilitates paired-associate learning over and above any non specific effects, such as warm-up or learning-to-learn.

Discussion

The results are consonant with a two-phase conception of verba learning. It should be clear that the present results are direct relevant only to the first phase – the response-learning phas Nothing is given in the present findings as to how the associati phase – the second phase – takes place. Nor is there any intent suggest that, all items considered, the two phases can be clear separated in the over-all learning process. It has been asserted only that the early trials have a heavy component of response learning and the present results show that response similarity may be viewed as a variable influencing the rate at which this response learning takes place. Furthermore, the results indicate that if the necessity for response learning in paired-associate learning is removed by teaching *S* the responses before they become a part of the paired-associate list, paired-associate learning is facilitated. Concerning this latter finding it should be noted that Hovland and Kurtz (1952) have shown that familiarization training will facilitate serial learning. However, serial learning tends to confuse stimulus and response functions of the items. While stimulus learning before paired-associate learning (given in the same manner that response learning was given here) might influence subsequent paired-associate learning, it would be through other mechanisms (e.g. stimulus differentiation) than those being dealt with here for response learning.

It might be suggested that the response-learning procedures used produced a differentiation among the responses (reduced intralist similarity), hence facilitating learning. A number of facts argue against this interpretation. (a) If differentiation among responses is involved, response learning of the lists of low similarity should have little or no effect in paired-associate learning. (b) If differentiation among responses is the critical factor, it should have produced a much greater facilitation in the learning of the paired-associate lists for responses with high similarity than for responses with low similarity. The results showed that there was no appreciable difference between the effect for responses of low similarity and responses of high similarity. In fact, the mean differences for the initial part of learning favored the lists with low response similarity. (c) Finally, there is no reason to believe that the *method* used for response learning would produce a differentiation among responses in the sense that associations were differentially reinforced. All facts considered, therefore, it does not seem likely that response differentiation is of much moment in the present studies.

The present materials probably do not allow an optimum effect to be produced by response learning. That is, since adjectives were used, response learning should take place much more rapidly than if, say, nonsense syllables of low-association value had been employed. (It will be recalled that pure response learning in the R L groups took place very rapidly.) It would be expected that if response learning were given before paired-associate learning with material of low meaningfulness, subsequent paired-associate learning would be facilitated more than was true in the present results.

What is the stimulus for the recall of each item in the response-learning phase? There is no satisfactory answer to this question. But, it should be pointed out that the question is relevant not only to the present procedures but also to any learning situation in which S is shown a group of items and is then asked to recall them in any order. The stimulus for such recall may be the gross stimulus complex of the laboratory room, the memory drum, the instructions, etc. No resolution of this systematic problem seems possible. At the same time it must not be inferred that the initial recall of a given response is never instigated by the particular stimulus with which it is paired in the list. The fact that it is possible to set up pairs in which already established associations obtain between the stimulus and response, and that learning is very rapid in such situations, suggests that response recall can be tied to the specific stimulus and that this is a very effective arrangement. It is therefore quite possible that in the present experiment the initial recall of some items by some Ss is entirely tied to a specific stimulus.

The present findings on the role of intralist response similarity have some implications for the role of both stimulus and response similarity in over-all paired-associate learning. Although available data are not completely conclusive on this matter (Underwood, 1953a; 1953b), the best evidence is that a given range of intralist stimulus similarity produces a greater variation in learning than does a corresponding range of response similarity. Such a finding is understandable in light of the present results and the conception of two stages in learning. It could be assumed that increasing interference produced by increasing similarity would affect the associative phase of learning and would have an equal effect in this phase for stimulus and response similarity. But increasing response similarity has an increasing positive effect for response learning in the first phase (as seen in the present results) which has no counterpart in stimulus similarity. Therefore, the over-all effect of stimulus similarity should be greater than the effect of response similarity.

Summary

Verbal learning may be conceptualized as a two-stage process. In the first phase S must learn the responses, in the second he must attach them to specific stimuli. The present experiments dealt directly with the first stage only. It was hypothesized that: (a) response learning is initially more rapid the higher the response similarity in a paired-associate list; and (b) teaching S the responses before he learns a paired-associate list would initially faciliate the learning of this list.

Two paired-associate lists were used. The stimuli for both lists were nonsense syllables, the responses, adjectives. In one list the adjectives were all similar in meaning, in the other, dissimilar. In one set of conditions (control), Ss merely learned the paired-associate lists by standard procedures for fifteen trials. In a second set of conditions, Ss were taught the responses prior to learning the paired-associate list for fifteen trials. In the third set of conditions standard paired-associate learning was used but different groups of Ss were stopped after 1, 2, 3, 5, 8 and 13 trials and were asked to write down all the responses they could remember. These three sets of conditions required sixteen groups of Ss. There were twenty in each group, all naïve to verbal learning experiments.

The results show that:

a) Teaching S the responses prior to paired-associate learning facilitates the learning of lists with both high and low similarity among the responses. A second experiment showed that this effect cannot be ascribed to warm-up or learning-to-learn resulting from the procedure of teaching S the responses before paired-associate learning. In both experiments the positive effect was evident throughout the entire fifteen trials for lists of high response similarity. For low similarity the effect was only in initial learning for one comparison but present throughout learning in the other.

b) In response learning (prior to paired-associate learning) items with high similarity are learned initially more rapidly than are items of low similarity, although for both lists learning was very rapid. When Ss are tested for free recall at various points in learning a paired-associate list, more responses are given from a high-similarity list than from a low-similarity list even though over-all level of paired-associate learning is higher for the low-similarity list. The difference in this response recall was clearly evident for the first few trials.

The results confirm the expectation that high intralist response similarity would facilitate response learning. Thus, the results are consistent with the two-stage conception of learning. Furthermore, the present results aid in understanding certain previous findings on the roles of stimulus similarity and response similarity in verbal learning.

References

BOUSFIELD, W. A., and COHEN, B. H. (1955), 'The occurrence of clustering in the recall of randomly arranged words of different frequencies of usage', *Journal of General Psychology*, vol. 52, pp. 83–95.

FELDMAN, S. M., and UNDERWOOD, B. J. (1957), 'Stimulus recall following paired-associate learning', *Journal of Experimental Psychology*, vol. 53, pp. 11–15.

GLAZE, J. A., (1928), 'The association value of nonsense syllables', *Journal of Genetic Psychology*, vol. 35, pp. 255–69.

HAAGEN, C. H., (1949), 'Synonymity, vividness, familiarity, and association-value ratings of 400 pairs of common adjectives', *Journal of Psychology*, vol. 30, pp. 185–200.

HOVLAND, C. I., and KURTZ, K. H. (1952), 'Experimental studies in rote-learning theory: X. Pre-learning syllable familiarization and the length-difficulty relationship', *Journal of Experimental Psychology*, vol. 44, pp. 31–9.

SHEFFIELD, F. D. (1946), 'The role of meaningfulness of stimulus and response in verbal learning', *Doctoral dissertation, Yale University*.

THORNDIKE, E. L., and LORGE, I. (1944), *The Teacher's Word Book of 30,000 Words*. Teacher's College, Columbia University.

UNDERWOOD, B. J. (1953a), 'Studies of distributed practice: VIII. Learning and retention of paired nonsense lists as a function of intralist similarity', *Journal of Experimental Psychology*, vol. 45, pp. 133–42.

UNDERWOOD, B. J., (1953b), 'Studies of distributed practice: IX. Learning and retention of paired adjective lists as a function of intralist similarity', *Journal of Experimental Psychology*, vol. 45, pp. 143–9.

UNDERWOOD, B. J., and GOAD, D. (1951), 'Studies of distributed practice: 1. The influence of intra-list similarity in serial learning', *Journal of Experimental Psychology*, vol. 42, pp. 125–34.

7 V. J. Cieutat, F. E. Stockwell and C. E. Noble

The Interaction of Ability and Amount of Practice with Stimulus and Response Meaningfulness (m, m') in Paired-Associate Learning

V. J. Cieutat, F. E. Stockwell and C. E. Noble, 'The interaction of ability and amount of practice with stimulus and response meaningfulness (m, m') in paired-associate learning', *Journal of Experimental Psychology*, vol. 56 (1958), pp. 193–202.

The present program on the role of meaningfulness (m) in verbal learning began with the development of the m scale of association frequency (7), and proceeded to experimental studies of the effects of this variable upon serial learning (8) and paired-associate learning (10). Using either method, Ss' rate of memorizing two-syllable nouns and paralogs is a positive function of m.[1] The latter two investigations also discovered interactions between Ss' initial ability and their reactivity to differences in m. In all previous studies, however, the m values of the stimuli and responses were deliberately co-varied, so the relative contributions of the S and R terms to the variance in performance have not yet been measured. There exists the possibility of an $S \times R$ interaction with respect to m, as well as interactions with amount of practice if wide ranges in proficiency are produced.

Variants of the m scale have also been applied to consonant-vowel-consonant or 'CVC' material (11) with similar effects on paired-associate acquisition (4, 5, 6, 11, 13, 14). In this second group of experiments the association values of S and R were separately manipulated in two cases (5, 13), but no attempt was made simultaneously to evaluate the role of individual differences. To determine the extent to which initial ability interacts with the locus of meaningfulness in paired-associate CVC learning, the

1. These findings have been confirmed for serial learning by Dowling and Braun (1), and for paired-associate learning by Kimble and Dufort (2). As further index of the m scale's reliability (10, p. 16), Rocklyn, Hessert, and Braun (12) have shown that the defining operations (7) yield measurements which are practically invariant over age differences from 20 to 66 yr: $= 0.96$.

S and R terms must be independently varied with respect to this factor. Because of its methodological status, known reliability, and current relevance to the population available to the writers, the m' scale (11) will be employed for the second objective. This x/σ scale consists of a random sample of 100 CVC syllables, rated for number of associations by 200 Ss, whose measurements were transformed into deviates of the normal curve by the method of successive intervals. It has been shown (11) that the relationship between m and m' is positive, thus rationalizing the definition of m' as an estimate of m. This implies that both operations reflect quantitative changes in the same hypothetical concept: the number of habit connexions evoked by a given stimulus (7).

The two experiments described here will investigate (a) the nature of S and R combination in paired-associate learning under manipulations of m and m', (b) the interaction of each of these measures with amount of practice, and (c) the role of initial ability in determining the type and extent of such interrelationships when m' is varied. Experiment I uses the m scale and the pronunciation method, whereas Experiment II uses the m' scale and the spelling method.

Experiment I

After considering evidence from earlier studies of the influence of meaningfulness, Noble and McNeely proposed the S–R motor-patterning hypothesis that 'differential facilitation is primarily connected with responding (articulation) and that stimulus factors are of secondary importance' (10, p. 21). The following predictions were made for a 2×2 factorial design employing four independent groups of Ss practicing homogeneous paired associate lists: '(a) the simple effect favoring high S-high R meaningfulness (e.g. $m = 6$–9) over low S-low R meaningfulness (e.g. $m = 0$–2) will be greater than for any other comparison, and (b) the difference in the main effect of m on the response side will be greater than the comparable difference on the stimulus side. Given (a) and (b), the likelihood of intrinsic S–R interaction with respect to m is slight' (10, p. 21).

The last sentence reveals the uncertainty of current knowledge about the nature of S and R combination in paired-associate learning. If the relationship is intrinsically *non-additive* when *m* is varied, and if this interaction should itself interact with number of trials (N), then it is conceivable that the S × R variance in a simple factorial experiment might be averaged out in criterion scores due to ignoring the trend factor N. Data reported in an unpublished study by Sheffield (13) indicate such a possibility, as pointed out earlier (8, p. 443).

For this reason, the present experiment will test these implicates in an S × R × N mixed factorial design (3, Type III), thereby jointly evaluating the three-factor interaction in addition to the main effects and two-factor interactions. As far as the basic issue underlying so-called 'perceptual' (2, p. 363) and 'motor' (10, p. 22) principles of verbal learning is concerned, it is evident that when the N classification is disregarded this more complex design includes the 2 × 2 factorial conditions proposed above.

Method

Apparatus. The learning device consisted of a Patterson memory drum set to present the paired associates at a 4-sec rate with a 4-sec intertrial interval.[2] The S term was exposed for 2 sec, followed by S and R together for 2 sec. An idler attachment permitted four sets (trials) of ten pairs to be presented in series to *S* without changing tapes. Six tapes were constructed, each containing a practice and an experimental list typed in capital letters. There were four different random trial sequences for each list, and the series was repeated on trials 5 and 9. On each tape the practice list appeared on the right side, the experimental list on the left. Sliding shutters over the aperture of the memory drum permitted one list to be covered while the other was being presented.

For the *practice* list, ten pairs of three-syllable adjectives were used as in a previous study (10), the four trial sequences being the same for all *S*s. This practice period was intended to reduce variability due to learning-to-learn and to provide comparisons of the initial ability and predictability of the four groups. For the *experimental* lists, forty items were drawn from the high (H) and low (L) extremes of the *m* scale (7) such that the mean median *m*

2. Photographs of this device appear in Wickens and Meyer (15, p. 59).

value of the twenty H items was 7·50 and that of the twenty L items was 0·29. Each of these lists consisted of ten pairs of two-syllable nouns or paralogs, combined so as to avoid mediated associations and similar sources of bias (10).

Subjects. The Ss consisted of eighty undergraduate students at Louisiana State University. There were forty-four women and thirty-six men, whose ages ranged from 18 to 31 (mean = 20·7 yr). All were naïve with respect to paired-associate learning.

Procedure. Four experimental groups were formed in terms of the possible combinations of the *m* values of the S and R items: H–H, L–H, H–L, and L–L. In groups L–L and H–H the pairs were reversed for half the Ss, and the pairs learned by group L–H were reversed for group H–L, giving six lists in all. There were twenty Ss in each group, assigned consecutively by fives to the six lists in a counterbalanced order. Each time a list was repeated, it began with a different trial sequence. Thus, all four sequences appeared equally often for the four experimental groups.

Each S received twelve trials on the practice list. After a 2-min rest, this was followed by twelve trials on the appropriate experimental list. During the rest period between lists E engaged S in conversation. The experiment was performed in an air-conditioned laboratory, so the temperature and humidity conditions were quite constant.

The instructions to Ss were the same as in the earlier study (10) On the first presentation of the list (trial 1), S merely read the paired words aloud and standard pronunciations were estab lished. Attempted anticipations of the correct responses began on the second presentation (trial 2). The correction procedure wa used, and both S and R were pronounced.

Results

To evaluate the comparability of the four groups before introduc tion of the experimental treatments, a simple 4 × 1 analysis o variance was performed upon the total number of corre responses (R+) made during trials 2–12 on the practice list. Th *F* ratio is only 0·13, which for $df = 3/76$ is not significant. Th experimental groups, therefore, may be considered to be of equal initial ability.

Table 1 presents a 2×2 analysis of the average performance of each group on the experimental lists. The order of increasing difficulty in terms of cell means is: H–H, L–H, H–L, L–L. From the main effects of the S and R terms, it can be seen that the average difference due to R is greater than that due to S.

Table 1

Mean Total Correct Responses (R+) During Trials 2–12 in Experiment I

m value of S term	m value of R term		Row means	S difference
	L (0·29)	H (7·50)		
L (0·29)	34·00	85·40	59·70	
H (7·50)	71·60	92·75	82·18	22·48
Column means	52·80	89·08		
R-Difference		36·28		

Figure 1 shows the percentage of correct responses as a function of practice, with type of S–R pair as the parameter. The curves are quite regular with no inversions during the entire training period. There is a tendency for negative acceleration to occur when the R term has high m value, and for the curves to be near or slightly positively accelerated when the R term has low m value. Group L–L is markedly inferior to the other three groups, but it seems to be approaching the same asymptote.

A $2 \times 2 \times 11$ analysis of variance of the number of correct responses made by the four groups during trials 2–12 is summarized in Table 2. All main effects and interactions are significant. In variance terms, the relative magnitudes of the *inter*individual comparisons are: $\sigma^2_R > \sigma^2_S > \sigma^2_{SR}$. For the *intra*individual comparisons the order is: $\sigma^2_N > \sigma^2_{SRN} > \sigma^2_{RN} > \sigma^2_{SN}$. It is interesting to observe that the variance of R exceeds the variance of S, and that R interacts more with N than S does.

Acquisition

To determine the predictability of each group from initial ability measures, product-moment correlations (r) were computed between the total correct responses (R+) on the practice list and the same score on the experimental lists. The correlations are as follows: 0·45 (H–H), 0·51 (L–H), 0·72 (H–L), and 0·81 (L–L).

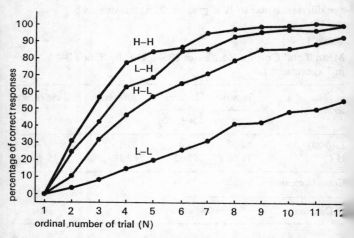

Figure 1 Acquisition curves for lists of ten paired associates as a function of practice (N) in Experiment I. The four S–R combinations of low (L) and high (H) meaningfulness (m) represent the parameter. Each curve contains 20 Ss

This systematic progression could mean that validity increase with difficulty, but the observed trend is probably due merely to greater restriction of range in the easier lists. The average calculated by Fisher's Z transformation is 0·65, which is consistent with the 0·50 reported previously (10) using trials-to criterion scores.

Discussion

Sheffield's (13) experiment is rather closely akin to Experiment He employed so-called 'nonsense' CVC's and familiar three letter words to constitute two levels of high (H) and low ('meaningfulness'. The Ss practiced heterogeneous lists containing the four possible S–R combinations of the H and L items: H–H, L–H, H–L, and L–L. Both S and R were pronounced and ten trials were given. The pairs were learned with the increasing rank order of difficulty stated above. Regardless of the nature of the S term, greater over-all proficiency was attained when the R

Table 2

Analysis of Variance of Number of Correct Responses (R+) During Trials 2–12 in Experiment I

Source	df	MS	F
Between Ss	79		
Stimulus (S)	1	918·41	49·46 *
Response (R)	1	2392·50	128·84 *
S × R	1	415·94	22·40 *
Error (b)	76	18·57	
Within Ss	800		
Trials (N)	10	400·61	328·37 *
S × N	10	5·10	4·18 *
R × N	10	8·42	6·90 *
S × R × N	10	8·55	7·01 *
Error (w)	760	1·22	
Total	879		

* $P < 0.001$.

term was an actual word than when it was a CVC syllable. Specifically, the difference between the mean levels of the two high-R and two low-R conditions exceeded the difference between the mean levels of the respective high-S and low-S condition. This implied the dominance of response factors over stimulus factors in paired-associate learning.

Unfortunately, Sheffield did not report a statistical test of × R interaction, due probably to nonindependence of the four conditions. Graphs of his Ss' curves indicated, however, that the initial separation of H–H and L–H was greater than that of H–L and L–L but tended to become equalized with practice. This suggests the possibility of interaction, but artifacts could have resulted since the H and L items were not actually quantified by means of common operations. Reviewing this experiment in 1952, Noble (8) proposed using the m scale in an appropriate design to determine whether a significant S × R interaction is present.

Turning now to the present data, we recall that the first prediction from the S–R motor-patterning hypothesis (10) was that there would be a greater difference between groups H–H and L–L than between any other two groups. This is confirmed by Table 1 and Figure 1, and is in general agreement with five other paired-associate experiments (6, 10, 11, 13, 14). Two exceptions are a study by Kimble and Dufort (2, Experiment II), in which the order of proficiency was L–H, H–H, H–L (no L–L condition being given), and a study by Mandler and Campbell (5, Experiment I), in which the order was H–H, L–L, L–H, H–L. Both sets of results, however, are difficult to compare with Table 1. Aside from the complications of a confounded design (10, p. 21), half the Kimble–Dufort items were unscaled three-letter words, and the Mandler–Campbell CVC data came from three different groups of Ss ($N = 12$) unmatched for ability. In a more adequate follow-up study (5, Experiment II) using a larger sample ($N = 30$) and a constant-trials design, however, Mandler and Campbell obtained the following ranking: H–H, H–L, L–H, L–L. The extremes are as predicted but the middle groups are reversed.

The second expectation (10) was that the variance attributable to R would be greater than that attributable to S. This is confirmed by Table 1, where the main effect (mean difference) of R is 36·28 correct responses versus 22·48 for the main effect of S. Although Sheffield's (13) findings agree, the Mandler–Campbell (5) data do not; and the Kimble–Dufort (2) design is inappropriate. Such equivocal reports are not surprising in view of the methodological differences among these experiments. This constitutes one reason for performing Experiment II below. From Table 2 it may be seen that the size of σ^2_R is approximately 2 times that of σ^2_S, indicating that the meaning-learning correlation is primarily a response effect and that the stimulus factor is secondary. If our rationale linking m and m' is correct (7, 11), a similar phenomenon ought to occur in the learning of CV pairs.

The remaining issue concerns the interactions. According

Figure 1 and Table 2, there is a significant tendency for an increase in the m value of the S term to cause a greater difference in rate of acquisition when the R term has low m value than when the R term has high m value. Referring to Table 1, the difference between the simple effects (cell means) of groups L–L and H–L is 37·60 correct responses whereas the difference between groups L–H and H–H is only 7·35. (There is a related tendency for increases in R to produce more facilitation when S is low than when it is high: 51·40 versus 21·15 correct responses.) In Figure 1 these interacting trends appear as differential acquisition rates, and Table 2 shows that both S and R as well as S × R interact significantly with amount of practice (N). Consistent with the motor-patterning hypothesis, but not explicitly stated therein, is the fact that $\sigma^2_{RN} > \sigma^2_{SN}$. The ratio is about 1·6/1.

Unlike Sheffield's (13) curves, the S × R interaction in Figure 1 is of a different type and does not disappear late in practice. Furthermore, due to the use of independent Ss and homogeneous lists, the level and range of difficulty are greater than when the same Ss and heterogeneous lists are used (10). This leads to the problem of *extrinsic* versus *intrinsic* interaction (3, p. 124). In view of the fact that all our groups were well matched for ability, the Ss tested individually, procedural factors equalized for each group, and the H and L items quantified by means of common operations, it is unlikely that the significant S × R interaction is caused by extraneous decremental factors associated, say, with group L–L and not with the other groups. We conclude, therefore, that the observed interaction is intrinsic; i.e. due only to the treatments and not to uncontrolled factors.

Experiment II

Our analysis of experiments using CVC syllables indicated that inadequate attention had been paid to the importance of initial ability (A) in determining the influence of S and R meaningfulness. There is also a need for greater procedural comparability between 'verbal' and 'syllable' experiments than has existed up to now.

In order to perform a more comprehensive test of the Noble–McNeely hypothesis (10), Experiment II will expand the

$2 \times 2 \times 11$, $S \times R \times N$ design of Experiment I to a $3 \times 3 \times 20 \times 2$, $S \times R \times N \times A$ mixed factorial (3, Chap. 13), and apply it in the context of paired-associate CVC learning. A prediction favoring the facilitative effect of the R term over that of the S term, when high (H), medium (M), and low (L) levels of m' are used, suggests the following rank order of proficiency for the nine experimental groups disregarding ability: H–H, M–H, L–H, H–M, M–M, L–M, H–L, M–L, L–L. Assuming next that the same hypothetical factors are operating in learning items from the m' scale as from the m scale, Ss' level of pre-experimental ability (A) should interact with the S, R, and N factors (8, 10), and the main effects and interactions observed in Experiment I will be given an opportunity to be confirmed or refuted.

Method

Apparatus. The memory drum and time constants were the same as in Experiment I. A *practice* list was constructed of ten pairs of CVC syllables selected from Mandler's (4) table to avoid overlapping with the m' scale. The *experimental* lists were taken from the Noble–Stockwell–Pryer m' norms (11). Both the practice list and the experimental lists were presented in five random trial sequences and the series was repeated on trial 6. The practice period was intended to reduce variability due to learning-to-learn and to serve as an estimate of initial ability as in Noble and McNeely (10) and in Experiment I.

Nine tapes were prepared, each having the 10-pair practice lis and one of the 10-pair experimental lists typed in capital letters The mean m' values of the S and R terms in the experimental list varied from low (L = $\bar{m}'$ of 0·68) to medium (M = $\bar{m}'$ of 1·72) t high (H = $\bar{m}'$ of 2·91) in all possible combinations: H–H M–H, L–H, H–M, M–M, L–M, H–L, M–L, and L–L. Lis H–M, H–L, and M–L were composed of pairs formed reversals of the items in the M–H, L–H, and L–M lists, respe tively.

The following criteria governed the construction of the list no consonant or vowel letters were duplicated in any pair (e. MOF–DOQ); no alphabetical sequence of consonants occurre within a single syllable (e.g. MEN) or from syllable to syllable any pair (e.g. KEP–QAD); and no pairs constituted meaning associations (e.g. BOR–DAL, GUD–YIR). In the randomization of the lists the following criteria were adopted: each list was considered a circular series and no pair appeared twice within any five consecutive positions (i.e. there were at least four intervening pairs before a repeat); no pair occupied the same serial position on any two adjacent lists; and no two pairs were in the same relative positions on two adjacent lists.

Subjects. The *S*s consisted of ninety undergraduate students at Louisiana State University. There were thirty-five men and fifty-five women, whose ages ranged from 17 to 27 (mean = 19·9 yr). All were naïve with respect to paired-associate learning. On the basis of the total number of correct responses (R+) made on the practice list, *S*s were classified as either Fast (R+ ≥ 6) or Slow (R + ≤ 5) learners (*N* = 45 each). A pilot study was conducted to determine the median (cut-off) score on this list. The mean of the Slow group was 2·0(R+)s, while that of the Fast group was 12·5(R+)s.

Procedure. Each *S* received ten trials on the practice list. After a 2-min rest, this was followed by twenty trials on the appropriate experimental list. During the rest period between lists, *E* engaged *S* in conversation. Five *S*s in each of the two ability levels (A) were then randomly assigned to each of the nine lists in a counterbalanced order of trial sequences. To effect the matching, *E* had to change tapes occasionally and to reject a number of *S*s.

The instructions to *S*s were similar to those in prior studies (10, 11), especially Experiment I. The correction procedure was used, and both S and R were spelled aloud.

Results

To evaluate the comparability of the nine groups within each A level before introduction of the experimental treatments, simple 9×1 analyses of variance were performed upon the total number of (R+)s made during trials 1–10 on the practice list. Both *F* ratios are less than unity (*df* = 8/36). Even the combined *F* ratio is only 0·34, which for 8/81 *df* is not significant. The experimental groups, therefore, may be considered to be of equal initial ability, either preserving or disregarding the Slow versus

Acquisition

Fast classification. Differences in ability between men and women were also tested by comparing their cumulated R+ scores on the practice list. The t ratio was 1·16 for 88 df, which is not significant. The average product-moment r between total $(R+)$s on the practice list and the same measure on each of the experimental lists is 0·63. This correlation is significant at the 5 per cent point for 8 df. For computation of the individual rs the scores of both ability groups were combined ($N = 10$) for each experimental list.

Table 3

Mean Total Correct Responses (R+) During trials 1–20 in Experiment II

m'value of S term	m'value of R term			Row means	S difference (H–L)
	L (0·68)	M (1·72)	H (2·91)		
L (0·68)	6·0	16·7	30·5	17·7	
M (1·72)	17·4	31·4	77·5	42·1	23·3
H (2·91)	21·0	47·2	54·8	41·0	
Column means	14·8	31·8	54·3		
R-Difference (H–L)		39·5			

Fisher Z transformations were then used to compute the average of the nine rs. The predictability of the present data is very similar to that reported previously (10) and in Experiment I.

Table 3 presents a 3 × 3 analysis of the average performance of each group on the experimental lists. From the main effects of the S and R terms, exactly as in Table 1, it is clear that the average difference due to R is greater than that due to S.

A 3 × 3 × 4 × 2 mixed factorial analysis of variance (3) was computed on the R+ scores of each subgroup ($N = 5$), arranged in four blocks of five trials each. The four factors in this S × R × N × A design were stimulus meaningfulness (m') at three levels (H, M, L), response meaningfulness (m') at the same three levels (H, M, L), number of practice blocks (N) at four levels, and initial ability (A) at two levels (Slow, Fast). There were thus $9 \times 2 = 18$ independent treatment groups of five Ss each practicing for twenty trials. The summary analysis is shown in Table 4.

Table 4

Analysis of Variance of Number of Correct Responses (R+) During Four 5-trial Blocks in Experiment II

Source	df	MS	F
Between Ss	89		
Stimulus (S)	2	1424·32	16·30‡
Response (R)	2	2934·51	33·59‡
Ability (A)	1	4396·01	50·31‡
S × R	4	348·87	3·99†
S × A	2	417·22	4·78*
R × A	2	1025·14	11·73‡
S × R × A	4	132·36	1·51
Error (b)	72	87·37	
Within Ss	270		
Trial blocks (N)	3	2340·84	208·26‡
S × N	6	116·18	10·34‡
R × N	6	151·63	13·49‡
N × A	3	246·43	21·92‡
S × R × N	12	25·90	2·30†
S × N × A	6	37·88	3·37†
R × N × A	6	48·69	4·33‡
S × R × N × A	12	11·47	1·02
Error (w)	216	11·24	
Total	359		

* $P < 0.025$. † $P < 0.01$. ‡ $P < 0.001$.

It is evident that all main effects (S, R, N, A), all two-factor interactions (S × R, S × A, R × A, S × N, R × N, N × A), and all three-factor interactions except S × R × A (S × R × N, S × N × A, R × N × A) are significant; but the four-factor S × R × N × A interaction is not. These results confirm all of the findings in Experiment I which pertain to the m scale and extend them to the domain of the m' scale. In addition to verifying the main effect of A, the three two-factor interactions involving A and the three three-factor interactions involving N clearly reflect the intimate relationships existing between initial ability and amount of practice in paired-associate learning when meaningfulness is independently varied. In variance terms, the relative magnitudes of the significant *inter*individual comparisons are: $\sigma^2_A > \sigma^2_R > \sigma^2_S > \sigma^2_{RA} > \sigma^2_{SA} > \sigma^2_{SR}$. These inequalities agree perfectly with Experiment I. For the significant *intra*-individual comparisons the order is: $\sigma^2_N > \sigma^2_{NA} > \sigma^2_{RN} > \sigma^2_{SN} > \sigma^2_{RNA} > \sigma^2_{SNA} > \sigma^2_{SRN}$. These latter variances agree with Experiment I except for the placement of σ^2_{SRN}, a point to which we shall return later.

The major hypothesis generalized from the previous study (10) was tested by computing a rank-difference correlation coefficient between the predicted order of proficiency and the obtained order. The latter was based on the cell means of Table 3 ($N = 10$), disregarding the ability classification. For 8 df, rho $= 0.88$, which is significantly greater than zero at the 1 per cent point. Taking account of individual differences, the motor-patterning hypothesis is about equally tenable for high and low A levels. The two rho values ($N = 5$) are 0.70 for the Slow group and 0.75 for the Fast group, both of which are significant at the 5 per cent point.

Discussion

The present results generally confirm earlier studies in this series with respect to the meaning-learning correlation (8, 10, 11), the differential importance of S and R and their nonadditive combination (Experiment I), the interaction of meaningfulness with initial ability (8, 10), and the dependence of these various relationships upon amount of practice (8, 10, 11). With respect to the four combinations of H and L tested in Experiment I, the rank-order agreement in Tables 1 and 3 is perfect. This fits with the Sheffield (13) data, but conflicts with the Kimble–Dufort (2) and Mandler–Campbell (5) studies mentioned above. In the light of previous methodological comments, however, one should not take these disagreements too seriously. For instance, the Mandler–Campbell experiments (5, Experiment I versus Experiment II) do not even agree with each other. Using rank-correlation again, the ce means for the two sets of nine combinations of H, M, and L in their paper yield a rho of only 0·03. It should be added, however, that both sets of data are positively, though not significantly, related to our hypothesized rank order of the nine groups: rho $\approx$ 0·60, which for 8 df fails to reach significance at the 5 per cent point.

The correspondence between fact and hypothesis in Table 4 (rho = 0·88) is not as close as expected by the writers. One curious inversion is the superiority of the M–H group over the H–H group. Upon investigation of this discrepancy, it was found to be an experimental artifact caused by a slightly greater average m' value for the R terms in the M–H list ($\bar{m}' = 3·04$) than in the H–H list ($\bar{m}' = 2·79$). The mean difference in $\bar{m}'$ scale values of 0·25 is not significant ($t = 1·51$; $df = 18$; $P > 0·10$), but apparently it was powerful enough to produce the obtained reversal. There is no a $priori$ reason to expect any intrinsic superiority for the M–H combination.

Aside from testing the S–R motor-patterning hypothesis at more points along the meaningfulness continuum, the present study was designed to clarify the role of individual differences. The predicted interaction of the A factor was found with S as well as with R, and the magnitude of σ^2_{RA} exceeded that of σ^2_{SA}. Because Experiment I found the ratio σ^2_R/σ^2_S to be approximately 2·6/1 and the ratio $\sigma^2_{RN}/\sigma^2_{SN}$ to be 1·6/1, it is interesting to note that in Table 4 the analogous σ^2_R/σ^2_S ratio is about 2·1/1 and the quantity $\sigma^2_{RN}/\sigma^2_{SN}$ is roughly 1·3/1. The inference is clear that at least twice the variance in performance due to meaningfulness is attributable to R as to S, and that nearly one and a half times the interaction variance with practice can be similarly identified. That S × R interacts more with N in Experiment I than in Experiment II is probably due to the greater ease of learning m scale items; i.e. the general law covering all types of material is × R × N.

In previous experiments (8, 10) the significant interactions between m and A suggested that 'slow learners are more sensitive differences in meaningfulness than are relatively fast learners' (0, p. 19). The present situation, however, produces trends which are exactly the opposite. If one calculates the mean number of R+'s during trials 1–20 for the Slow and Fast Ss in the

L–L, M–M, and H–H groups, it appears that Fast Ss profit more by increases in m' than do Slow Ss. The average correct anticipations increase with m' as follows: Slow (5·0, 24·8, 20·2) versus Fast (7·0, 38·0, 89·4). Rather than assigning this reversal to scale differences between m and m', or perhaps to other procedural factors such as pronouncing versus spelling, the writers believe that the principal variable is the extreme difficulty of the CVC syllable learning task, as mentioned earlier (11). Comparing the present H–H, L–H, H–L, and L–L conditions with those in Experiment I, one finds that the acquisition curves during trials 1–12 proceed more slowly in every case in this experiment. A similar comparison was true of two earlier studies (10, 11) which did not involve independent variation of S and R, and in which all pairs were learned by the same Ss.

The foregoing discussion of individual differences may be summarized by the principle that relatively difficult paired-associate material (e.g. CVC syllables) produces *diverging* slopes for Fast versus Slow Ss, whereas easier material (e.g. dissyllabic words) produces *converging* slopes. The general curve form is of the sigmoid family. If one now imagines a graphical plot of R per cent $= f(m')$ with A as the parameter, it is clear why the form of the meaning-ability interaction should differ in the two experimental situations. A comprehensive investigation of this problem, employing several levels of A and either a wider range of m' or greatly extended practice, is needed. Since the effects of familiarization on *serial* learning (9) imply that variations in the m (hence m') value of paired associates must also reflect the transfer of prior frequencies of experience (n), the suggested experiment might reveal that meaningfulness is a secondary phenomenon derivable from the same basic variable which controls all learning. This coordination would be demonstrated neatly if one could produce similar acquisition curves by manipulating either n or m'. The empirical question is whether familiarization would affect the S and R terms differentially. In 1921 Winzen (16) reported the S-effect to be greater than the R-effect, but Sheffield (13) got the reverse; Mandler and Campbell (5) found no difference. Greater amounts of familiarization in the latter study, however might have produced significant facilitation. Available data (5) indicate a continuous function.

V. J. Cieutat, F. E. Stockwell and C. E. Noble

Summary

In Experiment I, four independent groups of twenty Ss practiced homogeneous lists of ten pairs of dissyllables for twelve trials. Two levels of meaningfulness (m) were employed, high (H = 7·50) and low (L = 0·29), giving the following stimulus-response m values: H–H, L–H, H–L, and L–L. In agreement with prediction, the lists were learned with the rank order of proficiency shown above when practice (N) was varied. The mean total correct responses made by each group during trials 2–12 were 92·75, 85·40, 71·60, and 34·00, respectively. Greater facilitation was attributable to the m value of the R term than to the m value of the S term, and there were significant S × R, R × N, S × N, and S × R × N interactions.

Experiment II evaluated the influence of scaled meaningfulness (m') upon paired-associate syllable learning together with the interaction of the S and R factors with initial level of ability (A) and amount of practice (N). Ninety Ss first received ten trials on a practice list used to classify them as Fast or Slow on the A factor. This was followed by twenty trials on one of nine experimental lists in which the m' values of S and R were independently varied at three levels: 0·68, 1·72, and 2·91.

A rho of 0·88 was obtained between the observed rank order of experimental groups and that expected from the hypothesis favoring the influence of the R term over that of the S term. The effects of S, R, N, and A were significant, as were all two-factor interactions and all three-factor interactions except S × R × A. The relative magnitudes of the variances in Experiment I and Experiment II agreed in six out of seven cases.

From these two experiments it was concluded that at least twice the variance in performance due to meaningfulness (m or m') is attributable to R as to S, and that S–R combination in paired-associate learning is intrinsically nonadditive. The degree to which learning ability interacts with meaningfulness (m or m') depends upon the difficulty of the material and the amount of practice. The results generally confirm earlier experiments in this series, thus supporting the S–R motor-patterning hypothesis. Contradictory findings of recent studies were discussed.

References

1. R. M. DOWLING and H. W. BRAUN, 'Retention and meaningfulness of material', *Journal of Experimental Psychology*, vol. 54 (1957), pp. 213–17.

2. G. A. KIMBLE and R. H. DUFORT, 'Meaningfulness and isolation as factors in verbal learning', *Journal of Experimental Psychology*, vol. 50 (1955), pp. 361–8.

3. E. F. LINDQUIST, *Design and Analysis of Experiments in Psychology and Education*, Houghton Mifflin, 1953.

4. G. MANDLER, 'Associative frequency and associative prepotency as measures of response to nonsense syllables', *American Journal of Psychology*, vol. 68 (1955), pp. 662–5.

5. G. MANDLER and E. H. CAMPBELL, 'Effect of variation in associative frequency of stimulus and response members on paired-associate learning', *Journal of Experimental Psychology*, vol. 54 (1957), pp. 269–73.

6. G. MANDLER and J. HUTTENLOCHER, 'The relationship between associative frequency, associative ability and paired-associate learning', *American Journal of Psychology*, vol. 69 (1956), pp. 424–8.

7. C. E. NOBLE, 'An analysis of meaning', *Psychology Review*, vol. 59 (1952), pp. 421–30.

8. C. E. NOBLE, 'The role of stimulus meaning (m) in serial verbal learning', *Journal of Experimental Psychology*, vol. 43 (1952), pp. 437–46; Erratum, vol. 44 (1952), p. 465.

9. C. E. NOBLE, 'The effect of familiarization upon serial verbal learning', *Journal of Experimental Psychology*, vol. 49 (1955), pp. 333–8.

10. C. E. NOBLE and D. A. MCNEELY, 'The role of meaningfulness (m) in paired-associate verbal learning', *Journal of Experimental Psychology*, vol. 53 (1957), pp. 16–22.

11. C. E. NOBLE, F. E. STOCKWELL and M. W. PRYER, 'Meaningfulness (m') and association value (a) in paired-associate syllable learning', *Psychology Report*, vol. 3 (1957), pp. 441–52.

12. E. H. ROCKLYN, R. B. HESSERT and H. W. BRAUN, 'Calibrated materials for verbal learning with middle- and old-aged subjects', *American Journal of Psychology*, vol. 70 (1957), pp. 628–30.

13. F. D. SHEFFIELD, 'The role of meaningfulness of stimulus and response in verbal learning', *Unpublished Ph.D. dissertation, Yale University*, 1946.

14. T. UMEMOTO, Y. MORIKAWA and M. IBUKI, 'The non-associatio values and meaningfulness of 1892 Japanese two-letter syllables and words', *Japanese Journal of Psychology*, vol. 26 (1955), pp. 148–55.

15. D. D. WICKENS and D. R. MEYER, *Psychology*, Dryden, 1955.

16. K. WINZEN, 'Die Abhängigkeit der paarweisen Assoziation von der Stellung des besser haftenden Gliedes', *Zeitschrift für Psychologie m Zeitschrift für angewandte Psychologie*, vol. 86 (1921), pp. 236–52.

8 W. N. Runquist and M. Freeman

Roles of Association Value and Syllable Familiarization in Verbal Discrimination Learning

W. N. Runquist and M. Freeman, 'Roles of association value and syllable familiarization in verbal discrimination learning', *Journal of Experimental Psychology*, vol. 59 (1960), pp. 396–401.

Paired-associate and serial verbal learning may be conceived of as consisting of two stages. The first stage consists of delimiting the population of responses, i.e. learning what the responses are. The second stage consists of pairing each response with its correct stimulus or learning the correct order of these responses. Although logically the first stage must precede the second, it is likely that the two occur concomitantly in the ordinary learning situation.

Several studies of the role of association value and familiarization of syllables in paired-associate and serial learning have suggested that factors associated with responding are more important than 'perceptual' factors in acquisition of verbal lists (e.g. Deutat, Stockwell and Noble, 1958; Mandler and Campbell, 1957; Noble, 1952, 1955; Noble and McNeely, 1957). One hypothesis which may be advanced concerning these results is that the primary influence of association value and familiarization is in the first stage (the response-learning phase) of acquisition. According to this hypothesis, the letters making up a nonsense syllable must be integrated into a single response before correct anticipations can occur (Mandler, 1954). Syllables of high association value and familiarity are conceived of as representing verbal habits established outside the experiment and thus are more readily integrated. The number of responses available on any given trial is then determined by how far this integration time has progressed.

However, suppose a learning task is used in which the total number of available responses is determined by the task, rather than the rate of response integration. This may be accomplished by using a procedure called verbal discrimination learning, where presented with a pair of syllables and must select the response arbitrarily designated as 'correct' from these two. The response population from which S must make his choice is thus restricted to the two syllables presented, and integration in the sense described above is unnecessary. It might then be expected that neither association value nor familiarization would have much effect upon acquisition in this task.

The following experiments are designed to investigate the role of both association value and familiarization on the verbal discrimination learning of nonsense syllables.

Experiment I

The first two experiments were concerned with the effects of association value. Two methods of varying association value are available for verbal discrimination learning: A pair may be made up of one high and one low association value syllable, or the two syllables making up a pair may both be high or both low association value. According to the hypothesis, there seemed to be no reason to favor one method or the other. Although this conclusion later appeared to be in error, for the first experiment the first method (heterogeneous pairs) was used.

Method

Design and materials. Two sets of eight pairs of syllables were constructed from Glaze's lists (1928). In each pair one syllable was 80 per cent to 100 per cent association value and one syllable was 0 per cent to 27 per cent association value. Formal similarity was kept to a minimum both within and between sets, and the same number of letters was duplicated within a set. These sets were then combined to make a list of sixteen pairs of syllables. For half of the Ss, the high association value syllables of set I and the low association syllables of set II were correct. For the other half of the Ss, the low association value syllables of set I and the high association value syllables of set II were correct. This reduced the chances of extraneous factors such as different difficulty or interference with specific syllables influencing results. It was felt that having both high and low association value syllables correct in the same list would avoid Ss recognizing, for example, that all the 'word-like' ones were correct.

Procedure. The sixteen pairs in each list were arranged in three orders and presented with a 16-mm filmstrip projector. The pairs were flashed from the back of the screen so that S could not see E or the projector during the presentation. General illumination was reduced to minimize distraction. Syllables appeared black on a white background and were $\frac{3}{8}$ in high. They appeared on an 3×8 in milk glass piece in the center of a 3×3 ft wooden screen. The two syllables were presented one above the other for sec followed by the correct syllable for 2 sec. The intertrial interval was 4 sec. The position of the syllables in a pair varied from trial to trial. All Ss were given fifteen trials unless they went three consecutive trials with no error. They were then stopped and given a perfect score for the remaining trials. The Ss, twenty volunteers from Hobart and William Smith Colleges, were instructed to select and spell aloud the syllable designated as correct on each presentation including the first trial. All Ss were naïve to verbal learning experiments.

Results

The percentages of correct anticipations for the high association value syllables and low association value syllables on each trial are shown in Figure 1. The hypothesis that variations in association

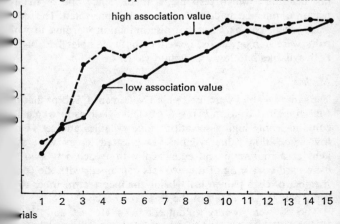

Figure 1 Percentage of correct responses on each trial for high and low association value syllables in Experiment I (heterogeneous pairs)

value would not produce performance differences is not supported by these data. Statistically, the mean total correct anticipations for the high association value syllables is significantly greater than for the low association value syllables ($t = 3.65$). Seventeen of the twenty Ss gave more correct responses to the high than to the low association syllables.

Experiment II

Rather than completely reject the hypothesis on the basis of this single experiment, explanation was sought in terms of other factors associated with making the response. The facilitation in performance obtained here may have been due to greater ease of responding with the high association syllables. Essentially the notion is what Noble (1955) has called 'motor patterning'. If it is easier to learn to make the high association value responses than the low association value responses, some facilitation might be expected. This is a kind of response integration although only the motor aspect is being referred to here. If the pairs, however, are constructed of two high or two low association value syllables greater ease of responding to high association value syllables can not determine which response is made, since one of the two responses must be made each time a pair is presented. The second study, then, compared verbal discrimination learning in which pairs were homogeneous, i.e. either both syllables had high or both syllables had low association value.

Method

The same syllables were used as in Experiment I, except that they were re-paired to form two sets of eight syllables in which set I contained only high association value syllables and set II of low association value syllables. Duplicated letters were again kept at a minimum and equalized within each set. Two lists were used consisting of the two sets combined, with the correct member of each pair in list 1 being the incorrect member of the same pair in list 2. Half of the Ss learned each list.

The Ss were twenty volunteers from Hobart and William Smith Colleges. All were naïve with respect to verbal learning. The procedure was identical to that in Experiment I.

Results

The acquisition curves for the high and low association value pairs are presented in Figure 2. Although there is some evidence for better performance on the high association value pairs, the differences are much smaller than those obtained in Experiment I. Comparison of the mean total correct responses for the two kinds of syllables resulted in a t of 2·07, which is just short of significance at the 0·05 level for 19 df. Although a constant number of

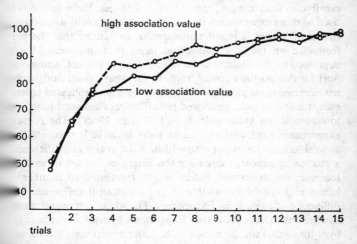

Figure 2 Percentage of correct responses on each trial for high and low association value syllables in Experiment II (homogeneous pairs)

als was used, all Ss obtained all eight items within each set rect on at least one trial. Thus trials to 8/8 criterion may be d as a measure of acquisition rate. Seventeen of the twenty Ss ched this criterion first on the high association value pairs. A nparison of the mean trials to this criterion for the two kinds pairs resulted in a t of 3·45. It thus appears that the difference erformance shown in Figure 2 is reliable, although a small

comparison was made between Experiments I and II of the n difference between the total correct responses to high and low association value pairs. The value of t obtained was 1·73 which is only significant at about the 0·08 level.

The results of Experiments I and II do not support the hypothesis that the facilitative effects of association value can be attributable solely to the response-learning phase. Although there are several interpretations of these differences, the one favored here is suggested by Underwood and Richardson (1958). High association value syllables may provide some sort of extra cue value, often called 'meaning', thus making them less susceptible to interference from duplicated letters. Since in the lists used in these experiments it was impossible to avoid some duplication of letters, it is not unreasonable to assume that the performance on the low association items in Experiment II was depressed by the slight amount of interference present. Some support for this position comes from the fact that a pilot study using ten homogeneous pairs in which there were no duplicated letters except a few vowels, produced no differences between high and low association value pairs ($t = 1·27$ with 19 df). The present experiments used lists of sixteen pairs because it was felt that acquisition was too rapid with a 10-item list to give any difference a chance to appear. Increasing the length of the list necessarily increases the duplicated letters due to the restricted number of letters and syllables available, thus increasing interference. The difference obtained in Experiment II, while not significant, smaller than that obtained in Experiment I, tends to support the hypothesis that the difference in the latter experiment was mostly due to differential ease of making the response.

Experiments III and IV

The purpose of these two studies was to compare the effects produced by the familiarization of nonsense syllables (Noble, 19 with those produced by association value.

Method

Design and materials. The rules for the construction of lists were the same as those in the previous experiments, with the exception that all syllables were from 0 per cent to 27 per cent association value (Glaze, 1928). The number of duplicated letters within a was slightly higher for these lists than in Experiments I and II. As in the previous studies, a given syllable in each pair was correct for half the Ss and incorrect for the other half.

Procedure. Prior to learning the list each S was given familiarization training on half the syllables.

Half the syllables were correct in learning and half the syllables were incorrect. For Experiment III, one syllable was chosen from each pair; for Experiment IV, both syllables of half of the pairs were used. Two different familiarization lists were employed in each experiment so that syllable difficulty, etc. was partially counterbalanced between the familiarized and nonfamiliarized syllables. In familiarization training each syllable was exposed ingly on the screen for 2 sec. The S was instructed to spell out ach syllable as it appeared. The sixteen syllables were arranged in six different orders, but there was no interval between orders. No syllable preceded or followed any other syllable more than nce. Each syllable was seen and spelled twelve times by each S.

The verbal discrimination learning procedure was identical ith that in Experiments I and II. Twenty volunteers from the obart and William Smith students served as Ss in each study. one of the Ss had served in a verbal learning experiment before.

esults

e percentage of correct responses on each trial for familiarized d non-familiarized syllables in Experiment III is shown in gure 3. With heterogeneous pairs performance level is higher en the familiarized syllable is correct than when it is incorrect, h the advantage being particularly marked in the early trials. test comparing the mean total correct responses for the two ds of syllables resulted in a value of $3 \cdot 78$ ($P < 0 \cdot 01$).

he acquisition curves for Experiment IV are presented in ure 4. In this experiment, however, there is no difference in formance between pairs of familiarized and nonfamiliarized ables. Comparison of the mean total correct responses gave a $0 \cdot 33$, which is clearly not significant.

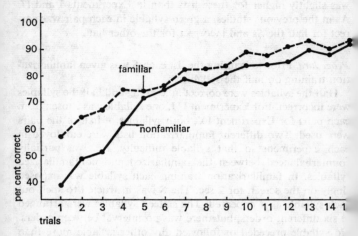

Figure 3 Percentage of correct responses on each trial for familiar and nonfamiliar syllables in Experiment III (heterogeneous pairs)

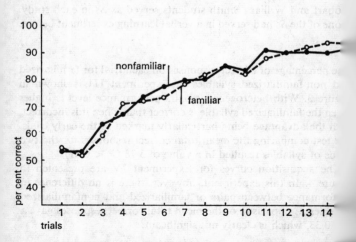

Figure 4 Percentage of correct responses on each trial for familiar and nonfamiliar syllables in Experiment IV (homogeneous pairs)

Discussion

The effects of familiarization training on verbal discrimination learning are not the same as the effects of association value. The fact that familiarization produced facilitation in the case of heterogeneous pairs is consistent with the effects produced by association value, although there are some slight differences. In the case of association value, performance on the two kinds of pairs starts at the same level, then diverges before converging again near the asymptote. Familiarization, on the other hand, produces large differences on the first trial. This large initial difference in the case of familiarization is probably produced by a tendency to guess and to keep guessing the syllables which have just been seen. This is clearly shown by the fact that performance on the nonfamiliarized syllables begins below the chance level (at 39 per cent), while performance on the familiarized syllables begins at 57 per cent. These results are also consistent with the hypothesis attributing facilitation to differential ease of responding for the two kinds of syllables. Since the differential ease of responding might not be established until after a few trials when association value was varied, facilitation did not take place until later in learning, whereas familiarization training established these habits prior to learning the list.

The striking result of these studies, however, is the failure of familiarization training to produce differences in performance when homogeneous pairs are used. This result is also consistent with the interpretation given the association value experiments. If the differences which occurred in the homogeneous pairs association value experiment are attributed to the cue value of association or 'meaning', familiarization training should not produce differences since it can be shown that familiarizing operations, in general, do not increase association value (Riley and Phillips, 1957). It might be argued that a difference would have been obtained in Experiment IV had familiarization training been continued. This cannot, of course, be denied; however, the twelve trials given here were sufficient to produce large differences in Experiment III when conditions for producing these differences were allowed. In fact, the purpose of Experiment III was to ensure that the familiarizing operations were sufficient to produce performance differences in one situation where these differences might be expected.

It is felt that, over-all, the results support a response-oriented interpretation of the effects of association value and familiarization, although they do indicate some cue effect of association value. The results of Experiment IV represent the only real support for the original predictions from the response integration hypothesis that association value and familiarization would not facilitate verbal discrimination learning. Nevertheless, an attempt has been made to show that complicating factors were present in the case of heterogeneous pairs.

Summary

Four verbal discrimination learning experiments were performed to test the hypotheses that association value and familiarization with the syllables would not facilitate performance. Two experiments varied association value and two gave familiarization training on the syllables. In one experiment each pair of items to be learned consisted of one high and one low association value syllable (heterogeneous pairs), while in the other experiment, both syllables were either high or low association value. The same held true for the familiarization studies.

The results showed that both association value and familiarization facilitated performance with the heterogeneous pairs, while only association value facilitated performance with the homogeneous pairs. These results were discussed in relation to an interpretation of the role of association value and familiarization in learning in terms of their effects on response availability.

References

CIEUTAT, V. J., STOCKWELL, F. E., and NOBLE, C. E. (1958), 'The interaction of ability and amount of practice with stimulus and response meaningfulness (*m*, *m'*) in paired-associate learning', *Journal of Experimental Psychology*, vol. 56, pp. 193–202.

GLAZE, J. A. (1928), 'The association value of non-sense syllables', *Journal of Genetic Psychology*, vol. 35, pp. 255–69.

MANDLER, G. (1954), 'Response factors in human learning', *Psychological Review*, vol. 61, pp. 235–44.

MANDLER, G. H., and CAMPBELL, E. H. (1957), 'Effects of variation in associative frequency of stimulus and response members on paired-associate learning', *Journal of Experimental Psychology*, vol. 54, pp. 269–73.

NOBLE, C. E. (1952), 'The role of stimulus meaning (*m*) in serial verbal learning', *Journal of Experimental Psychology*, vol. 43, pp. 437–46.

NOBLE, C. E. (1955), 'The effect of familiarization upon serial verbal learning', *Journal of Experimental Psychology*, vol. 49, pp. 333–8.

NOBLE, C. E., and MCNEELY, D. A. (1957), 'The role of meaningfulness (*m*) in paired-associate verbal learning', *Journal of Experimental Psychology*, vol. 53, pp. 16–22.

RILEY, D. A., and PHILLIPS, L. W. (1957), 'The influence of syllable familiarization on association value, serial rote learning, and reminiscence', *American Psychology*, vol. 12, pp. 425 (abstract).

UNDERWOOD, B. J., and RICHARDSON, J. (1958), 'Studies of distributed practice: XVIII. The influence of meaningfulness and intralist similarity of serial nonsense lists', *Journal of Experimental Psychology*, vol. 56, pp. 213–19.

9 R. L. Erickson

Relational Isolation as a Means of Producing the von Restorff Effect in Paired-Associate Learning

R. L. Erickson, 'Relational isolation as a means of producing the von Restorff effect in paired-associate learning', *Journal of Experimental Psychology*, vol. 66 (1963), pp. 111–19.

One S–R pair in each of eight 9-pair lists of syllables and numbers was isolated solely on the basis of the relationship between its members. Stimulus and response elements of the isolated pairs were each individually more massed than isolated among their respective counterparts. An obtained isolation effect ($p < 0.001$) was interpreted to indicate that S–R intralist associative interference explanations based solely upon reduced stimulus and/or response generalization are inadequate to account completely for the von Restorff effect. Additional isolation was produced for some Ss by printing critical elements in red. Color isolation of both S–R elements produced an effect greater than that of response isolation alone ($p < 0.05$) but not greater than that of stimulus isolation alone. Stimulus and response color isolation did no produce different effects. Ss were 176 undergraduates.

The existence of the von Restorff, or isolation, effect has been clearly demonstrated. H. von Restorff (1933), using both serial and paired-associate lists, found that when relatively isolated items of one type were embedded in lists containing other 'massed' material, the recall of the isolated items was superior. Subsequent investigations (e.g. Kimble and Dufort, 195; Nachmias, Gleitman and McKenna, 1961; Newman and Salt 1958; Pillsbury and Raush, 1943; Saltz and Newman, 1959; Sa and Osgood, 1950; Siegel, 1943) have confirmed the existence an isolation effect in both paired-associate and serial learning.

Although the isolation effect is clearly demonstrable at empirical level, marked differences have evolved with regard the theoretical explanation of the phenomenon. The Gestalti contend that the effect is to be understood in terms of the Gest laws of perceptual organization. The basic precept of the Gest approach is that, in the case of the isolation phenomenon elsewhere, perceptual processes persist in and determine m monic processes (Koffka, 1935, pp. 481–506; von Restorff, 1933). Green (1958), on the other hand, maintains that the isolation effect does not depend upon structural *isolation* of items within a list. He contends that the 'isolation' effect results from increased attention given any element that introduces a change into the structure of a list, so that in serial lists the subsequent massed material is not relevant to the effect. 'Attention', for Green, is a primitive notion, similar in a sense to the Gestalt concept of figure-ground, and he does not explain why increased attention should produce more rapid learning. Finally, current S–R explanations of the effect are based largely upon Gibson's (1940, 1942) principles of stimulus generalization and differentiation. They attribute the isolation effect to reduced intralist interference, resulting from reduced stimulus and/or response generalization (e.g. Kimble and Dufort, 1955; Postman and Phillips, 1954; Saul and Osgood, 1950; Siegel, 1943). Newman and Saltz (1958) and Saltz and Newman (1959), in particular, extended Gibson's principles to include response generalization and differentiation in an attempt to explain several aspects of the isolation effect in serial learning, although they were not satisfied with the success of their attempt.

Any S–R explanation that attributes the isolation effect solely to a reduction in intralist interference resulting from reduced stimulus and/or response generalization will be referred to here as the S–R intralist associative interference explanation. To date, no investigation has demonstrated an isolation effect in multitrial learning under such a condition that the S–R intralist associative interference explanation is clearly inapplicable. The major purpose of the present investigation was to demonstrate such an isolation effect by constructing paired-associate lists in which the only basis for isolation would be the *relationship* between the stimulus and response of each critical pair.

Table 1 shows two examples of the eight sets of items used in the lists. The critical pair in list 1 (KSC-ZNH) is isolated because both the stimulus and response are consonant syllables, whereas each of the other eight pairs of items in the list consists of a consonant syllable and a number, the syllables functioning as stimuli for half the eight pairs and as responses for the other half. The critical pair in list 2 (CTG-472) is isolated because it is composed of a consonant syllable and a number, whereas all the other pairs consist of pairs of consonant syllables or of numbers. In such lists, both the stimulus and the response of each critical pair are individually more massed than isolated among their respective counterparts; hence neither member of the critical pair is subject to reduced generalization tendencies.

An additional purpose of the present study was to investigate the differential effects of individually isolating either the stimulus, the response, or both elements of each critical pair along the dimension of color.

Method

Materials and apparatus

Eight basic nine-pair lists, each containing a different relationally isolated pair, were used. Each isolated pair appeared in one of the other lists as a nonisolated pair.

List 3 was identical to list 1 (in Table 1), except that a number-number pair constituted the isolated pair. List 4 was identical to list 2, except that a number–syllable combination functioned as the isolated pair. Lists 5 through 8 replicated the first four, except that different syllables and numbers were used. Hence, there was a complete counterbalancing of syllable–syllable, syllable–number, number–number, and number–syllable combinations in the isolated position.

Each relationally isolated pair of items appeared under four color conditions: (a) black–black: both stimulus and response in black; (b) red–black: stimulus in red, response in black; (c) black–red: stimulus in black, response in red; (d) red–red: both stimulus and response in red. All nonisolated pairs appeared in black only. Condition black–black thus provided the experimental condition for evaluating the relational isolation effect, while the other three color conditions permitted evaluation of the differential stimulus-response isolation effects.

All consonant syllables used came from the 50 per cent association level of Witmer's (1935) list of association values. The lists were printed on 80-lb fotolith paper by means of rubber stamps with symbols $\frac{3}{8}$ in in height. Each list appeared on endless tape in nine different orders, with no spaces separating the orders. A Gloric memory drum with a 2–2–1 sec time sequence was used.

Design and procedure

The first replication of the experiment used 128 Ss assigned in equal numbers to each color condition. In the second replication,

Table 1

Two of the Eight Sets of Items Used in the Experimental Lists

List 1	List 2
SWJ–217	SWJ–DXR
BJN–821	BJN–GDP
RKD–764	RKD–JPZ
CTG–472	KSC–ZNH
KSC–ZNH *	CTG–472 *
086–DXR	086–217
590–GDP	590–821
305–JPZ	305–764
153–LFS	138–649

Note: Lists were not presented in the order shown here. An original random order of the pairs was determined and nine subsequent arrangements of this random order were selected such that each pair appeared once at each of the nine positions and there was only one repetition of any adjacent pairs in running through eighty-one presentations. The nine orders were the same for all lists.

* Isolated pairs. The basis for isolation is the S–R *relationship* between the items of the critical pair. In list 1, for example, KSC–ZNH is a syllable–syllable pair in a list otherwise composed of syllable–number and number–syllable pairs.

which was temporally contiguous with the first and had as its major purpose acquiring additional data for Cond. black–black, thirty-two additional Ss were run under Cond. black–black and additional sixteen Ss were run under Cond. red–red as a check on replication effects. Lists were counter-balanced within or conditions in both replications.

Each S first practiced to a criterion of one perfect recitation on

143

a list of six pairs of two-syllable nouns. He was then presented with his appropriate experimental list, on which learning continued to a criterion of one errorless trial or twenty-five presentations, whichever took longer. The Ss were instructed to spell out their responses to the consonant syllables, and were told not to be afraid to guess and make mistakes. Responses were recorded verbatim.

In addition to the above independent variables, three minor variables were included in the design. The Ss were divided into four groups on the basis of their College Entrance Examination Board (CEEB) scores, and the Ss from each CEEB level were randomly assigned to the thirty-two list-color conditions. Eight of the nine different orders of each list were used as initial orders of presentation, and these eight starting orders were counterbalanced within lists, color conditions, and CEEB levels. Finally, each S was specifically assigned to be run among the first, second, third, or fourth quarter of the Ss and these tempora groups were counterbalanced in a like fashion. For a more detailed description of procedure, see Erickson (1962).

The design confounded certain higher order interactions o these three minor variables. Since these interactions would b expected to be negligible on *a priori* grounds, and since the mai effects were not significant (with the single exception of a barel significant F for CEEB level), the procedure seems justified.

Subjects

The Ss were 176 volunteer undergraduate psychology studen at Whittier College. There were fifty-six males and 120 female

Results

The dependent variables extracted for analysis were: (a) numb correct responses to the isolated pair over trials 1–25; (b) me number correct responses to the nonisolated pairs over tri 1–25. The 'nonisolated pairs' were defined for each list as th pairs whose stimulus and response elements were used son where in other lists as elements in isolated pairs. Consequen six rather than eight nonisolated pairs were scored for each l the remaining two pairs being ignored.

Table 2 shows mean correct responses for isolated and non-isolated pairs in each of the four color conditions. Figure 1 presents the learning curves for isolated and nonisolated pairs within each of the four color conditions.

Table 2

Mean Correct Responses per S per Pair over trials 1–25 for Isolated and Nonisolated Pairs in Each of the Four Color Conditions

Color Cond.	Isolated Pair	Nonisolated Pairs
Black–black	10·23	6·92
Red–black	16·28	7·58
Black–red	14·06	6·98
Red–red	16·96	6·92

The most important results are from the black–black condition. As both Table 2 and Figure 1 indicate, the isolated pairs were learned more easily than the nonisolated pairs under Cond. black–black. The difference of 3·31 correct responses is significant, as shown by the F ratio for Isolation in the analysis of variance of Table 3.

Variations along the color dimension produced no detectable effect on the ease of learning the nonisolated pairs, but did produce effects on the ease of learning the isolated pairs, and hence on the magnitude of the isolation effect. An analysis of variance of isolated scores alone yielded a significant F for color effects, $F(3, 144) = 12·23$, $p < 0·001$, indicating that at least one of the four means for isolated pairs shown in Table 2 differed significantly from the others. A similar analysis of nonisolated scores alone indicated no significant differences among the four non-isolated score means shown in Table 2, $F(3, 144) = 0·23$.

A more precise indication of color effects was obtained by applying a Duncan multiple-range test to the four color condition group means of the isolated scores. The mean isolated score under Cond. black–black was significantly lower ($p < 0·05$) than each of the other three means, but the means of conditions in which color was used did not differ significantly from each other.

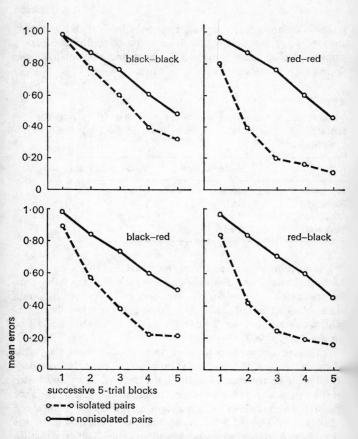

Figure 1 Mean errors per *S* per pair per trial made to isolated and nonisolated pairs averaged over five-trial blocks for each color condition

Since the analysis of variance of nonisolated scores alone ha shown that the use of color produced no detectable effect on t rate of learning the nonisolated pairs, it was considered appr priate to use the nonisolated scores as a covariable for the th conditions in which color was used. A second Duncan multip range test analysed the differences among these three means the isolated scores as adjusted by the covariance analysis. The adjusted mean of Cond. red–red was significantly larger ($p < 0.05$) than that of Cond. black–red, but no other differences were significant.

Table 3

Analysis of Variance of Total Correct Responses over trials 1–25 for Isolated and Nonisolated Pairs under Cond. black–black

Source	df	F
Between Ss		
Lists (L)	7	1·08
Replications (R)	1	0·03
L × R	7	1·16
Error (b)	48	(1,474·71)
Within Ss		
Isolation (I)	1	21·48 *
I × L	7	0·93
I × R	1	0·54
I × L × R	7	1·59
Error (w)	48	(588·59)

Note: Error MSs in parentheses. For computational convenience, isolated scores were multiplied by 6 rather than dividing the nonisolated scores by 6.
* $p < 0.001$.

In summary, any addition of color to the critical pairs of items produced a significant increase in the magnitude of the isolation effect compared to that obtained from relational isolation alone. The isolation effect under Cond. red–red was found to be greater than that under Cond. black–red, but not greater than that obtained under Cond. red–black. Conditions red–black and black–red did not produce detectably different effects.

As Table 3 shows, the Lists × Isolation interaction for Cond. black–black was not significant. Hence, the highly significant F obtained for relational isolation cannot be attributed to idiosyncratic characteristics of particular lists. The only significant

Table 4

Analysis of Mean Errors per S over trials 1–25 for Isolated Pairs in Each of the Four Color Conditions

Color Cond.	Incorrect responses to critical stimulus							Incorrect elicitations of critical response	
	Total errors	No response	Extra-list responses	Partial correct responses*	Partial incorrect responses†	Homogeneous intrusions‡	Heterogeneous intrusions‡	By homogeneous stimuli§	By heterogeneous stimuli§
Black–black	14·77	9·82	0·50	2·34	0·96	0·31	0·84	0·78	0·25
Red–black	8·72	5·06	0·22	2·19	0·75	0·34	0·16	0·09	0·44
Black–red	10·94	7·97	0·19	1·75	0·69	0·03	0·31	0·69	0·34
Red–red	8·04	3·55	0·40	3·21	0·40	0·42	0·06	0·08	0·29

* Partial correct responses defined as responses containing two elements from the critical response.

† Partial incorrect responses defined as responses containing two elements from any noncritical response.

‡ Homogeneous intrusions defined as intralist responses from same class as critical response; heterogeneous from opposite class. (Classes were numbers and syllables.)

§ Homogeneous stimuli defined as stimuli from same class as critical stimulus; heterogeneous from opposite class.

List effect in any of the analyses was a Lists × Isolation inter-action, $F (7, 144) = 2.78$, $p < 0.01$, obtained in an analysis of scores from all four color conditions. Inspection of isolated and nonisolated means for each list showed that the isolation effect was in the same direction for all lists and that the significant interaction reflected the fact that the isolation effect was greater for some lists than for others. The cause of this difference is not known.

Table 4 presents an analysis of the errors made to isolated pairs. Of interest is the high proportion of 'no response' to the critical stimulus; intralist intrusions constituted only about 6 per cent of the total errors. Although the isolated pairs were learned more rapidly under Cond. red–red than under Cond. black–red, there were fewer intralist intrusions to the critical stimulus under Cond. black–red then under Cond. red–red, whether these are measured in absolute numbers or as proportions of total errors.

It is also of interest to note that Cond. black–red did not produce fewer elicitations of the critical response by inappropriate stimuli than did Cond. black–black. This holds true even when only incorrect elicitations by heterogeneous stimuli (i.e. stimuli associated with responses from which a maximum of response generalization could be expected) are considered. On the other hand, trends evident in the intralist intrusion data are consistent with the interpretation that both stimulus and response color isolation produced a greater reduction in intralist interference resulting from like elements than that resulting from unlike elements.

The effects of the minor variables require only brief comment. Analyses of variance of the main effects of each minor variable were carried out separately on isolated and nonisolated scores. All effects were found to be nonsignificant with the single exception of CEEB level on nonisolated scores, which was just significant at the 0.05 level. However, there was no orderly relationship among the performances at the four CEEB levels. No significant were obtained for replications, nor for any replication inter-actions. Hence, combining data from the two replications was considered to be appropriate.

Discussion

The results of the present investigation are best considered in two parts: those from Cond. black–black, and those from the other three color conditions. The black–black results will be considered first.

The important finding here was that relational isolation facilitated the learning of the critical pairs. Pairs of items that possessed a unique S–R *relationship* within a list were learned more readily than pairs of items not possessing this unique relationship. Both Gestalt theory and Green's attention hypothesis can easily account for this effect. According to the Gestalt explanation, the trace systems of the relationally isolated pairs would constitute a figure on the ground of the trace systems of the nonisolated pairs. The isolated pairs would be learned more easily because their unique relationship causes their traces to 'stand out' as a figure, while the traces of the nonisolated pairs become assimilated with each other into a ground. If it is assumed that the relationally isolated pairs constitute a perceptible 'structural change' in the lists, according to Green they would then receive increased attention and would be learned more rapidly for that reason.

However, the traditional S–R intralist associative interference explanation does not account for the relational isolation effect. According to this explanation, the more differentiated a stimulus item is from other list stimuli, the fewer inappropriate responses that stimulus will elicit. This follows because its greater differentiation (isolation) is equivalent to less stimulus generalization. Similarly, a response item that is more differentiated from the remainder of the response items than the latter are from each other will evoke less response generalization. Consequently the stimulus for the isolated response item will elicit few responses that are appropriate elsewhere in the list. The isolation effect in paired-associate learning is held to result, then, from reduced intralist interference, the basis for which is either reduced stimulus generalization or reduced response generalization both.

It is apparent that such an S–R explanation cannot account the relational isolation effect found here. Under Cond. bla black, both the stimulus and the response items of the isolated pairs were individually more massed than isolated among their respective counterparts. There is thus no basis for assuming a reduction in either stimulus or response generalization for the critical pairs. It seems clear, therefore, that even if the more rapid learning of the relationally isolated pairs is attributed to a reduction in intralist interference, explanatory principles in addition to stimulus and/or response generalization will have to be utilized to account for this reduction in interference. It would be premature to infer that the results cannot be explained within the framework of general S–R theory, but account must somehow be taken of the pattern of relationships obtaining between the stimuli and the responses making up a given list.

One additional explanatory S–R principle would involve the concepts of mediating response and response-produced cues. Such a mediating response hypothesis would hold that the relational isolation effect is produced by a covert response made to the unique characteristic of the relationally isolated pair of items. The precise nature of this mediating response would be impossible to specify at this point. However, it would be assumed that the mediating response, whether conscious and well-articulated or not, is a response made to the relationally isolated pair of items because the presentation of that critical pair disrupts the tendency to respond to that type of stimulus item with the *type* of response that has received reinforcement throughout the rest of the list. It is assumed that this response functions as a typical mediating response, in that it provides discriminable cues. While the original evocations of the mediating response depend upon the prior appearance of the response item of the relationally isolated pair, the mediating response comes, as learning processes, to be associated with the critical list stimulus alone. One chain of associations, then, is from the critical stimulus item to the mediating response, and from the response-produced cues to the critical response item.

The distinctive characteristic of the hypothesized mediating response is that it is a response brought about by a particular attribute of the list. Mediating responses utilized by Ss in learning the nonisolated pairs, on the other hand, would depend upon each S's idiosyncratic associations to particular elements and pairs. The advantage for the isolated pair of items results from the fact that the list structure makes it possible for all Ss to share a common mediating response to the critical pair.

The main result from the remaining three color conditions was that any addition of color increased the size of the isolation effect. This raises some interesting questions. The most parsimonious S–R explanation would be to attribute the increased effect to a reduction in stimulus and/or response generalization, since with any introduction of color, either the stimulus or the response element of the critical pair, or both, were individually isolated. However, the error data relevant to Cond. black–red and red–red presented in Table 4 seem inconsistent with an interpretation that ascribes increased ease of learning of the isolated pairs solely to reduced stimulus and/or response generalization. Furthermore, there is no logical reason to assume that the factors that produced an isolation effect under Cond. black–black ceased to operate in the three conditions in which color was used. Granted the appropriateness of the mediating response hypothesis to account for the effect obtained in Cond. black–black, it may be assumed that similar mediating responses were operating in the other three color conditions. According to this argument, the addition of color may not only have reduced stimulus and/or response generalization, but it may also have changed the characteristics of the mediating response in that Ss were now responding to the atypical color as well as to the difference in relationship of the critical pair. This could either have made the mediating response more discriminable, or increased the probability of its occurrence, or both.

Such a use of the mediating response hypothesis as an additional explanatory principle is related to an interpretation made by Gleitman and Gillett (1957), who proposed that the von Restorff effect may be a composite of two factors. The first of these they held to result from Ss' deliberate efforts to organize the materials. They maintained that while the cues for organization may be inherent in the materials, their utilization perhaps depends upon intentional structuring, in a manner akin to the use of rhythm and other organizational devices. The second factor they presumed to depend upon lowered interference effects from other items in the list, and to operate regardless of intent

While mediating responses of the type hypothesized here need not depend upon intentional structuring, when intent is involved they would appear to be closely akin to what Gleitman and Gillett call organizing responses.

The results of the present investigation, together with those of Newman and Saltz (1958) and Saltz and Newman (1959), indicate that the von Restorff effect is more complex than intralist interference theories based solely upon the principles of stimulus and/or response generalization would allow. Since the existence of mediating responses in verbal learning seems well established (e.g. Bugelski, 1962; Bugelski and Scharlock, 1952; Russell and Storms, 1955; Underwood and Schulz, 1960, pp. 296–300), the mediating response explanation for the relational isolation effect found here has a certain plausibility. The extent to which mediating responses may be involved in all isolation phenomena remains to be determined.

References

BUGELSKI, B. R. (1962), 'Presentation time, total time, and mediation in paired-associate learning', Journal of Experimental Psychology, vol. 63, pp. 409–12.

BUGELSKI, B. R., and SCHARLOCK, D. P. (1952), 'An experimental demonstration of unconscious mediated association', Journal of Experimental Psychology, vol. 44, pp. 334–8.

RICKSON, R. L. (1962), 'Further investigation of the von Restorff effect in paired-associate learning: Relational isolation', Unpublished doctoral dissertation, University of California.

IBSON, E. J. (1940), 'A systematic application of the concepts of generalization and differentiation to verbal learning', Psychology Review, vol. 47, pp. 196–229.

IBSON, E. J. (1942), 'Intra-list generalization as a factor in verbal learning', Journal of Experimental Psychology, vol. 30, pp. 185–200.

LEITMAN, H., and GILLETT, E. (1957), 'The effect of intention upon learning', Journal of General Psychology, vol. 57, pp. 137–49.

REEN, R. T. (1958), 'Surprise, isolation and structural change as factors affecting recall of a temporal series', British Journal of Psychology, vol. 49, pp. 21–30.

MBLE, G. A., and DUFORT, R. H. (1955), 'Meaningfulness and isolation as factors in verbal learning', Journal of Experimental Psychology, vol. 50, pp. 361–8.

FFKA, K. (1935), Principles of Gestalt Psychology, Harcourt, Brace.

CHMIAS, J., GLEITMAN, H., and MCKENNA, V. (1961), 'The effect of isolation of stimuli and responses in paired associates', American Journal of Psychology, vol. 74, pp. 452–6.

NEWMAN, S. E., and SALTZ, E. (1958), 'Isolation effects: Stimulus and response generalization as explanatory concepts', *Journal of Experimental Psychology*, vol. 55, pp. 467–72.

PILLSBURY, W. B., and RAUSH, H. L. (1943), 'An extension of the Koehler–Restorff inhibition phenomenon', *American Journal of Psychology*, vol. 56, pp. 293–8.

POSTMAN, L., and PHILLIPS, L. W. (1954), 'Studies in incidental learning: I. The effects of crowding and isolation', *Journal of Experimental Psychology*, vol. 48, pp. 48–56.

RUSSELL, W. A., and STORMS, L. H. (1955), 'Implicit verbal chaining in paired-associate learning', *Journal of Experimental Psychology*, vol. 49, pp. 287–93.

SALTZ, E., and NEWMAN, S. E. (1959), 'The von Restorff isolation effect: Test of the intralist association assumption', *Journal of Experimental Psychology*, vol. 58, pp. 445–51.

SAUL, E. V., and OSGOOD, C. E. (1950), 'Perceptual organization of materials as a factor in influencing ease of learning and degree of retention', *Journal of Experimental Psychology*, vol. 40, pp. 372–9.

SIEGEL, P. S. (1943), 'Structure effects within a memory series', *Journal of Experimental Psychology*, vol. 33, pp. 311–16.

UNDERWOOD, B. J., and SCHULZ, R. W. (1960), *Meaningfulness and Verbal Learning*, Lippincott.

VON RESTORFF, H. (1933), 'Über die Wirkung von Bereichsbildungen im Spurenfeld', in W. Köhler and H. von Restorff, 'Analyse von Vorgängen im Spurenfeld. I.', *Psychologische Forschung*, vol. 18, pp. 299–342.

WITMER, L. R. (1935), 'The association value of three-place consonant syllables', *Journal of Genetic Psychology*, vol. 47, pp. 337–60.

10 C. I. Hovland

Experimental Studies in Rote-Learning Theory. V. Comparison of Distribution of Practice in Serial and Paired-Associate Learning

C. I. Hovland, 'Experimental studies in rote-learning theory. V. Comparison of distribution of practice in serial and paired-associate learning', *Journal of Experimental Psychology*, vol. 25 (1939), pp. 622–33.

Introduction

A decrease in the rate of presentation of syllables in serial learning has been shown to be accompanied by a decrease in the amount of reminiscence obtained (5). It has also been found that material learned at a rate which shows no reminiscence requires as many trials to learn by distributed as by massed practice, but material learned at a rate where reminiscence is obtained is greatly benefited by distributed practice (6). The problem arises as to whether this relationship between reminiscence and distribution of practice efficacy is a general one – whether distributed practice is only efficient with conditions and materials which produce reminiscence. This is the contention of Bunch and Magdsick (1). A comparison between the efficacy of distributed practice with serial and with paired-associate materials would give evidence on this point, since a recent study by the writer (7) showed that paired-associate materials give much less reminiscence than serial lists learned under identical conditions. It would be predicted from the above relationships that paired-associate learning, which shows little reminiscence, would be much less benefited by distribution of practice than serial learning, where reminiscence is more pronounced. This prediction was tested in the present experiment.

Experimental Procedure

Subjects learned on successive days both paired-associate and serial lists by massed and by distributed practice. The relative efficacy of distribution of practice for the two types of learning could thus be determined. To permit satisfactory comparison, the difficulty of the two types of materials was equated in a preliminary experiment (7). The results indicated that approximately the same number of trials are required to learn eleven units by the serial method as are required to learn nine pairs by the paired-associate method. These two lengths were consequently employed in the present experiment.

The details of the experimental procedure have been previously described (4, 7). The Hull exposure apparatus was employed. The experiments were performed in a sound-proof chamber to eliminate distractions. The anticipation method was used for both types of learning. The customary rules for construction of nonsense syllable lists were followed. For the paired-associate procedure the bands were prepared in such a way that the succession of the pairs was changed on successive presentations. Four experimental and two practice bands were employed for each learning method.

During massed practice only six seconds elapsed between successive presentations of the list. During distributed practice, a learning trial and a rest pause were regularly alternated. The rest pauses were two minutes in length. During the pause the subject named colors automatically presented on the memory drum.

The rate of presentation was two seconds per syllable for both learning methods. This meant that in the paired-associate method four seconds were devoted to each pair. The instructions used with serial learning were identical to those given in (4); those used with paired-associates were the same as those given in (7). The schedule was prepared in advance in such a way that balanced practice orders were employed throughout to equalize practice effects and average out constant errors.

Thirty-two Yale college students, paid for their services, were employed. They had all been employed previously in memory experimentation and consequently only required four practice periods (one for each experimental program). During the main experiment the subjects learned two lists with each procedure, total of eight lists in all. The subjects reported at the same hour every day except Sunday. They did not know the purpose of the experiment nor were they told in advance which experimental program would be employed on a given day.

Results

Data on the number of trials required to learn to the criterion of
one perfect recitation by massed and distributed practice with
paired-associate and with serial learning methods are given in
Table 1. It will be observed that distribution of practice shows its

Table 1

Mean Number of Trials Required to Reach Criterion of One
Perfect Recitation of Serial and Paired-Associate Lists by
Massed and Distributed Practice. Each Mean Based upon
Sixty-four Learning Scores—Two Trials for Each of
Thirty-Two Subjects

Serial

	Massed practice		Distributed practice
Mean number of trials	12·05		9·23
σ_M	0·48		0·43
Diff.		2·82	
r		+0·43	
$\sigma_{diff.}$		0·49	
CR_σ		5·76	

Paired-Associate

	Massed practice		Distributed practice
Mean number of trials	13·03		12·81
σ_M	0·51		0·58
Diff.		0·22	
r		+0·38	
$\sigma_{diff.}$		0·63	
CR_σ		0·35	

stomary effectiveness in reducing the number of trials required
for learning in the case of the serial method. Learning by distributed practice resulted in a 23 per cent saving in number of trials
required for learning. In the case of paired-associates, however,
the advantage is very little (2 per cent), the difference in the number of trials required for learning by the two methods lacking

statistical significance. Closely similar results are shown in Table 2 where the percentages of subjects for whom distributed practice is superior, equal, or inferior to massed are given for the two learning methods.

Table 2

Percentages of Subjects for Whom Distributed Practice is Superior, is Equal, or Inferior to Massed with Serial and Paired-Associate Learning (Thirty-two Subjects)

Serial

	Per cent	σ_P
1. Subjects learning more rapidly with distributed practice	62·5	0·086
2. Subjects learning equally rapidly with massed and with distributed practice	15·6	0·064
3. Subjects learning more rapidly with massed practice	21·9	0·073
Difference in per cent between 1 and 3, 40·6		

Paired-Associate

	Per cent	σ_P
1. Subjects learning more rapidly with distributed practice	43·8	0·088
2. Subjects learning equally rapidly with massed and with distributed practice	18·7	0·069
3. Subjects learning more rapidly with massed practice	37·5	0·086
Difference in per cent between 1 and 3, 6·3		

The difference between the paired-associate and serial learning with respect to distribution of practice is brought out clearly Figures 1 and 2, where the numbers of trials required to read successive criteria of syllable performance are given. The gra for serial learning is presented in Figure 1, and for paired-ass ciate learning in Figure 2. Massed practice is inferior to distribut at every criterion with serial learning, but with the paired-associate material the two curves cross and are practically superimposed. The close agreement in the total number of trials required to reach mastery by massed practice with the two learning methods supports the results of the preliminary equating experiment.

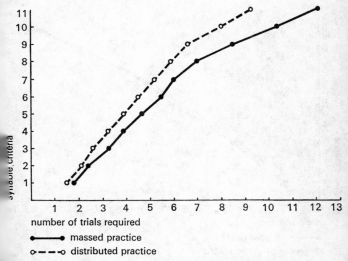

Figure 1 Graph showing mean number of trials required to reach successive criteria of performance by massed and distributed practice with *serial* learning. (For example, it required an average of 6·6 trials to get nine syllables correct by massed practice, 8·5 trials by distributed.) Each point is based upon the mean of sixty-four learning scores (two from each of thirty-two subjects)

Comparison of the curves obtained with the paired-associate and serial methods shows the former to be more nearly linear than the latter. This is in support of Kjerstad's (9) results. He found that additional syllables are progressively more difficult to learn at later stages of learning in the case of serial learning, but not to such a great extent in the case of paired-associates. Another way of stating the decreased rate of learning during the latter phases of learning with serial material is to point out that in the present experiment only about a third (36 per cent) of the material was

Acquisition

learned during the last half of the massed practice serial-learning, whereas nearly half (46 per cent) of the paired-associate materials was learned during the last half of the trials. Distribution of practice with the serial method appears to make the learning curve much more linear, but distribution apparently does not greatly affect the paired-associate curves.

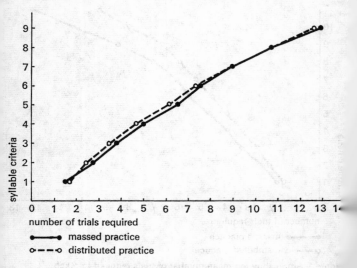

Figure 2 Graph showing mean number of trials required to reach successive criteria of performance by massed and distributed practice with *paired-associate* learning. Each point is based upon the mean of sixty-four learning scores (two from each of thirty-two subjects)

Discussion

Paired-associates have seldom been used in studying the effect distribution of practice upon the rate of learning. In Jost's widely quoted study a paired-associate method of testing w employed, but the experimental variable was not the time betwe repetitions, as in the present experiment, but the number of repe tions in a block of trials. A constant number of repetitions we given but distributed over a varying number of days. The o numbered syllables were the stimulus words, and the even numbered syllables the associates to be recalled. He presents his results in terms of the number of correctly recalled associates and their reaction times. Distributed practice increased the number of associates which could be recalled. Since the data are not given in terms of the number of trials required to learn, the results cannot be compared with the present experiment. Similarly, the present results cannot be compared with Lorge's (11) experiment employing paired-associates for studying distribution of practice. The material used for memorizing consisted of twelve pairs of three-place numbers as stimuli with two-place numbers as associates. In contrast to the present experiment, a constant time (one minute) was allowed for study of the page upon which the pairs were printed. Another minute was allowed for written recall. A group which was given one minute between trials was only 'slightly and regularly superior' (p. 26) to an equated group learning by massed practice. Comparison with his results is not possible because of the marked difference in the method of presenting the words and testing recall and because each trial involved the learning of a different list of words.

Lyon (12) found the same clear-cut difference between the effect distributed practice upon learning serial nonsense syllables and on memorization of poetry and prose that was obtained in the present experiment between serial and paired-associate learning. He attributes the difference to the nature of the connexions: 'For digits and nonsense syllables, *i.e. material in which there is but le logical connexion*,[1] there is considerable saving (by distributed practice)' (p. 91). While it is true that there is a difference in the nature of the logical connexion, no explanation is given as to why this difference should be systematically relevant.

Theories advanced for explaining results upon distribution of practice have changed little since the competent review by Warden). The implication of a number of these formulations has been discussed in relation to paired-associate learning by the writer in analysing results on reminiscence (7). *Rehearsal* is often used to explain the efficacy of distributed practice (10). This explanation cannot be applied to the present results since with both the paired-associate and serial learning the rest pause during distributed

Hovland's italics.

practice was spent in color-naming, an activity which obviates rehearsal.

Differences in the *motivation* (2) involved in the learning of the two types of material could similarly only be considered explanatory if such differences had been experimentally demonstrated. There is at present no evidence that there is an increased motivation to learn after a rest pause with serial learning but not after paired-associates. Such an explanation would have a greater probability if, for example, a greater number of trials were required to reach the criterion. But it will be observed that the massed trials were closely equated with respect to this factor. It will also be recalled that the differential effect of the rest-pause upon serial and paired-associate learning appears after even a single repetition (Hovland, 7). Essentially the same considerations apply to explanations based upon *fatigue* (3).

Perseveration (neural 'setting') is frequently used as an explanatory principle for distribution of practice results. It has been espoused most recently by Woodworth (20) who uses the term 'consolidation'. The theory may be regarded either as a neurological explanation, as originally intended by Müller and Pilzecker (15), or as merely descriptive. In its neurological aspect the theory has been vigorously attacked, notably by Lashley (10). No experimental evidence has been obtained to support the hypothetic persistence of neural activity following learning. Furthermore, the theory were to explain the present results it would have to assumed that differences exist in the perseverative effect following serial and paired-associate learning. No experimental confirmation of this additional postulate has been presented. If the theory of perseveration is restricted to be purely descriptive, it becomes circular and of no value (13). Thus, the appearance of distributed practice efficacy would be used as evidence of perseveration, and perseveration would then be used to explain the advantage distributed practice.

In its present form the theory of *stimulus-maturation* (19), also (16) is difficult to apply to the present results. It predicts that at certain stages of learning distributed practice is advantageous because the interpolated time permits maturation to take place a later stage and with greater complexity the interpolated time ineffective. With learning of the type employed in the present experiment the theory gives us no clue as to whether the learning is at a stage where it would or would not be subject to maturation. Furthermore, it would have to be assumed that with serial learning maturation takes place; with paired-associates it does not. While this formulation *describes* the present results, there is no independent evidence of this assumption.

Distributed practice efficacy has also been explained on the grounds that the rest pauses permit recovery from *decremental effects* inherent in the learning (6). This theory stresses the close relationship between learning and work performance. In expositions of this explanation the concept of *refractory phase* (7) is sometimes employed. Applied to the present results these formulations would say that there were factors in the serial learning which would cause decrement which would not be found in paired-associate learning. Two such factors appear possible: (a) the greater uniformity in the mode of presentation of the serial compared with the paired-associate lists might cause greater decrement in performance. The successive syllables always appear in the same window and in a constant order, whereas with the paired-associates the stimulus word first appears in the left-hand window and subsequently the associate appears in the right-hand window. This method of exposure might be less monotonous to the subject and hence cause less decrement. This explanation would be closely allied to formulations based on motivation. (b) The other possibility of decremental differences (after the analogy of *refractory phase*) would be based on the fact that even though paired-associates are presented at a two second rate, the response on the part of the subject only has to be made every four seconds in paired-associates, while with serial materials the response must be made at two second intervals. The more rapid rate of making responses would cause decrement in response. A close connexion between the present experiment and an earlier one concerning the effect of rate of exposure upon distribution of practice (6) would then be indicated. A theory of this type would cover the fact that with massed practice the learning of additional units is progressively more difficult, while with distributed practice the units are more nearly equal in difficulty.

The last principal theory explains the advantage of distributed practice as due to the fact that it permits the *conflicting habits* and

interferences to be forgotten (14). It is assumed that the interfering associations are weaker than the ones which are being
learned and that they therefore weaken at a more rapid rate.
Thus the *effective strength* of response (strength of correct response minus strength of conflicting response) increases for a shor
interval of time following learning. This is the *reminiscence* phenomenon. Utilization of successive reminiscence effects would then
be the basis of distributed practice efficacy. If this theory were t
explain the present results it would have to be assumed that seri
associations give rise to stronger interference than paired-asso
ciates. It is very plausible that the interferences are in the for
of the remote associations which occur in serial learning. Here the
are the well-known *forward* and *backward associations*. In paire
associate learning, in contrast, the present technique prevents to
large extent the formation of remote associations by consta
rotation of the order in which pairs are presented. This theo
would be broad enough to also cover the results of Lyon (1
quoted above, since Thorndike (17) and others have shown th
remote associates are exceedingly rare in learning of the type
emplified by poetry and prose. Rest pauses would then be relati
ly ineffective with these materials, which is the result obtained
Lyon. His explanation of his results as due to the *logical c
nexion* between the words in the two situations (see above) wo
thus be subsumed under conflicting associations, since with str
logical connexions the possibility of remote associations would
greatly reduced. The differences in the form of the learning cur
for these various types of material reported by Kjerstad (9) mi
then be closely related to the amounts of interference present.

From the foregoing survey of theories[2] it appears that a nu
ber of the commonest theories such as rehearsal, motivation,
fatigue cannot be applied to the present results. The theorie
perseveration and stimulus-maturation are phrased in forms
make them extremely difficult to prove or disprove, although
are descriptively adequate. Decremental factors, principally of
refractory phase type, are doubtless involved in many exp

2. Explanations have also been advanced on the basis of Jost's law (8)
the Zeigarnik effect (21). These are not independent theories, but are re
which must themselves be explained by an adequate and comprehe
theory of learning.

ments on distribution of practice and may be partially involved here. But it would appear that the most important factor of difference in the two types of learning is the nature of the interferences or conflicting associations. Further study of this theory appears to be indicated.

Summary

Thirty-two subjects learned both serial and paired-associate lists on successive days by massed and by distributed practice. The anticipation method was used for both types of learning. The number of trials required for learning both types of material by massed practice was equated in a preliminary experiment. During distributed practice a two minute rest pause (during which the subjects named colors) was interpolated between successive learning trials.

Learning by distributed practice resulted in a pronounced reduction in the number of trials required for mastery in the case of serial materials. No superiority of distributed over massed practice was found in the case of paired-associates.

The learning curve obtained with massed practice of serial materials shows that progressively more trials are required to reach successive criteria of performance, but with distributed practice the learning curve is more nearly linear. The curves for *paired-associates* were nearly identical for massed and distributed practice, and both approached linearity to a much greater degree than the curve for massed serial learning. These findings agree with the results of Kjerstad (9).

The various theories of distributed practice efficacy are discussed in relation to the present results. Differences in the nature of the decremental factors are probably involved, but it appears that the most likely explanation of the difference in the effectiveness of distribution of practice with the two materials is the difference in the nature of the interferences involved. Long associational bonds which are prominent in serial learning have little opportunity to become formed in the present paired-associate technique. If these give rise to conflicting associations and weaken more rapidly during a short interval than do the correct associations, which are presumably stronger, distribution of practice would naturally be more effective than massed practice.

Acquisition

References

1. M. E. BUNCH and W. K. MAGDSICK, 'The retention in rats of an incompletely learned maze solution for short intervals of time', *Journal of Comparative Psychology*, vol. 16 (1933), pp. 385–409.
2. J. F. DASHIELL, *Fundamentals of Objective Psychology*, Houghton, Mifflin, 1928.
3. E. R. GUTHRIE, *The Psychology of Learning*, Harper, 1935.
4. C. I. HOVLAND, 'Experimental studies in rote-learning theory. I. Reminiscence following learning by massed and by distributed practice', *Journal of Experimental Psychology*, vol. 22 (1938), pp. 201–24.
5. C. I. HOVLAND, 'Experimental studies in rote-learning theory. II. Reminiscence with varying speeds of syllable presentation.' *Journal of Experimental Psychology*, vol. 22 (1938), pp. 338–53.
6. C. I. HOVLAND, 'Experimental studies in rote-learning theory. III. Distribution of practice with varying speeds of syllable presentation', *Journal of Experimental Psychology*, vol. 23 (1938), pp. 172–90.
7. C. I. HOVLAND, 'Experimental studies in rote-learning theory. IV. Comparison of reminiscence in serial and paired-associate learning', *Journal of Experimental Psychology*, vol. 24 (1939), pp. 466–84.
8. A. JOST, 'Die Assoziationsfestigkeit in ihrer Abhängigkeit von der Verteilung der Wiederholungen', *Zeitschrift für Psychologie mit Zeitschrift für Angewandte Psychologie*, vol. 14 (1897), pp. 436–72.
9. C. L. KJERSTAD, 'The form of the learning curves for memory', *Psychological Monographs*, vol. 26 (1919), no. 116.
10. K. S. LASHLEY, 'A simple maze: with data on the relation of the distribution of practice to the rate of learning', *Psychobiology*, vol. 1 (1918), pp. 353–67.
11. I. LORGE, 'Influence of regularly interpolated time intervals upon subsequent learning', *Teachers College, Contr. Educ.*, vol. 438 (1930)
12. D. O. LYON, 'The relation of length of material to time taken for learning, and the optimum distribution of time', *Journal of Educational Psychology*, vol. 5 (1914), pp. 1–9, 85–91, 155–63.
13. J. A. MCGEOCH, 'Studies in retroactive inhibition. II. Relationship between temporal point of interpolation, length of interval and amount of retroactive inhibition', *Journal of General Psychology*, vol. 9 (1933), pp. 44–57.
14. J. A. MCGEOCH, Chapter 13 in E. G. Boring, H. S. Langfeld, and H. P. Weld, eds., *Psychology*, Wiley, 1935.
15. G. E. MÜLLER and A. PILZECKER, 'Experimentelle Beiträge zur Lehre vom Gedachtniss', *Zeitschrift für Psychologie mit Zeitschrift für Angewandte Psychologie*, vol. 1 (1900), pp. 1–300.
16. G. S. SNODDY, *Evidence for Two Opposed Processes in Mental Growth*, Science Press, 1935.
17. E. L. THORNDIKE, *The Fundamentals of Learning*, Bureau of Publications, Teachers College, Columbia University, 1932.

18. C. J. WARDEN, 'The distribution of practice in animal learning', *Comparative Psychological Monographs*, vol. 1 (1923), no. 3.

19. R. H. WHEELER and F. T. PERKINS, *Principles of Mental Development*, Crowel, 1932.

20. R. S. WOODWORTH, *Experimental Psychology*, Henry Holt, 1938.

21. B. ZEIGARNIK, 'III. Über das Behalten von erledigten und unerledigten Handlungen', (Untersuchungen zur Handlungs- und Affekt-Psychologie, K. Lewin, ed.), *Psychologische Forschung*, vol. 9 (1927), pp. 1–85.

11 B. J. Underwood and J. Richardson

Studies of Distributed Practice: XVIII. The Influence of Meaningfulness and Intralist Similarity of Serial Nonsense Lists

B. J. Underwood and J. Richardson, 'Studies of distributed practice XVIII. The influence of meaningfulness and intralist similarity of seria nonsense lists', *Journal of Experimental Psychology*, vol. 56 (1958), pp 213–19.

The primary purpose of the present experiment is to determine intertrial interval interacts with meaningfulness and with intrali similarity in the learning of serial nonsense lists. It was unde taken in the belief that no available data give uncontaminate tests of these two interactions. The following discussion gives th bases for this belief.

Certain lines of evidence could be advanced in support of t principle that the lower the meaningfulness of the material t greater the likelihood that distributed practice will facilita learning.

(a) Tsao (3) has pointed out that the older studies using pro materials commonly found that massed practice was as good better than distributed practice for learning, whereas w syllables the opposite was usually true. Tsao also points o however, that one cannot be sure that a difference in meaningf ness is the only critical difference between prose material a nonsense syllables.

(b) In two previous reports in this series (4, 5), both of wh were performed under identical conditions except that se adjectives were used in one case and syllables in the other, dis buted practice appeared to exert a greater facilitating effect the learning of syllables than on the learning of adjectives. H ever, since it is now known that intralist similarity and mean fulness interact in that the lower the meaningfulness the greater influence of a given degree of intralist similarity (9), the differe in the effect of intertrial interval in the two experiments ma due to differences in intralist similarity and not meaningfulne

(c) The one direct attack on the problem was made by

(3). Two serial lists of syllables of high meaningfulness were constructed and two with low meaningfulness. One list from each level was presented by massed practice and one by distributed practice, the latter consisting of a 1-min rest after every two trials. All lists were presented for ten trials and all *S*s served in all conditions by counterbalancing. The low meaningful lists were significantly facilitated by distributed practice, the high-meaningful lists were not. Thus, if Tsao had performed an analysis of variance on his data it would be expected that the interaction term (Intertrial interval × Meaningfulness) would have been significant. Yet, two facts about Tsao's study make it seem desirable to have further work on this interaction phenomenon. First, an examination of Tsao's lists shows that the low-meaningful lists have greater intralist similarity (fewer different letters used) than the high-meaningful lists. Thus, meaningfulness and intralist similarity may be confounded. Second, all *S*s served in all conditions. It is now known that such designs may introduce considerable interference between lists and this interference may well be different for different levels of meaningfulness. Thus, it is possible that Tsao's results might be due to differences in intralist or interlist similarity, or both.

The primary implication of the above comments is that intralist similarity may have confounded tests of the interaction between meaningfulness and intertrial interval. Such a criticism is not valid, of course, unless intralist similarity and intertrial interval do indeed interact in learning. In two studies (4, 5) in which intertrial interval has been varied, intralist similarity has also been manipulated. No interaction was apparent. But, neither of these studies was a satisfactory test of the interaction because they were counter-balanced designs which are now known (7) to result in a reciprocal relationship between intralist and interlist similarity. Therefore, if distributed practice facilitates learning when interference is high (produced either by intralist or interlist similarity) the two experiments are simply not adequate tests.

It appears, therefore, that both meaningfulness and intralist similarity must be manipulated independently. Interlist similarity can be eliminated by using *S*s naive to verbal learning who serve in only one condition of the experiment. The present study attempts to meet these specifications.

Method

Materials

Four serial lists of ten syllables each were used. These lists have been used in a previous study and are reproduced there (9). Two lists were made up of Glaze (1) syllables of from 0·0 per cent to 20·0 per cent association value, and two with syllables of from 93·3 per cent to 100 per cent association values. One of the lists at each level of meaningfulness had high intralist similarity and one low intralist similarity. The two lists with high intralist similarity had only four consonants, each being used five times. In the lists with low intralist similarity each consonant was used only once. All vowels were used twice in each list. The four lists are designated as follows: HM–HS (high meaningfulness, high intralist similarity); HM–LS (high meaningfulness, low intralist similarity); LM–HS (low meaningfulness, high intralist similarity), and LM–LS (low meaningfulness, low intralist similarity). (In the previous publication, where the lists are reproduced, the fourth syllable in the HM–LS list was given as MEK; this should have been MEX.)

Each list was preceded by three asterisks as the anticipator cue for the first syllable. As in the previous study, ten different serial orders of each list were used so that each syllable occurred equally often at each serial position. The rate of presentation was 2 sec and S spelled the syllables, using the anticipation method.

Subjects and procedure

Eight groups of fifty Ss were used. Two groups were assigned each list, one learning by massed practice and one by distributed practice. Massed practice consisted of an 8-sec blank period between each trial. Distributed practice consisted of 38 sec between each trial, this interval being filled with symbol cancellation. With two levels of meaningfulness, two levels of intralist similarity, and two intertrial intervals, the experiment becomes a $2 \times 2 \times 2$ design with independent groups in each cell.

A random order of the eight conditions (four lists, with massed and distribution for each) was made up subject to the restriction that each condition occur fifty times. The Ss were then assigned in succession in order of their appearance at the laboratory. When an *S* was dropped for any reason he was replaced with the next *S*. A total of thirty-five *S*s was dropped for a variety of reasons. No appreciable bias can result from this since the minimum number dropped from any one condition was 2 and the maximum 7. To avoid bias in selection of *S*s due to differential difficulty produced by the different conditions, a constant number of trials was used for all lists. Under this procedure only two *S*s were dropped for failure to learn. One *S* became so emotionally upset in learning that it seemed advisable to dismiss her. The other *S*, when he experienced difficulty in learning, simply quit and walked out of the room. All *S*s used in the present evaluation were naïve to laboratory verbal learning experiments.

Each list was always presented for thirty anticipation trials with *S* instructed to give as many correct responses as possible on each trial. The *S* returned for five relearning trials 24 hr after learning.

Results

Learning

The basic response measure used was the mean number of correct responses over the thirty trials. Table 1 shows the means for each condition and Table 2 shows the summary of the analysis of variance.

As in the previous study using these lists (9), meaningfulness and intralist similarity produced highly significant effects. The interaction between these two variables is also significant, i.e. the lower the meaningfulness the greater the effect of intralist similarity.

Turning next to the major data, with special reference to the intertrial-interval interactions, on the basis of the statistical evidence the following conclusions would be reached: (a) over-all *S*s, distributed practice is superior to massed practice beyond the 1 per cent level of significance; (b) the interaction between meaningfulness and intertrial interval does not even approach significance; (c) interaction between intertrial interval and intralist similarity is significant between the 1 per cent and 5 per cent levels, and (d) the triple interaction approaches the 5 per cent level. While these conclusions cannot be gainsaid, they do not fully impart the effects produced by the variables. The complete picture can best be perceived through an inspection of the acquisition curves (Figure 1) together with the means in Table 1.

Table 1
Mean Number of Correct Responses for Trials 1–30

List	Massed*	Distributed*
HM–HS	157·12	188·86
HM–LS	206·42	203·70
LM–HS	110·64	123·62
LM–LS	165·46	176·38

* Estimate of σ_M, based on the within-groups variance, is 6·08.

Considering first the effect of distributed practice, it can b seen that the greatest effect was produced in learning list H M HS (this is reflected in the triple interaction which approache

Table 2
Analysis of Variance of Correct Responses in Trials 1–30

Source	df	MS	F*
Interval (I)	1	17,503·54	9·48
Meaningfulness (M)	1	202,500·25	109·65
Similarity (S)	1	184,298·74	99·80
I × M	1	163·84	—
I × S	1	8,335·69	4·51
M × S	1	11,793·96	6·39
I × M × S	1	6,560·25	3·55
Within	392	1,846·75	
Total	399		

* With 1 and 400 df, F at 0·05 level is 3·86, and at 0·01, 6·70.

the 5 per cent level of significance). Indeed, when t ratios w calculated between massing and distribution for each of the t low-meaningful lists the null hypothesis could not be rejecte either case. However, it would not seem appropriate to concl that intertrial interval had no influence in learning these two li

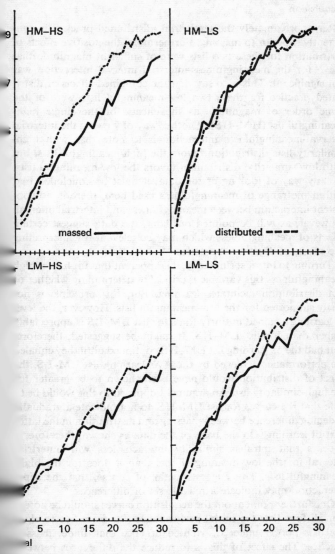

Figure 1 Acquisition curves for each list by massed and distributed practice

After approximately the tenth trial, distributed practice is consistently superior to massing. Furthermore, the positive effects of distribution for these two lists were of sufficient magnitude that the F for the meaningfulness-intertrial interval interaction was not significant. This is to say that the combined effects of distributed practice for these two low-meaningful lists were of the same order of magnitude as the effects for the single high-meaningful list (HM–HS). Another way of viewing the intertrial interval-meaningfulness interaction is to note that with high-similarity lists distribution favors the high-meaningful lists, but with low similarity, distribution favors the low-meaningful lists. By any way of looking at the data, it must be concluded that within the range of meaningfulness used here, there is no consistent interaction between meaningfulness and intertrial interval. However, as will be pointed out later, the data suggest certain effects of meaningfulness which may be relevant for interpreting the effects of distributed practice.

Turning to intralist similarity, it is apparent that for lists of high meaningfulness this variable is critical in determining whether or not distribution facilitates learning. But, this principle is not easily supported for the low-meaningful lists. However, the level of learning attained in thirty trials for list LM–LS is appreciably higher than for list LM–HS. It might be suggested, therefore, that had the Ss learning list LM–HS continued until they equaled the performance achieved by those Ss learning list LM–LS, the effect of distribution would have been shown to be greater for the high-similarity list. An argument opposed to this would be to note that the curves for list LM–HS do not indicate a gradually widening difference between massing and distribution in the latter part of learning. On the basis of the data as shown, therefore, it appears that intralist similarity interacts less with intertrial interval for the low-meaningful lists than it does for the high-meaningful lists. This suggests again, of course, that the triple interaction may indicate a reliable set of differences.

One further point about the acquisition curves should be noted. For all four lists the initial performance (for from five to eight trials) is poorer under distributed practice than under massed practice. The effect of this is to reduce the differences between massed and distributed practice when total correct responses over

all trials is used as the response measure. This cross-over phenomenon will be discussed in the next section.

Retention

Due to the fact that the level of learning at the end of thirty trials
was quite different for the different lists, the retention measurements primarily reflect these differences in original strength.
However, certain facts will be mentioned briefly. First, there is no
difference in recall as a function of massing and distribution for
any list when adjustments are made for differences in associative
strength at end of learning. The massed and distributed conditions
are combined, therefore, for further comparisons.

Table 3

Percentage Recall Based on Number of Items Correct on the
Last Learning Trial

List	Correct on last trial	Correct on recall	Per cent recall
HM–HS	8·73	7·12	81·6
HM–LS	9·35	8·39	89·7
LM–HS	6·45	4·63	71·8
LM–LS	8·55	7·06	82·6

The high recall under all conditions is worth noting. As
pointed out elsewhere (8), if naïve Ss are used so that no proactive interference from previously learned lists is present, very
little loss should occur over 24 hr. To demonstrate this for the
present data, the mean number of items correct on the last learning trial has been used as a base for calculating percentage recall.
It can be seen from Figure 1 that little if any error is introduced
by using this base. That is, if Ss had been given one more trial
their performance would have been only slightly higher than it
was on trial 30. As shown in Table 3, percentage recall varies
from approximately 72 per cent for the most poorly learned list
(LM–HS) to nearly 90 per cent for the strongest (HM–LS).

In confirmation of the previous study using these lists (9), no
difference in recall is observable as a function of meaningfulness
when adjustments are made for differences in associative strength

at the end of learning. Concerning intralist similarity and recall, the two experiments require discussion. In the previous study, more loss was reported for lists of high intralist similarity than for low when both were of low meaningfulness. The difference occurred primarily with items of weak associative strength. That is, weak items in the high-similarity list were forgotten more rapidly than comparably weak items in the low-similarity list. When the present data were examined no such difference was apparent. Two possibilities for the discrepancy seemed possible. First, the difference in the earlier experiment may have been a chance phenomenon. The other possibility was that the method used to compare retention was biased against the high-similarity list. In the previous study a gross probability analysis (6) had been used to equate for associative strength. Since the time that those data were so evaluated, a more precise method of probability analysis has been worked out. It had been discovered that the gross method did produce some bias in some situations. The more refined method avoids this bias. Without detailing this method it is sufficient to say that it makes estimates of associative strength at the end of learning for items by using for this estimation only items which have approximately the same strength as determined by number of times given correctly during learning. In the gross probability analysis this was not true. In the present data the refined method was used and no difference was obtained in recall as a function of intralist similarity at any level of associative strength. Therefore, the data from the earlier experiment were reanalysed by the newer technique and the difference in recall as a function of intralist similarity was no longer present. The conclusion must be, therefore, that intralist similarity as manipulated here does not influence retention as measured by recall.

In summary of the retention data, the only variable found to influence recall was associative strength. Meaningfulness, intralist similarity and intertrial interval are not relevant variables in the recall of the present lists.

Discussion

The present data leave no doubt that intralist similarity is a highly important variable in determining whether or not distribut practice facilitates learning. While meaningfulness and intertrial interval did not interact in any simple way, the argument will be advanced that meaningfulness cannot be ignored entirely in considering the effects of distribution. With high-meaningful lists facilitation by distribution occurred only when intralist similarity was high. If meaningfulness is irrelevant, and only intralist similarity relevant, why was not distribution as effective for the list of high intralist similarity and low meaningfulness as it was for the list of high intralist similarity and high meaningfulness (HM–HS versus LM–HS)?

It has already been pointed out that both in this study and in the previous one using the same lists, meaningfulness and intralist similarity interact. Given a constant degree of intralist similarity as determined by amount of duplication of consonants, learning will be more retarded with low-meaningful lists than with high-meaningful lists. The reason for this, it is believed, lies in the nature of the task presented S when given high- and low-meaningful syllables. Most high-meaningful syllables will be perceived as words. This is not true for low-meaningful syllables. In the latter case S must learn to integrate (in the Mandler sense, 2) the individual letters into a unitary response. Therefore, it may well be that letter duplication in the high-meaningful syllables will produce less interference than in the low-meaningful syllables. The high-meaningful syllables provide a discriminative cue of 'wordness' not frequently present in the low-meaningful syllables. Thus, the same formal degree of intralist similarity could produce more interference among low-meaningful syllables than among high. The argument is, therefore, that interference is a critical variable determining whether or not distribution facilitates. Meaningfulness enters only because a given degree of intralist similarity produces more interference in low-meaningful lists than it does in high-meaningful lists. The fact that distributed practice affected the learning of the low-meaningful list with low intralist similarity (LM–LS) even a small amount could be attributed to the fact that in these low-meaningful lists the duplicated vowels produce an interference which does not occur in the high-meaningful list.

The question still remains, however, as to why list LM–HS did not show greater facilitation under distribution than it

177

actually did. If interference is a critical factor, this list, which produced more interference than any other list, should certainly have been facilitated by distribution of practice more than the other lists. A simple hypothesis that amount of facilitation by distributed practice and amount of interference are directly related cannot account for this discrepancy. Thus, while the present data leave no doubt that interference produced by intralist similarity is a highly important factor determining whether or not distributed practice facilitates learning, some additional factor must be eventually included as a modifying agent.

It was noted that for every list massed practice was initially superior to distributed practice (Figure 1). The main question concerning this observation is whether or not systematic relevance should be attributed to it. That is, does it have implications for a theory of distributed practice? The evidence, while not conclusive, suggests a negative answer. The Ss in the distributed-practice group had no previous experience in switching from the learning task to the cancellation task and back. The poorer performance may simply represent the retardation in learning as S learned to make the transitions. It might, too, represent slower warm-up than occurs under massed practice. An examination of the serial-position curves shows that the Ss having distributed practice are poorer on the initial items in the list than are those Ss having massed practice. If the Ss having distributed practice were having trouble in switching from cancellation to learning, it would be expected that the initial items in the list would be adversely affected. The fact that the phenomenon occurs in list HM–LS which is not facilitated by distributed practice also suggests that the initial decrement of the distributed group should not be given theoretical relevance.

Summary

The major purpose of this study was to determine if meaningfulness and intralist similarity interact with intertrial interval in learning serial nonsense lists. Eight groups of fifty Ss each learned a single list of ten serial syllables. The eight cells of the experiment were made up of two levels of meaningfulness (thus, a total of four lists), and two intertrial intervals for each list (massed and distributed practice). Learning was carried for thirty trials for all lists with recall after 24 hr.

The major results were (a) Meaningfulness does not interact with intertrial interval. (b) Intralist similarity does interact with intertrial interval but in a complex fashion. With high meaningfulness, high intralist similarity is clearly necessary to produce facilitation by distributed practice. With low meaningfulness, intralist similarity does not influence learning by massed vs. distributed practice. (c) Recall was affected only by strength of association.

The results indicate that intralist interference is necessary before distributed practice facilitates serial learning. However, the relationship is not simple; the data do not indicate that the greater the intralist interference the greater the facilitation in learning by distributed practice. Some factor(s) modifies this relationship when a certain degree of interference is reached.

References

J. A. GLAZE, 'The association value of non-sense syllables', *Journal of Genetic Psychology*, vol. 35 (1928), pp. 255–69.

G. MANDLER, 'Response factors in human learning', *Psychological Review*, vol. 61 (1954), pp. 235–44.

J. C. TSAO, 'Studies in spaced and massed learning: II. Meaningfulness of material and distribution of practice', *Quarterly Journal of Experimental Psychology*, vol. 1 (1948), pp. 79–84.

B. J. UNDERWOOD, 'Studies of distributed practice: VII. Learning and retention of serial nonsense lists as a function of intralist similarity', *Journal of Experimental Psychology*, vol. 44 (1952), pp. 80–87.

B. J. UNDERWOOD, 'Studies of distributed practice: X. The influence of intralist similarity on learning and retention of serial adjective lists', *Journal of Experimental Psychology*, vol. 45 (1953), pp. 253–9.

B. J. UNDERWOOD, 'Speed of learning and amount retained: A consideration of methodology', *Psychological Bulletin*, vol. 51 (1954), pp. 276–82.

B. J. UNDERWOOD, 'Intralist similarity in verbal learning and retention', *Psychological Review*, vol. 61 (1954), pp. 160–66.

B. J. UNDERWOOD, 'Interference and forgetting', *Psychological Review*, vol. 64 (1957), pp. 49–60.

B. J. UNDERWOOD and J. RICHARDSON, 'The influence of meaningfulness, intralist similarity, and serial position on retention', *Journal of Experimental Psychology*, vol. 52 (1956), pp. 119–26.

12 B. R. Bugelski

Presentation Time, Total Time, and Mediation in Paired-Associate Learning

B. R. Bugelski, 'Presentation time, total time, and mediation in paired associate learning', *Journal of Experimental Psychology*, vol. 63 (1962), pp 409–12.

The present experiment deals with a neglected variable in th
systematic study of memorization; namely, item presentatio
time per trial in relation to total learning time. This variable
obviously important in the interpretation of claims such as that c
Rock (1957) for one-trial learning, claims that were based on a
inter-item time of 8 sec. For Rock, a trial consisted of 96 s
during which 12 nonsense pairs were exposed. During this peric
S was free to repeat any item for the entire period, but even if I
merely used the 8 sec per item interval, he could still repeat a
item quite frequently. The claim that repetition has no merit
obviously improperly drawn from such a study. Time per trial
also involved directly in studies of massed vs. spaced learni
where massing is defined as a rapid interitem rate (Hovland, 193
Using a rate of 2 sec per item Hovland found learning infer
(14·89 trials) to a rate of 4 sec per item (6·78 trials). A sim
multiplication of trials by time, however, shows the two p
cedures to involve about the same total time (29·98 and 27
sec). Even when a long intertrial interval is employed, total tin
appear to be about the same (22·36 and 23·40 sec) for 2-sec a
4-sec presentation rates although the number of trials diffe
significantly (11·18 and 5·85).

It is the present hypothesis that in at least some areas
memorization, and under some conditions of presentation,
degree of learning will be a function of total time, regardles
the duration of the individual trials or interitem times.
hypothesis does not appear to be without support. Murd
(1960), employing free recall of words in lists of varying len
found total time to be a determining factor in how much
learned regardless of presentation rate. Attempts to com

total learning times from published studies have also proved suggestive for a variety of learning situations but the many variations in kinds and length of material and associated learning conditions prevent adequate comparisons. It is hoped that the present study will focus more attention on the various temporal factors in learning such as exposure time per item, interitem interval, intertrial interval, and total learning time. The essence of the problem is: what is a learning trial?

Method

Apparatus

The Hunter Card Master was used to expose pairs of nonsense syllables at varying presentation times. The stimulus syllable was always exposed for 2 sec and remained visible while the response syllable was exposed for either 2, 4, 6, 8, or 15 additional sec. Two seconds always elapsed before a new stimulus syllable appeared. Eight pairs of syllables which had been used by Rock (1957) for his control group (see Table 2), were presented in three different random orders. The total time available to S for reacting to or learning a given pair, including the time before a new stimulus was presented, varied, therefore, from 6 sec for the 2-sec response to 19 sec for the 15-sec response, with the other times lasting 8, 10, and 12 sec per pair. The time allowed for anticipation of the response term was, of course, always 2 sec.

It will be noted that the total time for presentation of eight pairs of syllables, i.e. one trial, would last either 48, 64, 80, 96, or 152 sec depending upon the exposure time of the response syllable. There was no rest period between trials.

Procedure

Each S learned the same eight pairs of syllables to a criterion of two successful anticipations of the complete list. The apparatus used did not allow for the elimination of pairs as they were learned, but this was done in the computations so that the total learning times reported are based on the time taken to learn each pair to the criterion. Upon completion of learning each S was asked specifically how he happened to learn each pair, what made

181

Acquisition

him think of the correct response, why some pairs were easy and some difficult.

Subjects

One hundred sophomore students in experimental psychology courses, naïve with respect to nonsense syllable learning, were assigned to one of the five experimental conditions, thereby making up five groups of twenty. Assignment to groups depended only on order of arrival at the laboratory; the first S was assigned to Group 1, the next to Group 2, etc.

Results

Both trials and total time to learn are shown in Table 1 for each of the five different presentation times. The total times are obtained by multiplying the total number of trials to learn each pair

Table 1

Mean Trials and Total Times to Learn Lists

Presentation time	N	Trials		Total exposure tim	
		Mean	SD	Mean	SD
6 sec	20	10·2	4·1	61·2	24
8 sec	20	8·8	3·8	70·1	30
10 sec	20	5·8	1·9	57·9	19
12 sec	20	4·7	2·5	56·1	29
19 sec	20	3·3	1·2	62·2	22

in the series by the presentation time. As expected, the longer t presentation time per pair, the fewer the number of trials criterion. Analysis of variance for the trials yields $F = 18$ ($p = 0·01$, $df = 99$). Total time, however, is not significan different among the five conditions ($F = 0·845$). The cor spondence between total times for the most rapid presentati time and the longest presentation time is striking. Although former required more than three times as many trials as latter, the mean time difference is hardly more than 1 sec. Ext

182

polating roughly from these findings, it might be possible for similar Ss to learn all eight pairs in one trial with a presentation time of about 25 sec per pair. Within the limits, then, of the intervals and conditions used, the conclusion appears reasonable that presentation time multiplied by trials amounts to a constant value, $T_p \times T = k$.

Table 2

Mean Trials to Learn Each Pair of Associates and the Corresponding Number of Mediators Volunteered by Ss, with Breakdown by Type of Mediator

Syllables	Trials		Total (out of a possible 100)	Mediators					
	Mean	S D		Types					
				I	II	III	IV	V	None
EY–NUR	5·02	5·2	81	54	12	8	2	5	19
AR–WEH	5·51	5·8	84	7	68	4	3	2	16
IH–XIR	5·53	4·6	73	18	2	16	29	8	27
EZ–MUN	6·79	6·2	70	6	31	13	4	16	30
AX–SOQ	6·94	4·7	57	1	11	26	15	4	43
OF–LAH	7·13	5·6	54	5	19	7	9	14	46
UP–TEZ	7·16	5·8	52	2	1	32	5	12	48
AC–QET	8·24	5·6	66	25	0	15	21	5	34

During the postexperimental interrogation every S reported spontaneously that one kind of association, mediator or bridge occurred to him and was used to fix the responses. They did not, of course, use such terms and their explanations were ordered into a tentative and arbitrary classification of five seemingly discriminable groups such as the following:

The S formed one word of the two syllables, as, for example, from DUP–TEZ, he would create DEPUTIZE; from GAC–QET, he would form RACQUET or JACKET.

The syllables would be formed into two separate words or a phrase that could be initiated by the stimulus syllable: CEZ–MUN becomes SAYS MAN or C'EST MAN or SEND MONEY.[1]

Categories I and II appear to be 'sound bound'. The associations appear to derive from the sounds of the syllables. The sounds are modified into words.

Acquisition

III. The S would manufacture or imagine appropriate phrases or words that sound like the syllables, e.g. GEY–NUR becomes A GENERAL NURSE or KAR–WEH becomes KAREN–WAYWARD. This category involves largely personal experience.

IV. Some Ss would attempt abstract analyses of the syllables to get at some lead to the response, e.g. BIH–XIR becomes BI = 2, X = 10, *one number goes with another number, or they both had an* 'I'.

V. The Ss would report some vague association with one part of the combination, e.g. GAC–QET becomes translated into TOURNIQUET. BIH–XIR becomes SOMETHING LIKE BICEPS.

Not all pairs aroused reportable mediators for all Ss (see Table 2). Some mediators were forgotten after being used. Useless mediators were also commonly mentioned but those were impossible to classify and frequently forgotten. Many Ss reported inability to learn until a mediator of some type did occur. The longer the interitem interval the more likely the occurrence of mediator. The five intervals in order from shortest to longest aroused respectively 94, 96. 109, 111, and 127 mediating associations.

Discussion

The findings support the original hypothesis that total learning time is a significant variable to consider in at least some kinds learning. While it may be convenient to break up a learning session into some kinds of units of time, and label these 'trials', it may be a questionable practice in trying to get at appreciation of what S is actually learning or doing. If a presentation time is anything upwards of 1 sec, he may very well repeat the material to himself within the trial. To count period as one trial may be quite inappropriate. To conclude where S learns after one such interval, that he learned in one t (implying no repetition) may be quite incorrect.

On the other hand, the reports from Ss support the interpretation that on many of the trials nothing effective is learned. Wrong responses may occur because inadequate mediators occurred S or the mediators misled S into an inappropriate response. After varying amounts of search, which takes more or less time an appropriate mediator might be generated or stimulated i functioning. Once this occurs, S might be able to respond correctly and meet the learning criterion. In a sense, then, learning does occur in one trial in such situations. It must be remembered that about a third of the time S is unable to report any mediator. On such occasions he reports 'working on the pair' with a 'it just came to me' type of answer. It may be that such unassignable associations are of an unconscious nature, as suggested by Bugelski and Scharlock (1952), Russell and Storms (1955), and Ryan (1960).

The vast amount of research done on lists of pairs and on serial lists must be viewed from the limited viewpoint of how *lists* are learned, and not how pairs or other units are learned. From the viewpoint of a learning theory, it is the latter question that is of greater importance, however practical the former may be.

While the present study was not directed at the question of massed as opposed to spaced learning it does suggest that such studies too might take into consideration the question of total time involved in the learning sessions. Typically such studies provide some rest interval between trials for the spaced group while the massed Ss carry on with the activity. Commonly enough it is found that the spaced group performs at a higher level than the massed group after the same number of trials. When the spaced group's rests are included, however, it might be found that the total time was far in excess of the apparent advantage in trials, and the massed Ss have learned proportionally more than the spaced.

The present finding must be interpreted as restricted to the experimental conditions involved, particularly with respect to the time intervals employed, the method of exposure, and the nonsense material task. This report must be considered more suggestive than conclusive and other tasks must be examined before greater confidence can be placed in the constant time principle.[2]

[2]. It has been suggested to the writer by the linguist, Henry Lee Smith, that there is a striking similarity in the ages at which children of different nationalities learn to speak their native language to about the same level of proficiency.

Summary

Five groups of twenty Ss learned eight pairs of nonsense syllables under conditions where the stimulus syllable was always presented for 2 sec while the response syllable was presented for an additional 2, 4, 6, 8, or 15 sec depending on the group. A 2-sec interval preceded each new stimulus. The total exposure times for the several groups were 6, 8, 10, 12, or 19 sec per syllable pair. A significant difference was found between trials to learn with the fastest learning occurring with the longest presentation times. When presentation time was multiplied by trials, however, no significant differences were found. It was concluded that T_p (presentation time) $\times T$ (trials) is a constant value.

Interrogation of Ss after learning revealed that in 67 per cent of the total possible learning units, Ss made use of mediational devices. Those pairs that lent themselves most readily to translation into two meaningful words or could be combined into one word, or could initiate some imagery were most easily learned. These findings are discussed in terms of their significance for studies of 'one-trial' learning.

References

BUGELSKI, B. R., and SCHARLOCK, D. (1952), 'An experimental demonstration of unconscious mediation', *Journal of Experimental Psychology*, vol. 44, pp. 334–8.

HOVLAND, C. I. (1938), 'Experimental studies in rote-learning theory. III. Distribution of practice with varying speeds of syllable presentation', *Journal of Experimental Psychology*, vol. 23, pp. 172–90

MURDOCK, B. B. (1960), 'The immediate retention of unrelated words' *Journal of Experimental Psychology*, vol. 60, pp. 222–34.

ROCK, I. (1957), 'The role of repetition in associative learning', *American Journal of Psychology*., vol. 70, pp. 186–93.

RUSSELL, W. A., and STORMS, L. H. (1955), 'Implicit verbal chaining paired-associate learning', *Journal of Experimental Psychology*, vol. 4? pp. 287–93.

RYAN, J. J. (1960), 'Comparison of verbal response transfer mediated meaningfully similar and associated stimuli', *Journal of Experimental Psychology*, vol. 60, pp. 408–15.

13 A. Mechanic

The Responses Involved in the Rote Learning of Verbal Materials

A. Mechanic, 'The responses involved in the rote learning of verbal materials', *Journal of Verbal Learning and Verbal Behavior*, vol. 3 (1964), pp. 30–36.

Ss in incidental learning studies are required to perform an orienting task which ensures their exposure to the incidental stimuli. For purposes of comparison, intentional learners may be required to perform the same orienting task. Both incidental and intentional learning have been shown to vary as a function of the nature of the orienting task (Mechanic, 1962b; Postman and Adams, 1956). It has been suggested that rote learning of nonsense materials – both intentional and incidental – takes place as a result of 'pronouncing' responses made by S to the stimulus items (Mechanic, 1962 a and b). Different types of orienting tasks may facilitate or inhibit these pronouncing responses to varying degrees, thereby determining the amount of learning which takes place.

Pronouncing responses refer to hypothetical responses by S so that he reacts to each set of letters as a single pronounceable unit. Underwood and Schulz (1960, especially pp. 291–2) suggest that emitted spoken frequency is of fundamental importance for the learning of verbal units. These writers note that experiments, such as that of Gates (1917), have shown the superiority of active recitation over passive reading. Although Underwood and Schulz only refer to actual spoken responses, Mechanic (1962b) has described several experimental operations related to manipulation of pronouncing responses on a hypothetical (i.e. nonspoken) basis. It is suggested here that such responses are critical in rote verbal learning, whether the items be spoken or unspoken, and whether the learning be intentional or incidental. The pronouncing response is viewed here as being an important vehicle for the inter-sequence integration of response units. The critical role of such integration in verbal learning has been analysed by

Underwood and Schulz (1960), who indeed suggest that vocal emission is of fundamental importance for response integration. While response integration may take place in the absence of pronouncing responses, as with nonpronounceable trigrams, it is believed that these responses serve to short-circuit the integration process whenever the stimuli are pronounceable.

If pronouncing responses are viewed as being equally critical for both intentional and incidental learning, it is still necessary to explain the well-established finding that intentional learners are superior to incidental learners in the retention of low-meaningful materials. It is hypothesized that instructions to learn have this facilitating effect because they serve to increase the frequency of critical pronouncing responses made by S. That is, when S is instructed to learn the items, he instructs himself to make the appropriate integrative (i.e. pronouncing) responses, thereby increasing the frequency of these responses. This hypothesis has a rather interesting implication. If incidental Ss somehow can be induced to make pronouncing responses at a high enough rate, they should learn as efficiently as intentional learners. This should be true even for those materials which in the past have always resulted in superior intentional learning. This hypothesis can be tested experimentally by manipulating the orienting task so as to produce either high or low rates of pronouncing response. Keeping the learning items constant for the two orienting tasks, we should predict that: (a) intentional learning will show considerable superiority over incidental learning when the orienting task does not require a high rate of pronouncing response; (b) there will be no significant difference when the orienting task requires both kinds of learners to make pronouncing response at a very high rate of frequency.

These predictions were tested in Experiment I by varying both instructions (intentional or incidental) and orienting task (low-pronouncing or high-pronouncing) in a standard 2×2 factorial design. It was predicted that: (a) intentional learners would be superior to incidental learners with the low-pronouncing orienting task; (b) no significant difference would be found with the high-pronouncing orienting task; (c) the high-pronouncing task would be superior to the low-pronouncing task regardless of instructions; and (d) there would be a significant interaction between instructions and orienting task. It may be noted that this last prediction, which combines the first two predictions, is critical for the hypothesis which has been outlined.

In Experiment I, an immediate recall test was given 10 sec after the completion of the stimulus-list presentation. In order to facilitate the interpretation of the obtained data, they have been supplemented by those of Experiment II in which recall is measured after an interval of 6 min. Experiment III involves comparisons between the learning of incidental Ss, who are required by the orienting task to make pronouncing responses, with intentional learners, who are not asked to perform any orienting task at all. It is well established that the performance of an orienting task reduces the amount of learning which takes place (Gleitman and Gillett, 1957; Postman and Adams, 1956; Postman, Adams and Bohm, 1956; Saltzman, 1953). It will be of interest to ascertain whether this generalization is applicable to the specific orienting tasks used here.

Experiment I

Method

Materials. The learning materials consisted of a heterogeneous list of twenty-four pronounceable trigrams. The list was composed of twelve high-frequency trigrams and twelve low-frequency trigrams taken from Underwood and Postman (1960). The high- and low-frequency items were pooled and then drawn out individually to make up the random order of twenty-four trigrams used in the experiment. All Ss were exposed to the list for single presentation.

Conditions of learning. Individual Ss were seated at a desk in front of a microphone which was connected to a tape recorder. The tape recorder was started in a conspicuous manner at the onset of the stimulus-list presentation. The twenty-four trigrams were presented individually by means of an automatic slide projector. Each item was exposed for 9 sec with a $2\frac{1}{4}$-sec interval between exposures. During exposure of the list, different groups of Ss were required to perform the different orienting tasks described in the next section. Both an intentional and an incidental learning group were exposed to the list with each orienting task. These groups differed only in that the intentional group was given additional instructions. They were told that we were also interested in how their performance on the task was related to learning the items, and that they would be tested for the total number of items that they could remember regardless of order. No mention of learning was made to the incidental Ss.

Orienting tasks. Two orienting tasks were designed to produce pronouncing responses to different degrees: (a) pronouncing each item over and over; and (b) guessing a number presumably associated with each item. These two tasks will be referred to as 'High Pronouncing' (HP) and 'Low Pronouncing' (LP), respectively.

The HP groups were told we were interested in the effects of repetition on the pronunciation of certain kinds of verbal units. To obtain credibility, Ss were told that we had a mathematical model of linguistic functioning, and were testing predictions concerning the effects of fatigue and practice on pronunciation. As each item appeared on the screen, they were required to pronounce it into the microphone over and over again until the next item appeared. This necessitated continued pronouncing of the item even after it was no longer on the screen during the slide change interval. With a 9-sec presentation period and a $2\frac{1}{4}$-sec interval, each item was pronounced for slightly over 11 sec. The Ss pronounced item after item with no rest at all between items. This precluded the possibility of intentional Ss using the interval for rehearsal while incidental Ss rested. In order to test the experimental hypotheses, it was necessary to prevent, as far as possible, any differential rehearsal for intentional and incidental learners in the HP condition.

The Ss were told that there were no 'correct' or 'incorrect' pronunciations, and that they were to use whichever pronunciation seemed most natural to them. They were also told to repeat each item at a rate which seemed natural to them. It was stated that a rate about the speed of one's normal conversation seemed right for most people. It was requested that they try to be consistent both in their rate of pronouncing and in their pronunciation of each individual item. For each S a count was made of total number of pronunciations made to the middle two items in the list. It was found that, with these instructions, individual Ss varied from slightly less than one to slightly more than two responses per sec.

The LP groups were told that this was an experiment on extrasensory perception and that they were to guess what number between zero and 99 had been assigned previously to each item. They were required to look at each item for 9 sec and announce their guess into the microphone after the item had gone off the screen (during the slide-change interval). No information was given to LP Ss with regard to how they were to make the number assignments. Previous data (Mechanic, 1962b) are consistent with the assumption that many Ss use pronouncing responses to help them make such guesses. However, such responses are clearly much less frequent than they are with the HP orienting task.

Experimental design. With two variations of orienting task (HP and LP) and two variations of instructions (Intentional and Incidental), four groups of twenty Ss each were used in a standard 2×2 factorial design. The Ss, who were all students in lower-division psychology courses at Northwestern University, were assigned to the four conditions by rotation, with the initial order being determined randomly.

Recall test. Both intentional and incidental Ss were given a 5-min test of free recall 10 sec after the completion of stimulus presentation. The Ss were told that their score would be the number of items correctly recalled regardless of order. They were encouraged to guess if they were not sure of an item. A postexperimental inquiry was made of the incidental Ss to ascertain whether they suspected a memory test or attempted to learn the syllables for any other reason. None of the incidental Ss reported this to be the case. However, four Ss had to be discarded and replaced for not following the instructions of the experiment. Two of these Ss were in the LP-Intentional condition, and one each was in the LP-Intentional and HP-Incidental conditions.

Results and discussion

The mean number of items recalled by the four experimental
groups are given in Table 1. Although there is no difference
between intentional and incidental learning in the HP condition
the over-all effect of instructions to learn is significant ($F = 7.04$

Table 1

Average Numbers of Items Recalled as a Function of Orientin
Task and Instructions

Condition	Instructions			
	Incidental		Intentional	
	Mean	SD	Mean	SD
Low Pronunciation Task (LP)	3·50	1·69	6·95	2·09
High Pronunciation Task (HP)	8·85	4·15	8·85	2·78

$df = 1/76$, $p < 0.01$). The difference between the LP and I
orienting tasks is also highly significant ($F = 31.09$, $df = 1/$
$p < 0.01$). This confirms the prediction that learning, b
incidental and intentional, will be facilitated by an orienting ta
requiring a high rate of pronunciation responses. The gaps
tween the individual means for the two orienting tasks
significant for both incidental ($p < 0.01$) and intentio
($p < 0.05$) learning.

The critical comparison for the pronouncing-response hy
thesis is the interaction between orienting tasks and instructi
It may be seen in Table 1 that while instructions to learn ha
great effect in the LP situation, they have no effect at all in
HP situation. This interaction is highly reliable ($F = 7$
$df = 1/76$, $p < 0.01$). In fact, the influence of the high-

ouncing condition is so great that HP Ss learn more items ncidentally than LP Ss learn intentionally ($p < 0.05$).

Production of emitted responses. The number of pronouncing esponses to the two middle items in the list was recorded for ach HP S. The means were 27·30 responses for incidental earners and 28·75 for intentional learners. It is clear that instructions to learn do not influence the production of spoken esponses in the HP condition ($t = 0.65$). The correlation between number of items correct and number of spoken responses not significant for either incidental or intentional learning s $= 0.096$ and -0.166, respectively). While the high-pronouncing orienting task facilitates learning, the variation in *tual number* of spoken responses by HP Ss is not an important ctor.

xperiment II

Experiment I, the test of recall was given immediately after mulus presentation. The critical finding of this experiment, th regard to the pronouncing-response hypothesis, was the lack a difference between intentional and incidental learners performing the HP task. In order to test the stability of this finding, 1 its persistence when the HP-incidental Ss are subjected to reased interference, data on delayed recall were obtained.

thod

eriment II involved a comparison between two new HP ups. The two groups, one intentional and the other incidental, e made up of thirty-five Ss each. The materials and conditions earning were identical to those for the comparable groups in eriment I. Only after the stimulus presentations had been npleted did the experimental procedures deviate from those of eriment I.

all test for incidental learners. After presentation of the final ulus item, Ss were delayed in the experimental room for a n retention interval before being given the recall test. To ent rehearsal during this interval, Ss were given a written attitude test (California F-scale) in which they were required to agree or disagree with various statements. During a 35-sec instruction period prior to the test, Ss were told that we were interested in the relationship between pronouncing habits and social attitudes. The Ss worked on the test for 5 min. At this point, they were stopped and told that they were not expected to come even close to finishing the social-attitude scale. They were then asked to write down as many of the syllables as they could remember. The interval between termination of work on the F-scale and the start of the 5-min test of free recall was 25 sec.

Recall test for intentional learners. The intentional Ss had been told previously that they would receive a test of recall after the presentations. Immediately after presentation of the final stimulus item, they were told that there would be no test in spite of earlier instructions. The earlier instructions were justified as a method for permitting E to see what effect 'trying to learn' would have upon S's pronunciations. Ss were then given the F-scale in the same manner as the incidental Ss. At the completion of the 6-min retention interval, they were given the recall test with instructions identical to those given the incidental Ss. During a postexperimental inquiry, intentional Ss were asked whether they continued to expect a memory test after they were told that there would none. Those answering affirmatively, or those reporting that they rehearsed during the retention interval, were discarded and replaced. A similar inquiry was made of the incidental Ss. There were only one S in the intentional group and one S in incidental group who had to be replaced for the reasons cited above.

Results and discussion

The intentional group recalled an average of 6·71 items while incidental group recalled an average of 5·49 items. The SDs were 3·29 and 2·80, respectively. This difference between means did not reach marginal significance ($t = 1·65$, $df = 68$). The failure to find an intentional-incidental difference with the high-pronouncing orienting task in Experiment I is therefore confirmed Experiment II.

The data of both experiments support the pronouncing-response hypothesis. When the orienting task requires S to make pronouncing responses at a high enough rate, instructions to learn have no effect. This is true whether the recall test is immediate or delayed. However, with the same stimulus materials, instructions have a powerful effect when the orienting task does not require a high rate of pronouncing responses on the part of S. It appears that instructions to learn have this facilitating effect in the latter case (LP) because they serve to increase the frequency of critical pronouncing responses made by S. In the former case (HP), a comparably high rate of responding is required by the orienting task with or without instructions to learn.

Experiment III

The findings in Experiments I and II indicate that, when compared with other orienting tasks, the HP task strongly facilitates those responses necessary for learning. In order to ascertain the limits of this facilitation, additional comparisons were made between HP-incidental Ss and intentional Ss who were not required to perform any orienting task at all. It is of interest to examine whether the HP orienting task facilitates pronouncing responses to such an extent, that it actually compensates for the usual inhibitory effects of orienting task *per se*.

Experiment III was carried out at the same time as Experiment I. An additional group of twenty Ss was tested along with the four basic groups in Experiment I. The Ss were assigned to this group in rotation with the assignment of Ss to the conditions of Experiment I. They were shown the stimulus items for the same periods as all other Ss but were not asked to perform an orienting task. They were told only that E was interested in how well they could remember the syllables, and that they would be tested after the presentations. Like all Ss in Experiment I, they were given an immediate test of free recall. The mean number of items correctly recalled was 11·75 with an SD of 2·75. As may be seen in Table I, both HP groups averaged 8·85 items. The intentional Ss not given an orienting task were superior to both the incidental ($t = 2.54$, $df = 38$, $p < 0.05$) and intentional ($t = 3.23$, $df = 38$, $p < 0.01$) Ss given the HP task.

195

Acquisition

From the point of view of a pronouncing-response hypothesis, these data indicate that Ss given instructions to learn without an orienting task are able to program their pronouncing responses in a manner more efficient than the HP Ss. It is not surprising that the arbitrarily devised HP procedure is not as efficient a response programmer as the learning habits which S brings with him into the experimental situation. Alternatively, it may be argued that there are other essential differences between intentional and incidental learning which favor the intentional learner in this comparison. Postman (1964) points out that the instruction stimulus determines the frequency and intensity of differential cue-producing responses which occur during the practice period. Among such differential responses, he includes 'categorizing responses such as naming or labeling, other responses elicited through stimulus generalization, and responses serving as associative links among the members of a series.' Undoubtedly, such factors may favor intentional learning over and above the influence of pronouncing responses. However, it appears unlikely that these kinds of responses played a significant role in the experimental situation under consideration. These responses would be expected to favor the HP-intentional Ss just as well as the intentional learners without an orienting task. However, the HP-intentional Ss did not perform more efficiently than incidental learners in Experiments I and II. The question remains as to why the intentional learners without an orienting task learned more than the HP-intentional Ss. Even when learning instructions are given to HP Ss, their learning habits are superseded by the requirements of the orienting task.

The HP orienting task required S to keep pronouncing the items aloud without allowing him an opportunity to rest his voice at all during the entire procedure. It may be suggested that the physical requirements placed upon the speech apparatus were so great as to produce a deleterious effect upon learning. To check this possibility, two new groups of twenty Ss each were tested after the other experiments had been completed. One group was given learning instructions but no orienting task, while the other group was given a modified-HP task but no learning instructions. The modified-HP task involved having S alternate between pronouncing the item aloud and silently. He was instructed to first

A. Mechanic

pronounce the item aloud, then to himself, then aloud, and so on. This was intended to mitigate the physical requirements placed upon the speech apparatus. If the superiority of the intentional learners, without an orienting task, over the HP-incidental learners in Experiment I is due to the actual physical requirements placed upon the latter, then the modified-HP task could be expected to eliminate this difference. The obtained data make it clear that this is not the case. For this experimental comparison, the exposure period was increased from 9 to 14·5 sec. The intentional Ss learned an average of 12·10 items with an SD of 2·39, while the modified-HP Ss learned an average of 6·66 items with an SD of 2·37 ($t = 7·50$, $df = 38$, $p < 0·01$). Even with a greatly increased stimulus-exposure time, the modified-HP Ss do not perform as well as the original HP-incidental Ss in Experiment I ($t = 2·00$, $df = 38$, $0·05 < p < 0·06$). It appears that the alternating task has an effect opposite to that intended. Even with longer exposure times, it is inferior to the continuous pronouncing task in the amount of learning which takes place. This is consistent with postexperimental reports by Ss that the silent-aloud alternation task is a difficult one to perform.

Theoretically it should be possible to devise an orienting task in which the required pronouncing responses are programmed as efficiently as are the responses of the intentional learner without an orienting task. It is clear that this has not yet been achieved. Perhaps by decreasing stimulus-exposure times to a minimum, it will be possible to obtain incidental learning equal to that of intentional learning without an orienting task. In such situations, intentional Ss may have minimal opportunity to utilize the response programs (i.e. learning habits) which they bring with them into the experimental situation.

Summary

It was hypothesized that rote learning, both intentional and incidental, takes place as a result of 'pronouncing' responses made by S to the stimulus items. In this view, instructions to learn facilitate learning because they serve to increase the frequency of typical pronouncing responses made by S. This implies that, incidental learners can be induced to make pronouncing

197

responses at a high enough rate, they should learn as efficiently as intentional learners.

Two orienting tasks were designed to produce pronouncing responses to different degrees: (a) pronouncing each item over and over (HP); and (b) guessing a number presumably associated with each item (LP). Two groups of twenty Ss each, one intentional and one incidental, were tested with each task. It was predicted that: (a) intentional learning would show considerable superiority over incidental learning when the orienting task does not require a high rate of pronouncing responses (LP); and (b) there would be no significant difference when the orienting task requires both kinds of learners to make pronouncing responses at a very high rate of frequency (HP). That is, a significant interaction between instructions (intentional or incidental) and orienting task (LP or HP) was predicted.

Instructions and orienting task were varied in a 2 × 2 factorial design. Both independent variables produced significant variation in the learning scores. In accordance with the critical theoretic prediction, the interaction between the main variables was also significant. These findings support a pronouncing-response hypothesis and appear to be independent of whether recall is measured immediately or after a 6-min retention interval.

References

GATES, A. I. (1917), 'Recitation as a factor in memorizing', *Archives of Psychology*, vol. 6, no. 40.

GLEITMAN, H., and GILLETT, E. (1957), 'The effect of intention upon learning', *Journal of General Psychology*, vol. 57, pp. 137–49.

MECHANIC, A. (1962a), 'The distribution of recalled items in simultaneous intentional and incidental learning', *Journal of Experimental Psychology*, vol. 63, pp. 593–600.

MECHANIC, A. (1962b), 'Effects of orienting task, practice, and incentive on simultaneous incidental and intentional learning', *Journal of Experimental Psychology*, vol. 64, pp. 393–9.

POSTMAN, L. (1964), 'Short-term memory and incidental learning', in A. W. Melton, ed., *Categories of Human Learning*, Academic Press.

POSTMAN, L., and ADAMS, P. A. (1956), 'Studies in incidental learning IV. The interaction of orienting tasks and stimulus materials', *Journal of Experimental Psychology*, vol. 51, pp. 329–33.

POSTMAN, L., ADAMS, P. A., and BOHM, A. M. (1956), 'Studies in incidental learning: V. Recall for order and associative clustering', *Journal of Experimental Psychology*, vol. 51, pp. 334–42.

SALTZMAN, I. J. (1953), 'The orienting task in incidental and intentional learning', *American Journal of Psychology*, vol. 66, pp. 593–7.

UNDERWOOD, B. J., and POSTMAN, L. (1960), 'Extraexperimental sources of interference in forgetting', *Psychological Review*, vol. 67, pp. 73–95.

UNDERWOOD, B. J., and SCHULZ, R. W. (1960), *Meaningfulness and Verbal Learning*, Lippincott.

Part Two Organization in Recall

The common thread running through the papers in this section is the demonstration of the effects on memory of pre-experimental habits – associative, linguistic, and conceptual – which are brought into play by the presentation of the learning materials. New learning must necessarily build on old; the subject may be expected to call whenever he can on the armamentarium of his language and its schemata for classifying and ordering objects and events. In recent years there has been a great upsurge of interest in the exploration of the systematic influences of pre-experimental habits and in particular of the role of linguistic processes in learning and memory. This activity has been stimulated and sustained by the rapid advances in the analysis of associative hierarchies and structures and by important developments in linguistic theory. Thus, investigators have been acquiring increasingly refined and theoretically relevant tools for specifying the pre-existing habits which have a bearing on a given experimental task.

The method which has lent itself most readily to the analysis of the effects of pre-experimental habits is free-recall learning. The essential feature of this procedure is that subjects are permitted to recall the lists of words presented to them in any order they wish. It should be emphasized that the defining characteristic of free recall is the removal of restrictions on the order of output of the responses. The items may be presented only once, or if more than once, either in a fixed or in a varying order (the latter is the common procedure when there are multiple trials). Regardless of the conditions of input, the subject may or may not reproduce the items in the order in which they were presented. Because recall is that sense free, the reproductions can reflect whatever relations or groupings have been developed among the items. In short, there is an opportunity for recall to be organized, and the sources of organization are likely to be the learner's pre-experimental habits.

Inter-Item Associations

Norms of free association are used widely to specify the inter relations among words established through linguistic usage. Th first paper in this section, Reading 14 presents a convincin demonstration of the fact that normative associative relation among the words in a list significantly influence the amount r called. Variations in the degree of inter-item associative strengtl as measured by the average relative frequency with which th items in the list elicit each other as free associates, predict tl level of recall with considerable accuracy. The mechanism r sponsible for the enhancement of recall is best described as tl convergence of inter-item associations on the responses includ in the list. Associates elicit each other at the time of the test (a perhaps during the presentation of the list as well, thereby i fluencing the frequency of rehearsal), and the probability of particular item being given depends on the number of differe associations converging upon it. This interpretation is strengt ened by its ability to predict both the relative frequency and t nature of intrusions from outside the list. The correlation l tween the degree of inter-item associative strength and the f quency of intrusions is negative; the stronger the relations amc the items within the list, the more likely it becomes that associations which are aroused will converge on a correct rat than an incorrect response. However, the more cohesive the l the more agreement there is among subjects on the particu errors that are given. Correct responses and errors are com mentary manifestations of the same process. As Deese (1959) able to show in another study, the frequency of an individual portation can be predicted reliably on the basis of the converg probabilities that items within the list will elicit that partic response.

Deese's experimental lists consisted of items all of which v related to each other to at least some degree. The effectivenes associative convergence in enhancing recall is not, howe limited to this special case. In a study by Rothkopf and Coke (1961), subjects were given a single exposure to a list of ninety-nine words; within that very long list associative relations among individual words varied widely. The probability of recall of a particular word was found to be a direct function of the number of other items which were known to elicit it as an associative response. Thus, associative convergence determines the probability of recall even if there is no constraint on the range of possible responses, i.e. the list as a whole lacks any apparent organization. This finding supports the conclusion that the positive relation between inter-item associative strength and recall is not attributable to the subjects' success in editing their responses and reconstructing the list.

The very multiple associations which serve to increase the number of correct responses in free recall become a potential source of interference when reproduction of the items in an arbitrary serial order is required. The more numerous and the stronger the pre-existing linkages among non-adjacent items, the more the prescribed sequences should be subject to competition. In agreement with this expectation, speed of serial anticipation learning does not increase with inter-item associative strength; in fact, the observed difference is in the opposite direction (Postman, 1967). The difficulty of the serial task depends on the strengths of the non-adjacent associations relative to those of the adjacent ones (Weingartner, 1963). These results underline the fact that the influence of pre-existing associations on performance will depend on the requirements of the experimental task; response recall is facilitated, but the sequential ordering of items is likely to be inhibited. Hence inter-item associative strength may be expected to have dual and opposed effects when correct performance requires not only response recall but also the reproduction of serial order. Inter-item associative strength is a fundamental property of verbal lists whose possible influence should be considered carefully even when it has not been manipulated directly. That is, whenever manipulation of a variable entails correlated changes in inter-item associative strength, it is necessary to ask whether the latter are responsible for the observed effects on performance. The variable of word frequency is a case in point. Free recall is shown to increase as a function of the frequency of usage of the

words in the list (Bousfield and Cohen, 1955; Hall, 1954; Underwood, Ekstrand and Keppel, 1965). However, it is more likely
that at least some of the items in the list will be associatively related when the word frequency is high than when it is low. In a
study by Deese (1960) the expected correlation between word
frequency and inter-item associative strength was, in fact, found.
Moreover, when the associative factor was held constant, there
was no residual effect of word frequency on recall.

Clustering in Recall

Direct behavioural evidence for the influence of pre-experimenta
habits on the process of recall is providing by the phenomeno
of clustering. Suppose a list comprises several groups of words
each of which falls into a distinct category, e.g. names of countries
professions, parts of the body, and vegetables. The list is pre
sented in a random order so that members of the same categor
follow each other with no more than chance frequency. In recal
ing the list, most subjects show a pronounced tendency to grou
the words by category. The extent to which the amount of cate
gorical grouping exceeds the level to be expected by chance defin
the degree of clustering. The systematic exploration of the cond
tions and characteristics of clustering was initiated by Bousfie
and his associates some fifteen years ago and has since bee
carried on both by this group and by many other investigato
The literature is by now voluminous and contains a considerab
amount of information about the dependence of clustering on t
characteristics of the stimulus lists, the methods of presentati
and the conditions of testing. (For selective reviews of t
literature see Cofer, 1965; and Postman, 1964.)

   The point of departure in a study of clustering is the definiti
of the categories to be included in the list and the assignment
instances to each of them. A standard source of categorized ite
are the 'cultural norms' of Cohen, Bousfield, and Whitma
(1957). The procedure used for obtaining these norms is describ
by the same authors in Reading 15. The experiment reporte
this reading also shows that the amount of clustering increase
a function of the frequency with which the stimulus words
given as free associates to the category names. The authors c

lude from this finding that degree of organization in free recall epends on the readiness with which subjects can categorize the timulus words. This conclusion calls attention to a critical issue a the interpretation of clustering phenomena. In a typical experiment on clustering, the experimenter provides the subject with ulturally defined categories for grouping the individual words in the list and then determines the extent to which these categories ere in fact used in recall. If a significant amount of clustering is ound, the organization of recall on the basis of categorical groupings has been demonstrated. However, if there is little or no clustering, it would be hazardous to conclude that the items were not ouped systematically in recall: the categories used by the bject may have been different from those defined by the experimenter (see Tulving, 1968). The categories provided by the experimenter will be used when they are readily recognized and applied individual instances and thus are more useful in the organization recall than alternative groupings the subject himself may be le to generate (see Cofer, 1965). It may be reasonable, therefore, regard an index of clustering not so much as a measure of the gree to which recall is organized as of the usefulness of the egories defined by the experimenter. The fact that the correlations between the degree of clustering and the amount recalled not pronounced is consistent with the view that items may quently be grouped into idiosyncratic rather than normative egories. These considerations lead us to the question of subive organization.

bjective Organization

all may be described as organized when the subject's output is aracterized by systematic features which are not present in the t. Thus, clustering is an instance of organization in recall ause the categorical grouping of words first occurs in the outphase. The organization reflected in clustering can be identiand measured because the categories are known. As was ady pointed out, however, the groupings which impose organon on recall may be generated by the subject. To the extent such is indeed the case, there arises the problem of developing ctive criteria for the existence of such subjective groupings.

Consider, for example, the case in which a list of 'unrelated' word is presented to the subject. The words are unrelated in the sens that there are no known normative relations among them, e.g they do not fall into any obvious taxonomic categories nor d they elicit each other as free associates. There is a possibility, how ever, that the subject can devise ways of grouping these words int a limited number of higher-order units on the basis of similaritie and relations among them which he was able to discover or in vent. As Tulving (1968) put it, there may be a discrepancy be tween E-units and S-units, i.e. between 'single items defined such by the experimenter and those that are handled as sing items by the memory system' (p. 8). The development of S-uni which are distinct from the E-units constitutes subjective organiza tion in recall.

An objective method for measuring the degree of subjecti organization (SO) in free recall was proposed in an influent paper by Tulving (1962). The logic of Tulving's measure of SO related to the concept of clustering. The basic assumption is th E-units (individual words) which are subjectively organized in higher-order S-units will be grouped together on successive te of recall even though a different random order of the word used in each presentation of the list. That is, the words cluster in recall but the basis of clustering is devised by the subj rather than provided by the experimenter. The index of devised by Tulving is based on concepts derived from informat theory and is essentially a measure of redundancy. It asks h predictable the sequences of items are from one output to next, given the number of words the subject is able to recall. index of SO increases as a function of trials and thus co-va with the level of recall, and it also correlates positively ac subjects with the number of items recalled (Tulving, 1962, 19

These correlations pose the usual interpretive problem: is development of subjective units responsible for the progres improvements in recall, or are the increases in SO a consequ of the mastery of the list? Or are both manifestations of a t underlying process? Tulving has argued for the first alterna the number of S-units that can be recalled is strictly limited, an increase in the number of E-units recalled over trials reflect progressive expansion of the size of the S-units. The ques cannot, however, be answered decisively on the basis of correlations alone. To provide direct support for the assumption that organization determines performance, it is necessary to manipulate subjective organization and to demonstrate that the predicted changes in recall performance do in fact occur. The study by Tulving which is presented here as Reading 16 represents a successful attempt to do just that. In a subsequent study Tulving (1965) used a different approach to demonstrate the effectiveness of subjective organization in enhancing recall. In the first phase of this study, the protocols obtained in an experiment on free-recall learning were examined, and sequences which were common to the outputs of a relatively high proportion of the subjects were identified. Such sequences were assumed to represent instances of efficient subjective organization. New groups of subjects then learned serial lists which comprised either common sequences or uncommon ones. The expected difference in speed of acquisition favouring the common sequences was obtained.

The development of measures of subjective organization – other indices supplementing Tulving's have been devised (e.g. Bousfield, Puff, and Cowan, 1964) – represents an important advance in the analysis of the recall process. The theoretically useful distinction between E-units and S-units has been given operational meaning, and the potentially critical role of subjective organization as a determinant of recall has been brought into focus. Nevertheless, certain limitations of existing analyses of subjective organization should be recognized. Apart from the fact that the quantitative indices are based on the recurrence of short (two-item) sequences, a question must be raised about the basic assumption that the growth of subjective organization is necessarily reflected in an increasing consistency of the sequential order of output. When there is a network of relations and associative connexions among a group of items, alternative sequences may be activated on successive tests, precisely because of the cohesiveness of the organization. Thus, consistency of output order must be viewed as but one of the possible manifestations of subjective organization.

Contextual Constraints

One of the outstanding characteristics of the system of language habits which the subject brings to the laboratory is the constraint on the choice of particular words exerted by the preceding verbal context. Any given sequence of words of length n entails a distribution of transitional probabilities which specifies the likelihood that each of a number of possible alternatives will occupy the position $n+1$. The longer the prior sequence the greater is the degree of constraint on the word that may follow; and as the contextual constraint increases, the word sequences approximate the statistical structure of English more and more closely. The relation between degree of approximation to English represented by the learning materials and the amount recalled was first examined in an important paper by Miller and Selfridge which appears here as Reading 17. The article contains a description of the method used to construct strings of words of different orders of approximation to English. The experimental results show a clear relation between order of approximation and amount recalled. A noteworthy feature of the findings is the pronounced negative acceleration of the function relating recall to order of approximation. Thus, there is little difference between the highest-order approximations and English text. The authors' interpretation of the latter finding that recall is facilitated to the extent that the learning material preserve short-range associations established through linguistic usage; in that respect higher-order approximations are as effective as English text.

The study of Miller and Selfridge aroused considerable interest and their type of material has been used widely by other investigators. The basic findings have been confirmed repeatedly (e Postman and Adams, 1960; Richardson and Voss, 1960; Sha 1958). In subsequent studies special attention was given to shape of the function relating recall to the order of approximation and in particular to the apparent absence of a difference between the higher orders and text. The available evidence now indicates that this result is attributable to the method of scoring recall u by Miller and Selfridge who counted the number of words called without regard to order. When scores are based on rep ductions in the correct serial order, textual material shows expected advantage over the higher-order approximations (Marks and Jack, 1952); the longer the sequence which must be reproduced in order, the greater is the superiority of the textual material (Coleman, 1963). These findings show that increases in contextual determination imply progressively greater sequential constraints.

It is likely that several processes contribute to the observed increases in recall as a function of order of approximation. In a recent review of the literature, Johnson (1968) points out that various characteristics of the materials change concomitantly as the statistical structure of English is approached; there are increases in the relative meaningfulness (in the sense of semantic appropriateness) of the word strings, in the degree of conformity to grammatical rules, and probably in the strength of word-to-word associations. Each of these changes favours the transfer of pre-experimental habits to the learning task.

The experiment by Marks and Miller (1964), reported in Reading 18, was designed to distinguish between the syntactic and the semantic factors which underlie the contextual constraints. In the construction of the materials to be recalled, semantic and syntactic rules were violated singly and in combination. The results show that the two factors can, indeed, be varied independently and that both contribute to the mastery of the material.

References

BOUSFIELD, W. A., and COHEN, B. H. (1955), 'The occurrence of clustering in the recall of randomly arrayed words of different frequencies of usage', *Journal of General Psychology*, vol. 52, pp. 83–95.

BOUSFIELD, W. A., PUFF, C. R., and COWAN, T. M. (1964), 'The development of constancies in sequential organization during repeated free recall', *Journal of Verbal Learning and Verbal Behavior*, vol. 3, pp. 449–59.

COFER, C. N. (1965), 'On some factors in the organizational characteristics of free recall', *American Psychologist*, vol. 20, pp. 261–72.

COHEN, B. H., BOUSFIELD, W. A., and WHITMARSH, G. A. (1957), 'Cultural norms for verbal items in 43 categories', *Technical Report No. 22*, Office of Naval Research and University of Connecticut.

COLEMAN, E. B. (1963), 'Approximations to English: Some comments on the method', *American Journal of Psychology*, vol. 76, pp. 239–47.

DEESE, J. (1959), 'On the prediction of occurrence of particular verbal intrusions in immediate recall', *Journal of Experimental Psychology*, vol. 58, pp. 17–22.

DEESE, J. (1960), 'Frequency of usage and number of words in free recall: The role of association', *Psychological Report*, vol. 7, pp. 337–44.

HALL, J. F. (1954), 'Learning as a function of word frequency', *American Journal of Psychology*, vol. 67, pp. 138–40.

JOHNSON, N. F. (1968), 'Sequential verbal behavior', in T. R. Dixon and D. L. Horton, eds., *Verbal Behavior and General Behaviour Theory*, Prentice-Hall.

MARKS, M. R., and JACK, O. (1952), 'Verbal context and memory span for meaningful materials', *American Journal of Psychology*, vol. 65, pp. 298–300.

POSTMAN, L. (1964), 'Short-term memory and incidental learning', in A. W. Melton, ed., *Categories of Human Learning*, Academic Press.

POSTMAN, L. (1967), 'The effect of inter-item associative strength on the acquisition and retention of serial lists', *Journal of Verbal Learning and Verbal Behavior*, vol. 6, pp. 721–8.

POSTMAN, L., and ADAMS, P. A. (1960), 'Studies in incidental learning: VIII. The effects of contextual determination', *Journal of Experimental Psychology*, vol. 59, pp. 153–64.

RICHARDSON, P., and VOSS, J. (1960), 'Replication report: verbal context and the recall of meaningful material', *Journal of Experimental Psychology*, vol. 60, pp. 417–18.

ROTHKOPF, E. Z., and COKE, E. U. (1961), 'The prediction of free recall from word association measures', *Journal of Experimental Psychology*, vol. 62, pp. 433–8.

SHARP, H. C. (1958), 'Effect of contextual constraint upon recall of verbal passages', *American Journal of Psychology*, vol. 71, pp. 568–72.

TULVING, E. (1962), 'Subjective organization in free recall of "unrelated" words', *Psychological Review*, vol. 69, pp. 344–54.

TULVING, E. (1964), 'Intratrial and intertrial retention: Notes towards a theory of free recall verbal learning', *Psychological Review*, vol. 71, pp. 219–37.

TULVING, E. (1965), 'The effect of order of presentation on learning of "unrelated" words', *Psychonomic Science*, vol. 3, pp. 337–8.

TULVING, E. (1968), 'Theoretical issues in free recall', in T. R. Dixon and D. L. Horton, eds., *Verbal Behavior and General Behavior Theory*, Prentice-Hall.

UNDERWOOD, B. J., EKSTRAND, B. R., and KEPPEL, G. (1965), 'An analysis of intralist similarity in verbal learning with experiments on conceptual similarity', *Journal of Verbal Learning and Verbal Behavio* vol. 4, pp. 447–62.

WEINGARTNER, H. (1963), 'Associative structure and serial learning', *Journal of Verbal Learning and Verbal Behavior*, vol. 2, pp. 476–9.

14 J. Deese

Influence of Inter-Item Associative Strength upon
Immediate Free Recall

J. Deese, 'Influence of inter-item associative strength upon immediate free
recall', *Psychological Reports*, vol. 5 (1959), pp. 305–12.

A number of recent studies have pointed to the associative
strength of particular items within the context of the material
presented to Ss as a fundamental determinant of the organization
and amount of recall in immediate free recall. Of particular
interest to the problems examined in the present study are those
experiments dealing with clustering and association strength. Two
experiments (3, 4) have demonstrated that when stimulus–response pairs from free association norms are randomly separated in
presentation, they are reunited in recall and recalled in proportion
to the strength of the association. The large and consistent clustering effects obtained in these experiments suggest that it may
be fruitful to examine the more general case of associative relationships between all items, not just particular pairs of items.

The principal independent variable examined in the present
study may be described as inter-item associative strength. The
experiment examines the influence of this variable upon some
characteristics of immediate free recall. Inter-item associative
strength is defined as the average relative frequency with which
all items in a list tend to elicit all other items in the same list as
free associates. The hypothesis concerning inter-item associative
strength which are examined in the present experiment are: (a)
the number of items recalled is proportional to inter-item associative strength; (b) extraneous intrusions are inversely related to
inter-item associative strength; and (c) the number of different
intrusions is inversely related to inter-item associative strength.
The last hypothesis stems from the results of an earlier experiment
1. In this experiment it was demonstrated that the frequency of
occurrence of a particular intrusion was proportional to the probability of that intrusion's occurring as a free associate to items on

the list. It turns out, for reasons explained below, that if inter-item associative strength is high, the items on the list tend to elicit the same free associates from outside of the list. Thus, the number of different high strength free associates from outside the list is relatively small. If the inter-item associative strength is low, on the other hand, there are few if any free associates in common between different items on the list. Thus, if intrusions are determined by associative strength to items on the list, there will be little overlap between different associations and the intrusions will be variable.

In general, these hypotheses may be described by the assertion that lists with high inter-item associative strength are more highly organized than those with low inter-item strength. High organization means that the number of items recalled is increased and that resistance to outside intrusion is relatively high.

One important question in the interpretation of the relationship between associative strength and recall concerns the immediacy of the influence of associative strength. There are at least two possibilities. Associative strength may have a direct influence upon recall; thus, in part, free recall may be described as free association. On the other hand, associative strength may be used, through the intervention of a secondary or mediating activity, as a mnemonic device. That is to say, Ss may deliberately seek appropriate associations and actively reject associations that are inappropriate. While a definitive test for any given situation as to whether S behave in one way or the other is almost impossible, a test wa built into the present study which tells the extent to which S actually do use an associative mnemonic device available to ther outside of the items to be remembered. This mnemonic device con sists of a name given to each list, a name which Ss write down o their data sheets before beginning recall. Under certain conditio of the experiment the name provides an associative cue for iten on the list; under other conditions the name provides no such cu A comparison of recall with and without appropriate names su gests the extent to which Ss use such a device.

Procedure

The experiment was conducted in two phases. In one phase data on immediate free recall for lists of words were obtained. In the second phase free association norms were established with a new sample of Ss for the words used in the recall experiment. The specific procedures were as follows:

Immediate free recall

Eighteen lists of fifteen words each were used for the free recall tests. Six of the lists consisted of words frequently given as associations to particular Kent–Rosanoff stimuli. Each list consisted of high frequency response items to a single Kent–Rosanoff stimulus. Six lists consisted of low frequency associations to the same six stimuli, and six lists consisted entirely of words never given as associations to those stimuli. The association frequencies were determined from the Minnesota norms (5). The lists were all matched for Thorndike–Lorge frequency on the L count (6). Associated with each list was a list name. For half of the Ss the list name was the appropriate Kent–Rosanoff stimulus; for the remaining Ss the name was an irrelevant word matched in Thorndike–Lorge frequency with the appropriate Kent–Rosanoff word. All lists together with their names are shown in Table 1. These particular lists were chosen because preliminary data suggested a great range of variation in inter-item associative strength for the lists. Preliminary investigation had shown that in general high frequency response items to Kent–Rosanoff stimuli tend to elicit one another as free associates, while low and 'zero' frequency response items do not tend to elicit one another as free associates. Ss ($N = 144$) drawn from the Introductory Psychology course at the University of California, Berkeley, were divided into six groups of twenty-four Ss each. Each group of Ss was given two high frequency lists, two low frequency lists, and two zero frequency lists (as defined above). For half of the Ss the name given the list was relevant (although, of course, the relevancy of the name was of no significance for the zero frequency lists), and for half of the Ss the name given the list was irrelevant.

All Ss were tested in groups. The following instructions were given after introductory remarks: 'I will read a short list of words

Table 1

Word Lists Used

1. (Butterfly, Deliberate) H.F.* moth insect wing bird fly yellow net pretty flower bug cocoon color stomach blue bees.
2. (Butterfly, Deliberate) LF. garden sky flutter sunshine nature chase spring collection beautiful caterpillar summer light wasp colorful grace.
3. (Butterfly, Deliberate) ZF. book tutor government study early velvet winter payroll line zebra spray arrow help arithmetic typical
4. (Slow, Sold) HF. walk speed quick lazy drive skid run work fast down stop snail sign poke traffic.
5. (Slow, Sold) LF. go tortoise drag slide late crawl country motion dull steady caution stream halt sticky accident.
6. (Slow, Sold) ZF. home exactly step devotion morning wave fire paper improve cat glitter company weapon watch evening.
7. (Music, National) HF. art sweet play tone soft instrument symphony sing note song sound piano noise band horn.
8. (Music, National) LF. beautiful hear enjoyment ear nice fun co emotion string silence page charm ballet pretty drum.
9. (Music, National) ZF. determine person story depth projection desert body mood check headache mongrel rest attract for various.
10. (Whistle, Propose) HF. stop train noise sing blow tune sound d song shrill boy wolf loud mouth woman.
11. (Whistle, Propose) LF. ring ear low watch speech game sig fellow pierce talk tone teeth shout music referee.
12. (Whistle, Propose) ZF. plant nation kindly wish student chief na coat indication early forget opera position cut hat.
13. (Command, Contract) HF. general halt voice soldier harsh attention sharp navy order army obey officer performance tell shou
14. (Command, Contract) LF. firm head direct sword change stu agreement forward post repeat strong chief demand yell anarch
15. (Command, Contract) ZF. fight add oven shed class true libr report matter bank ordinary exhibit dollar tempo optimistic.
16. (Chair, Possible) HF. sofa wood cushion stool comfort rest pill rung table sit legs seat soft desk arm.
17. (Chair, Possible) LF. small paint straight study lazy cozy h couch modern upholstery glue high cloth relax rocker.
18. (Chair, Possible) ZF. lake ride tonight enemy subtract turtle theory legal family delicious low school race insurance.

* The two words at the beginning of each list in parenthesis are the appropriate inappropriate names for that list. The code HF refers to high frequency (associa appropriate name), LF to low frequency and ZF to zero frequency.

to you. You are to listen carefully to the words and try to remember them. Immediately after I read the list, I will say "begin" and you are to write down, in the order in which you remember them, as many of the words as you can. It is extremely unlikely that you will remember all of the words, but on some lists you will probably remember a good many, and on other lists you will remember few. For the first lists of words write the words in the first column. Then fold over this column and use the second column for the second list. If you are not sure about how to spell a word, write it down the best way you can. Each of the lists of words will have a name. I will read the name of the list first, and you are to write down the name of the list in the box at the top of each column before I begin reading the list. Do you understand?'

Word association tests

The use of inter-item associative strength as a variable in this experiment made it necessary to obtain free association norms for the words used in the recall experiment. Therefore, the words presented in Table 1 were given to fifty Ss drawn from the same population as those Ss used in the recall tests. Previous evidence showed that a group this size yielded stable norms (2). The instructions given to Ss in this part of the study were those used in obtaining the Minnesota norms for the Kent–Rosanoff words. The test consisted of 260 items administered in two forms of 130 items each. Half of the Ss received each form first. The results of the test were tabulated as the per cent frequency of every item in each list occurring as a free association to other items on the same list. These percentages were summed and averaged to obtain the index of inter-item associative strength. While the frequencies for any given item, particularly for low frequency responses, may be relatively unreliable, the inter-item association index itself is very stable (2).

Results

Number of items recalled

There is a larger number of items recalled for high frequency associates to Kent–Rosanoff stimuli than for low or zero frequency associates. However, the mean and standard deviations presented in Table 2 clearly show that giving to Ss the appropriate Kent–Rosanoff stimulus as a name has *no* effect upon the number of items recalled. If the Kent–Rosanoff stimulus had been effective when presented at the beginning of the list, it should have produced an interaction in Table 2 such that there would have been a difference in mean number of items recalled between the

Table 2

Means and Standard Deviations of Numbers of Items Recalled for High Frequency, Low Frequency, and Zero Frequency Lists of Associates to Appropriate List Name

	High frequency		Low frequency		Zero frequency	
	Mean	SD	Mean	SD	Mean	SD
Appropriate name	7·17	1·53	6·02	1·62	5·38	1·4
Inappropriate name	7·52	1·44	6·14	1·54	5·61	1·4

relevant and irrelevant name conditions for the high frequenc lists (and perhaps for the low frequency lists) but not for the ze frequency lists. No such interaction exists, however; in point fact, recall for Ss given irrelevant names is very slightly superic for all lists.

The failure of the stimulus name to make a difference in numb of items recalled suggests that the major variable associated wi the different numbers of items recalled for the three kinds of lis is the inter-item associative strength of the individual lists. direct examination of this variable can be seen in the correlati between the inter-item associative strength index and the numb of items recalled per list. For this correlation, the two conditic of list name were combined.

The number of items recalled per list is shown in column 2 Table 3, while the inter-item associative strength is shown column 1. The r between these variables is 0·88, significant beyond the 1 per cent level for 17 df. This relationship is consist with the clustering effects discovered by Jenkins, Mink a Russell (3) with particular pairs of associates. The conclusio

at the likelihood of a particular item's occurring in free recall is
function of the associative strength of that item to other items
the list. This conclusion, of course, may be extended to words
ot actually presented by *E* but occurring as intrusions (2).

able 3

ter-item Associative Strength, Items Recalled per *S*,
trusions per *S* and Commonality of Intrusions for All Lists

st		Inter-item assoc. strength	N *items recalled*	N *Intrusions*	Common-ality
tterfly	HF	28·3	7·9	0·18	17·27
tterfly	LF	4·3	6·7	0·33	6·43
tterfly	ZF	1·0	5·6	0·50	7·51
w	HF	15·1	6·5	0·40	5·80
w	LF	0·2	5·8	0·59	11·09
w	ZF	2·7	5·8	0·40	6·84
istle	HF	22·8	7·3	0·39	7·79
istle	LF	4·0	5·6	0·61	4·30
istle	ZF	2·3	5·4	0·60	2·70
sic	HF	20·5	7·7	0·21	9·09
sic	LF	9·3	6·1	1·14	3·70
sic	ZF	0·0	5·1	0·69	3·79
nmand	HF	13·0	7·1	0·13	23·61
nmand	LF	0·7	5·6	0·53	4·17
nmand	ZF	0·0	5·2	0·57	6·31
ir	HF	17·0	7·8	0·43	14·04
ir	LF	2·0	6·6	0·82	4·39
ir	ZF	0·0	6·1	0·39	5·88

a-list intrusions

adjusted mean number of extra-list intrusions per list occur-
in recall is shown in column 3 of Table 3. The adjustment
isted of multiplying all occurrences of the appropriate Kent–
noff stimulus as an intrusion by two. This was necessary
for half of the *S*s this word was artifically excluded as an
sion. The correlation between the adjusted mean intrusions
nter-item associative strength is -0.48, significant at between
per cent and the 1 per cent level. The correlation is materially

lowered by one list. This list consisted of low frequency associate to the Kent–Rosanoff word 'Music'. In the case of this list bot the inter-item associative strength and the frequency of intrusio were relatively high. This case is so deviant from the general re gression that it suggests this list may have unique properties. Thu while we may accept the generalization implied in the obtaine correlation, it can be applied to individual collections of iten only with caution.

The fourth column in Table 3 shows an index of commonali for the extra-list intrusions given by different Ss. This inde which can vary from 0 to 100, expresses as a percentage the ratio agreements in giving particular words as intrusions to the to number of possible agreements among all of the intrusions giv by different Ss. This index is independent of the absolute numt of intrusions, though its variance is not. The correlation betwe the commonality index and inter-item associative strength for different lists is 0·55, significant at approximately the 1 per c level. Thus, not only is there a tendency for the intrusions to somewhat less frequent for lists high in inter-item associat strength but also the intrusions given by different Ss tend m often to agree for such lists. This is in accord with other data The absolute frequency of intrusions is considerably higher, he ever, and the absolute degree of commonality for particu intrusions is considerably less than that expected on the basi earlier work (2).

Discussion

Despite ample evidence for the importance of verbal associat in the recall process, there are many undecided questions at the exact role these associations play. Two related questions cern (a) whether or not the associations occur as delibe mnemonic devices and (b) whether or not there is a selection cess after the association such that Ss reject some association emit others as items in recall. In general, these questions invo distinction as to whether associations in recall are primary o secondary mediated processes. The present data bear or adequacy of the alternate answers to these questions.

The possible influence of the list name upon recall is signif for the first question. The fact is that there is not an increase in recall frequency as a result of the availability of a list name which has high associative strength for the items on the list. Thus, it is clear that Ss in this study did not use an extra-list mnemonic device available to them. In view of their failure to use a well-labelled, high frequency associative device from outside of the list, it seems unlikely that they deliberately set about to improve recall by the use of considerably weaker intra-list associative connections. It is difficult to see how Ss would deliberately use a weaker associative mnemonic device from within the list rather than a stronger one readily available to them at the top of the recall data sheets.

Considerably more positive evidence bears on the question of selectivity after association has occurred. The greatest stumbling block to the view of association in recall as a primary, simple process of free association is the fact that recall is generally more appropriate or relevant than the purely associational view would seem to imply. Previous verbal associations that Ss bring into experiments on verbal processes are so strong and pervasive that is impossible to avoid them, even if it is desired. Despite these associations, however, the responses in free recall of English words are fairly well restricted to the items given to Ss in the original presentation. In the category clustering phenomenon, for example, extraneous intrusions are few, despite the fact that the items presented to Ss by no means exhaust the categories involved (1). Thus, it has seemed likely that Ss edit their associations before producing them as overt items in recall. This implies that Ss must have available to them a faint copy of the original material or the general context imported by the material originally presented against which they may judge the relevancy of their associations.

This assumption proves to be quite unnecessary for the present aim, however. In the present case it is only necessary to assume that Ss are able to reproduce from immediate memory a small set of items (the 'immediate memory span') and that to these items free associations occur, the strongest of which are emitted as responses in recall. It is not necessary to assume that Ss pick and choose among their associations. The appropriateness or inappropriateness of recall will be determined by the list of words itself. If the list is an 'organized' one (obtained, for example, by picking popular free associations to particular words, as was done in this experiment), the inter-item associations tend to converge on the items in the list and upon a few restricted responses outside of the list. If, on the other hand, the list of words is composed of items chosen randomly from the dictionary or a large word count there is no convergence on items in the list, and only by rare chance will two words on the list elicit the same response as a strong association. In this case the total number of responses in recall is reduced slightly because the scattered associations given by the items on the list cannot jointly reinforce any particular response enough to make intrusions occur frequently enough to offset poor recall of items on the list. Those intrusions that do occur should be, more often than not, popular associations to particular individual items on the list. Because the number of different popular associations is large (equal to the number of items on the list the most popular association defines popularity), the number of intrusions may be relatively large. Because these associations do not converge on common responses, however, the commonality of the intrusions will be low.

Thus, the results of the present study can be described by the assumption that recall consists of a small core of words directly available through immediate memory and of strong free associations to these. Recall is good or poor depending, then, upon the tendency of free associations from items within the list to converge upon other items within the list.

Will this assumption describe the results, say, of category clustering? It at least implies that frequency of intrusions (as well as tendency to cluster) will vary with inter-item associative strength within a category of items both within and without the list. Thus it is implied that category clustering depends upon associative strength and should vary with it. Bousfield (1) has argued for an interpretation of category clustering in terms of superordinate functions, and it is possible that such an interpretation may lead to conclusions quite different from those implied by the association hypothesis.

ummary

ists consisting of fifteen words each were presented to Ss for mmediate free recall. For each of the eighteen lists a measure of ter-item associative strength was obtained; this consisted of the erage relative frequency with which all items in a list tend to cit all other items on the list as free associates. Inter-item asso-tive strength was positively correlated (0·88) with the number words recalled per list, negatively correlated (− 0·48) with the mber of extra-list intrusions in recall, and positively correlated 55) with the commonality of the extra-list intrusions that did :ur. In general, these results are consistent with an interpreta-n of free recall in terms of free association. Free association, as ccurs in recall, is probably a direct, unmediated activity with le or no active editing of the material being recalled. The data intrusions from the present experiment are consistent with the umption of lack of editing. The fact that Ss in the present ex-iment gave no evidence of using an extra-list associative emonic device made available to them suggests that the free ociation from item to item in recall is not the result of Ss' ructing themselves to free associate in order to increase recall.

rences

'. A. BOUSFIELD, 'The occurrence of clustering in the recall of ndomly arranged associates', Journal of General Psychology, vol. 49 953), pp. 229–40.

DEESE, 'On the prediction of occurrence of particular verbal trusions in immediate recall', Journal of Experimental Psychology, l. 58 (1959), pp. 17–22.

J. JENKINS, W. D. MINK and W. A. RUSSELL, 'Associative ustering as a function of verbal association strength', Psychological port, vol. 4 (1958), pp. 127–36.

J. JENKINS and W. A. RUSSELL, 'Associative clustering during :all', Journal of Abnormal and Social Psychology, vol. 47 (1952), pp. 8–21.

A. RUSSELL and J. J. JENKINS, The Complete Minnesota Norms Response to 100 Words from the Kent–Rosanoff Association Test, chnology Report No. 11, Office of Naval Research and University Minnesota.

L. THORNDIKE and I. LORGE, The Teacher's Word Book of 000 Words, Bureau of Publications, Teacher's College, Columbia iversity, 1944.

15 W. A. Bousfield, B. H. Cohen and G. A. Whitmarsh

Associative Clustering in the Recall of Words of Different Taxonomic Frequencies of Occurrence

W. A. Bousfield, B. H. Cohen and G. A. Whitmarsh, 'Associative cluster ing in the recall of words of different taxonomic frequencies of occurrenc *Psychological Reports*, vol. 4 (1958), pp. 39–44.

Associative clustering may be defined as the occurrence sequences of related words in the recall of a randomized stimu word list. As indicated in an earlier study (3), the operations inducing and measuring clustering have typically involved following steps: (a) the compiling of two or more sub-lists equal lengths, of words with each sub-list representing words i different taxonomic category; (b) the randomization of all words thus chosen to form a stimulus list; (c) the presentatior the stimulus list for learning; (d) the obtaining of free rec (e) the analysis of the recalled words to determine the incide of clusters of two or more words falling in the same taxono category. The unit for the measurement of clustering is a rej tion which is defined as a sequence of two words in the s; operational category. In applying this measure, the numbe repetitions in a cluster is designated as one less than the numbe words in the cluster.

The convention established in the original study of cluste (1) was to rely upon E's judgement for the choice of words in operational categories. To equate the response strengths of words in the specified categories use was made of the Thornc Lorge (7) frequencies of usage. It was assumed that both the r and the range of the frequencies of the words in each cate should be similar. The feasibility of these operations was der strated in a study (2) employing two stimulus lists with the : categories in each. One comprised words with relatively Thorndike–Lorge frequencies and the other words with rela low Thorndike–Lorge frequencies. The data indicated a si cant difference in both clustering and the number of v recalled in favor of the list with the higher frequencies.

W. A. Bousfield, B. H. Cohen and G. A. Whitmarsh

The present study was based on the choice of words selected from the tables of Cohen, Bousfield and Whitmarsh (4). These tables comprise taxonomic norms obtained on the following basis. Ss were given mimeographed forms on which appeared forty-three classes of items (categories) such as *a fish, a type of human dwelling, an insect*, etc. Each class of items was followed by four blank spaces. Ss were instructed to list the first four specific items which occurred to them for each class of items. Data were collected from 200 male and 200 female undergraduate students at the University of Connecticut. Since each S gave four responses, the total number of responses to any one category was 600, i.e. 800 male responses and 800 female responses. Frequencies of occurrence of the various responses to a class of items were tabulated. In general, the method of collecting these forms was similar to that used in the Minnesota revision of the Kent–Rosanoff Word Association Test (6) but with two exceptions: (a) Ss were required to give associates to specified classes of items rather than to specific stimulus words; (b) for each item, Ss were required to give four associates rather than one.

Method

Stimulus items and apparatus

Eight categories of verbal items were chosen from the taxonomic norms of Cohen, Bousfield and Whitmarsh (4). Four of these categories were identical with those used in an earlier study (2), namely, *animals, vegetables, names* and *professions*. The other four categories chosen were *birds, countries, cloths* and *musical instruments*. From each category, ten frequently occurring and ten infrequently occurring items were chosen. In this manner four lists of stimulus words were constructed. Each list comprised ten words in each of four categories as follows: List I, ten high frequency words from the *animals, names, vegetables* and *professions* categories, (ANVP-high); List II, ten high frequency words from the *birds, cloths, countries* and *musical instruments* categories, (BCCM-high); List III, ten low frequency words from the *animals, names, vegetables* and *professions* categories, (ANVP-low); and List IV, ten low frequency words from the *birds, cloths, countries* and *musical instruments* categories,

(BCCM-low). The stimulus word lists are shown in Table 1. Also presented in Table 1 are the geometric means of the frequencies of occurrence of the verbal items for each list. The words of each list were randomized and a separate 2×2 in slide was prepared for each word. The slides were exposed singly in their randomized order by means of a Selectroslide projector at 2·5-sec intervals.

Table 1
Stimulus Word Lists

ANVP-*High*

Animals	f	Vegetables	f	Names	f	Professions	f
dog	369	carrot	240	John	189	doctor	3
cat	326	pea	199	Bob	105	lawyer	1
horse	209	potato	175	Joe	79	professor	
cow	164	bean	118	Bill	69	dentist	
bear	66	corn	112	Jim	54	teacher	
lion	48	lettuce	93	Tom	48	reverend	
deer	47	spinach	90	Richard	39	nurse	
fox	33	squash	62	George	38	engineer	
rabbit	33	cabbage	51	Jack	31	carpenter	
tiger	30	turnip	38	Frank	27	salesman	

Geometric mean = 74·7

ANVP-*Low*

Animals	f	Vegetables	f	Names	f	Professions
wolf	16	radish	15	Michael	12	accountant
squirrel	10	cauliflower	13	Arthur	11	farmer
leopard	6	cucumber	12	Carl	10	banker
raccoon	4	pepper	7	Harold	7	chemist
donkey	3	parsnip	2	Stephen	7	plumber
zebra	3	pumpkin	2	Ralph	5	mechanic
beaver	2	mushroom	1	Philip	5	painter
kangaroo	1	artichoke	1	Walter	2	butcher
buffalo	1	melon	1	Bernard	1	grocer
camel	1	yam	1	Dennis	1	janitor

Geometric mean = 3·5

Table 1—*Continued*

BCCM-*High*

Birds	f	Cloths	f	Countries	f	Musical instruments	f
robin	344	cotton	330	France	224	piano	286
sparrow	190	wool	270	England	214	violin	214
bluejay	160	silk	249	Germany	134	trumpet	175
canary	72	rayon	149	Russia	111	clarinet	106
crow	70	nylon	109	Spain	81	flute	94
wren	54	linen	108	Canada	76	trombone	53
eagle	53	satin	64	Italy	66	oboe	47
oriole	42	dacron	40	Mexico	43	harp	42
hawk	35	orlon	35	Japan	35	guitar	40
parrot	31	velvet	25	Sweden	26	cello	35

Geometric mean = 84·3

CCM-*Low*

Birds	f	Cloths	f	Countries	f	Musical instruments	f
pigeon	17	flannel	12	Scotland	16	bugle	12
owl	12	muslin	11	Poland	14	banjo	11
ark	10	gingham	9	Egypt	8	bassoon	9
dove	7	corduroy	9	Holland	7	fife	9
chickadee	6	burlap	7	Belgium	7	piccolo	8
ostrich	4	denim	4	Finland	7	cornet	7
falcon	3	chintz	3	Greece	4	harmonica	5
peacock	3	calico	3	Turkey	2	lute	2
lark	2	poplin	1	Denmark	2	mandolin	2
penguin	1	khaki	1	Cuba	1	zither	1

Geometric mean = 4·8

Procedure

Four groups of undergraduate students in psychology served as Ss. They were randomly assigned to the four stimulus lists as follows: List I, eighty-four Ss; List II, eighty Ss; List III, seventy-six Ss; and List IV, seventy-two Ss.

The instructions to all groups of Ss were identical. Briefly, they were told that a list of words would be projected one at a time on the screen in front of the room. After completion of the projection, they were to write down as many of the words as they could recall in the order in which the words occurred to them. Blank sheets of paper were distributed to Ss to use in writing the words they could recall. After completion of the projection of the words, E gave the signal to start writing. Ss were allowed 5 min for recall.

Table 2

Means and Standard Deviations of Recalls and Ratios of Repetition with Critical Ratios of the Differences Between Means

Recall

| | ANVP *categories* | | BCCM *categories* | |
	High	Low	High	Low
Mean	23·67	17·37	25·99	20·10
SD	5·22	3·56	4·64	3·86
CR		8·87		8·54
N	84	71	80	72

Ratio of repetition

| | ANVP *categories* | | BCCM *categories* | |
	High	Low	High	Low
Mean	0·516	0·404	0·574	0·496
SD	0·208	0·175	0·200	0·167
CR		3·64		2·61
N	84	71	80	72

Results

For each S two scores were recorded: first, the total number words recalled from the stimulus word list (n), and second, ratio of the number of repetitions of words belonging in the sa category (r) to the total number of words recalled minus ($n - 1$). This ratio, $r/(n - 1)$, is referred to as the *ratio of rep tion*.[1] The rationale of this ratio as a measure of clustering is

1. This ratio is one of the simpler of the measures of associative cluste Its distribution is approximately normal for four-category lists. The re for using $n - 1$ in the denominator derives from the fact that in no cas the first word in a recall sequence be counted as a repetition.

ussed in an earlier study (5). Table 2 gives a general summary of
ιe data for both the number of words recalled and clustering as
ιeasured by the ratio of repetition. The critical ratios are for the
ifferences between the means. A critical ratio of 2·58 would be
ignificant at the 0·01 level. All the ratios exceed this level.

iscussion

is evident that significant differences in both recall and cluster-
ɡ were obtained from the use of frequently occurring and in-
·quently occurring items selected from the taxonomic norms of
ɔhen, Bousfield and Whitmarsh (4). These norms may be
·d to indicate the readiness with which various words are
ociated with the specified categories. Our findings imply that
more readily Ss can categorize groups of words, the more
dily will the words be recalled and the greater will be organiza-
ι of recall. In considering these conclusions the question
es of the relationship between two methods of appraising the
ɔonse strengths of words selected for the categories of stimulus
used for measuring associative clustering. Thorndike–Lorge
frequencies of usage were employed in the earlier studies,
·reas the present study employed what we have termed taxo-
ιic frequencies with which the words are associated with
ified categories. If we can regard the Thorndike–Lorge
:uencies as indices of what may be termed the gross response
ιgths of words, it may be supposed that in general, words
high gross response strengths would be favored when Ss are
·d to associate words with specified categories; conversely,
ls with low gross strengths would be less favored. With the
ɔ associate words with categories, Ss would be expected to
: from words made available to them in part on the basis of
gross strengths. It would follow that there should be some
ε of positive correlation between the results obtained from
ɔe of these two methods for selecting stimulus words. As a
·d test of this assumption we recorded the Thorndike–
· frequencies of the words comprising our four stimulus lists.
:eometric means of these frequencies along with the geo-
: means derived from the taxonomic norms appear in
3 along with the means of the recalls and of the ratios of

repetition. It may be seen from inspection that the Thorndike Lorge frequencies are indeed greater for the high taxonomic fre quency forms of the ANVP and BCCM stimulus lists than fo the low taxonomic frequency forms of these lists. It may also b seen that both the mean recall scores and the mean clusterin scores are in a perfectly ordered relationship to the geometr

Table 3

Mean Recalls and Mean Ratios of Repetition as Functions of the Means of the Taxonomic and Thorndike–Lorge Frequencies of the Stimulus Words

Stimulus word list	Geometric mean of taxonomic frequencies	Geometric mean of T–L frequencies	Mean recall	Mean ratio o repeti
ANVP-high	74·7	38·9	23·67	0·516
ANVP-low	3·5	9·4	17·37	0·404
BCCM-high	84·3	13·0	25·99	0·574
BCCM-low	4·8	5·6	20·10	0·496

means of the taxonomic frequencies. On the other hand, ordering of these means in relationship to the geometric mear the Thorndike–Lorge frequencies of the items of the stim lists is somewhat discrepant. It should be noted, however, tha direct comparisons can be made between the Thorndike–L and the taxonomic frequencies.

It appears safe to conclude that the taxonomic norms of Co Bousfield, and Whitmarsh may be used for selection of stin words for studies of associative clustering. Furthermore, are some grounds for assuming that the taxonomic frequenci measures of the response strengths of words used for studi associative clustering are probably preferable to the Thorn Lorge frequencies of usage.

Summary

This study was planned as a test of the validity of the taxon norms of Cohen, Bousfield, and Whitmarsh. These norms cate the cultural frequencies with which a large sample associated various verbal items with specified categories of objects. Words were selected from these norms to represent 2 groups of categories: (a) *animals, names, professions, vegetables;* and (b) *birds, cloths, countries, musical instruments.* For each group of categories 2 stimulus word lists were prepared, one comprising items having high taxonomic frequencies and the other comprising items having low taxonomic frequencies. For each stimulus word list the words representing the specified categories were equated in terms of their taxonomic frequencies. The experiment made use of the 4-word lists for the measurement of associative clustering and recall, each list being given to a different group of Ss. Analyses of the data show that the lists comprising items with high taxonomic frequencies induced significantly more clustering and recall than the lists made up of words with low taxonomic frequencies. The findings were interpreted as indicating that the more readily Ss can categorize groups of words, the more readily will the words be recalled and the greater will be the organization of the recall.

References

W. A. BOUSFIELD, 'The occurrence of clustering in the recall of randomly arranged associates', *Journal of General Psychology*, vol. 49 (1953), pp. 229–40.

W. A. BOUSFIELD and B. H. COHEN, 'The occurrence of clustering in the recall of randomly arranged words of different frequencies-of-usage', *Journal of General Psychology*, vol. 52 (1955), pp. 83–95.

W. A. BOUSFIELD and B. H. COHEN, 'Clustering in recall as a function of the number of word-categories in stimulus-words lists', *Journal of General Psychology*, vol. 54 (1956), pp. 95–106.

B. H. COHEN, W. A. BOUSFIELD and G. A. WHITMARSH, *Cultural Norms for Verbal Items in 43 Categories*, Technical Report No. 22, University of Connecticut, 1957.

B. H. COHEN, J. M. SAKODA and W. A. BOUSFIELD, *The Statistical Analysis of the Incidence of Clustering in the Recall of Randomly Arranged Associates*, Technical Report No. 10, University of Connecticut, 1954.

W. A. RUSSELL and J. J. JENKINS, *The Complete Minnesota Norms for Responses to 100 words from the Kent–Rosanoff Word Association Test*, Technical Report No. 11, University of Minnesota, 1954.

E. L. THORNDIKE and I. LORGE, *The Teacher's Word Book of 30,000 Words*, Teacher's College, Columbia University, 1944.

16 E. Tulving

The Effect of Alphabetical Subjective Organization on Memorizing Unrelated Words

E. Tulving, 'The effect of alphabetical subjective organization on memorizing unrelated words', *Canadian Journal of Psychology*, vol. 16 (1962), pp. 185–91.

This paper reports an experimental demonstration of the effect of subjective organization on memorizing unrelated words. Subjective organization refers to subjects' tendency to recall in an invariant order verbal items presented in varying orders from trial to trial. It has been discussed and a method for its measurement has been described elsewhere (Tulving, 1962).

There is some evidence (Tulving, 1961; 1962) that subjective organization and frequency of correct responses are positively correlated: subjects who achieve high scores on subjective organization recall more words than subjects with low organization scores, and increasing recall over trials is accompanied by increasing organization. While it seems plausible enough to assume that such a correlation between the two response variables results from the effect of organization on performance, alternative interpretations are not excluded. One could argue, for instance, that organization and performance are two parallel, but independent manifestations of 'intelligence'. Thus, more intelligent subjects might not only organize their recall more systematically than subjects of lower intelligence, but also recall more words. Nor do other experiments, in which recall is shown to be a function of organization inherent in the material (for example Bousfield, 1953; Miller and Selfridge, 1950), provide unequivocal evidence as to the nature of the relation between the two variables. When learning materials differ in degree of organization, they may also differ in other variables relevant to ease of learning.

A more direct approach to the problem involves experimental manipulation of subjective organization independently of changes in learning materials or conditions of practice. If under these conditions changes in organization lead to changes in per formance, the latter variable can be said to be dependent on the former. The experiment reported in this paper used this general approach.

The design of the experiment was simple. Two groups of subjects learned identical material under identical conditions of presentation and recall, but under different sets of instructions. One group was told to recall as many words as possible, the other group was given instructions to organize their recall alphabetically.

Method

Subjects

Ninety-nine second-year, pre-medical students enrolled in an introductory psychology course served as Ss. The experiment was conducted as a part of the regular classroom procedure.

Materials

A list of twenty-two English nouns, covering a wide range of frequency of occurrence values, constituted the learning material for both groups. The words, listed alphabetically, were: answer, buyer, cherub, despot, ether, fasces, gorget, hermit, journal, ker, mantel, natron, orphan, person, question, rennin, satin, tapest, umbra, vulture, windrow, and xylem. As can be seen, all words were five- to seven-letter disyllables, and no two words had the same initial letter.

Procedure

Prior to the experiment, each S received a set of twelve recording slips with twenty-two consecutively numbered lines, and a folded sheet. The latter contained additional instructions. The Ss were not to look at these sheets.

The instructions given to all Ss before the first trial informed them that their task was to memorize a list of twenty-two nouns which would be projected one by one on the screen in front of the room. After all twenty-two words had been shown, they were to record as many of the words as possible on the first recording slip. Then, when time was called by E, they were to draw a line under the last word they had recorded, place the slip, face down,

under the pile of other slips, and be ready for the next trial. Th
Ss were also informed that there were no restrictions on the orde
in which they recalled the words, their main task was to recall a
many words on each trial as possible.

Words were projected with a Kodak Cavalcade 520 projecto
at the rate of approximately 1·5 sec per word. The Ss had 90 se
after each trial to record their recall. The order of words in th
stimulus list was changed after each trial in a non-systemat
manner. A total of eleven trials was given.

Differential instructions

All Ss worked under identical instructions for the first three tria
After the Ss had finished recording their recall following the th
trial, E asked them to look at the folded instruction sheets. F
one-half of the total group, hereafter called the Standard (
Group, the instructions were: 'This is just to inform you that y
have been assigned to the experimental group "S". You shou
simply continue as before, trying to do your very best on ea
recall trial and put down as many words from the list as you ca

For the other half of the Ss, hereafter referred to as the Alp
betical (A) Group, the instruction sheets contained the followi
'Try to organize your recalled words alphabetically. When
look at the words on the screen, note their first letters, and m
an attempt to associate the word with the letter. When you w
the words down, go through the letters of the alphabet one
time and try to remember the word that goes with each lette

30 sec were given Ss to read these additional instructions.

Results

In this experiment we were interested in comparing the
formance of two groups of subjects distinguished in terms o
organization of recall. The differential instructions given to
groups were designed to produce clear-cut differences in orga
tion. For some reason, seven subjects in the A group did no
low instructions and did not organize their recall alphabetic
In the light of the primary objective of the experiment it
decided to exclude their data from the analysis. For the
reason the data of two subjects in the S group, who had orga

heir recall alphabetically, were also omitted from consideration.
To equalize and round off the numbers in the two groups, the
recall records of forty subjects in each were randomly selected for
analysis from among the remaining subjects.

Figure 1 shows the learning curves for the two groups. On the
abscissa are eleven trials, on the ordinate the mean number of
words correctly recalled.

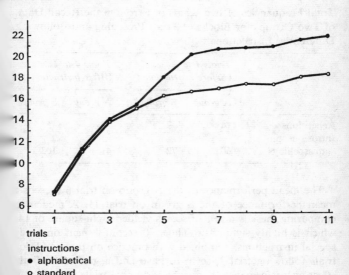

trials

instructions
● alphabetical
○ standard

Figure 1 Mean number of words recalled as a function of trials. Each
curve is based on an independent group of forty subjects. Immediately
preceding trial 4, different instructions were given to the two groups

For the first three trials, when both groups worked under
identical standard instructions, the curves are very similar. Thus
there seem to be no systematic differences between the two
groups as to their learning 'ability'. On trial 4, immediately after
the differential instructions were given, there still is no obvious
difference in performance. Beginning with trial 5, however, the
two curves draw rapidly apart. The slopes of the curves are quite
different between trials 4 and 6. It seems reasonable to assume

that the upper limit imposed on performance by the length of the list attenuates the score of the A group on later trials. With longer lists, the advantage of the Alphabetical Group over the Standard Group may well be greater than it was in this experiment.

Table 1

Total Frequencies of two Kinds of Errors in the Recall Data of Two Groups for Blocks of Trials Preceding and Following Differential Instructions

	Trials 1 to 3 (Before instructions)		Trials 4 to 11 (After instructions)	
	A group	S group	A group	S group
Repetitions	14	9	0	55
Intrusions and misspellings	60	72	41	103

The mean performance of the A group on trial 6 exceeds the mean performance of the S group on trial 11. A median test comparing these two sets of scores yielded a chi-square of 14 which is highly significant. Thus, 30 seconds spent on reading special instructions, combined with practice on three additional trials following trial 3, seem to have had a greater facilitating effect on performance than eight additional trials in the absence of special organizing instructions. It should also be mentioned that on trial 11 the perfect score of twenty-two correct was achieved by thirty-seven subjects in the A group, but only 5 subjects in the S group.

An analysis of the erroneous responses reflected a similar difference in favour of the A group. Table 1 shows the total frequencies of two kinds of errors: (a) repetitions of list words within a trial, and (b) misspellings and extra-list intrusions. The data are shown separately for the blocks of the first three and last eight trials.

It is difficult to evaluate the data in Table 1 statistically, since the frequencies are combined for subjects and trials. The uencies of errors are too small to justify a more detailed breakown. These error data, however, do suggest that alphabetical rganization completely eliminates repetitions and considerably educes the probability of other errors.

No attempt was made in this experiment to examine the sequenal organization in the recall records of the S group. It is well nown that the order of immediate free recall is related to the robability of recall of individual items (Bousfield, Cohen and lva, 1956), to the organization inherent in the material (Bousld, 1953; Deese and Kaufman, 1957; Rothkopf and Coke, 61), and to the instructions as to the order of recall (Deese, 57). Previous research at Toronto has also sufficiently demonated that subjects tend to subjectively organize recall of experintally unorganized materials even in the absence of any specific structions to do so (Arbuckle, 1961; Marshall, 1961; Tulving, 51; 1962). Organization of recall, therefore, undoubtedly curred in the S group of this experiment, but in view of the viously reported findings it need not be elaborated in the sent context. The experimentally produced difference between two groups clearly was not that between alphabetical anization and no organization, but rather between alphaical organization and other, apparently less effective, forms of anization. This fact, however, does not change the main conion drawn from the experiment: performance is a function of iective organization.

cussion

ious experiments (Tulving, 1961; 1962) have shown that ated presentations and attempts at free recall have at least readily observable consequences. First, the frequency of ect responses increases systematically over trials – subjects n' the material. Second, the tendency to recall items in the order from trial to trial also increases – subjects 'organize' naterial. When repetition is held constant, a positive coron between learning and organization is found. A plausible nation of these concomitant effects is that changes in perance are dependent upon changes in organization. The main se of this experiment was to test an implication of this explanation and thereby clarify the relation between the two variables.

The findings of the experiment leave little doubt that subjective organization is an important determinant of performance in free recall learning. The superiority of performance of subjects who organized their recall alphabetically over that of those who used different, apparently less powerful methods of organizing was both large and obvious. In the light of this finding it is entirely reasonable to assume that correlations between performance and subjective organization, under conditions where methods of organizing are not under the experimenter's control, reflect nothing more nor less than the same functional relation demonstrated in this experiment.

The experiment and its findings have several implications for theory and research in the field of verbal learning and memory. On the theoretical side, the results of the experiment add further support to Miller's conceptual analysis of remembering (Miller, 1956a and b; Miller, Galanter and Pribram, 1960) which holds that improvement in recall under conditions of practice, and of sequentially structured materials (for example, Miller and Selfridge, 1950), is a consequence of organization of initially unrelated items into larger units of information. In view of the present results as well as the results from previous studies (Tulving, 1962; Tulving and Patkau, 1962) Miller's unitization hypothesis can be regarded as a very promising beginning of comprehensive theory of memory.

Implications of the present experiment for research have to do with the problem of individual differences and the problem of the effect of repetition on recall. Consider again the two learning curves shown in Figure 1. Remember that all subjects learned identical material under identical conditions of practice. Now suppose that differences in organization between the two groups are not known, as would in fact be the case in most experiments in verbal learning. Under these conditions most researchers would probably interpret the differences between the two groups of subjects in terms of their learning 'ability': there are 'fast' learners and 'slow' learners. The tendency may also be strong to attempt to understand these between subject differences in terms of their psychometric correlates (Noble, 1961). As we do in know about the underlying differences in organization in this experiment, these remarks are admittedly irrelevant. But they are possibly quite relevant to other experiments in which subjective organization has been neither manipulated nor measured. It is quite reasonable to assume that in those experiments, too, a certain proportion of between subject variability, perhaps a large proportion, is attributable to variability in methods of organization. It follows that if we wish to add to our understanding of 'individual differences' in learning 'ability', a good place to begin looking for the source of these differences is the learner's own behaviour in the learning situation and his subjective strategies of remembering.

As to the effects of repetition on recall, the two learning curves in Figure 1 are again instructive. It is obvious that the curves reflect much more than the effects of repetition or practice, even if we limit the question about these effects entirely to the given material under the given conditions of learning. One could say, for instance, that the learning curve of the S group reflects not only the effects of repetition, but also the effects of the subjects' ignorance of effective methods of organizing the material. Because of such an intimate relation between repetition and organization, the specification of the effects of repetition on recall necessarily involves the specification of the methods of organization that the subject uses. That is, because of the interaction between repetition and methods of organization, there may be no such thing as a 'pure' effect of repetition. The limiting case of such a hypothesized interaction is the situation in which no subjective organization of any kind is possible. Under these conditions, repetition would have no effect on recall. It is very probable, of course, that with normal adult human beings as subjects, subjective organization cannot ever be completely prevented. But other implications of the hypothesized relation between repetition and organization do pose new and interesting problems for research.

Summary

A demonstration experiment has been reported on the effect of alphabetical subjective organization on memorizing words. Two groups of Ss learned an identical list of twenty-two nouns on eleven trials. After the first three trials one group was instructed to organize recall alphabetically, while the other group proceeded under standard instructions to recall as many words as possible. A considerable difference in the rate of learning favouring the alphabetical organization group was discussed in terms of the role of subjective organization in memorizing. The experimental findings have implications for the problem of individual differences in learning and the problem of the effect of repetition on recall.

References

ARBUCKLE, T. Y. (1961), 'The role of meaningfulness and subjective organization in verbal learning and retention', *Unpublished M.A. thesis, University of Toronto.*

BOUSFIELD, W. A. (1953), 'The occurrence of clustering in the recall of randomly arranged associates', *Journal of General Psychology.*, vol. 49, pp. 229–40.

BOUSFIELD, W. A., COHEN, B. H., and SILVA, J. G. (1956), 'The extension of Marbe's law to the recall of stimulus-words', *American Journal of Psychology.*, vol. 69, pp. 429–33.

DEESE, J. (1957), 'Serial organization in the recall of disconnected items', *Psychology Report.*, vol. 3, pp. 577–82.

DEESE, J., and KAUFMAN, R. A. (1957), 'Serial effects in recall of unorganized and sequentially organized verbal material', *Journal of Experimental Psychology*, vol. 54, pp. 180–87.

MARSHALL, M. A. (1961), 'The development of subjective organization in verbal learning as a function of the time available to learn', *Unpublished M.A. thesis, University of Toronto.*

MILLER, G. A. (1956a), 'The magical number seven, plus or minus two: some limits on our capacity for processing information', *Psychological Review*, vol. 63, pp. 81–97.

MILLER, G. A., (1956b), 'Human memory and the storage of information', *IRE Transactions on Information Theory*, vol. IT-2, pp. 129–37.

MILLER, G. A., and SELFRIDGE, J. A. (1950), 'Verbal context and the recall of meaningful material', *American Journal of Psychology*, vol. 63, pp. 176–85.

MILLER, G. A., GALANTER, E., and PRIBRAM, K. H. (1960), *Plans and the Structure of Behavior*, Holt.

NOBLE, C. E. (1961), 'Verbal learning and individual differences', C. N. Cofer, ed., *Verbal Learning and Verbal Behavior*, McGraw-Hill, pp. 132–46.

ROTHKOPF, E., and COKE, E. U. (1961), 'The prediction of free recall from word association norms', *Journal of Experimental Psychology*, vol. 62, pp. 433–8.

TULVING, E. (1961), 'Subjective organization and the anatomy of the learning curve in free recall of "unrelated" words', *Paper presented at the meeting of the Canadian Psychological Association, Montreal, June.*

TULVING, E. (1962), 'Subjective organization in free recall of "unrelated" words', *Psychological Review*, vol. 69, pp. 344–54.

TULVING, E., and PATKAU, J. E. (1962), 'Concurrent effects of contextual constraint and word frequency on immediate recall and learning of verbal material', *Canadian Journal of Psychology*, vol. 16, pp. 83–95.

17 G. A. Miller and J. A. Selfridge

Verbal Context and the Recall of Meaningful Material

G. A. Miller and J. A. Selfridge, 'Verbal context and the recall of meaningful material', *American Journal of Psychology*, vol. 63 (1950), pp. 176–85.

Communicative behavior, perhaps more than any of man's other activities, depends upon patterning for its significance and usefulness. An accidental inversion of words or letters or sound can produce grotesque alterations of a sentence, and to scramble the elements at random is to turn a sensible message into gibberish. No attack upon the problems of verbal behavior will be satisfactory if it does not take quantitative account of the pattern of verbal elements.

We can dependably produce and distinguish only a small number of different letters or speech sounds. We must use these few elements to talk about millions of different things and situations. To stretch these few elements to cover these many needs we are forced to combine the elements into patterns and to assign a different significance to each pattern. Since the number of possible patterns increases exponentially as the length of the pattern increases, this proves to be an efficient method of solving the problem.

Not all the possible patterns of elements are used in any particular language. In English, for example, the sequence of letters *qke* does not occur. It is reasonable to ask, therefore, why we do not exploit the available patterns more effectively. Is it not more efficient to ignore some patterns while others are greatly overworked?

The preference for some patterns at the expense of others forces us to produce more elements – letters, sounds, words, etc. – in order to make the same number of distinctions that we could make with the same elements if we used all possible patterns. To illustrate: imagine a language with ten elementary symbols that is used to refer to 100 different things, events or situations we used all possible pairs of elements, we could refer to every one of the 100 things with one of the 100 pairs of ten symbols. If, however, we refuse to use some of the pairs and so rule them out of the language, it is necessary to make up the difference by using triads. Thus the language uses patterns of three elements to make distinctions that could be made with patterns of two elements.

On further consideration, however, this kind of inefficiency does not appear a complete waste of time. By favoring some patterns rather than others the language is protected against error (Shannon, 1948). More specifically, in English we recognize immediately that an error has occurred if we read in our newspaper, 'Man bites dxg'. The pattern *dxg* is not admitted in English, and so we catch the error. If, however, all patterns of elements were admissable, *dxg* would have some semantic rule and we would not be able to catch the mistake. The number system is an example of the efficient use of ten symbols, but it is highly susceptible to mechanical errors. If a man says that his telephone number is 9236 we have no way of recognizing that he has or has not made an error.

Patterns are unavoidable, and a preference for some patterns provides insurance against errors. Thus it seems reasonable that the statistical studies of different languages all show that some patterns of elements are greatly overworked while others occur rarely or not at all (Zipf, 1949). The present interest in verbal patterning, however, is in the light these observations can throw on the psychological problem of verbal context.

Verbal Context

Psychologists use the word context to refer to the totality of conditions influencing a behavioral event. For the present discussion want to restrict this broad definition and to consider only the antecedent verbal conditions. When a man talks, his choice of words depends upon his training, his needs and intentions, the situation and audience. These factors comprise the total context which his words must be studied. By verbal context, as opposed total context, we mean only the extent to which the prior occurrence of certain verbal elements influences the talker's present choice. If the talker has said 'children like to', his choice for the next word in this pattern is considerably limited – *elephant*, *punished*, *loud*, *Bill*, and many other words are highly unlikely continuations.

By verbal context, therefore, we mean the extent to which the choice of a particular word depends upon the words that precede it. In the statistical sense, this definition of verbal context is given in terms of dependent probabilities (Miller and Frick, 1949). The probability that event C will occur is not the same after A as it is after B. The statistical dependencies between successive units form the basis for a study of verbal context.

To illustrate the operation of conditional probabilities in our verbal behavior, consider the set of all possible sequences ten letters long. We could construct a table listing them. The first row of the table would be the pattern *aaaaaaaaaa*, ten consecutive *a*s. The second would be *aaaaaaaaab*, then *aaaaaaaab*, *aaaaaaaabb*, *aaaaaaabaa*, etc., until all possible arrangements of letters, spaces, commas, periods, hyphens, quotes, colons, numbers, etc., were exhausted. Altogether there would be about fifty different symbols, and the table would contain 50^{10}, or about 100,000,000,000,000,000 different patterns. Then we would examine some English writing and try to determine the relative frequencies of occurrence of the patterns. Only a small fraction of the 50^{10} alternatives actually occur in English. The table would show strong dependencies. For example, the letter *q* is always followed in English by the letter *u*, and so all those entries in the table that contained a *q* followed by anything but *u* would not occur in English. It is not possible to predict the relative frequency of *qe*, for instance, by multiplying the relative frequency of *q* and of *e*.

If such a table existed, along with the relative frequencies of occurrence, it would be possible to construct sequences of letters that reflected the statistical dependencies of English verbal patterns. We can imagine similar tables constructed for shorter or longer sequences of letters. A table for all patterns of two symbols would represent the relative frequencies of pairs; for three symbols, triads, etc. The longer the sequence, the more information the table contains about the pattern of dependencies in our molar verbalizations.

To illustrate the use of such information we shall borrow a device used by Shannon. Suppose we have no knowledge at all of the relative frequencies of occurrence, but only a list of the fifty different symbols. Then, for all we know, any sequence of symbols might be permissible. If we tried to construct a message in the language, the best we could do would be to draw at random from the fifty different symbols. We have no reason to think that one sequence of symbols is more likely than another. Proceeding in ignorance to construct a message, we might produce something like this: *cplp'rzw(p".:k!)"ntegznqO ?i6vlaur :8h*, etc.

Now suppose that we have a reliable tabulation of the relative frequencies of 'patterns' of one symbol. We know, therefore, that *e* and the space between words are more likely to occur than *?* and *z*. With this information we can increase the chance of constructing a meaningful message, although our chances are still very small. If we draw successive symbols according to their relative frequencies of occurrence in English, we might produce something like this: *wli bnrooye lricocnri mae c zg 2eaya*, etc.

The next step is to imagine that we have a tabulation of relative frequencies of occurrence of patterns of two symbols. Now it is possible to improve the statistical approximation to English by drawing in the following way. Begin by drawing any likely pair. Suppose the pair is *au*. Now look at all the pairs starting with *u* and draw from them according to their relative frequencies of occurrence. Suppose the result is *ud*. Now look at all pairs starting with *d* and draw one of those, and so proceed to build up the message. Notice that each draw depends upon the preceding draw – the preceding draw determines from which set the present draw is to be made. Drawing in this way reflects the conditional probabilities of successive symbols. A message constructed in this way might read *aud ren stiofivo omerk. thed thes bllale*, etc.

If we have a tabulation of sequences of three letters, we can construct a message that reflects the conditional probabilities of English triads. First we draw a likely triplet, say *ann*, then draw a letter from the triplets starting with *nn* and obtain *nna*, then from the triplets beginning *na*, etc. The preceding two symbols determine from which set the next triplet is drawn. In this way a message might be produced that would read: *annation ef to the was. Oth rested*, etc.

With a tabulation of sequences of four letters we might pro duce: *influst intradio be decay, the condive,* etc. By tabulating th relative frequencies of longer sequences and drawing successiv items so as to reflect these frequencies, we can construct message that reflect the statistical dependencies of English as extensivel as we please.

For convenience, we shall refer to these different ways of co structing a statistical English as orders of approximation, a shall number them from *0* to *n*. At the zero order we have knowledge of relative frequencies, at the first order we know t relative frequencies of individual symbols, at the second order know the relative frequencies of pairs, at the *n*th order we kn the relative frequencies of *n*.

Consider this statistical English now in terms of verbal conte With a zero-order approximation to English there are contextual influences whatsoever on the choice of success symbols. At the *n*th-order approximation, however, each sym is selected in the context of the preceding *n*−1 symbols. As order of approximation is increased, the amount of context each symbol is increased, and the contextual constraints (de dent probabilities) have a chance to operate. As the orde approximation is increased, the messages we can constr become more and more familiar, reasonable, meaningful. more we permit contextual restraints to operate, the better our chances of producing a message that might actually occu English.

We have, therefore, a scale for what can be loosely ca 'meaningfulness'. At one end are the random jumbles of sym we customarily call nonsense, and at the other end are patter symbols that could easily appear in our daily discourse. Equi with this quantitative estimate of 'the degree of nonsense 'amount of contextual constraint', we can proceed to s certain psychological problems that have been phrased in terr meaningfulness.

An Experimental Illustration

Briefly stated, the problem to which this concept of verbal text has been applied is, How well can people remember sequ of symbols that have various degrees of contextual constraint in their composition? The experimental literature contains considerable evidence to support the reasonable belief that nonsense is harder to remember than sense. This evidence has suffered, however, from a necessarily subjective interpretation of what was sensible.

In the present experiment, the learning materials were constructed at several orders of approximation to English. These materials were presented to Ss whose recall scores were then plotted as a function of the order of approximation (Selfridge, 1949).

Learning materials

In the preceding examples we have used patterns of letters to illustrate the effects of contextual constraints. There is, of course, no necessity to limit the argument to letters. It is possible to use words or even sentences as the component elements that are arranged according to the statistical structure of English. In the present experimental illustration the materials were constructed with words as the units of analysis.

In theory, the construction of materials to incorporate the statistical structure of English over sequences of several words requires a tabulation of the relative frequencies of such sequences. Such a tabulation would be exceedingly long and tedious to compile. An alternative method of construction is available, however, which makes the procedure practicable. Instead of drawing each successive word from a different statistical distribution indicated by the preceding words, we draw the word from a different person who has seen the preceding words.

At the second order, for example, a common word, such as *he*, or *the*, is presented to a person who is instructed to use the word in a sentence. The word he uses directly after the one given him is then noted and later presented to another person who has not heard the sentence given by the first person, and he, in turn, is asked to use that word in a sentence. The word he uses directly after the one given him is then noted and later given to yet another person. This procedure is repeated until the total sequence of words is of the desired length. Each successive pair of words would go together in a sentence. Each word is determined in the context of only one preceding word.

For higher orders of approximation the person would see a sequence of words and would use the sequence in a sentence. Then the word he used directly after the sequence would be added, the first word of the sequence would be dropped, and the new (but overlapping) sequence would be presented to the next person. By this procedure we constructed sequences of words at the second, third, fourth, fifth and seventh orders of approximation.

For the first order approximation to English a scrambling of the words in the higher orders was used. By drawing words at random from the contextually determined lists, we obtained as good an approximation to the relative frequencies of individual words in English as these higher order lists provided. The alternative method of selecting words at random from a newspaper might have given a sample quite different in difficulty (familiarity).

A zero order approximation to English could be obtained by drawing at random from a dictionary. Most dictionaries contain too many rare words, however, so we drew from the 30,000 commonest words listed by Thorndike and Lorge (1944). This source had the additional advantage that it listed separately all forms of the word, whereas the dictionary lists only the lexical units. Words drawn at random from this list of 30,000 words are selected independently and without any constraints due to adjacent words or the relative frequencies of appearance of the word in English.

A final set of words was taken directly from current fiction or biography. These lists represent a full contextual determination

By these devices we constructed sequences of words with eight different degrees of contextual constraint. In the following discussion we shall refer to these lists as 0, 1, 2, 3, 4, 5, 7, and text orders of approximation. At each order four lists of different length – 10, 20, 30 and 50 words – were constructed. Thus the experimental design called for thirty-two different lists. Two such sets of thirty-two lists were constructed. Since the lists require considerable time to compile and since they may be of some general interest, one of the sets of thirty-two is reproduced in full in the appendix to this paper.

G. A. Miller and J. A. Selfridge

Experimental procedure

Each set of thirty-two lists was read aloud and recorded on a wire recorder. A man's voice was used. The words were read slowly and distinctly in a near monotone, with a short pause between words. At the beginning of the recording the instructions were given and a single practice list was presented to make sure the Ss understood their task. They were to listen until a list was finished, at which time a bell sounded signalling them to begin writing what they had just heard. The Ss were instructed to write the words they remembered as nearly in their correct order as possible. Order was not used, however, as a criterion for scoring their responses. All eight of the 10-word lists were given first, proceeding from least to greatest contextual determination, then the 20-word lists in the same order, then the 30-word lists, and finally the 50-word lists. Short rest periods (5 min) were given between the 20- and 30-word lists and between the 30- and 50-word lists.

Two groups of ten Ss were used. One group heard and recalled one of the sets of thirty-two lists, the other group heard and recalled the second set. The Ss were principally students at Harvard and Radcliffe. It was E's impression that a larger number of Ss would not have reduced the irregularities in the results, for most of the variability seemed attributable to sampling peculiarities in the lists themselves. Several more sets of thirty-two lists would be needed before an accurate estimate of the functional relations could be made. The results are adequate, however, to indicate the approximate magnitudes and general trends of the functions.

Ss' answers were scored for the number of words that they had written that had occurred in the test material. The number recalled, regardless of order, was expressed as a percentage of the total number presented.

Results and discussion

The experimental data are summarized in Figures 1 and 2. In Figure 1 the recall-score, expressed as a percentage, is plotted as a function of the order of approximation to the statistical structure of English, with the length of the lists as the parameter. In Figure 2 the same data are replotted to show the relation of the

247

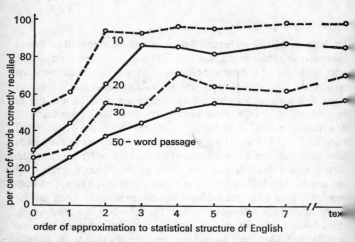

Figure 1 Percentage of words of the lists of different lengths that were correctly recalled at the various orders of approximation to the statistical structure of English

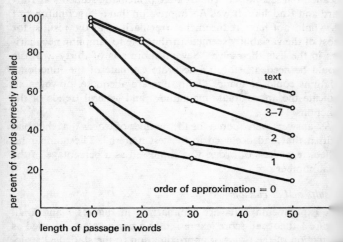

Figure 2 Percentage of words of the various orders of approximation to the statistical structure of English that were correctly recalled at the different lengths of passages learned

recall-score to the length of the list, with the order of approximation as the parameter. In both figures the functions represent the mean scores for all twenty Ss. It is clear from the results that percentage recalled increases as the order of approximation is increased and decreases as the length of the list is increased. Inspection of Figure 1 leads to a reasonable suspicion that the two variables, length and order of approximation, interact. With the short, 10-word lists there is little to be gained from contextual bonds extending over more than two words. With the 20-word lists the Ss remembered as well at the third order of approximation as they did for the textual material. With the 50-word lists, however, only orders 5 and 7 are comparable to the textual material in terms of percentage recalled. It would seem, therefore, that the longer the passage the greater is the usefulness of contextual associations extending over long sequences of items.

By a strict interpretation of the word 'nonsense', one is forced to conclude that all orders of approximation less than the full text are nonsense. Consider an example from Order 5:

house to ask for is to earn our living by working towards a goal for his team in old New York was a wonderful place wasn't it even pleasant to talk about and laugh hard when he tells lies he should not tell me the reason why you are is evident

The experimental results show that this kind of gibberish is as easily recalled as a passage lifted from a novel. Thus there are kinds of nonsense that are as easy to recall as are meaningful passages. The significant distinction is not to be drawn between meaning and nonsense, but between materials that utilize previous learning and permit positive transfer and materials that do not. If the nonsense preserves the short range associations of the English language that are so familiar to us, the nonsense is easy to learn.

The experiment shows, therefore, that the problem of meaning versus nonsense in verbal learning need not be approached in terms of a qualitative dichotomy, but can be studied as a functional relation between quantitative variables. The results indicate that meaningful material is easy to learn, not because it is meaningful *per se*, but because it preserves the short range associations that are familiar to the Ss. Nonsense materials that retain these short range associations are also easy to learn. By shifting the problem from 'meaning' to 'degree of contextual constraint' the whole area is reopened to experimental investigation.

Psychologists familiar with the problems of verbal learning will recognize the usefulness of the kind of material employed in this illustrative experiment. For example, is retroactive inhibition affected by interpolating different orders of approximation to English between the original learning and the recall? What is the effect of using original and interpolated materials of the same or of different orders of approximation to English? Do the higher approximations to English show the same differences between recall after sleep and recall after waking activity that the lower approximations show? Is it possible to show a continuum from the short-term reminiscence that can be demonstrated with syllables to the long-term reminiscence that can be shown with poetry? How does the span of immediate memory vary with the order of approximation? Is the superiority of distributed over massed practice a function of the order of approximation of the materials to the statistical structure of English? Can differences in learning and recalling different orders of approximation be demonstrated as a function of age?

The operational analysis of meaningfulness makes it possible to ask such questions and to see how one would proceed to answer them. The problem now is to collect the experimental data.

Summary

A quantitative definition for verbal context is given in terms of dependent probabilities. The definition is used to construct lists of words with varying degrees of contextual determination. When short range contextual dependencies are preserved in nonsense material, the nonsense is as readily recalled as is meaningful material. From this result it is argued that contextual dependencies extending over five or six words permit positive transfer, and that it is these familiar dependencies, rather than the meaning *per se*, that facilitate learning.

Appendix. Lists Used in Recall Experiment

-order approximation

10. byway consequence handsomely financier bent flux cavalry swiftness weather-beaten extent

20. betwixt trumpeter pebbly complication vigorous tipple careen obscure attractive consequence expedition pane unpunished prominence chest sweetly basin awoke photographer ungrateful

30. crane therewith egg journey applied crept burnish pound precipice king eat sinister descend cab Idaho baron alcohol inequality Illinois benefactor forget lethargy fluted watchtower attendance obeisance cordiality dip prolong bedraggle

50. hammer neatly unearned ill-treat earldom turkey that valve outpost broaden isolation solemnity lurk far-sighted Britain latitude task pub excessively chafe competence doubtless tether backward query exponent prose resourcefulness intermittently auburn Hawaii inhabit topsail nestle raisin liner communist Canada debauchery engulf appraise mirage loop referendum dowager absolutely towering aqueous lunatic problem

rder approximation

10. abilities with that beside I for waltz you the sewing

20. tea realizing most so the together home and for were wanted to concert I posted he her it the walked

30. house reins women brought screaming especially much was said ake love that school to a they in is the home think with are his before ant square of the wants

40. especially is eat objections are covering seemed the family I that ubstance dinner raining into black the see for will passionately and I after is window to down hold to boy appearance think with again om the beat go in there beside some is was after women dinner orus

der approximation

was he went to the newspaper is in deep and

sun was nice dormitory is I like chocolate cake but I think that ok is he wants to school there

the book was going home life is on the wall of you are ready the waltz is I know much ado about it was a dog when it was

you come through my appetite is that game since he lives in ool is jumping and wanted help call him well and substance was iano is a mistake on this is warm glow in and girl went to write r turtledoves in my book is fine appearance of the

3-order approximation

10. tall and thin boy is a biped is the beat
20. family was large dark animal came roaring down the middle ⸢
my friends love books passionately every kiss is fine
30. happened to see Europe again is that trip to the end is comir
here tomorrow after the packages arrived yesterday brought goo
cheer at Christmas it is raining outside as
50. came from the beginning and end this here is the top spins in
house by the library is full of happiness and love is very nice of h
that fell from the window she went home from work to pass t
cigarettes down to earth he picked an apple

4-order approximation

10. saw the football game will end at midnight on January
20. went to the movies with a man I used to go toward Harva
Square in Cambridge is mad fun for
30. the first list was posted on the bulletin he brought home a turl
will die on my rug is deep with snow and sleet are destructive a
playful students always
50. the next room to mine silver in Pennsylvania is late in getti
home on time my date was tremendous fun going there skiing
day would end and have no more objections to his speech on
radio last night played the viola in the orchestra and chorus
formed the

5-order approximation

10. they saw the play Saturday and sat down beside him
20. road in the country was insane especially in dreary rooms w
they have some books to buy for studying Greek
30. go it will be pleasant to you when I am near the table in the di
room was crowded with people it crashed into were screaming
they had been
50. house to ask for is to earn our living by working towards a
for his team in old New York was a wonderful place wasn't it
pleasant to talk about and laugh hard when he tells lies he shoul
tell me the reason why you are is evident

7-order approximation

10. recognize her abilities in music after he scolded him before
20. easy if you know how to crochet you can make a simple s⸢
they knew the color that it

30. won't do for the members what they most wanted in the course an interesting professor gave I went to at one o'clock stopped at his front door and rang the

50. then go ahead and do it if possible while I make an appointment I want to skip very much around the tree and back home again to eat dinner after the movie early so that we could get lunch because we liked her method for sewing blouses and skirts is

Text

10. the history of California is largely that of a railroad

20. more attention has been paid to diet but mostly in relation to disease and to the growth of young children

30. Archimedes was a lonely sort of eagle as a young man he had studied for a short time at Alexandria Egypt where he made a life-long friend a gifted mathematician

50. the old professor's seventieth birthday was made a great occasion for public honors and a gathering of his disciples and former pupils from all over Europe thereafter he lectured publicly less and less often and for ten years received a few of his students at his house near the university

References

MILLER, G. A., and FRICK, F. C. (1949), 'Statistical behavioristics and sequences of responses', *Psychological Review*, vol. 56, pp. 311–24.

SELFRIDGE, J. A. (1949), *Investigations into the Structure of Verbal Context*, honours thesis, Harvard University.

SHANNON, C. E. (1948), 'A mathematical theory of communication', *Bell System Technical Journal*, vol. 27, pp. 379–423 and 623–56.

THORNDIKE, E. L., and LORGE, I. (1944), *The Teacher's Wordbook of 30,000 Words*, Teachers' College, Columbia University.

ZIPF, G. K. (1949), *Human Behavior and the Principle of Least Effort*, Addison-Wesley.

18 L. E. Marks and G. A. Miller

The Role of Semantic and Syntactic Constraints in the Memorization of English Sentences

L. E. Marks and G. A. Miller, 'The role of semantic and syntactic constraints in the memorization of English sentences', *Journal of Verbal Learning and Verbal Behavior*, vol. 3 (1964), pp. 1–5.

It has been shown by Miller and Isard (1963) that the intelligibility of strings of English words depends, at least in part, on their conformity to linguistic rules known by the listener. Other things being equal, intelligibility is highest for meaningful grammatical sentences, lower for semantically anomalous (grammatical but meaningless) sentences, and lowest for ungrammatical strings of words. Apparently, both syntactic and semantic rules provide psychologically effective constraints on the number of alternative messages that a listener expects to hear. When strings of words follow these rules, perceptual processing is facilitated and intelligibility is increased.

If adherence to syntactic and semantic rules increases the intelligibility of strings of words, it might be expected that memorizing such strings would likewise be facilitated. Miller and Selfridge (1953) reported that the recall of strings of words improves as their order of approximation to the statistical pattern of English increases. Statistical approximations to English, however, do not distinguish between the syntactic and semantic factors that underlie the sequential contingencies. In the present experiment, strings of words were constructed in which semantic and syntactic rules could be violated independently. Ss' performance in a free-recall type of learning situation was then compared for the various types of strings. We expected that, when syntactic and/or semantic rules were disrupted, the least disrupted string would be most easily recalled, and that specific and predictable types of errors would occur in the recall of the disrupted strings. These expectations were confirmed by the experimental data.

Method

Materials

The method of construction of meaningful grammatical sentences and semantically anomalous sentences has been described by Miller and Isard (1963), and thus will be treated here only briefly. Five normal sentences of five words each with identical syntactic structures (adjective–plural noun–verb–adjective–plural noun) were constructed. From these original sentences five more sentences were derived by taking the first word from the first sentence, the second from the second, and so on. The syntactic structure of these derivative sentences remained identical to that of the normal sentences, but, because of the word substitutions, the derivative sentences were semantically anomalous.

In addition, two other types of strings of words were derived. The first, which we shall call anagram strings, was constructed by taking each of the normal sentences and scrambling the word-order, each sentence being scrambled somewhat differently in order to avoid the possibility of Ss noticing any pattern, with care being taken that none of the scrambled sentences was grammatical. Thus nothing was done to the semantic components of these sentences, but the normal syntactic structure was destroyed. Finally, strings of words which we shall call word-lists were similarly formed by scrambling the word-order of the anomalous sentences. The word-lists preserved neither the syntactic structure nor the semantic components of the original sentences.

Five strings of each type were formed. Two sets of materials, each containing all four types of strings, were constructed. These materials are presented in full in the Appendix. It should be noticed that the words used are not in general high-frequency words in English. As Miller and Isard pointed out, high-frequency words have multiple syntactic and semantic roles which they can fill, so that scrambling or substituting them is less likely to produce ungrammatical or semantically anomalous derivatives.

Procedure

Each group of four strings was recorded on magnetic tape by one of the experimenters (LEM). They were read at the rate of about five words in $3\frac{1}{2}$ sec, with about 2 sec between strings. Since five

trials were run, each group of strings was recorded five times, th
order of the strings being varied from trial to trial according to
latin-square design.

The recorded strings were played to Ss in a quiet room. C
each trial Ss listened to all five strings, then had 2 min in which
write them down in any order as accurately as possible. Ss we
requested to guess if they were uncertain.

Twenty-four groups of four Ss were used. Ss were Harvard a
Radcliffe undergraduates and graduate students. Each group w
tested on two different types of strings, one from each of the tv
sets of materials. Each of the four types of string from each
was given first to three groups and was then followed by one
the other three types from the other set. Thus, each of the twen
four possible combinations of two sets of strings was presented
one group of four Ss.

Results

There was a marked warm-up effect for all groups of Ss from
first to the second set of materials learned. Since this effect
of secondary interest, and since the relative differences among
four types of test materials were essentially the same on both
first and the second tasks, the results of the same type of stri
for the two sets were combined. The counterbalanced desig
the experiment made such a combination possible.

Three alternative ways of scoring Ss' performance were u
the results for each are given in Figures 1 to 3. Figure 1 shows
median per cent of words correct on each trial for the four ty
of material. In order for a word to be correct, it had to be wr
as presented and in its correct position relative to the o
words recalled in the string. Clearly, learning was most rapid
the normal sentences and most difficult for the word-lists.
curves for the anomalous sentences and for the anagram str
are almost identical.

Figure 2 shows the median per cent of total words cor
That is to say, words counted as correct if they occurred tog
in a presented string, but regardless of the position in the s
in which Ss recalled them. These functions are similar to
of Figure 1, except that the anagram strings here are sli

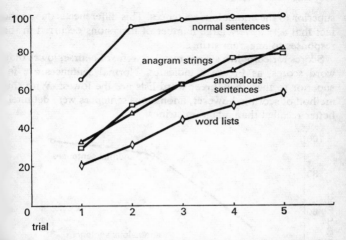

Figure 1 Median per cent of words correct for each of the four types of strings over five trials. A word was counted as correct only if it appeared its correct position in the string

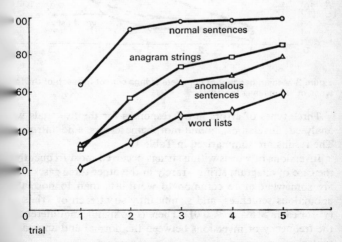

Figure 2 Median per cent of total words correct for each of the four types strings over five trials. A word was counted as correct regardless of its ition in the string

superior to the anomalous sentences. This difference is due to the fact that a relatively large number of inversions occurred in the responses to anagram strings.

Scores for complete strings recalled were, of course, lower than word scores, as Figure 3 indicates. Normal sentences are far superior to the other three; word-lists are the lowest. With this method of scoring, however, anomalous sentences were definitely better recalled than anagram strings.

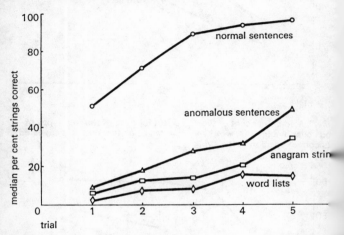

Figure 3 Median per cent of complete strings correct for each of the four types of strings over five trials

Three types of errors in Ss' responses for the five trials were analysed: inversions, bound-morpheme errors, and intrusions. The results are summarized in Table 1.

Inversions of words within strings occurred most frequently in the case of anagram strings, rarely in the other three cases. They are somewhat more common to word-lists than to normal or anomalous sentences, and significantly so at each of Trials (χ^2 for each ≥ 6.5, $p < 0.01$). There is no significant difference in the frequency of inversions between the normal and anomalous sentences.

Bound-morpheme errors refer to the omission or incorrect addition of prefixes and suffixes. The majority of these omissions of the plural — s. Again, these errors are most frequent in anagram strings. They are also common to word-lists but are relatively rare in normal and anomalous sentences, except for the former on Trial 1.

Table 1

Median Number of Three Types of Error for Each S for the Four Types of Strings over Five Trials

String	Trial	Inversions	Bound-morpheme error	Intrusions
Normal sentences	1	0·15	0·75	0·19
	2	0·04	0·17	0·12
	3	0·02	0·13	0·05
	4	0·00	0·09	0·02
	5	0·01	0·06	0·06
Anomalous sentences	1	0·10	0·27	1·42
	2	0·07	0·30	1·09
	3	0·07	0·13	1·00
	4	0·04	0·25	0·83
	5	0·04	0·30	0·50
Anagram strings	1	1·39	1·61	0·42
	2	2·70	2·63	0·21
	3	2·59	2·90	0·17
	4	1·94	2·77	0·09
	5	1·15	2·50	0·10
Word-lists	1	0·08	0·63	0·83
	2	0·32	1·44	1·29
	3	0·30	1·64	1·43
	4	0·30	1·37	0·94
	5	0·25	1·61	0·90

The final type of error studied was intrusions. These concern misplacing of words from one string to another in the group strings being learned. Intrusions are most common to the word-lists and anomalous sentences, and rare in normal sentences anagram strings. They are most frequent in word-lists, but difference is significant only with respect to anomalous sentences at Trial 1 ($\chi^2 = 5.44$, $p < 0.01$).

Discussion

It is clear that, in this experimental situation at least, syntactic and semantic structure facilitate learning. The role of the former has previously been studied by Epstein (1961, 1962), who concluded that the facilitation is apparently the result not of constraints which reduce the number of possible alternatives, but of some sort of 'chunking' according to grammatical rules (see Miller, 1956). As mentioned above, constraints due to transitional probabilities do not distinguish between semantic and syntactic factors. Yet these two seem distinguishable on the basis of error scores.

The three types of error scores may be placed into two categories: semantic and syntactic errors. Intrusions can be considered as semantic errors, related to decisions as to which words may combine in a sentence, and thus occur most frequently in anomalous sentences and word-lists, where semantic rules are violated. Bound-morpheme errors and inversions can be considered as syntactic errors: the first related to grammatical tags, the second to word-order. Both occur most frequently in anagram strings and word-lists, where syntactic rules are violated. Apparently, therefore, these errors give support to the contention that syntactic and semantic rules have psychological as well as linguistic reality.

Figure 1 indicates almost no difference between the relative frequencies of correctly placed words for anomalous sentences and anagram strings; using a more lenient scoring method that ignores order, however, the scores (Figure 2) for anagram strings are higher. It can be argued that the similarity between the two sets of scores is in line with the conclusion reached by Epstein: the facilitory effect on learning of syntactic and semantic structure is due to chunking, then, for these strings at least, one would conclude that the *average* size of the chunks is the same in anomalous sentences and anagram strings. However, string scores (Figure 3) show the anomalous sentences well above anagram strings. Thus, it would seem that the chunks formed in the recall of anomalous strings are more varied in length, more nearly 'all-or-none', and are more consistent than in the recall of anagram strings.

L. E. Marks and G. A. Miller

Summary

Ninety-six *S*s learned normal sentences, anomalous sentences, anagram strings, and word-lists for five trials by the method of free recall. The results demonstrate a differentiation between semantic and syntactic factors and a facilitory effect of both on learning.

Appendix. The Two Sets of Materials Used in the Present Experiment

Set I

Original sentences. Rapid flashes augur violent storms. Pink bouquets emit fragrant odors. Fatal accidents deter careful drivers. Melting snows cause sudden floods. Noisy parties wake sleeping neighbors.

Anomalous sentences. Rapid bouquets deter sudden neighbors. Pink accidents cause sleeping storms. Fatal snows wake violent odors. Melting parties augur fragrant drivers. Noisy flashes emit careful floods.

Anagram strings. Rapid augur violent flashes storms. Bouquets pink odors fragrant emit. Deter drivers accidents fatal careful. Sudden melting cause floods snows. Neighbors sleeping noisy wake parties.

Word lists. Rapid deter sudden bouquets neighbors. Accidents pink storms sleeping cause. Wake odors snows fatal violent. Fragrant melting augur drivers parties. Floods careful noisy emit flashes.

Set II

Original sentences. Furry wildcats fight furious battles. Respectable jewelers give accurate appraisals. Lighted cigarettes create smoky fumes. Gallant gentlemen save distressed damsels. Soapy detergents dissolve greasy stains.

261

Anomalous strings. Furry jewelers create distressed stains. Respectable cigarettes save greasy battles. Lighted gentlemen dissolve furious appraisals. Gallant detergents fight accurate fumes. Soapy wildcats give smoky damsels.

Anagram strings. Furry fight furious wildcats battles. Jewelers respectable appraisals accurate give. Create fumes cigarette lighted smoky. Distressed gallant save damsels gentlemen. Stains greasy soapy dissolve detergents.

Word lists. Furry create distressed jewelers stains. Cigarette respectable battles greasy save. Dissolve appraisals gentlemen lighted furious. Accurate gallant fight fumes detergents. Damsels smoky soapy give wildcats.

References

EPSTEIN, W. (1961), 'The influence of syntactical structure on learning', *American Journal of Psychology*, vol. 74, pp. 80–85.

EPSTEIN, W. (1962), 'A further study of the influence of syntactical structure on learning', *American Journal of Psychology*, vol. 75, pp. 121–6.

MILLER, G. A. (1956), 'The magical number seven, plus-or-minus two: some limits on our capacity for processing information', *Psychological Review*, vol. 63, pp. 81–97.

MILLER, G. A., and ISARD, S. (1963), 'Some perceptual consequences of linguistic rules', *Journal of Verbal Learning and Verbal Behavior*, vol. 2, pp. 217–28.

MILLER, G. A., and SELFRIDGE. J. A. (1953), 'Verbal context and the recall of meaningful material', *American Journal of Psychology*, vol. 63, pp. 176–85.

he study of transfer is concerned with the influence of prior
actice upon performance in a new learning task. The transfer
fects can be positive or negative; prior practice may be a source
facilitation or of interference in the acquisition of new
aterials. The analysis of transfer occupies a position of central
portance in the experimental investigation of verbal learning.
ost of the learning observed in the laboratory is significantly
uenced by the habits and skills which the individual brings to
experimental situation. In studies of transfer the prior habits
established in the laboratory and brought under experimental
trol. Thus it becomes possible to trace in detail the mechanisms
acilitation and interference which come into play as the learner
ves from one task to the next. In general, tests of transfer
stitute an important analytic device because they permit an
ssment of what has been learned during the acquisition of a
n task. For example, as was shown in an earlier section, the
urrence of stimulus selection is demonstrated by means of
sfer tests. After training with a compound stimulus the degree
ansfer to the separate components is determined. Whenever
assumed that a rule or a principle has been learned, the critical
is one of transfer.

continuing experimental objective is the identification of
components or sub-processes of transfer. A first basic
ion is provided by the distinction between specific and
ral transfer. Specific transfer effects reflect the operation of
esses which are dependent on known similarity relations
een the stimuli or the responses in the successive tasks.
ral transfer effects are produced by processes which are
endent of such specific similarity relations and thus are

attributed to the acquisition of highly generalizable habits and skills.

General Transfer

General transfer effects are typically positive. While one might expect prior practice to have some negative consequences, such as fatigue and boredom, there has been no convincing demonstration that such factors have a significant influence on performance in experiments on verbal learning; the possibility cannot be ruled out, however, that they reduce the observed amount of positive transfer.

Two sources of general transfer are conventionally distinguished, viz. warm-up (WU) and learning to learn (LTL). Warm-up refers to the establishment of a perceptual-motor or attentional set favourable to the performance of the experimental task. Familiarization with the exposure apparatus and the temporal order of events will contribute to the development of an effective set, i.e. a warm-up activity will prepare the subject for the reception of the relevant stimuli and leads him to adopt the required rhythm of responding. Warm-up does not depend on the performance of a learning task but is assumed to occur whenever the conditions to which the subject is exposed are favourable to the establishment of an appropriate set. Thus, a non-learning task, such as colour naming or number guessing, may serve as a warm-up activity for subsequent paired-associate learning as long as there is sufficient similarity between the experimental arrangements in the two situations. Learning to learn, on the other hand, refers to changes in the subject's mode of attack on the experimental task: the relevant habits and skills are carried over from one learning task to the next. These habits and skills are assumed to be nonspecific, since care is taken in studies of LTL to eliminate or minimize identical or similar elements in the successive tasks.

The role of warm-up

When a subject learns a task in the laboratory, both WU and LTL may be expected to occur. If speed of acquisition increases as a function of prior learning experience, the question must considered of how much each component contributes to the observed improvement in performance. One approach to this problem is represented by Thune's study (Reading 19). Thune's analysis takes its point of departure from the assumption that WU effects are relatively transitory and will dissipate rapidly during an interval separating successive tasks; by contrast, transfer effects derived from LTL are considered to be relatively permanent. Thune's subjects learned three lists on each of five successive days. Given the assumptions just mentioned, it was possible to estimate the amount of improvement resulting from LTL by comparing performance measures for corresponding lists on successive days; gains within sessions were interpreted as being largely a matter of WU. The substantial losses in learning efficiency from the third list on one day to the first list on the following day were attributed to the rapid dissipation of WU. The implication of these data is that WU both grows and declines more rapidly than LTL. However, the use of a criterion of temporal persistence for distinguishing between WU and LTL is open to question. It is possible that a portion of the effects of WU is transitory, but some of the perceptual-motor adjustments may become conditioned to the experimental context and thus be more persistent. Moreover, the assumption that LTL is not forgotten has not been tested. In fact, there are indications to the contrary in the literature (Newton and Wickens, 1956, exper. 3).

A second approach to the assessment of the contribution of WU has been the comparison of the transfer effects of a 'pure' WU activity and a learning task. The physical arrangements and the temporal order of events are made as similar as possible for the two tasks, but the WU activity does not involve any learning. Using such a design, Thune (1950) showed that there was as much transfer to a paired-associate test list from the performance of a colour-guessing task as from prior practice on another list of paired associates. It appeared, therefore, that WU accounted entirely for the observed increases in speed of learning. However, the subjects in Thune's experiment had had prior experience in paired-associate learning, and the WU activity may have served to reactivate the habits and skills acquired during the earlier experience with a learning task. In a more recent study (Schwenn and Postman, 1967) the transfer effects of a WU activity (number guessing) and a learning task were compared with naïve subjects. The improvement produced by WU was quite small, whereas the transfer effects of the prior learning task were substantial. It was concluded that for naïve subjects, familiarization with the learning task was of much greater importance than the establishment of an appropriate perceptual-motor set. The pronounced difference between the results obtained with naïve and with experienced subjects indicates that a sharp separation between the relative contributions of WU and LTL is difficult. Nevertheless, it now appears likely that WU *per se* is not a major factor in producing improvements in the performance of verbal tasks.

The conditions of learning to learn

Whatever the relative weight of WU and LTL, it is a fact that subjects learning successive tasks in the laboratory show impressive gains in performance. For example, the second paired associate or serial list is often acquired twice as fast as the first. However, improvement tends to slow down as the subject continues learning new lists (e.g. Meyer and Miles, 1953; Ward 1937). Speed of acquisition also increases as a function of the amount of training on a single prior list (e.g. Postman, 1962; Schwenn and Postman, 1967; Thune, 1950), but again the improvement diminishes at the higher levels of practice. The major portion of the habits and skills responsible for the gains in performance is acquired rapidly and protracted training yields diminishing returns.

It has been suggested that much of the progressive improvement is probably a matter of LTL. However, such an assertion says little about the characteristics of general transfer. It necessary to specify the habits and skills which constitute LTL. A first step in this direction is the systematic exploration of the relations between the conditions of prior training and the amount and manifestations of general transfer. This approach is illustrated in the study by Postman and Schwartz (Reading 20). The purpose of the experiment was to determine to what extent the skills developed through experience with learning tasks are specific to the method of practice and the type of material encountered in the course of prior training. The results show that improvement performance is greater when the method of practice (paired-associate versus serial learning) remains the same than when it changes. The continued use of the same class of materials also favours improvement, although this factor is of less importance than the method of practice, at least when the transfer list is composed of familiar English words. Such differential transfer effects show that LTL comprises specific and circumscribed habits. However, the fact that all conditions of training produced significant amounts of transfer points to important communalities among the habits and skills required for the mastery of the various tasks.

Systematic manipulation of the conditions of training has made it possible to identify some of the higher-order habits and skills which constitute LTL. A few representative findings may be mentioned briefly.

a) Experience with response terms which do not form well integrated units facilitates the acquisition of a new set of such materials. The ability to accomplish the process of response integration is, therefore, a component of LTL when the response units are outside the subject's normal repertoire (Postman, Keppel and Zacks, 1968).

b) More generally, as already noted, improvement is greater when the method of practice and the class of materials are kept constant than when they change.

c) Experience with transfer situations enhances the learner's ability to recognize similarity relations between successive tasks and to develop strategies of responding which serve to maximize inter-task facilitation and to minimize interference (Keppel and Postman, 1966; Postman, 1964).

d) As a result of prior exposure to the appropriate experimental paradigms, subjects learn to make effective use of the opportunities for mediation in the mastery of a new task (Postman, 1968). Findings such as these make it clear that LTL is subject to experimental manipulation and analysis into component habits and skills. In that sense the phenomena of general and specific transfer may be regarded as continuous.

Specific Transfer

Experimental operations

As was indicated earlier, transfer effects which depend on known
similarity relations between stimuli or responses in successive
lists are classified as specific. Hence the major experimental
manipulations in studies of specific transfer concern the similarity
relations between the terms in the successive lists. Paired-associate tasks are typically used because they permit the separation
of stimulus and response functions. Since any experimental
arrangement for the study of specific transfer provides an opportunity for WU and LTL to influence performance, a control
condition is usually required to assess the influence of the latter
factors. Changes in performance under the A–B, C–D paradigm
(unrelated stimuli and unrelated responses in the successive lists)
provide the control baseline for the evaluation of specific transfer
effects; this paradigm is also typically used in studies of general
transfer. If a particular transfer condition produces performance
which is superior to that under the A–B, C–D paradigm, we conclude that specific positive transfer has been demonstrated; if the
condition falls below the control baseline, the presence of specific
negative transfer is indicated.

Three kinds of similarity are commonly manipulated in experiments on verbal learning: formal, meaningful, and conceptual
(see Underwood, 1966, p. 476). Formal similarity is defined in
terms of the overlap of letters among items, i.e. the more letters
the items have in common, the higher is the similarity. The
variable of formal similarity is relevant primarily to nonwords,
for example trigrams. In the case of words, ratings of synonymity
(e.g. Haagen, 1949) make possible a graded manipulation of
meaningful similarity. For example, *stupid*, *foolish*, and *silly* are
progressively less similar in meaning to the word *absurd*. Another
procedure makes use of free-association norms to define associative similarity, with the magnitude of the relationship being
indexed by the frequency with which a word is given as an
association to a particular stimulus. For instance, *chair*, *food*, and
floor represent responses which are progressively weaker associates to the stimulus word *table*. Since it is usually assumed that
associative similarity is the dimension underlying meaningful

imilarity (see Haagen, 1949), we shall not distinguish between
hem further. Finally, conceptual similarity refers to membership
n a common taxonomic category, for example, *apple*, *pear*, and
lum are all members of the category *fruit*. All these types of
imilarity apply both to items within a list and to the relations
etween terms in successive lists.

As is shown in Reading 21 by Twedt and Underwood, either an
nmixed-list or a mixed-list design may be used in studies of
pecific transfer. In the unmixed design a single inter-list relation
represented by all the pairs in the transfer task, while in the
ixed design two or more relations are represented by different
irs. (In the latter case it is, of course, necessary to make sure
at all of the pairs are used in each of the transfer paradigms.
nless that is done, differential transfer effects may be counter-
ted or magnified by inherent differences in the difficulty of the
irs assigned to the various paradigms.) The mixed design has
e advantage of economy, since each subject serves in each
nsfer condition. The main disadvantage of this design lies in
e possibility that performance factors may come into play
ich cannot operate in the unmixed case. For instance, subjects
y choose to learn the different types of pairs in a mixed list in
articular order, for example, concentrating initially on those
ich maintain the stimulus terms of the first list. Such pre-
nces obviously cannot influence performance when the list is
nixed. The study by Twedt and Underwood exhibits in detail
problems of design and analysis which must be considered in
eriments concerned with comparisons between unmixed-list
mixed-list designs. Although these investigators found only
or differences between the two types of design, there is
ence in the literature for differential transfer effects when
r 'mixtures' of paradigms are used (e.g. Postman, 1966).
s, it is advisable as a rule to use the unmixed-list design, unless
known that the particular set of paradigms under study is not
eptible to mixed-list effects.

r-list similarity

ling 22 by Martin (1965) provides an excellent discussion
e effects of inter-list similarity upon transfer. At this point it
be useful to outline briefly the basic framework for the

experimental analysis of inter-list similarity. With the conditio
of maximal similarity – the A–B, A–B paradigm – as a point c
reference, it is possible to manipulate independently stimulus c
response similarity. Progressive decreases in stimulus similari
will eventually result in the A–B, C–B paradigm (differe
stimuli and identical responses in the two lists); in like fashio
progressive decreases in response similarity will eventually le;
to the A–B, A–D paradigm (identical stimuli and differe
responses). Finally, if the similarity of the response terr
in the A–B, C–B paradigm and of the stimulus terms in t
A–B, A–D paradigm is now varied, both sets of manipulatio
will terminate in the A–B, C–D paradigm (different stim
and different responses) which defines the point of extrer
dissimilarity. These four paradigms – A–B, A–B; A–B, C–
A–B, A–D; A–B, C–D – are anchor points in the schema
representation of interlist similarity. This fact is reflected
Martin's Figure 1 through the placement of these paradigms
the four corners of the transfer surface. Obviously, a large numl
of transfer paradigms may be located on this particular trans
surface. Moreover, other surfaces are possible. For instance,
initial starting point might be the A–B, A–Br transfer paradi
(see Dallett, 1965), rather than A–B, A–B as in the first case
the former paradigm the same stimuli and responses are also u
in the second list, but in this case they are re-paired. Nov
decrease in stimulus similarity will result in the A–B, C
paradigm and a decrease in response similarity will result in
A–B, A–D paradigm. (The re-pairing is irrelevant at the poir
stimulus or response dissimilarity.) As with the first surfac
decrease in the similarity of the remaining terms (response
stimuli, respectively) will also produce the A–B, C–D parad

  While transfer surfaces provide a convenient means of c
loguing interlist arrangements and their outcomes, they are
descriptive in function. An extremely useful further developr
is the introduction of *component* transfer surfaces by Marti
the present paper Martin hypothesizes that specific transfer
be broken down into components derived from (a) for
associations, (b) backward associations, and (c) response le
ing. The contribution of each component under various parad
is represented in a component surface. It is assumed tha

ansfer effects of first-list forward associations decline as stimulus
milarity decreases; as responses become less similar the effects
f both backward associations and of response learning diminish.
lartin's analysis shows that an application of these surfaces can
so account for the influence of two other variables, viz. response
eaningfulness and degree of first-list learning. Although there
ill remains the problem of ascertaining the relative weight of the
fferent components in determining performance, this approach
es go a long way towards identifying the sources of specific
ansfer.

ediation

s studied in the verbal-learning laboratory, mediation refers
any interlist relationship which will allow the subject to arrive
the current response to be learned on the basis of previously
rned associations. For example, suppose a subject is asked to
rn the following sequence of three lists: A–B, B–C, A–C.
ing to the presence of the common B term, performance in the
rd stage can be mediated by the previously learned string,
B–C. Mediation paradigms can be classified in terms of (a) the
rce of prior training, i.e. whether all or some of the stages are
rned in the laboratory, and (b) the number of separate stages
essary to form the paradigm. The example given above comes three stages and represents the paradigm of mediational
ining used in the experiment of Goulet and Postman which
be found in Reading 24. In their experiment all three stages
e acquired in the laboratory. In Reading 23 by McGehee and
ulz, a four-stage paradigm was used (A–B, B–C, C–D, A–D),
the middle two stages (B–C and C–D) being inferred on the
s of free-association norms.

oth these experiments are concerned with methodological
lems. For McGehee and Schulz the question was essentially
ther mediation is an associative phenomenon, dependent
the subject's actual use of the specific associative relations
ing a particular paradigm, or whether other factors, e.g.
ased availability of the response terms, are responsible for
observed facilitation. On the basis of two experiments, they
able to conclude that the mediation effect is attributable to

271

the assumed associative connexions (Experiment 1) and that it is also dependent upon the specific order of the training sequence (Experiment 2). In subsequent studies, Schulz (e.g. Schulz, Weaver, and Ginsberg, 1965) has focused upon the associative aspects of mediation by using a procedure (multiple-choice learning) which eliminates the necessity for the subject to recall the correct response in the final stage. Under these conditions any superiority of the experimental group is attributed to mediation rather than to a difference in response availability.

Recently Mandler and Earhard (1964) raised the question of whether mediational effects produced by associations acquired in the laboratory are an experimental artifact. Consider again the experimental paradigm of mediational chaining, A–B, B–C, A–C. The control treatment conventionally used to assess the amount of mediation is A–B, D–C, A–C. With the common B term eliminated, the latter sequence does not permit mediation to occur. Hence differences between the two treatments in the third stage (A–C) are attributed to the effects of mediation under the experimental arrangement. Mandler and Earhard argued that during the second stage of the experimental paradigm, there is indirect unlearning of the first-list forward association, A–B, because the acquisition of B–C leads to the direct unlearning of the backward association, B–A. As a result, the amount of interference from A–B with the critical third-stage association, A–C, is reduced. There is no comparable reduction in interference under the control treatment. Mandler and Earhard suggest that this alternative mechanism, which was termed 'pseudomediation', might be responsible for the superior performance of the experimental group previously attributed to mediation chaining. These authors presented experimental evidence in support of the hypothesis of pseudomediation. However, as a study by Goulet and Postman shows, recent research has brought into question the reliability of the phenomenon. While there is evidence on both sides (see Earhard and Earhard, 1967; Schulz, Weaver, and Ginsberg, 1965), it now appears extremely unlikely that pseudomediation can account for more than a negligible portion of the mediational phenomena reported in the literature.

These methodological studies indicate that mediational phenomena are complexly determined. Since mediation paradigms in essence transfer designs, they must be influenced by the same factors as have been identified in the simpler two-list situation. In comparison with the latter, however, the inclusion of one or more additional stages necessarily complicates the analytical picture of the transfer relations. Research in this area exhibits a continuing concern for methodological problems (see Earhard and Mandler, 1965). In addition, attention is being focused on the identification of methods and procedures which will encourage the use of mediated associations (see Jenkins, 1963). This objective has been accomplished by providing subjects with sufficient time to mediate during the test stage, by employing training techniques which emphasize associative relations, by choosing transfer tasks which are sufficiently difficult to encourage the productive use of mediated associations, and by using subjects who are aware of the possibility of mediation either as a result of instructions or of explicit training with the mediation paradigms being studied. Under these circumstances, mediation is often found to be an impressive phenomenon.

References

HALLETT, K. (1965), 'A transfer surface for paradigms in which second-list S–R pairings do not correspond to first-list pairings', *Journal of Verbal Learning and Verbal Behavior*, vol. 4, pp. 528–34.

EARHARD, B., and EARHARD, M. (1967), 'Role of interference factors in three-stage mediation paradigms', *Journal of Experimental Psychology*, vol. 73, pp. 526–31

EARHARD, B., and MANDLER, G. (1965), 'Mediated associations: Paradigms, controls, and mechanisms', *Canadian Journal of Psychology*, vol. 19, pp. 346–78.

HAAGEN, C. H. (1949), 'Synonymity, vividness, familiarity, and association-value ratings for 400 pairs of common adjectives', *Journal of Psychology*, vol. 27, pp. 453–63.

JENKINS, J. J. (1963), 'Mediated associations: Paradigms and situations', in C. N. Cofer and B. S. Musgrave, eds., *Verbal Behavior and Learning: Problems and Processes*, McGraw-Hill, pp. 210–45.

KEPPEL, G., and POSTMAN, L. (1966), 'Studies of learning to learn: III. Conditions of improvement in successive transfer tasks', *Journal of Verbal Learning and Verbal Behavior*, vol. 5, pp. 260–67.

MANDLER, G., and EARHARD, B. (1964), 'Pseudomediation: Is chaining an artifact?', *Psychonomic Science*, vol. 1, pp. 247–8.

RYER, D. R. and MILES, R. C. (1953), 'Intralist-interlist relations in verbal learning', *Journal of Experimental Psychology*, vol. 45, pp. 109–5.

Transfer

NEWTON, J. M. and WICKENS, D. D. (1956), 'Retroactive inhibition as a function of the temporal position of the interpolated learning', *Journal of Experimental Psychology*, vol. 51, pp. 149–54.

POSTMAN, L. (1962), 'Transfer of training as a function of experimental paradigm and degree of first-list learning', *Journal of Verbal Learning and Verbal Behavior*, vol. 1, pp. 109–18.

POSTMAN, L. (1964), 'Studies of learning to learn: II. Changes in transfer as a function of practice', *Journal of Verbal Learning and Verbal Behavior*, vol. 3, pp. 437–47.

POSTMAN, L. (1966), 'Differences between unmixed and mixed transfer designs as a function of paradigm', *Journal of Verbal Learning and Verbal Behavior*, vol. 5, pp. 240–48.

POSTMAN, L. (1968), 'Studies of learning to learn: VI. General transfer effects in three-stage mediation. *Journal of Verbal Learning and Verbal Behavior*, vol. 7, pp. 659–64.

POSTMAN, L. KEPPEL, G., and ZACKS, R. (1968), 'Studies of learning to learn: VII. The effect of practice on response integration', *Journal of Verbal Learning and Verbal Behaviour*, vol. 7, pp. 776–84.

SCHULZ, R. W., WEAVER, G. E., and GINSBERG, S. (1965), 'Mediation with pseudomediation controlled: Chaining is not an artifact!', *Psychonomic Science*, vol. 2, pp. 169–70.

SCHWENN, E., and POSTMAN, L. (1967), 'Studies of learning to learn: V. Gains in performance as a function of warm-up and associative practice', *Journal of Verbal Learning and Verbal Behavior*, vol. 6, pp. 565–73.

THUNE, L. E. (1950), 'The effect of different types of preliminary activities on subsequent learning of paired-associate material', *Journal of Experimental Psychology*, vol. 40, pp. 423–38.

UNDERWOOD, B. J. (1966), *Experimental Psychology*, Appleton-Century Crofts, 2nd edn.

WARD, L. B. (1937), 'Reminiscence and rote learning', *Psychological Monographs*, vol. 49, no. 4.

19 L. E. Thune

Warm-up Effect as a Function of Level of Practice in Verbal Learning

L. E. Thune, 'Warm-up effect as a function of level of practice in verbal learning', *Journal of Experimental Psychology*, vol. 42 (1951), pp. 250–56.

Recent studies have called attention to the role of a warm-up factor in verbal learning and retention (1, 3, 4, 7). Although each of these studies concerned itself with a unique problem, they all effectively demonstrated the presence and significance of a warm-up factor in paired-associate verbal learning with relatively unpracticed Ss. The primary aim of the present investigation is to determine the degree to which this warm-up factor operates in the performance of more highly practiced Ss in a similar verbal learning situation.

Only two studies have reported data on the relative rates with which comparable word lists (or other verbal materials) are learned under conditions which permit a separation of those transitory effects of practice which we call *warm-up* from the more stable *general practice* or learning-to-learn effects which carry over from one session to another. In 1928 Heron (2) reported a study in which he claimed to have found a significant warm-up effect in a verbal learning experiment which involved the learning of two related paired-associate lists on each of three days. The first list on the second experimental day required significantly more trials to learn than did the second list learned on the first day. Similarly, the first list learned on the third day was learned less rapidly than was the second list on either of the two preceding days.

Heron's conclusions regarding the presence of a valid warm-up effect have been questioned by Mitchell (6) on the basis that the four sessions which were employed were separated by such a long time interval (one week) that the general practice effect from one session was lost (forgotten) before the next. Mitchell then reports the pertinent data gathered incidentally while the author was investigating another problem. Although there were minor variations in experimental procedure for some Ss, the general design of the experiment has been stated as follows: 'The subjects learned at least two lists of 10 3-place numbers per day, five to six days per week for from 16 to 84 days . . .' (6, p. 139). Neither errors nor trials to reach one perfect repetition revealed any significant difference in the mean rate with which those lists which came first and those which came second were learned. Further, there was no tendency for the relative rate with which the second list was learned with respect to the first, to change with increasing days of practice.

It is possible that Mitchell's failure to obtain evidence for a warm-up effect arose because the design of her experiment, including the methods and materials employed, tended to suppress the appearance of such a factor. Thus, performance on the second list each day may have been influenced by proactive inhibition from the first list. This inhibitory factor may have been enough to offset any warm-up facilitation which might otherwise have occurred. This interpretation becomes all the more plausible when one considers the fact that Mitchell's Ss learned serial lists of 3-digit numbers with only a 45-sec or a 2-min rest interval between successive lists. The opportunities for proactive inhibition of the second list are large under these conditions. On the other hand, because of the relatively long (about 24-hr) time interval between it and the previous list, the first list learned each day may have been subject to only small amounts of proactive inhibition.

The present experiment may be regarded as an extension and refinement of the earlier work of Heron and Mitchell. The conditions have been arranged so as to permit the general practice and the warm-up effects to reveal themselves unambiguously. Further, it is possible to determine the form of the functional relationship existing between the warm-up effect and the S's level of practice.

Method

Procedure

All Ss served under the same experimental conditions. Fifteen lists of paired adjectives were learned, three lists being learned

276

successively on each of five days. Each list was presented for a minimum of ten trials. If S had not reached the criterion of one perfect repetition by the end of the tenth trial, additional trials were given until this criterion was attained. A 12-min rest interval was interpolated between the successive lists learned within each day. During this interval E changed the list of words on the memory drum and engaged S in conversation irrelevant to the experiment.

Because of conflicts with week-end holidays and individual class schedules, it was not always possible to arrange for the five experimental sessions to come on successive days. Of the 240 inter-session intervals (four for each of sixty Ss) 65 per cent involved a one day interval, and 18, 13, 3 and 1 per cent involved intervals of 2, 3, 4 and 5 days, respectively. Inter-session intervals which exceeded one day tended to distribute themselves evenly throughout the four inter-session intervals.

Apparatus and materials

All lists were presented on a modified Hull-type memory drum. The apparatus was mounted on a table in such a manner that the front of the drum projected through an opening in a plywood screen which served to shield E from S and to minimize the number of distractions to which S would be subjected. The stimulus word of each pair was presented for 4 sec, the stimulus and response words being jointly exposed during the last 2 sec of this interval.

Each list was composed of ten pairs of two-syllable adjectives. The lists were made as homogeneous as possible. Formal associations between stimulus and response words within a single list and between the various lists were minimized. Five different serial orders of presentation were employed for each list. There was an 8-sec rest interval between trials within a list. During this interval the drum continued to turn but only blank spaces appeared in the exposure window.

Although each S learned only fifteen lists, seventeen word lists were employed.[1] Which fifteen out of the seventeen lists would be

A total of seventeen lists was employed because these same Ss returned for a sixth experimental session during which they learned two additional lists. The activity on the sixth day constituted a separate study and will be

learned, and the particular order in which they would be learned
was determined separately for each S through the use of a tab'
of random numbers.

Subjects

Sixty undergraduate students (forty-four men and sixteen wome
enrolled in psychology courses served as volunteer Ss. None h
had previous experience in a memory drum experiment, and
were naïve with respect to the purpose of the experiment. T
topic of warm-up had not been discussed in any of their class

At the time of their first session, a set of written instructio
was read to each S. No further instructions were given other th
to say, 'Now learn this list as rapidly as you can,' just before ea
new list was presented. Since this study was primarily concern
with intra-day and inter-day practice effects, no prelimina
practice lists were employed.

Result and Discussion

The present experiment investigated rate of paired-assoc
verbal learning as a function of (a) the amount of prior prac
received within a single session (e.g. position within a sessi
and (b) the over-all amount of prior practice received on previ
sessions (e.g. session number within the series). The follow
three measures of performance were employed in the analysi
the data from the learning of each list: (a) the number of co
anticipations on the first five trials, (b) the number of co
anticipations on the first ten trials, and (c) the number of t
required to reach the criterion of one perfect repetition. Fig.
shows how performance measured by the mean correct antic
tions on the first five trials, varied as a function of position w
a session and of the session number within the series. The r
number of trials required to reach one perfect repetition on
of the three lists on each of the five days is given in Table 1.
based upon the mean number of correct anticipations on the

---

reported at a later time. However, it was important that the lists learn
the sixth day be comparable with those learned on the first five days re
in the present study, hence all seventeen lists were randomized toget

278

able 1

Table 1

Mean Trials Required to the Criterion of One Perfect Repetition for Lists Learned in Each of Three Positions on Each of Five Days

(*N* = 60)

Position within session	Learning session										All sessions	
	Day 1		Day 2		Day 3		Day 4		Day 5			
	Mean	S D	Mean	S D	Mean	S D	Mean	S D	Mean	S D	Mean	S D
1	21·62	9·63	17·98	8·11	17·15	9·99	15·23	6·73	14·17	7·15	17·23	8·82
2	13·70	5·99	10·73	4·74	9·78	4·17	9·93	5·15	9·10	4·02	10·65	5·08
3	11·20	6·62	9·87	4·50	9·10	4·67	7·97	3·33	7·42	2·89	9·11	4·99
Sessions	15·51	8·99	12·86	7·03	12·01	7·72	11·04	6·09	10·23	5·78	12·33	7·44

trials are not included here since this performance measure
related highly with each of the other two, and since a graphical
t of these data yielded a set of curves almost identical with
se shown in Figure 1.

he group data were subjected to an analysis of variance and
F-test applied to evaluate the significance of the within-
ions and between-sessions differences and of the inter-action
t between position-within-a-session and session-number-
in-the-series. The F-tests for within-sessions and between-
ons gains were significant at beyond the 0·001 level for all
e performance measures. (For within-sessions, $F = 155·73$
ean number correct in five trials, 251·96 for mean correct in
rials, and 139·48 for trials to reach one perfect repetition,
2 and 885 df in each case; for between-sessions, the cor-
nding F-ratios were 24·16, 32·19, and 18·78, with 4 and
df.) The interaction variance between position-within-a-
n and session-number-within-the-series lacked statistical
icance when tested on the basis of the total number of
t responses on the first five trials, and the number of trials
red to reach one perfect repetition. ($F = 0·24$ for mean
t in five trials and 1·10 for mean trials to reach one perfect
tion, with 8 and 885 df.) When performance was evaluated

in terms of the number of correct responses in the first ten trials this interaction test yielded an F-ratio of 2·34 which was significant at between the 0·01 and 0·05 levels of confidence for the 8 and 885 df involved.

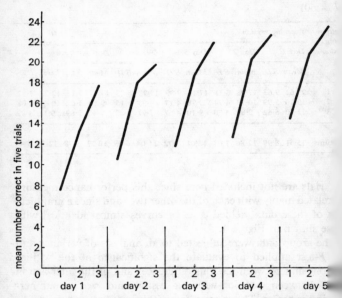

Figure 1 Mean total number of correct anticipations on the first five trials for each of the three lists learned on each of the five days ($N =$

The rate with which individual lists were learned was undoubtedly influenced by a multiplicity of psychological factors. Within the framework of the present experiment, some of the most important of these factors may have been:

(a) Facilitation of performance on successive lists within between sessions due to general practice or learning-to-l effects.

(b) Facilitation of performance on successive lists within session due to warm-up effects.

(c) Possible interaction between the general practice effect the warm-up effect.

d) Inhibition of performance due to proactive inhibition from lists learned previously within that same session and perhaps from earlier sessions.

Numerous studies, such as those of Ward (8) and of Melton and von Lackum (5), have reported a negatively accelerated relationship between rate of learning and general level of practice. Successive gains due to general practice effects tend to be largest during the early stages of practice and thereafter become progressively smaller. Presumably, in the present experiment, performance on all lists (both within and between sessions) was influenced by this general practice effect. Although this effect influenced successive lists within each session, it is shown most clearly by the general rise in performance efficiency on corresponding lists learned on successive days. The presence of a general practice effect is statistically demonstrated by the significant F-ratios obtained when the between-sessions differences were tested by the analyses of variance reported above.

It is obvious that only a small part of the total within-sessions gains on individual days can be attributed to general practice or learning-to-learn effects. The remainder is ascribed to the warm-up effect since it was lost during the interval, usually 24 hrs, which separated the individual learning sessions. Although the greatest gain in rate of learning within individual sessions occurred between performance on the first and second lists, in each case sizeable gains continued to take place between the second and third lists. Apparently an efficient or optimal state of warm-up is attained with small amounts of practice within an individual session.

The relative magnitudes of the warm-up effect and of the general practice or learning-to-learn effect are indicated by the fact that for two out of the three measures of performance employed (number correct in ten trials and number of trials to reach perfect repetition), the first list learned on the fifth day was mastered *less* rapidly than was the second list learned on the very first day.

The analyses of variance reported above suggest the possibility of there being a real interaction between position-within-a-session and session-number-within-the-series in determining level of performance on individual lists. At least part of this tendency can

281

be accounted for on the basis of the negatively accelerated relationship between rate of learning and general level of practice
General level of practice was increasing during or within each
session, although its effects are most readily observed by noting
the change in performance efficiency on corresponding lists from
one session to the next. The gain in efficiency on successive lists
due to general practice or learning-to-learn effects was greatest a
the lower levels of practice and became progressively less with th
learning of each additional list. Thus a larger proportion of th
increase in learning efficiency noted within the early sessions mus
be attributed to general practice effects, and hence less to warm
up effect, than for the later sessions. If, in interpreting the abov
data, allowance is made for the decreasing within-sessions gair
attributable to general practice we see that the magnitude of th
warm-up effect bears little relation to the S's total level of prac
tice.

It is evident from the data already presented that facilitatic
from general practice effects and from within-sessions warm-u
greatly outweighed any proactive inhibitory effects which m:
have been built up from practice on previously learned lists. T
the extent that inhibition was present, it would have tended
suppress the appearance of the warm-up effect and, to a less
extent, the general practice effect. It is not possible to determi
the absolute strengths of these opposing facilitory and inhibito
influences.

The only direct evidence for proactive inhibition comes fr
inter-list intrusion data. The total number of intrusions fr
prior lists was small. A total of only thirty-eight inter-list int
sions obtained from the sixty Ss each of whom learned fift
lists for an average of 12·3 trials. Of the eighteen Ss who gave :
intrusions, four gave one intrusion each, nine gave two int
sions, four gave three intrusions, and one S gave a total of f
intrusions. Of the total of thirty-eight intrusions, five occur
during the learning of a list that came first on its day, sixt
occurred in a second list, and seventeen occurred in a third
The tendency to carry over a response from a previous sess
bore no relationship to the amount of prior learning on
particular day. As would be expected, intrusions occurring du
the learning of the second and third lists each day were more li

282

to come from lists learned earlier on that same day than from lists learned on previous days. Approximately the same number of inter-list intrusions occurred on each of the five days. Thus, it appears that on later days, after the Ss learned numerous lists on previous sessions (and thus could be expected to have a larger number of interfering associations from prior lists), they were better able to isolate the list being learned from prior lists. It is perhaps worth noting that the smallest number of intrusions (five) occured on the fifth day, the day on which there were the greatest number of potentially competing responses.

Spontaneous comments given by Ss suggest that, although they recognized that the first list each day tended to require more trials than the second, and particularly the third list, they attributed this greater difficulty to something about *the lists themselves*. It was not uncommon to receive comments such as: 'The words in the first list are always a whole lot harder to associate than those in the other lists,' or, 'I wish that all of the lists were as short as the one I learn last each day.'

Warm-up effects are not something that involve only the naïve unpracticed learner. The warm-up effect was almost as prominent on the fifth day of practice as on the first. Evidently, Ss do not learn to overcome the handicap of lack of warm-up through self-instructions and self-induced sets. Had this been possible we might have expected that the within-sessions gains in learning efficiency would occur at progressively earlier stages *within successive sessions*. From inspection of Figure 1 and Table 1, this is not the case. With increasing days of practice, that portion of the within-sessions gains which took place between the first and second list did not become larger, relative to the gain from the second to the third list.

Other experiments (4, 7) have demonstrated that learning per se is not an essential aspect of those activities which serve to produce a favorable warm-up state in experiments such as this. Non-learning activities, such as color-guessing, carried out on a memory drum are virtually as effective as paired-associate or serial learning in producing a state of warm-up which aids performance in subsequent verbal learning tasks. On the other hand, spoon-sorting, carried out at a desk within the same experimental room, has no facilitating warm-up effect (7).

Transfer

As yet, we know very little about the fundamental nature of the warm-up state. Warm-up effects fall within the broad category of determiners of performance which we call *set*. However, the concept of set is so ill-defined and vague that it offers little as an explanatory principle. The warm-up state is most frequently thought of in terms of reinstatement of the postural and attentive adjustments necessary for optimal learning efficiency. It is suggested that one major aspect of this state may be readaptation to the rhythm of the apparatus and the establishment of a 'readiness' set to make a response just as soon as the next stimulus appears. The factors which influence the establishment of the facilitating response set appear to be relatively independent of the *S*'s general level of practice.

Summary

1. Sixty undergraduate students, working individually and serving under the same experimental condition, learned fifteen 10-item lists of unrelated paired-associate adjectives. The different lists were learned to the criterion of one perfect repetition on each of five days. A 2-min rest interval was interpolated between the successive lists learned on each day.

2. The efficiency with which the various lists were learned was determined by two major variables: (a) the number of lists previously learned within that session, and (b) the number of prior learning sessions.

3. Within each session there was a marked rise in learning efficiency as shown by performance on successive lists. Most of this rapid intra-session gain was lost during the interval (generally one day) between sessions.

4. The warm-up gain which took place within each session was consistently larger than was the general practice effect obtained from all five sessions taken together.

5. Amount of intra-session warm-up gain was relatively independent of general level of practice as measured by the number of prior sessions.

References

C. E. HAMILTON, 'The relationship between length of interval separating two learning tasks and performance on the second task', *Journal of Experimental Psychology*, vol. 40 (1950), pp. 613–21.

W. T. HERON, 'Warming-up effect in learning nonsense syllables', *Journal of Genetic Psychology*, vol. 35 (1929), pp. 219–28.

A. L. IRION, 'The relation of "set" to retention', *Psychological Review*, vol. 55 (1948), pp. 336–41.

A. L. IRION, 'Retention and warming-up effects in paired-associate learning', *Journal of Experimental Psychology*, vol. 39 (1949), pp. 669–75.

A. W. MELTON and W. J. VON LACKUM, 'Retroactive and proactive inhibition in retention: evidence for a two-factor theory of retroactive inhibition', *American Journal of Psychology*, vol. 54 (1941), pp. 157–73.

M. B. MITCHELL, 'The alleged warming-up effect in memorization', *Journal of Experimental Psychology*, vol. 16 (1933), pp. 138–43.

L. E. THUNE, 'The effect of different types of preliminary activities on subsequent learning of paired-associate material', *Journal of Experimental Psychology*, vol. 40 (1950), pp. 423–38.

L. B. WARD, 'Reminiscence and rote learning', *Psychological Monographs*, vol. 49 (1937), no. 220.

20 L. Postman and M. Schwartz

Studies of Learning to Learn. I. Transfer as a Function o‹
Method of Practice and Class of Verbal Materials

Abridged from L. Postman and M. Schwartz, 'Studies of learning
learn. I. Transfer as a function of method of practice and class of ver‹
materials', *Journal of Verbal Learning and Verbal Behavior*, vol. 3 (196·
pp. 37–49.

When Ss learn a series of unrelated verbal lists in the laborato›
speed of acquisition typically shows progressive increases. Su‹
cumulative practice effects occur in paired-associate learni›
(e.g. Hamilton, 1950; Thune, 1951) and in the acquisition
serial lists (Melton and von Lackum, 1941; Postman, 19‹
Ward, 1937). The degree of improvement is a negatively acc·
erated function of the amount of practice. The interlist pract·
effects which do not represent the transfer of specific associat·
habits have been attributed to warm-up and learning to le‹
(McGeoch and Irion, 1952, p. 308 ff.; Thune, 1951). Warm·
refers to the development of a set which maximizes S's efficie›
in the performance of a rote-learning task. An effective set ‹
sumably involves such factors as postural adjustments and
adoption of an optimal rhythm for observing stimuli and gi›
overt responses. Learning to learn, on the other hand, has ‹
taken to imply the acquisition of instrumental habits w‹
facilitate the mastery of new tasks, e.g. the developmen·
successful techniques of mediation. The basic criterion used
distinguishing between warm-up and learning to learn has ‹
the degree of temporal persistence of the practice effects.

The criterion of temporal persistence provides an uncer·
basis for the distinction between warm-up and learning to le‹
The instrumental habits which constitute learning to learn·
undoubtedly subject to interference and hence may be forg‹
between experimental sessions. On the other hand, some o·
adjustments which enter into an effective response set ma·
conditioned to the experimental situation and have long-·
effects on performance. A classification of practice effects mu·
based in the first instance on a determination of the sp·

...anges in performance which are responsible for S's progressive ...provement and the conditions of training on which these ...anges depend. Once the conditions and characteristics of the ...anges in performance have been identified, their temporal ...rsistence can be assessed in turn.

The present experiment investigates the degree of specificity of ...terlist practice effects. In studies of warm-up and learning to ...arn, the method of practice and the nature of the materials have ...pically been held constant, e.g. successive paired-associate lists ... adjectives or serial lists of nonsense syllables have been used. ... the extent that the response sets and habits which produce ...provements in performance are specific to a given condition of ...actice, variations in the learning task should influence the ...ount and characteristics of transfer. For purposes of the pre... t experimental analysis three components of interlist practice ...cts will be distinguished: (a) transfer specific to the method of ...actice, e.g. paired-associate or serial learning; (b) transfer ...cific to the class of verbal materials, e.g. trigrams or words; ... (c) situational transfer. The third category is a residual one ...er which will be subsumed improvements in performance ...ch are independent of the manipulated conditions of prior ...ning.

...hod

...erimental design

...h S learned a training list (list 1) and a test list (list 2). Four ...s of tasks were used for list 1; paired-associate adjectives, ...ed-associate trigrams, serial adjectives, and serial trigrams. ...se tasks will be designated as PA(A), PA(T), S(A), and ..., respectively. The task for list 2 was either PA(A) or S(A). ...eight combinations of first and second tasks were used. ..., for a given type of list 2 there were two conditions in which ...nethod of practice on list 1 was the same and two in which it ...different; similarly, there were two conditions in which the ...of materials was the same and two in which it was different. ...order to minimize differences in speed of list-1 learning by the ...nethods of practice, lists of 10 paired associates and 12-item ...lists were used. Acquisition of list 1 was inevitably slower for trigrams than for adjectives. For the purposes of the presen study it was considered preferable to carry list 1 to a commo criterion of complete mastery under all conditions rather tha to use a constant number of trials. The nature of S's task change progressively during the approach to complete mastery of a lis the common criterion insured that S had progressed through a stages of acquisition on each training list. In addition, the streng of list-1 associations which might become sources of specif transfer effects was equated as closely as possible.

Lists

Intralist similarity was kept as low as possible for all materia In the construction of lists of adjectives, interlist similarity w minimized for all combinations of training and test lists to learned in succession by the same Ss.

Paired-associate adjectives. There were two basic lists of ten pa of two-syllable adjectives each. The relationship between the t lists conformed to the A–B, C–D paradigm. The entire pool adjectives was selected from Haagen's tables (1948) and contai no synonyms. Within a given list there were no duplications first letters on the stimulus or the response side. Stimulus a response members had four first letters in common, but pai members never shared the same first letter. The stimulus memb and response members of the two lists each had four first letter common. There were two pairings of the stimuli and response each list. Thus, there were four different lists which were equally often as the test list and, in the appropriate conditions the training list. Successive lists learned by the same Ss, i.e condition PA(A)–PA(A), always conformed to the A–B, C paradigm.

Serial adjectives. There were two serial lists of twelve adjec each. The items were drawn from the adjectives used in the lis paired associates. Nine response terms and three stimulus t of each paired-associate list were used in the construction o two serial lists. No first letters were duplicated within a list the two lists had four first letters in common. There were erial orders of each list, chosen so that each item occupied a given position only once and there were no repetitions of identical sequences of two or more items. The four different lists were used equally often as the training and test list. Lists learned successively in condition S(A)–S(A) were, of course, composed of different items.

aired-associate trigrams. Only one basic list of ten paired-associate trigrams was used due to the limited number of items which satisfied the desired criteria of intralist similarity and meaningfulness. The same formal rules governed the construction of the series of stimulus members and response members. A total of nineteen letters was used to generate the ten three-letter items; ten different letters were used in the first position, eight in the second position, and ten in the third position. Stimulus and response members had no first letters in common. There were six second letters and two third letters in common. The mean frequency of the trigrams in the Total Count of Underwood and Schulz (1960, appendix D) was 61·3 for the stimulus members and 8 for the response members. Four different pairings of the stimulus and response members were used equally often.

ial trigrams. Two serial lists of twelve trigrams each were constructed from the twenty items used in the paired-associate list s four additional ones. Both lists conformed to the same rules of formal similarity. There were twelve different letters in the first tion, eight in the second position, and ten in the third position. The total number of different letters used was twenty for one and twenty-one for the other. The mean frequencies of the rams in the Total Count were 65·3 and 65·2. There were two rs of each list conforming to the rules described for serial ctives. The four different lists were used equally often.

edure

ed-associate learning. The paired-associate lists were presented Hull-type memory drum at a 2:2 rate, with an inter-trial val of 8 sec. Four different random orders of presentation used to minimize serial learning. For a given pairing of

289

stimulus and response members each order was used as t**
starting order equally often.

Serial learning. The serial lists were presented at a 2-sec rate, wi**
an intertrial interval of 8 sec. The conventional method of an**
cipation was used.

Training and test lists. The training list (list 1) was learned to**
criterion of one perfect recitation. Practice on the test list (list**
began 3 min 45 sec after the end of list 1. Instructions for lis**
were given during that interval. List 2 was learned to a criteri**
of one perfect recitation or for ten trials, whichever took **
longer.

Subjects

With four types of training and two kinds of test list, there w**
eight groups of sixteen Ss each. The Ss were assigned to co**
tions in blocks of eight, with one S from each condition per blo**
The running orders within blocks were determined by mean**
a table of random numbers as were the assignments to spe**
lists. The Ss were undergraduate students who were naïve to r**
learning experiments. No Ss were lost because of failure to le**

Results

First-list learning

An analysis of the numbers of trials to criterion on list 1 sho**
that (a) trigrams were learned more slowly than adjec**
($\overline{X} = 26\cdot12$ and $15\cdot94$, respectively) and (b) groups which**
treated identically were of equivalent learning ability.

Transfer in paired-associate learning

We shall consider first the transfer effects in the acquisiti**
test list $PA(A)$. For purposes of this and all subsequent ana**
it will be assumed that the amount of situational transfer (**
would conventionally be designated as warm-up) is equiv**
under all conditions of pretraining. For each measure of **
formance, a comparison will first be made between the co**
group and the pretrained groups to evaluate the amoun**

gnificance of situational transfer. The differences among the
etrained groups will then be considered in detail. Variations
nong the pretrained groups will be attributed to differences in
arning to learn.

able 1

:quisition of Paired-Associate Test List: Mean Numbers of
ials to Criterion and of Correct Responses on First Ten
ials

| | Trials to criterion | | Correct responses | | | |
| | | | Trials 1–5 | | Trials 6–10 | |
adition	Mean	SD	Mean	SD	Mean	SD
trol	16·75	7·77	14·44	7·88	—	—
(A)–PA(A)	7·38	3·10	28·62	8·63	45·44	4·03
(T)–PA(A)	9·62	5·60	26·00	10·46	41·19	9·53
)–PA(A)	11·25	8·02	25·12	10·31	40·38	10·08
–PA(A)	13·00	7·79	21·44	9·73	37·06	12·16

ed of learning. Table 1 shows the mean numbers of trials re-
ed to reach criterion on test list PA(A) after the different
ditions of prior training. As measured against the control
line, all types of training produce increases in speed of learn-
The difference between the control group and the combined
rained groups is significant beyond the 0·01 level ($F = 14·38$,
1/76).[1]
ie improvement in performance is greater when the method
ractice is the same on both lists (PA–PA) than when it is
rent (S–PA). The difference between the two methods of
ice is significant ($F = 6·08$, $df = 1/56$, $p < 0·02$). The mean
ion scores are also lower when the class of materials remains
ant than when it changes. However, neither materials nor

'or purposes of increasing the precision of the evaluation of transfer,
group was evenly divided into fast and slow Ss on the basis of the
r of trials to criterion on list 1, and the variable of ability and its
tions with the experimental treatments were included in the statistical
s.

the interaction of method of practice with materials is a sign
ficant source of variance (Fs of 1·85 and less than 1·00 respe
tively). It should be noted, however, that the mean criteri
scores form an orderly array, and that the largest separation
between the condition in which both method and materials are t
same on the one hand, and that in which both are changed on t
other.

An analysis of successive criteria curves indicated that t
differential effects of prior training develop rather slowly; t
curves of the pretrained groups show a substantial amount
divergence only when about half the list has been learned. Th
differences in the conditions of prior training appear to have th
full effect relatively late in the acquisition of the test list.

Total correct responses. The mean numbers of correct respon
on trials 1–5 and 6–10 of list 2 are presented in Table 1. The d
for the control group are limited to trials 1–5 since some of
Ss in that group reached criterion in fewer than ten trials.
trials 1–5, the difference between the control group and the co
bined pretrained groups is highly significant ($F = 20·14$, $df = 1$
$p < 0·001$).

The pattern of variation among the experimental gro
parallels that obtained for trials to criterion. The difference
tween methods of practice is significant for trials 6–10 ($F = 4$
$df = 1/56$, $p < 0·05$) but not for trials 1–5 ($F = 3·36$). Differe
in the conditions of prior practice again have their most
sistent effects late in the acquisition of the test list. As bef
materials and the interaction of materials with method
practice are not significant sources of variance.

Overt errors. The percentages of overt errors were base
opportunities, i.e. total numbers of presentations minus
numbers of correct responses. The error rates vary systemati
with the conditions of prior training, being reliably lower
the method of practice remains the same than when it cha
($\bar{X} = 16·6$ per cent and 22·7 per cent, respectively), and
when the class of materials remains the same ($\bar{X} = 16·3$ pe
and 23·0 per cent, respectively). Two classes of resp
accounted for the large majority of overt errors, misp

esponses (correct responses elsewhere in the list), and stimulus rrors (stimulus terms given as responses). The difference between he two methods of practice is apparent for both types of errors, hat between classes of verbal materials only for response errors. rior experience with the paired-associate method, regardless of lass of materials, increase Ss' success in differentiating the imulus and response terms within the list.

able 2

cquisition of Serial Test List: Mean Numbers of Trials to riterion and of Correct Responses on First Ten Trials

| | Trials to criterion | | Correct responses | | | |
| | | | Trials 1–5 | | Trials 6–10 | |
ndition	Mean	SD	Mean	SD	Mean	SD
ntrol	15·50	2·85	17·69	4·86	—	—
A)–S(A)	9·31	3·35	29·56	7·73	50·38	7·50
)–S(A)	9·75	4·39	28·62	7·32	49·12	7·92
(A)–S(A)	12·44	7·37	28·38	8·88	49·00	9·87
(T)–S(A)	11·44	5·94	28·00	9·29	46·75	9·24

nsfer in serial learning

ed of learning. The mean numbers of trials to criterion on test S(A) are shown in Table 2. The first-list performance of the up trained on S(A) and tested on PA(A) provides the control on the acquisition of the test list without prior training. in all conditions of pretraining produce substantial increases e speed of learning. The difference between the control group the combined pretrained groups is highly significant = 13·73, $df = 1/76$, $p < 0.01$). The use of the same method of tice on both lists results in better test performance than does se of different methods. This difference falls, however, short gnificance ($F = 3·82$, whereas 4·00 is required at the 0·05 with 1/56 df). The class of verbal materials used in pre- ing has no apparent effect on the acquisition of the test list, loes it interact with the method of practice.

ccessive criteria curves indicated that the control group is clearly separated from all other groups. The slow emergence of differences as a function of conditions of training is again in evidence. It is only after a criterion of 8/12 that differences related to the method of practice become apparent.

Total correct responses. Table 2 shows the mean numbers of correct responses on trials 1–5 and 6–10. There is a large separation between the control groups and the pretrained groups on trials 1–5 ($F = 30.21$, $df = 1/76$, $p < 0.01$). The differences among the pretrained groups are small throughout and do not approach statistical significance.

Table 3

Correct Responses as Mean Percentages of Opportunities (C/O) after First Correct Anticipation during Acquisition of Serial Test List

Condition	Terminal items (pos. 1–3, 10–12)	Central items (pos. 4–9)
Control	86·8	65·4
S(A)–S(A)	92·6	82·2
S(T)–S(A)	91·4	86·6
PA(A)–S(A)	92·9	76·2
PA(T)–S(A)	89·2	75·8

The small variation in the total numbers of correct respon and the slow divergence of the learning curves suggest that differential effects of pretraining on rate of acquisition may limited to differences in the stability of the most difficult item the list. To test this implication of the results, the index C/O determined for the terminal items (positions 1–3 and 10–12) the central items (positions 4–9) of the serial test list. This in which was developed by Schulz and Runquist (1960), expre the numbers of correct responses after the first anticipation percentage of the opportunities for the occurrence of responses. Thus, the index reflects the stability of items after initial stages of acquisition have been completed. The m percentages of C/O are shown in Table 3. The values of the i for the terminal items are uniformly high and do not vary sistently as a function of conditions. For the central items the percentages are clearly lower for the control group than the pretrained groups ($F = 20.55$, $df = 1/76$, $p < 0.01$). When the latter are compared, groups trained and tested by the same method have a significant advantage over those learning the two lists by different methods ($F = 13.31$, $df = 1/56$, $p < 0.01$). This analysis shows that the specific conditions of pretraining have reliable but strictly circumscribed effects on speed of learning.

Serial-position analysis. The relationship between serial position and rate of acquisition appears to have been influenced by the specific conditions of prior learning. Figure 1 shows the mean numbers of trials required for the first correct anticipation of a response as a function of serial position. There is considerable variation in the shape of these serial-position curves: (1) The bimodality which is apparent in the curve of the control group suggests that these Ss tended to subdivide the total list into two subseries. (2) The curves of the two groups pretrained on adjectives, but by different methods, differ from that of the control group and from each other. After serial training a bow-shaped curve showing only slight segmentation is obtained. After pairedassociate training the central portion of the curve is characterized by pronounced inversions. The alternation of rises and falls suggests that Ss continued to apply the method which they had practiced on list 1 and learned adjacent items in the middle of the series as paired associates. On this interpretation a rise in the curve followed by a sharp drop in the next position would indicate a functional stimulus-response pair. Two adjacent cycles of such alternations appear to be present. (3) The curves of the two groups pretrained on trigrams again differ from that of the control group and from each other. After serial learning there is little evidence of bimodality; a sharp rise to a peak is followed by slow and regular drops. A marked degree of bimodality is present after paired-associate training, with the segmentation into subseries more clearly defined than in the case of the control group.

Since further analyses indicated that there is considerable variation in the serial-position curves of individual Ss, the average trends shown in Figure 1 must be interpreted with caution. We do conclude, though, that practice by the serial

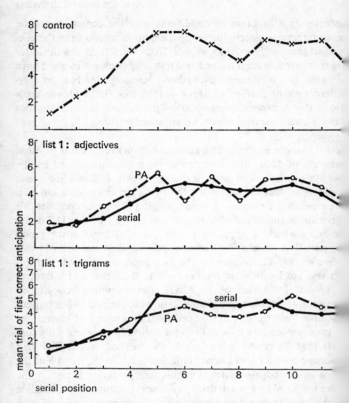

Figure 1 Serial-position curves of mean trials of first correct anticipation in acquisition of the serial test list

method reduces S's disposition to segment the list. By cont practice by the paired-associate method maintains or incre this tendency, leading to the selection of functional stimu response pairs within the series when the class of mate remains the same.

One more feature of the serial-position curves deserves c ment. As Figure 1 shows, the relative recency effect increases that of the control group after training on adjectives but ren minimal after training on trigrams. One possible mechanisr

e recency effect is mediation through backward association
tween the last and next to the last items (Ribback and Under-
ood, 1950). The last item serves as an anchor point and S then
arns the identity of the stimulus appropriate for it; the direction
the association has to be reversed to result in a correct anti-
pation. Prior mastery of a list composed of the same class of
aterials and also involving forward and backward associations
both serial and paired-associate learning are assumed to do)
uld appear to facilitate this process.[2]

ert errors. The error rates are comparable under all conditions.
us the level and distribution of overt errors are stable charac-
stics of serial performance which are not readily modified by
or training.

mparison of transfer in paired-associate and serial learning
re are large and significant differences in speed of learning
ween the control group and the pretrained groups on both the
red-associate and serial test lists. The question now arises
ther prior practice produces comparable amounts of improve-
t in both types of task. The most direct answer to this
stion is provided by a comparison of groups PA(A)–PA(A)
S(A)–S(A), which holds method of practice and class of
al materials constant in each case. Since speed of first-list
ing was comparable on the paired-associate and serial lists
= 16·25 and 15·25, respectively), there were approximately
l opportunities for transfer effects to be observed. The
ees of improvement shown in the acquisition of the second
lid not differ substantially. The mean number of trials to
rion decreased from 16·25 to 7·38 for the paired-associate
and from 15·25 to 9·31 for the serial list. The difference be-
n the amounts of interlist transfer is not significant ($t = 1·24$).
er the conditions of the present experiment, in which the
ulty of the paired-associate and serial lists was equated as
y as possible, the practice effects for the two types of task are
same order of magnitude.

he variations in the shape of the serial-position curves are greatly
d when total correct responses rather than trials of first correct antici-
s are plotted. The differences in mode of attack reflected in the latter
thus appear to be largely restricted to the early stages of practice.

Discussion

The most general finding of this study is that all conditions
pretraining produced a substantial improvement in performan
on a given test list. Much of the interlist transfer is, therefo
situational in the sense of being independent of the speci
method of practice and class of verbal materials used in pr
learning. The results of the present experiment do not prov
information about the common characteristics of the varie
conditions of training which are responsible for the nonspec
transfer effects. The fact that performance improves under
conditions of practice is consistent with the view that nonspec
transfer reflects the acquisition of response sets appropriate t
rote-learning task. Habituation to a laboratory situation is
likely to be a major factor in view of Thune's (1950) finding
the performance of a neutral task, viz. cartoon sorting, had
effect on speed of subsequent learning.

The results obtained on the paired-associate test list pro
clear evidence for transfer effects which are specific to the met
of practice. Speed of learning to criterion and total numbe
correct responses are greater when the method of practice
mains constant than when it changes. Analysis of the cours
acquisition suggests that the locus of this difference is primari
the associative stage. There were no significant differences
function of the method of prior practice in the speed of resp
recall whereas there was a clear effect on the duration of
associative stage. It appears that the specific skills acquired i
course of paired-associate learning include the ability to
stable associative links between the members of a pair a
differentiate stimulus and response terms within the list.
differences in the rate of overt errors indicate that prio
perience with the specific method of practice reduces int
generalization tendencies. The relatively late divergence c
learning curves is consistent with this interpretation sinc
stability of associative connexions and the reduction of int
interferences may be expected to have their most pronoi
effects in the terminal stages of acquisition.

The class of verbal materials used in pretraining had c
limited influence on the amount of transfer in paired-ass

arning. The basic measures of speed of learning do not change
liably as a function of this variable. The only significant effect
tributable to constancy of the materials is a reduction in the
rcentage of overt errors. This finding suggests that there
is transfer of differentiation from one group of adjectives to
other. The beneficial effects of prior experience with the
ss of materials used in the test may well be counteracted by
ociative interferences which occur because of uncontrolled
ilarities between the items in the two lists. The fact that the
asures of learning consistently favor the groups for which
class of materials was constant lends some support to this
ssibility.

here were no significant differences in speed of serial learning
a function of either the method of practice or the class of
terials used in pretraining. Nevertheless there is evidence for
erential transfer effects in the acquisition of the serial list. As
variations in the C/O index (Table 3) indicate, prior practice
a serial list increases the stability of the most difficult items in
terminal stages of acquisition. As a consequence, there is a
divergence of the learning curves, and the differences in trials
riterion as a function of method closely approach statistical
ificance. In addition, the differences in the serial-position
es of first correct anticipations suggest that the conditions of
raining influenced Ss' initial mode of attack on the serial
, with prior paired-associate practice favoring segmentation
he list into subseries. When the first list consisted of paired
ctives there was an apparent tendency to form functional
ulus-response pairs within the serial list. In a study of specific
sfer effects, in which a serial list was constructed of previously
ed stimulus-response pairs, Jensen (1963) found a similar
ency to carry over the technique of paired-associate learning
e serial task. By contrast, serial pretraining reduces seg-
ation and hence the differences in speed of learning between
ent items in the center of the list. The present results show
early in learning, the different modes of attack on the serial
were equally successful. It is only in the final stages of
isition that serially pretrained Ss had a discernible ad-
ge. This delayed separation between the groups may result
the fact that prior serial learning leads Ss to distribute their

efforts more evenly over all items in the list than does paire
associate pretraining. A steady build-up in the strength of a
items facilitates attainment of the criterion of complete master
Thus, variations in the conditions of pretraining are reflected
subsequent serial learning, but it is necessary to emphasize tl
highly limited nature of these effects. Clearly the amount ar
characteristics of interlist transfer are less subject to manipul
tion in serial than in paired-associate learning, although the ove
all magnitude of improvement is comparable on the two types
task.

We conclude that interlist practice effects in rote learning ca
not be adequately described as entirely a matter of nonspeci
warm-up and generalized learning to learn. The method of pra
tice and the class of materials used in prior learning systematica
influence subsequent performance, and these differential trans
effects can be attributed to specific instrumental habits which
carried over from one task to another. It is true that much of
transfer observed in the present study was independent of
manipulated conditions of prior training. The antecedent con
tions responsible for this situational transfer require furt
analysis and experimental manipulation.

Summary

This study investigated interlist transfer as a function of
method of practice and the class of verbal materials use
successive tasks. Each of eight groups learned a training
(list 1) and a test list (list 2). Four kinds of tasks were used
list 1: paired-associate adjectives, serial adjectives, pai
associate trigrams, and serial trigrams. List 2 consisted eithe
paired adjectives or serial adjectives. All combinations of first
second tasks were used. Intralist and interlist similarity
minimized throughout.

All conditions of training produced substantial improvem
in performance on list 2 as compared with first-list learning o
same task. In addition, transfer effects specific to the condi
of prior learning were demonstrated. Such differential tra
effects were more extensive in the acquisition of the pa
associate than the serial test list. The method of practice us

he first task consistently influenced subsequent learning more han did the class of verbal materials. The results support the :onclusion that interlist practice effects are based in part on pecific instrumental habits which are carried over from one task o the next.

references

IAAGEN, C. H. (1948), 'Synonymity, vividness, familiarity and association value ratings of 400 pairs of common adjectives', *Journal of Psychology*, vol. 27, pp. 453–63.

AMILTON, C. E. (1950), 'The relationship between length of interval separating two learning tasks and performance on the second task', *Journal of Experimental Psychology*, vol. 40, pp. 613–21.

NSEN, A. R. (1963), 'Transfer between paired-associate and serial learning', *Journal of Verbal Learning and Verbal Behavior*, vol. 1, pp. 269–80.

cGEOCH, J. A., and IRION, A. L. (1952), *The Psychology of Human Learning*, Longmans Green.

ELTON, A. W., and VON LACKUM, W. J. (1941), 'Retroactive and proactive inhibition in retention: evidence for a two-factor theory of retroactive inhibition', *American Journal of Psychology*, vol. 54, pp. 157–73.

»STMAN, L. (1962), 'The temporal course of proactive inhibition for serial lists', *Journal of Experimental Psychology*, vol. 63, pp. 361–9.

BBACK, A., and UNDERWOOD, B. J. (1950), 'An empirical explanation of the skewness of the bowed serial position curve', *Journal of Experimental Psychology*, vol. 40, pp. 329–35.

HULZ, R. W., and RUNQUIST, W. N. (1960), 'Learning and retention of paired adjectives as a function of percentage of occurrence of response members'. *Journal of Experimental Psychology*, vol. 59, pp. 09–13.

UNE, L. E. (1950), 'The effect of different types of preliminary activities on subsequent learning of paired-associate material', *Journal of Experimental Psychology*, vol. 40, pp. 423–38.

UNE, L. E. (1951), 'Warm-up effect as a function of level of practice a verbal learning', *Journal of Experimental Psychology*, vol. 42, pp. 50–56.

EDT, H. M., and UNDERWOOD, B. J. (1959), 'Mixed vs. unmixed ts in transfer studies', *Journal of Experimental Psychology*, vol. 58, ɔ. 111–16.

DERWOOD, B. J., and SCHULZ, R. W. (1960), *Meaningfulness and erbal Learning*, Lippincott.

RD, L. B. (1937), 'Reminiscence and rote learning', *Psychological onographs*, vol. 49, no. 220.

21 H. M. Twedt and B. J. Underwood

Mixed versus Unmixed Lists in Transfer Studies

H. M. Twedt and B. J. Underwood, 'Mixed versus unmixed lists in trans
fer studies', *Journal of Experimental Psychology*, vol. 58 (1959), pp. 111–1(

In relatively recent years there has been an increase in the fre
quency with which mixed lists (ML) have been used to stud
transfer with verbal materials. In ML a single group of Ss ma
be used. Each S learns only two lists in which different relatio
ships between subgroups of items allow the simultaneo
observation of the transfer effects produced by these differe
relationships. Thus, if each of two lists consisted on nine pair
associates, three pairs in each list could form the A–B, A-
paradigm, three the A–B, C–B, and three an A–B, C–D paradig

The ML procedure may be contrasted with the classical o
in which unmixed lists (UL) are used. With UL the relationshi
between all items in the two lists are the same. Thus, if the pa
digm was A–B, A–C, all stimuli in the two lists would be the sa
and all responses different. Obviously, to study transfer effe
for more than one paradigm requires as many different sets
lists as there are paradigms.

Certain contradictions in the facts of transfer could be at
buted to the possibility that UL and ML produce differe
transfer effects. The clearest example of this possibility is seer
the work of Mandler and Heinemann (1956) and Porter
Duncan (1953). In both of these studies an A–B, A–C paradi
was used, and also a paradigm that will be called A–B, A–Br
this latter paradigm the same stimuli and same responses
used in both lists (UL) or among a subgroup of items in the t
lists (ML), but they are re-paired in the second list. Porter
Duncan, using UL, found poorer second-list performance
A–B, A–Br than on A–B, A–C, while Mandler and Heinem
found just the opposite. There are other differences between
two studies over and above UL vs. ML which could account

this discrepancy. Indeed, a study (1958) published after the present one was completed essentially confirmed the Porter–Duncan results using ML. Therefore, other differences between the studies may be responsible for the different results. In other contradictions in the literature (e.g. Bugelski and Cadwallader, 1956 versus Osgood, 1946) ML versus UL is again one of several possible factors involved. Therefore, a direct test of the transfer effects for the two kinds of lists is indicated to decide whether or not ML versus UL is a variable of importance in the study of transfer. The major purpose of the present study is to make such test.

There was an *a priori* reason to suggest that ML versus UL is a variable influencing the relative amount of transfer among different paradigms. This may be seen by considering the situation in which S learns A–B, A–C with UL. While this paradigm can produce negative transfer, it has always been puzzling why (a) the negative effects are small, and why (b) so few B responses intrude during the learning of A–C. This would be less puzzling if it is assumed that two relatively independent response systems are maintained, differentiated by temporal or first and second list distinctions. If this differentiation is possible, S could instruct himself *not* to give responses from the first list and a relatively small amount of negative transfer would be expected. However, if the ML procedure is used in which some of the first-list responses are appropriate in the second list (A–B, C–B or A–B, A–Br) and some are not (A–B, A–C), the maintenance of the independent response systems is not possible. The prediction would be, therefore, that negative transfer would be greater for ML than for UL in the A–B, A–C paradigm. It is also possible that other interactions among effects of other paradigms could occur in ML and not in UL.

Method

Lists

The transfer effects for four paradigms were studied, each by the use of both UL and ML. If A–B represents the first list, the four paradigms may be symbolized in the second list (UL), or in subgroups of items in the second list (ML), as A–C, A–Br, C–B, and

C–D. The last paradigm may be considered the control condition, in that no systematic identities obtain between the items in the two lists (UL) or between the particular subgroup of items for ML.

The materials were paired-associate lists of twelve pairs of two-syllable adjectives. All Ss in all conditions with both UL and ML learned exactly the same *second* list. Therefore, any differences in transfer resulting from ML versus UL cannot be attributed to differences in list or pair difficulty. This second list consisted of the following twelve pairs: *honest–frantic, senior–rotten, certain–aloof, ready–severe, human–unshut, complex–valiant, single–noonday, zigzag–absurd, luke-warm–stubborn, profane–bitter, famous–exact, filthy–rising.* These twelve pairs were selected by use of a table of random numbers from a pool of twenty-four pairs used by Young (1955) in his low-similarity conditions. The items forming the remaining twelve pairs were used as necessary to construct the first list: for UL, all twelve pairs were used for the A–B, C–D paradigm, none was used for A–B, A–Br, and twelve items were necessary for A–B, A–C, and A–B, C–B.

For ML, with four conditions and twelve pairs in a list, each condition was represented by three pairs. The use of four groups of Ss for ML made it possible to use all twelve pairs in the second list for each paradigm. Thus, in UL, four groups of Ss were needed, each group having a given paradigm, and this paradigm held between all twelve pairs in the two lists. In ML, four groups were also used, and for all four groups combined, the relationship between the first and second lists was exactly the same as for UL.

Procedure

The first list was presented until one perfect trial was attained. After 1 min the second list was presented for ten trials. Learning was by the anticipation method, with the stimulus being presented for 2 sec and the stimulus and response together for 2 sec as timed by a Hull-type memory drum. The intertrial interval was 4 sec. Three different orders of the lists were used to minimize serial learning. In ML the three pairs representing a given paradigm were not grouped; that is, the ordering of the pairs was such that those representing one paradigm were mixed up with the representing other paradigms. In neither ML nor UL was *S* instructed concerning the nature of the relationships between the two lists.

Four groups of eighteen *S*s each learned under the ML procedure and four other groups of the same number learned under the UL procedure. An order of conditions was made up such that each of the eight conditions was represented once by each block of eighteen *S*s. Within each block the ordering was random. The *S*s were simply assigned in order of their appearance at the laboratory. All *S*s had previous experience in verbal-learning experiments.

It should be emphasized that all *S*s learned the same second list. Therefore, it is of little or no consequence whether or not first lists differed in difficulty; this would be true for comparisons within UL or within ML, and it would be true for comparisons between UL and ML. In actual fact, for eight groups, the over-all mean number of trials to learn the first list was 12·7 trials, with a range of from 10·5 to 15·2. An analysis of variance yielded an F 1·46, which is far from significant. This does not mean, of course, that these first lists did not differ in difficulty since possible ability differences among groups and possible list differences are confounded.

Results

The results will be presented first in graphical form and then attention will be given to statistical analyses. In Figure 1, the mean total correct responses on the ten transfer trials are shown for each condition for both UL and ML. For UL, each condition represents the mean performance of eighteen *S*s on twelve pairs. For ML, each condition represents the performance of twenty-two *S*s, each learning three pairs. To coordinate the values for UL and ML, the total correct responses were summed for successive groups of four *S*s each on ML, such that all twelve pairs representing a condition for UL were likewise represented for each subgroup of four *S*s in ML. Thus, in a sense, eighteen *S*s were 'constructed' out of the seventy-two *S*s learning under ML, and this was done for each transfer condition.

In Figure 1, it may first be noted that differences between UL

Transfer

and ML are very small. The second fact shown in Figure 1 is tha
if C–D is considered the control condition, all three other condi
tions show negative transfer, the amount of this negative transfe
increasing from C–B, to A–C, to A–Br.

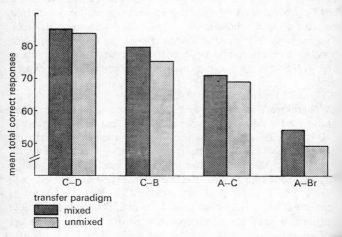

Figure 1 Total correct responses over ten transfer trials as a function of
mixed and unmixed lists and four transfer paradigms

In Figure 1, the values represent the total correct respon
over all 10 transfer trials. It is conceivable that a different order
of the conditions could occur at various stages in learning
second list. That this is not true is shown by Figure 2, where i
seen that the ordering of conditions remains relatively const
throughout all 10 trials. Also, Figure 2 shows quite clearly t
the differences between UL and ML are of small consequer
The coordination between UL and ML was handled the sa
way for Figure 2 as for Figure 1.

The first statistical analysis consists of a direct test of
results for UL versus ML. The measure used was the numbe
correct responses over the ten transfer trials. These compari
were made for the total correct for each group of three it
For example, in ML one group of eighteen Ss had a partic
group of three pairs for A–Br. These same three pairs were

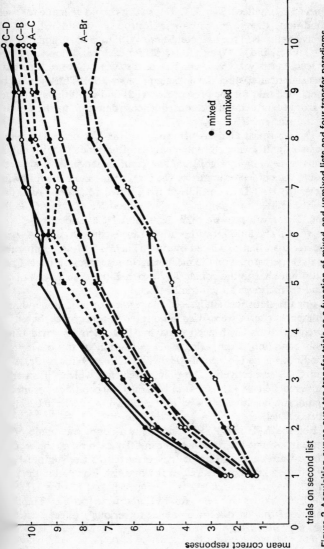

Figure 2 Acquisition curves over ten transfer trials as a function of mixed and unmixed lists and four transfer paradigms

learned by eighteen Ss in UL. Four t tests could be made for each condition, therefore, and these four tests would exhaust all twelve items used for that condition. With four conditions (A–Br, A–C, C–B, and C–D) and four tests for each condition, a total of sixteen t tests was involved. The results were that not a single was significant, using the 0·05 significance level. Thus, it may be concluded that for the present materials and conditions, whether UL or ML is used is of no consequence in determining the amount of transfer.

The statistical analysis of results for the UL procedure alone was straightforward. Simple analysis of variance showed conditions to be a highly significant source of variance. Several t tests (using the pooled estimate for the error term) show the following facts: (a) If C–D is considered the control condition, A–C and A–Br resulted in significant negative transfer whereas C–B did not. The t values were 6·29, 2·68, and 1·52, respectively, with 34 df. (b) The amount of negative transfer produced by A–Br is greater than that produced by A–C. The t is 3·61. A comparable analysis performed on the mean correct responses on trials 1 and 2 did not change the conclusions reached for the analysis of the total correct over all ten trials.

For the statistical analysis of the results for ML alone, direct difference t tests were used among conditions, each based on seventy-two Ss, with each S having three items learned under each condition. Comparing C–D with each of the other three conditions gave t values of 10·09, 4·59, and 2·40, for A–Br, A–C, and C–B, respectively. The only conclusion which differs from those reached for UL is that in ML the C–B condition resulted in significant negative transfer (the t of 2·4 is at the 0·02 significance level).

For the A–C and A–Br conditions, a count was made of intrusions of first-list responses during the learning of the second. These were counted only if they occurred to the stimulus with which they had been paired in the first list. For A–Br, the total intrusions over ten trials was 182 for ML and 154 for UL. For A–C, the values were five for ML and four for UL. Thus, the nature of the list does not appear to seriously affect intrusion making tendencies.

Discussion

The results have shown that UL and ML produce essentially the same transfer results. Indeed, it is not likely that correspondence would have been higher had the two experiments used the same method (either UL or ML). One implication of these results is that contradictions in the facts of transfer, noted in the introduction, are probably not due to ML versus UL. A second implication is that the possibility that S maintains independent response systems (also suggested in the introduction) in the A–B, A–C paradigm is untenable. The third implication is that it appears that investigators may choose either ML or UL procedures, depending upon circumstances which make one more desirable than another for a particular investigation, without serious concern that the transfer results will be affected by this choice. It is possible, of course, that the present near-identity of results for UL and ML will not hold with all materials, e.g. consonant syllables, although there is no obvious reason why they should not.

Concerning the transfer effects, the present experiments confirm Porter and Duncan (1953) and Besch and Reynolds (1958) in showing that A–Br produces more negative transfer than A–C. That Mandler and Heinemann (1956) actually found positive transfer with A–Br and negative transfer with A–C may be attributed (as suggested by Besch and Reynolds) to the low meaningfulness of the responses used by Mandler and Heinemann. However, this matter will not be pursued here. It is sufficient to say that it does not appear that the source of contradiction is in the nature of the lists (ML versus UL).

The one finding that does not fit current theory on previous findings is that the A–B, C–B paradigm produced negative transfer when evaluated against A–B, C–D. It is true that the amount of negative transfer is small, but it is consistent in both experiments and is present throughout most of the ten transfer trials. Furthermore, there is reason to believe that the negative factor (or factors) may be greater in extent than actually appears in the performance. It is known (Underwood, Runquist and Schulz, 1959) from other research that teaching S responses before learning a list of paired associates will facilitate the learn- In effect, when S learns A–B he has learned the responses required in learning C–B; therefore, the learning of C–B should be facilitated. In the present results, this positive factor is more than counteracted by negative effects. The question remains, therefore, as to the source of this interference. The best guess is that it results indirectly from backward learning. It is known (Feldman and Underwood, 1957) that as S learns A–B, an association develops between B and A so that B will elicit A with much greater than chance probability. It may be assumed that such backward associations developed in the learning of the first list in the present study; B will have some tendency to elicit A. The S then proceeds to learn C–B. As this association develops, it is possible that when C is presented it makes S 'think of' B, but that B (via backward association) makes him think of A (the stimulus in the first list) leading to an erroneous 'conclusion' that B does not go with the present stimulus – C. It would not require many such confusions to produce the negative transfer observed.

Summary

This study was designed to investigate the transfer effects in verbal paired-associate learning using a mixed design (in which subgroups of pairs in the second list form various transfer paradigms with pairs in the first) and an unmixed design (in which all pairs in the second list relate in the same way to the pairs in the first). Four paradigms were studied by each of these two procedures: A–B, A–Br (second-list pairs constitute a repairing first-list pairs); A–B, A–C; A–B, C–B; and A–B, C–D. The latter paradigm constituted the control condition. For all paradigms for both mixed and unmixed designs all Ss learned the same second list. The various paradigms were formed by changing the pairs in the first list. Eight groups of eighteen Ss each were used. The first list of paired adjectives was presented until all items were correctly anticipated on a single trial; the second or transfer list was presented for ten trials.

The results show no difference in the transfer effects as a function of mixed versus unmixed lists. Thus, the use of various paradigms among subgroups of items within a single list does not produce interactions among the transfer effects for the various paradigms. It was concluded, therefore, that investigators may use either type of design without serious concern that the transfer effects will be different.

Using A–B, C–D as a control, the results show that all paradigms produce negative transfer throughout the ten trials on the second list. The greatest negative transfer was produced by A–B, A–Br, the next greatest by A–B, A–C, and the least by A–B, C–B. A possible source of interference in the latter paradigm was discussed.

References

BESCH, N. F., and REYNOLDS, W. F. (1958) 'Associative interference in verbal paired-associate learning', *Journal of Experimental Psychology*, vol. 55, pp. 554–8.

BUGELSKI, B. R., and CADWALLADER, T. C. (1956), 'A reappraisal of the transfer and retroaction surface', *Journal of Experimental Psychology*, vol. 52, pp. 360–66.

FELDMAN, S. M., and UNDERWOOD, B. J. (1957), 'Stimulus recall following paired-associate learning', *Journal of Experimental Psychology*, vol. 53, pp. 11–15.

MANDLER, G., and HEINEMANN, S. H. (1956), 'Effect of overlearning of a verbal response on transfer of training', *Journal of Experimental Psychology*, vol. 52, pp. 39–46.

OSGOOD, C. E. (1946), 'Meaningful similarity and interference in learning', *Journal of Experimental Psychology*, vol. 36, pp. 277–301.

PORTER, L. W., and DUNCAN, C. P. (1953), 'Negative transfer in verbal learning', *Journal of Experimental Psychology*, vol. 46, pp. 61–4.

UNDERWOOD, B. J., RUNQUIST, W. N., and SCHULZ, R. W. (1959), 'Response learning in paired-associate lists as a function of intralist similarity', *Journal of Experimental Psychology*, vol. 58, pp. 70–78.

YOUNG, R. K. (1955), 'Retroactive and proactive effects under varying conditions of response similarity', *Journal of Experimental Psychology*, vol. 50, pp. 113–19.

22 E. Martin

Transfer of Verbal Paired Associates

Abridged from E. Martin, 'Transfer of verbal paired associates', *Psychological Review*, vol. 72 (1965), pp. 327–43. [*Editors' note:* Owing to the inclusion of McGovern's paper, 'Extinction of associations in four transfer paradigms' (Reading 29), portions of the following article have been deleted in order to conserve space. It is recommended that the reader study both papers concurrently.]

The problem of transfer of verbal paired associates originated with Müller and Schumann (1894), whose law of associative inhibition was essentially a specification of the negative transfer paradigm A–B, A–D, and Müller and Pilzecker (1900), who developed the method of 'right associates'. A closely related problem, one with which transfer is, in many respects, inextricably intertwined, is that of retroactive inhibition, which also originated with Müller and Pilzecker (1900) in conjunction with their perseveration theory of reproduction inhibition. In 1949, Osgood attempted to organize the many facts and insights that had been accruing in this general problem area since Müller's time by proposing a transfer and retroaction surface. Thus the period from Müller to Osgood is a historical package, so to speak, with the most articulate summary being Osgood's paper. The purpose of the present paper is a reorganization based on additional facts and insights, some of which have accumulated since 1949, with the restriction that only transfer problems will be considered.

In an analysis of the effects of having learned one set of paired associates on the subsequent learning of another, four experimentally controllable variables emerge for which there are sufficient data to draw definitive conclusions. Two of these, interlist stimulus and interlist response similarity, have received considerable attention and were incorporated into Osgood's (1949) transfer theory. The other two, degree of first-task learning (L) and response meaningfulness (M), have been treated experimentally but not explained theoretically. To grasp the empirical relationships among these four variables, it seems best to first examine

Osgood's theory and then to describe how L_1 and M underlie systematic departures.

Osgood's (1949) contribution to transfer theory can be seen to resolve into two components: (a) the invention of a coordinate system in which all paired-associate paradigms can be arranged, and (b) a summary of available data in the form of a surface which describes how amount of transfer and position in the coordinate system are related.[1] The coordinate system has the important feature of formally distinguishing the separate roles of interlist stimulus and interlist response dissimilarity. These two

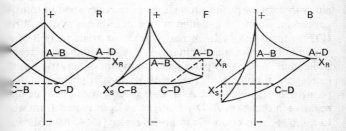

ure 1 Component transfer surfaces. (The surfaces R, F and B represent transfer of response availability, forward associations, and backward associations, respectively)

variables are expressed as orthogonal axes, the X_S and X_R axes Figure 1F, with the origin representing complete similarity, or entity. Thus, for example, the negative transfer paradigm A–B, D, has the coordinates $X_S = 0$ and X_R some sufficiently large ue to indicate complete dissimilarity (or unrelatedness) between the responses of the first- and transfer-task lists. All transfer paradigms are assigned a unique position in joint accordance the dissimilarity between the stimuli and the dissimilarity between the responses of the two lists. Surface points above the X_R plane represent positive transfer; points below, negative sfer.

At approximately the same time, and apparently independently, rwood (1949) made an equivalent proposal based on the same data, expectations from generalization theory, in the form of four curves. His s are essentially the surface edges given by Osgood.

A perusal of the transfer studies whose designs constitute a te:
of Osgood's surface, however, reveals that although the genera
shape of the surface is fairly well substantiated, there are a numbe
of systematic discrepancies which can be attributed to specif
experimental factors, namely, L_1 and response M. (In the ensuir
discussion, only experiments utilizing the A–B, C–D contr
paradigm for nonspecific effects will be cited; thus amount ar
sign of transfer at other positions in the coordinate system a
always with respect to transfer-task performance at the A–
C–D position.)

The effect on transfer-task performance of increasing L_1
either to decrease positive transfer or to increase negative transfe
depending upon the position in the coordinate system. Bru
(1933) found that as L_1 increased from six trials to twelve, t
amount of positive transfer in the A–B, C–B paradigm decrease
while in the A–B, A–D paradigm the amount of negative trans
increased. In Jung's (1962) experiment, transfer progressed fro
positive to negative in the A–B, C–B paradigm and became m
negative in the A–B, A–D paradigm as L_1 increased from a
to a 6/6 + 5 criterion. Dean and Kausler (1964) have show
striking shift from positive transfer with a first-task criterion
$L_1 = 3/6$ to negative transfer with $L_1 = 6/6 + 5$ in the A
C–B paradigm. Further substantiation of this role of degree
L_1 is provided by Spiker (1960) for the A–B, A–D paradigm
by Postman (1962b) for several paradigms.

If overlearning of the first task is considered, the foregoing cl
picture of the role of degree of L_1 becomes somewhat clou
Postman (1962b), while reporting an increase in negative tran
with a change from a 6/10 to a 10/10 criterion for L_1 in both
A–B, C–B and A–B, A–D paradigms, finds a sharp reductio
amount of negative transfer for a 10/10 + 50 per cent criter
Mandler and Heinemann (1956) report negative transfer in
A–B, C–B paradigm after ten errorless L_1 trials but positive tr
fer after thirty and fifty such trials, with a return to negative tr
fer after 100 trials. In the A–B, A–D paradigm, transfer rem
negative throughout but shows fluctuation similar to that ir
A–B, C–B. These results are difficult to reconcile both with
other and with data not involving overlearning. Mandler (1
has presented a systematic argument for negative transfer

-shaped function of degree of L_1, transfer becoming more nega-
ve then less negative in the A–B, A–D paradigm. It should be
oted, however, that in making that argument, Mandler cites his
wn data (Mandler and Heinemann, 1956) but leaves out the data
oint for his greatest-degree-of-overlearning condition, a data
oint which denies the V-shaped function. Other data cited by
andler in support of a V-shaped function are not relevant in the
esent context because they do not include A–B, C–D control
aradigms for nonspecific effects. Thus, although degree of L_1
versely affects transfer in the A–B, A–D and A–B, C–B para-
gms in a regular manner at ordinary degrees of L_1, a definitive
nclusion regarding the role of over-learning does not seem
ssible at this point.

Where M is taken as a generic term referring to the core attri-
te of verbal units reflected by such highly intercorrelated scales
meaningfulness, association value, and pronunciability (Noble,
63), the effect of first-list response M on transfer-task perform-
ce is to increasingly impede that performance as M is increased.
g (1963) showed that when responses are low-M trigrams, con-
erable positive transfer and barely negative transfer are ob-
ved in the A–B, C–B and A–B, A–D paradigms respectively;
when responses are high-M trigrams, transfer in the A–B,
B becomes nearly zero, and transfer in the A–B, A–D becomes
y negative. Varying M over three levels (low – CCCs, medium –
Cs, high – words), Merikle and Battig (1963) showed that as
ncreases, transfer in the A–B, A–D paradigm decreases from
ly negative to considerably negative.

urther evidence on this matter can be had by categorizing
lable data according to whether transfer is positive or nega-
in the A–B, C–B paradigm. If this is done, it turns out that
tudies yielding positive transfer involve trigrams as responses
ce, 1933; Jung, 1963; Mandler and Heinemann, 1956), where-
ose yielding negative transfer involve meaningful responses,
as adjectives (Dallett, 1962; Harcum, 1953; Kausler and
oti, 1963; Keppel and Underwood, 1962; Twedt and Under-
d, 1959; Wimer, 1964). An exception to this categorization
e Bugelski and Cadwallader (1956) study, which reports
ive transfer at the A–B, C–B position with words as response
rials. Their procedure involved dropping out pairs from the

first-task list once given correctly twice in succession. Further they used visual patterns as stimuli.

Thus degree of L_1 and response M appear to be major experimental factors responsible for systematic deviations from Osgood's surface. There are, of course, other factors whose effect will eventually have to be accounted for, for example, intralist similarity, list length, and time between L_1 and the transfer task. At the present time, little is known about the effects of the first two on the transfer task; and, adhering to the restriction of considering only transfer data which includes the A–B, C–D control only one study, Newton and Wickens (1956), is known to the present writer concerning the last. If one is willing to compare per cent saving (the per cent the difference in the number of trials to criterion for the two tasks is of the number for the first task) in the A–B, A–D paradigm (their experiment I) with percentage saving in the A–B, C–D paradigm (their experiment II), it turns out that the differences obtained by subtracting the latter from the former for intertask delays of 0, 24, and 48 hours is −3, −8, and +5. Thus for the A–B, A–D paradigm there is evidence that the associations which are to interfere during transfer-task learning are lost over time. The studies customarily cited on this phenomenon, however, either do not employ the A–B, C–D control for nonspecific effects (Bunch and McCraven, 1938) or deal only with the nonspecific effects of the A–B, C–D paradigm (Hamilton, 1950).

Essentially, while the coordinate system is definitional in nature, the surface proposed by Osgood is an empirical law, an induction from the facts. In view of the growing complexity of the facts revealed, at least, by the roles of L_1 and M however, a revised induction does not seem feasible; instead it would appear easier to turn to the implications embedded in already extant verbal learning theory for an improved formalization of transfer phenomena. On this view, two developments are of special interest: the two-phase conceptualization of verbal learning and the notion of association bi-directionality.

The idea that verbal learning may profitably be viewed as more than one process seems to have originated with Thorndike (19— who notes that 'other things being equal, connexions are easier to form in proportion as the response is available' (p. 343), and much of learning consists in making certain responses more available' (p. 347). Current expression of this notion is well exemplified by Underwood and Schulz (1960): 'Logically speaking, the acquisition of a serial or paired-associate list can be divided into two stages. The first will be called *response-learning* or *response-recall* stage. It occurs temporally prior to the second stage which will be called the *associative* or *hook-up stage*' (p. 92).

The utility of distinguishing two phases of the total verbal learning process is readily discernible in the literature. For example, Underwood, Runquist, and Schulz (1959), Horowitz (1961), and Carterette (1963) have demonstrated that the two phases can be discriminated experimentally on the grounds that a single variable differentially affects certain response measures separately identifiable with the two phases. It was found that while variations in intralist response similarity had a direct effect on response learning (as measured by recallability), association formation (as measured either by responding to specific stimulation or by ordering performance) was inversely affected.[2] A more detailed consideration of these two components of learning, plus others, has been given by McGuire (1961). He argues cogently for their utility and demonstrates experimentally their distinguishability.

Since it is meaningful to view the acquisition of verbal paired associates as a composite of two processes, response learning and

Caution must be exercised in claiming that high intralist response similarity facilitates response learning. When similarity among items is induced by means of either (a) generating a list of trigrams from a limited alphabet or (b) basing similarity on the notion of synonymity, the possibility exists that given one response some of the others can be inferred. In such situations, it becomes problematic whether observed facilitation is effected by current learning or by transfer of previously acquired rules or strategies. It is not reasonable to suppose that response learning is the sole source of response availability measured by recall. Strictly speaking, response learning is the serial acquisition of the elements of the response (and hence itself an association-formation process). Response availability, however, involves also the contextual associations that support recall. Thus the recall measure is not a pure measure of response learning. In the transfer situation, context associations which tend to elicit responses are indistinguishable from specific transferred associations, hence in future references to response availability what is intended is availability arising from response learning association formation, it makes sense to conclude that at the end of L_1 in a transfer situation there are at least two 'things' available for transfer to the second, or transfer, task; namely, response availability and associative connexions, the former being the product of first-task response learning, the latter of the first-task association formation.

Admitting that associative connexions are available for transfer from task to task entails a consideration of the rather extensive literature on backward associations. Cognizance of this problem apparently begins with Ebbinghaus (1885), who wrote that 'as a result of the learning of a series certain connections of the members are therefore actually formed in a reverse as well as in a forward direction' (p. 112). Most of the early interest in backward associations was centered on the problem of remote association in serial learning, the first application to transfer apparently not occurring until the appearance of Harcum's paper in 195. Harcum's finding that backward associations are transferred has since been confirmed by Murdock (1958) with different material with further evidence provided by Keppel and Underwood (1962); hence a generality seems to be in order. The conclusion then, is that backward associative connexions are a component of what is transferred in a transfer situation and must be included in a formalization of transfer phenomena.

A Component-Surfaces Conceptualization

It has been argued that there are three components to that which is transferred from one paired-associate task to another, namely response availability, forward associations, and backward associations. An immediate implication of this position is that all the ordinary measures of transfer (number of trials to criterion the transfer task; number of correct responses, or errors, in many transfer-task trials; etc.) reflect what is best called a effect. In other words, a single transfer surface whose ordinate values are given by any one of the standard measures is essentially a net transfer surface and presumably can be analysed into other more specific component surfaces. This means that, since there are three effects transferred, there should be three transfer faces, each describing how its particular effect is transferred function of position in the coordinate system. The specification of such a triad of surfaces, at least schematically, follows from general paired-associate interference theory.

Consider first how response availability (that due to response learning) transfers from one paired-associate task to another. Any response learning evolved during the first task must transfer maximally to the transfer task of paradigms at positions in the coordinate system where first- and transfer-task responses are identical. This transfer is not perfect to the extent that response availability includes context and/or other nonparadigmatic associations not carrying over; in fact, such associations may even be a source of interference. Response availability due to first-task response learning, however, has a maximum and equal positive effect along the X_S axis, that is, at all positions from A–B, A–B to A–B, C–B. At the other extreme, none of the response learning of the first task is appropriate to the transfer task of paradigms involving completely new transfer-task responses. Response availability acquired extraexperimentally may certainly apply but not response availability from first-task learning. Therefore, a surface representing the transfer of first-task response learning must coincide with the X_S–X_R zero-transfer plane at positions from A–B, A–D to A–B, C–D.

Regarding positions between the maximally positive-transfer loci from A–B, A–B to A–B, C–B and the zero-transfer loci from A–B, A–D to A–B, C–D, intermediate amounts of response availability obtain. These varying degrees of transferred response availability are seen as arising from the applicability of first-task response learning to whatever characteristics or components of the transfer-task responses are responsible for the similarity (relatedness, including opposition) between the first- and transfer-task responses. This argument can be summarized by a hypothetical surface, called the R surface for response availability, that is shown in Figure 1R.

The second component of paired-associate acquisition, forward association, requires some degree of similarity between first- and transfer-task stimuli in order to introduce a nonzero effect. If associations A–B are acquired in the first task, then to the extent to which the stimuli of the transfer task are similar to A, the associates of A from the first task are elicited in transfer-task learning.

Thus, those positions on a line between A–B, C–B and A–B
C–D cannot involve transfer of forward associations becaus
completely new stimuli characterize the transfer task. In progress
ing from the A–B, C–B position toward the A–B, A–B position i
the coordinate system, first-task forward associations become in
creasingly more useful in the transfer task, until the A–B, A–
position is reached where the transfer task is but a continuation
the first task.

As the A–B, A–D position is approached (from any direction
however, the forward associations acquired in the first task b
come increasingly stronger sources of interference in transfe
task learning. This interference is inferred from the fact th
acquisition of A–D associations involves the extinction of A–
associations (Barnes and Underwood, 1959; Briggs, 1954; Po
man, 1961, 1962a). As will be pointed out below, the literature
unanimous that relative to the A–B, C–D control paradigm
A–B, A–D yields negative transfer. The point to be made here
that this negativity cannot be due to either transferred respo
availability or transferred backward associations (because the r
ponses of the transfer task are completely new) and hence m
be due to interfering forward associations. The F surface, dep
ing the transfer of forward associations, is shown in Figure 1F
is essentially the surface proposed by Osgood (1949).

The third, and final, component to be considered is that
backward association. The surface to represent this effect n
necessarily be symmetric in general form, if not in magnit
with the F surface where the axis of symmetry is the line betw
the A–B, A–B and A–B, C–D positions. Arguing in the rev
direction, there must be some degree of similarity (relatedn
including opposition) between the responses of the first and tr
fer tasks in order for backward associations acquired in the
task to be elicited in the transfer task. Now it has already
pointed out that backward associations are a component of
is acquired in paired-associate learning; hence if, as in the A
C–B paradigm, the backward B–A associations of the first
are elicited during transfer-task learning, then the acquisitic
the backward B–C associations will be impeded. Thus the su
representing the transfer of backward associations must be
tive at the A–B, C–B position. At the A–B, A–B position,

ver, the backward associations to be acquired in the transfer task re the same as those already practiced in the first task, hence the urface there must be positive. On a line between A–B, A–D and –B, C–D, the responses are completely different in the transfer ask, that is, the stimuli capable of eliciting the backward assoations of the first task are absent, hence the surface must coinde with the X_S–X_R zero-transfer plane. Such a surface is shown Figure 1B.

The three surfaces of Figure 1 are not entirely empirical (as was sgood's single surface) because the three concepts represented by em are indeed primarily concepts. The surfaces are intended to representative of expectations as to the nature of the componts of the two-task paired-associate situation (transfer) arising m the general interference theory of the single-task pairedsociate situation.

The locus of action of the experimental variables L_1 and M now be seen somewhat more clearly. In the degenerate case ere $L_1 = 0$, that is, where no first-task learning obtains, all faces collapse into X_S–X_R zero-transfer plane: Nothing is transred. With successive first-task trials, the associations which are transfer become stronger, and the F and B surfaces assume ir characteristic curvature. For example, at the A–B, C–B ition, as L_1 increases, the negativeness of the B surface inses, presumably asymptotically, until a maximum is reached earlier discussion of over-learning). With respect to the R ace, L_1 trials serve also to develop its curvature. In situations re first-task responses are of the highest M (e.g. familiar ns), only a few trials are required for full development of the R ace. Thus L_1 and M enter the analysis as factors determining developmental (over trials) dispositions of the surfaces *relative* e X_S–X_R *zero-transfer plane*. These relationships will emerge e clearly when applications of the model are discussed below. ach surface is thus a different function of the same two bles, X_S and X_R. For example, the R surface would be desd by some function, f, as

$$f(X_S, X_R; M, L_1),$$

e M and L_1 are parameters representing the response-M and e-of-L_1 characteristics, respectively, of the transfer situation.

If response M, say, were to be studied functionally at some fixed position in the coordinate system, then resulting variations in response availability would be represented by

$$R = f(M; X_S, X_R, L_1),$$

where f is the same function as before, but M is now taken as the variable and X_S, X_R, and L_1 as the parameters. Thus there are multiple experimental approaches to the ultimate specification of the three functions relating the component surfaces to X_S and X_R. The most formidable obstacle between the present state of transfer theory and such a goal, however, is the unavailability of suitable similarity (relatedness) measure for the X_S and X_R dimensions. If such a measure cannot be evolved, then the Osgood coordinate system view of transfer phenomena cannot develop into a quantitative theory.[3]

The decomposition of transfer phenomena into component effects has been given brief consideration by Postman (1962b). He distinguishes four sources of transfer: (a) learning to learn and warm-up, or nonspecific effects; (b) response learning, which is represented by the R surface in the present formulation; (c) associative interference, which has here been formally subdivided into the F and B component surfaces; and (d) differentiation between lists, a characteristic of transfer tasks represented by the X_S and X_R values assigned to the paradigm involved. Regarding the last source, if X_S and X_R are to adequately represent differentiation between lists, they must necessarily include more than scaled dissimilarity. Undoubtedly, Postman means to include the type of differentiation characterized by increased certainty as to which of the two tasks a given response item belongs. Postman draws further attention to the fact that second-task learning also has two phases and that the several effects being transferred from the first task should be expected to differentially affect them.

3. It is of interest to note that in a component model for stimulus compounding and generalization presented by Atkinson and Estes (196 statement can be derived which says that in general the similarity relation between two verbal units is not symmetric; for example, *abc* may be more similar to *ab* than *ab* is to *abc*. If this is in fact the case, it would make difference which list goes into which task in a transfer problem, hence introducing directionality into dissimilarity measure.

Before proceeding to applications of the component-surfaces conceptualization to specific transfer situations, it is necessary to ake one more step on the theoretical level: In addition to the efined coordinate system and the assumed component surfaces, here needs to be a statement about the temporal relationship be-ween the two phases of learning. The role of such a statement ould be to provide a conceptual mechanism by means of which he parameters of the transfer problem can specify dispositions of he component surfaces *relative to each other*. For example, sup-ose it were assumed that the response-learning phase precedes he association-formation phase; then for a sufficiently low degree f L_1 very little association formation could occur. Therefore, at a osition such as the A–B, C–B where the sign of transfer depends on the net effect of the positive R and the negative B effects ee Figure 1), positive transfer would be predicted because no B fects could have developed. But this is an example of a success- l application of the complete component-surfaces conceptualiza- n to actual data and hence is putting the cart before the horse, to speak. If the original plan of attack is to be adhered to, a tement about the temporal relationship between the two phases ould be evolved outside of transfer theory.

The facts insist that there is no clear temporal distinction be- een the response-learning and association-formation phases in bal acquisition. Three studies of particular interest on this re are those of Peterson and Peterson (1959, Experiment II), others (1962), and McGuire (1961). Peterson and Peterson died the short-term retention of consonant syllables and dis- ered that the dependent probabilities of subsequent letters ng correct, given that the preceding letters were correct, in- ased with the number of repetitions before recall. In other ds, parts of a unit may become available before the unit is ilable as a whole. Crothers, working in a paired-associate ation, found that when response items comprise more than one ponent, association formation may begin between the stimu- and whatever components are available before the entire onse is available as a unit. This conclusion for the paired- ciate situation finds further exemplification in the work of Mc- re. The import of these studies is: although response learning association formation may be effectively distinguished, they nevertheless overlap; for association formation may begin as soon as at least one of the components of the response item is available.

Certainly the entire response unit must be available before a correct response can be accredited, and certainly association for mation continues after responding has become correct; but these two arguments say nothing about when, relative to each other the bulks of the two processes occur. An adequate analysis of this problem requires first an agreement as to what is meant by 'the bulks of'. Pending such a step, it might be noted in the Under wood, Runquist, and Schulz (1959) data that whereas the effect of intralist response similarity on recall of the response items di appear after the first half-dozen trials, the effects on over-a learning carry on to the end, an indication that response learning may be a more rapid process than association formation in som situations. For theoretical purposes, it will be assumed that, general, response learning precedes, but overlaps, association formulation. [. . .]

The coordinate system, the component surfaces, and the a sumption just made comprise a clearly asymmetric formulation no mention has been made of stimulus learning or integration. view of the limited role of experimentally manipulated stimu availability in subsequent paired-associate learning (e.g. Sch and Martin, 1964; Schulz and Tucker, 1962), and because of small effect of stimulus M relative to response M (e.g. Underwo and Schulz, 1960), it does not seem profitable at the present ti to develop an accommodating structure within transfer theo That certain stimulus factors will prove to be of considera importance in paired-associate learning is clear from the work McGuire (1961) and Shepard (1963); however, the implicati for transfer situations are not yet clear.

Summary

The thesis of the present paper is that what is transferred from first to a second task in a paired-associate transfer situatio some combination of three effects: response availability, forv associations, and backward associations. Three transfer surf based on Osgood's coordinate system are proposed which scribe how each of the three effects is transferred individually. It is found that the principal results of nearly all experiments utilizing the A–B, C–D control paradigm can be accounted for.

References

ATKINSON, R. C., and ESTES, W. K. (1963), 'Stimulus sampling theory', in R. D. Luce, R. R. Bush, and E. Galanter, eds., *Handbook of Mathematical Psychology*, vol. 2, Wiley, pp. 121–268.

BARNES, J. M., and UNDERWOOD, B. J. (1959), '"Fate" of first-list associations in transfer theory', *Journal of Experimental Psychology*, vol. 58, pp. 97–105.

BRIGGS, G. E. (1954), 'Acquisition, extinction and recovery functions in retroactive inhibition', *Journal of Experimental Psychology*, vol. 47, pp. 285–93.

BRUCE, R. W. (1933), 'Conditions of transfer of training', *Journal of Experimental Psychology*, vol. 16, pp. 343–61.

BUGELSKI, B. R., and CADWALLADER, T. C. (1956), 'A reappraisal of the transfer and retroaction surface', *Journal of Experimental Psychology*, vol. 52, pp. 360–66.

LYNCH, M. E., and MCCRAVEN, V. G. (1938), 'The temporal course of transfer in the learning of memory material', *Journal of Comparative Psychology*, vol. 25, pp. 481–96.

CARTERETTE, E. C. (1963), 'A replication of free recall and ordering of trigrams', *Journal of Experimental Psychology*, vol. 66, pp. 311–13.

CROTHERS, E. J. (1962), 'Paired-associate learning with compound responses', *Journal of Verbal Learning and Verbal Behavior*, vol. 1, pp. 66–70.

DALLETT, K. M. (1962), 'The transfer surface re-examined', *Journal of Verbal Learning and Verbal Behavior*, vol. 1, pp. 91–4.

DEAN, M. G., and KAUSLER, D. H. (1964), 'Degree of first-list learning and stimulus meaningfulness as related to transfer in the A–B, C–B paradigm', *Journal of Verbal Learning and Verbal Behavior*, vol. 3, pp. 30–34.

EBBINGHAUS, H. (1885), *Memory: A Contribution to Experimental Psychology*, Duncker and Humboldt. Translated by H. A. Ruger, Teacher's College, Columbia University, Bureau of Publications, 1913.

HAMILTON, C. E. (1950), 'The relationship between length of interval separating two learning tasks and performance on the second task', *Journal of Experimental Psychology*, vol. 40, pp. 613–21.

MARCUM, E. R. (1953), 'Verbal transfer of overlearned forward and backward associations', *American Journal of Psychology*, vol. 66, pp. 2–5.

HOROWITZ, L. M. (1961), 'Free recall and ordering in trigrams', *Journal of Experimental Psychology*, vol. 62, pp. 51–7.

JUNG, J. (1962), 'Transfer of training as a function of degree of first-list learning', *Journal of Verbal Learning and Verbal Behavior*, vol. 1, pp. 7–9.

Transfer

JUNG, J. (1963), 'Effects of response meaningfulness (*m*) on transfer of training under two different paradigms', *Journal of Experimental Psychology*, vol. 65, pp. 377–84.

KAUSLER, D. H., and KANOTI, G. A. (1963), 'R–S learning and negative transfer effects with a mixed list', *Journal of Experimental Psychology*, vol. 65, pp. 201–5.

KEPPEL, G., and UNDERWOOD, B. J. (1962), 'Retroactive inhibition of R–S associations', *Journal of Experimental Psychology*, vol. 64, pp. 400–4.

MANDLER, G. (1962), 'From association to structure', *Psychological Review*, vol. 69, pp. 415–27.

MANDLER, G., and HEINEMANN, S. H. (1956), 'Effect of overlearning of a verbal response on transfer of training', *Journal of Experimental Psychology*, vol. 51, pp. 39–46.

MCGUIRE, W. J. (1961), 'A multiprocess model for paired-associate learning', *Journal of Experimental Psychology*, vol. 62, pp. 335–47.

MERIKLE, P. M. and BATTIG, W. F. (1963), 'Transfer of training as a function of experimental paradigm and meaningfulness', *Journal of Verbal Learning and Verbal Behavior*, vol. 2, pp. 485–8.

MÜLLER, G. E., and PILZECKER, A. (1900), 'Experimentelle Beiträge zur Lehre vom Gedächtniss', *Zeitschrift für Psychologie*, vol. 1, pp. 1–300.

MÜLLER, G. E., and SCHUMANN, F. (1894), 'Experimentelle Beiträge zur Untersuchung des Gedächtnisses', *Zeitschrift für Psychologie*, vol 6, pp. 81–190, 257–339.

MURDOCK, B. B., Jr. (1958) '"Backward" associations in transfer and learning', *Journal of Experimental Psychology*, vol. 55, pp. 111–14.

NEWTON, J. M., and WICKENS, D. D. (1956), 'Retroactive inhibition as a function of the temporal position of the interpolated learning', *Journal of Experimental Psychology*, vol. 51, pp. 149–54.

NOBLE, C. E. (1963), 'Meaningfulness and familiarity', in C. N. Cofer and B. S. Musgrave, eds., *Verbal Behavior and Learning*, McGraw-Hill, pp. 76–119.

OSGOOD, C. E. (1949), 'The similarity paradox in human learning: A resolution', *Psychological Review*, vol. 56, pp. 132–43.

PETERSON, L. R., and PETERSON, M. J. (1959), 'Short-term retention of individual verbal items', *Journal of Experimental Psychology*, vol. pp. 193–8.

POSTMAN, L. (1961), 'The present status of interference theory', in C. N. Cofer ed., *Verbal Learning and Verbal Behavior*, McGraw-Hill, pp. 152–79.

POSTMAN, L. (1962a), 'Retention of first-list associations as a function of the conditions of transfer', *Journal of Experimental Psychology*, 64, pp. 380–87.

POSTMAN, L. (1962b), 'Transfer of training as a function of experimental paradigm and degree of first-list learning', *Journal of Verbal Learning and Verbal Behavior*, vol. 1, pp. 109–18.

SCHULZ, R. W., and MARTIN, E. (1964), 'Aural paired-associate learning: Stimulus familiarization, response familiarization, and pronunciability', *Journal of Verbal Learning and Verbal Behavior*, vol. 3, pp. 139–45.

SCHULZ, R. W., and TUCKER, I. F. (1962), 'Stimulus familiarization and length of the anticipation interval in paired-associate learning', *Psychological Reports*, vol. 12, pp. 341–4.

SHEPARD, R. N. (1963), 'Comments on Professor Underwood's paper', in C. N. Cofer and B. S. Musgrave, eds., *Verbal Behavior and Learning*, McGraw-Hill, pp. 48–70.

SPIKER, C. C. (1960), 'Associative transfer in verbal paired-associate learning', *Child Development*, vol. 31, pp. 73–87.

THORNDIKE, E. L. (1932), 'The Fundamentals of Learning', Columbia University Press.

TWEDT, H. M., and UNDERWOOD, B. J. (1959), 'Mixed vs. unmixed lists in transfer studies', *Journal of Experimental Psychology*, vol. 58, pp. 111–16.

UNDERWOOD, B. J. (1949), *Experimental Psychology*, Appleton-Century-Crofts.

UNDERWOOD, B. J., RUNQUIST, W. N., and SCHULZ, R. W. (1959), 'Response learning in paired-associate lists as a function of intra-list similarity', *Journal of Experimental Psychology*, vol. 58, pp. 70–78.

UNDERWOOD, B. J., and SCHULZ, R. W. (1960), *Meaningfulness and Verbal Learning*, Lippincott.

WIMER, R. (1964), 'Osgood's transfer surface: Extension and test', *Journal of Verbal Learning and Verbal Behavior*, vol. 3, pp. 274–9.

23 N. E. McGehee and R. W. Schulz

Mediation in Paired-Associative Learning

N. E. McGehee and R. W. Schulz, 'Mediation in paired-associative learning', *Journal of Experimental Psychology*, vol. 62 (1961), pp. 565–70.

Russell and Storms (1955) have shown that language habits inferred from free-association norms are presumably capable of mediating the learning of verbal paired associates. Their Ss learned to associate a word (B) with a nonsense syllable (A) in learning the first two lists. The response unit B was the first word of an associative-chain (B–C–D) inferred from the norms. Following A–B learning, Ss learned a test list consisting of A–D and A–X pairs. The A–D pairs were learned significantly faster than the A–X control pairs. However, as Russell and Storms (1955) hasten to point out, 'The mere demonstration of mediation influences in learning . . . does not explain how the effect is achieved' (p. 292). One main purpose of the present experiment was to attempt to provide this explanation for the above situation.

As pointed out recently (Underwood and Schulz, 1960), it is analytically fruitful to conceive of verbal learning as a two-phase process. The first phase consists of a response-acquisition or response-recall phase where S is concerned with learning or recalling the response units per se. The second phase, the associative phase, involves learning to associate the response units with their appropriate stimulus units.

The usual interpretation of the Russell and Storms (1955) results has been the one that the associative phase of test-list acquisition was facilitated via the specific associative chains linking the A and D items of the respective pairs. An alternative interpretation, made apparent by the two-phase conception, is that facilitation occurred because the B items on the first list enhanced the availability of the D items during A–B learning by raising them in S's response hierarchy. Moreover, this enhanced availability could facilitate test-list acquisition in the absence of any specific associative link between A and D. That is, the increased ease of response recall which would accompany heightened availability should facilitate test-list acquisition. The latter expectation is consistent with the results of a recent study in which it was found that the acquisition of paired-adjective lists was facilitated when the availability of the response units was enhanced by deliberate pretraining (Underwood, Runquist, and Schulz, 1959). The availability hypothesis was tested in Experiment I.

A second purpose of Experiment I was to compare performance under Russell and Storms' (1955) mediated and nonmediated conditions with performance under a condition in which first and test lists were unrelated (i.e. the practice control of transfer experiments). This was done to determine, in somewhat more absolute terms, the amount of facilitation which results from mediation in this situation.

The third purpose of Experiment I was to extend the generality of the Russell and Storms' (1955) results by replicating them with a design consisting of independent random groups and homogeneous lists as well as including Ss of both sexes.

The results of Experiment I failed to support the availability hypothesis. However, for reasons too lengthy to detail here, we remained skeptical as to whether the failure of the availability hypothesis necessarily implied that mediation had taken place via specific associative chains. Therefore, Experiment II was undertaken to investigate the matter further. Namely, if there is specific linkage, then a test list in which the A and D items are inappropriately paired (i.e. the analogue of the $S_1–R_1$, $S_1–R_r$ paradigm in conventional transfer terminology) should be more difficult to learn than the nonmediated test list. Put another way, there should be mediated interference. Indeed, Norcross and Spiker (1958) have demonstrated just such mediated interference for associative links acquired entirely in the laboratory. In Experiment II an attempt was made to demonstrate mediated interference in the present situation.

A second purpose of Experiment II was that of determining the 'criticalness' of the free-association norms as predictors of the mediation effects obtained in Experiment I. That is, while the A and D items were selected so as to minimize the possibility of a direct free-associative link between them, the method of selection *did not* preclude the possibility of a meaningful relationship between these items (e.g. thief–take, wish–need, etc.). Similarly, it did not prevent the occurrence of interlist relationships between response units in terms of formal similarity (e.g. smell–stem, memory–matter, etc.). Hence, if the interlist relationships between response units, along dimensions *not* predictable from free-association norms, were stronger in the mediated condition than in the nonmediated condition, then the interpretation of the superior performance in the mediated condition would require revision. Therefore, Experiment II included a condition in which the first and test lists were learned in reverse order (A–D, A–B). The logic of this arrangement is based on the assumption that the associative linkage defined by the free-association norms is unidirectional (i.e. B–C–D, but not D–C–B). Thus, making A–D the first list and A–B the test list, should reduce substantially, or even eliminate, the facilitation presumed to be mediated by habits inferred from free-association norms. Contrariwise, a relationship between B and D based on interlist response similarity should be unaffected by the reversal of the lists because it would be expected to be a bidirectional relationship. Storms (1958) has proposed and tested a similar hypothesis for a situation involving a single mediating term. He found clear evidence for bidirectionality with normatively unidirectional materials.

Method

Lists: Experiment I

The relationships between first and test lists define the conditions of Experiment I, and are summarized in Table 1. The first-list designations shown in Table 1 will be used as abbreviations in subsequent references to the various conditions (e.g. the mediated condition will be called Cond. A2–B, the nonmediated condition will be Cond. A2–X, etc.).

The stimulus designations A1 and A2 are used to distinguish between the two sets of ten nonsense syllables required by the design of Experiment I. The syllables were selected so that interand intralist similarity would be at a minimum. Their association values ranged from 0 per cent to 27 per cent according to Glaze (Underwood and Schulz, 1960, appendix A). In minimizing similarity

larity it was impossible, with one exception, to retain the syllables used by Russell and Storms.

The B, D, and X response units were the same words as those used by Russell and Storms (1955) and are shown in table 3 of their article (p. 290). The details regarding the selection of these words may also be found there. In brief, C was the most frequent free-association response to B, and D the most frequent free-

Table 1

Relationships between First and Test Lists Defining Conditions of Experiment I

Condition	First list	Mediation chain	Test list	Inferred action
Mediated	A2–B	B–C–D	A2–D	$B \rightarrow C$ ↗ ↘ A2 - - - - - - D
Nonmediated	A2–X	X–Y–Z	A2–D	$X \rightarrow Y \rightarrow Z$ ↗ A2 - - - - - - D
Availability	A1–B	B–C–D	A2–D	? ↗ A2 - - - - - - D
Practice control	A1–X	X–Y–Z	A2–D	? ↗ A2 - - - - - - D

associate of C, but D was not among the 10 most frequent responses to B, e.g. B (trouble), C (bad), D (good). The members of the X–Y–Z chain are related to one another in the same manner as the members of the B–C–D chain; however, the members of the two respective chains were not related, and must not be related, to each other. Each list consisted of 10 paired associates.

Conditions A2–B and A2–X correspond to Russell and Storms' (1955) chained (A–D) and unchained (A–X) conditions, respectively. The availability hypothesis would be supported if test-list performance in Cond. A1–B is superior to that in Cond. A1–X. Similarly, comparison of A2–B with A1–X will determine if absolute positive transfer resulted from mediation.

Lists: Experiment II

Conditions A2–B and A2–X of Experiment 1 were replicated. The lists of cond. A2–D were the same as those of Cond. A2–B in Table 1 except that A2–D was the first list and A2–B the test list. Condition A2–Br is most easily described as follows. Let A_1–B, A_2–B_2, etc. represent the syllable-word pairings of the first list. Similarly, B_1 is the beginning of the free-association chain B_1–C_1–D_1. The test list represents a random re-pairing of the respective A and D items: A_1–D_4, A_3–D_{10}, A_5–D_1, etc. This test list was List A2–D – the same one used in Experiment I and in Cond. A2–B and A2–X of this study.

Mediated interference will be demonstrated if performance in Cond. A2–Br is inferior to that in Cond. A2–X. If mediation in these materials is unidirectional, performance in Cond. A2–D and A2–X should not differ.

Procedure: Experiments I and II

Each S was read standard instructions for paired-associate learning prior to learning the first list. This list was then learned to a criterion of three consecutive errorless recitations. Following the completion of first-list learning all Ss rested for 4 min. After brief instructions to proceed as before, Ss were presented the test list for ten anticipation trials. For those Ss not reaching a criterion of one errorless recitation during the first ten trials, test-list acquisition was continued until this criterion was reached. The lists were presented on a memory drum at a 2:2-sec rate with a 4-sec intertrial interval. The ten pairs in each list were presented in four random orders to prevent serial learning of the response units. The experimental session was limited to fifty min for all Ss.

Subjects

The Ss, Northwestern University undergraduates, were randomly assigned to conditions, with thirty and twenty-four Ss per condition in Experiment I and II, respectively. The Ss were naïve with respect to the materials used, although most of them had served in other verbal learning experiments prior to their present service. When an S did not complete the experiment he was replaced by the next S appearing at the laboratory. There was no relationship between failure to complete the experiment and conditions.

Results and Discussion

First-list acquisition: Experiments I and II

Performance, in terms of mean number of trials to reach the criterion of three consecutive perfect recitations, did not differ significantly under the four respective conditions of either experiment (Experiment I: $F = 1.77$, $P > 0.10$; Experiment II: $F < 1$). In Experiment I the means were 18·33, 19·23, 18·90, and 15·43 for Cond. A2–B, A2–X, A1–B, and A1–X, respectively. The respective means for Cond. A2–B, A2–D, A2–X, and A2–Br of Experiment II were 13·62, 14·75, 14·71, and 15·87. The comparable difficulty of Lists A2–B and A2–D as first lists permits direct comparisons of test-list performance under Cond. A2–D with the other conditions of Experiment II, since the test list for this condition was List A2–B while List A2–D served as test list for the other conditions.

Test-list acquisition: Experiment I

Test list performance is shown in Figure 1. It is apparent from Figure 1 that performance under Cond. A2–B, A1–B, and A1–X is essentially equivalent. Performance under Cond. A2–X was consistently inferior to performance under the other three conditions. The mean total number of correct responses during Trials 0 was 78·23, 65·43, 79·50, and 81·30 for Cond. A2–B, A2–X, A1–B, and A1–X, respectively. The standard error of these means ranged from 1·64 to 2·75. The only reliable ($P < 0.01$) differences among these means are those involving a comparison between Cond. A2–X and each of the other three conditions. The results for mean number of trials to reach the criterion of one perfect recitation were in complete agreement with those for total correct responses.

From these results it seems clear that Russell and Storms' (1955) findings were reliable and of some generality. The significantly ($t = 3.79$, $P < 0.01$) superior performance under mediated as contrasted with nonmediated conditions in the present study represents a reproduction of their results. The interlist relationship in these two conditions – S_1–R_1, S_1–R_2 – is such that negative transfer would ordinarily be expected. Hence, the failure to find positive transfer under the mediated condition and the presence of a substantial amount of negative transfer in the nonmediate condition indicates that the inhibitory effects of the interlis relationship were somehow overcome in the mediated condition However, comparison of performance under mediated an practice-control conditions makes it clear that the facilitatio produced by mediation was not of sufficient magnitude to produc absolute positive transfer (see Figure 1).

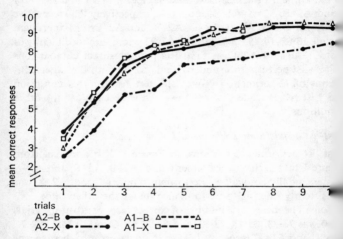

Figure 1 Test-list performances in Experiment I as a function of variou relationships between the stimulus and response units of the first and test lists. (See text for a complete description of these relationships)

Finally, it is apparent that the availability hypothesis was supported by the results of the present study. That is, had availability of the D units of the test list in cond. A1–B b enhanced during first-list acquisition, then test-list performa under Cond. A1–B should have been superior to performa under Cond. A1–X. As can be seen from Figure 1, it was Moreover, an analysis of overt errors failed to adduce any evid indicating enhanced response availability in Cond. A1–B. Th fore, mediation effects, at least in the present situation, canne attributed to facilitation of the response-recall phase of tes acquisition via enhanced response availability.

334

est-list acquisition: Experiment II

he performance on the test list for trials 1–10 is shown in Figure
The means for the total number of correct responses over the
n trials were 83·04, 66·37, 71·62, and 61·54 for Cond. A2–B,
2–X, A2–D, and A2–Br, respectively. The standard error of
ese means ranged from 1·75 to 2·57. The overall differences
nong means are highly reliable ($F = 10.55$, $P < 0.01$).

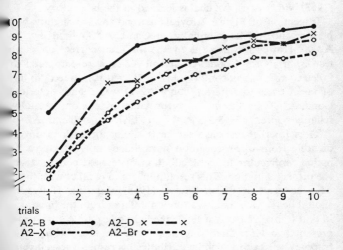

trials

A2–B ●━━━●   A2–D ×━━━×
A2–X ○━·━·━○   A2–Br ○━━━○

re 2 Test-list performance in Experiment II as a function of
us relationships between the stimulus and response units of the
and test lists. (See text for a complete description of these
ionships)

gnificant ($t = 5.12$, $P < 0.01$) superiority of performance in
. A2–B over cond. A2–X again replicates Russell and Storms'
5) results along with those of Experiment I.
s can be seen from Figure 2, performance was initially com-
ble in Cond. A2–X and A2–Br, but after trial 3 the curves
ge with performance under Cond. A2–X remaining consist-
superior on trials 4 through 10. The conditions did not
r significantly ($t = 1.45$, $P > 0.10$) in terms of total correct
trials 1–10. However, the difference in mean performance is

clearly in the expected direction. Furthermore, consistent with the divergence in the curves of Figure 2 for these conditions, the means for the number of trials to reach the criterion of one perfect recitation were 8·92 for Cond. A2–X and 11·87 for Cond. A2–Br. This difference in trials to reach criterion is highly significant ($t = 2·65$, $P < 0·01$). It appears justifiable to conclude that mediated interference has been demonstrated in cond. A2–Br. This result agrees with the one obtained by Norcross and Spiker (1958) with associative chains learned in the laboratory.

Inspection of Figure 2 reveals a trend toward slightly better performance, at least initially, in Cond. A2–D than in Cond. A2–X. However, when the means for total correct on the test-list trials for Cond. A2–D and A2–X were compared they failed to differ significantly ($t = 1·61$, $P > 0·10$). Indeed, in terms of mean trials to criterion cond. A2–D was slightly inferior to Cond. A2–X. Furthermore, performance under Cond. A2–D was reliably poorer ($t = 3·51$, $P < 0·01$) than under Cond. A2–Br.

Thus interlist response similarity along dimensions not predictable from free-association norms does not appear to be a major contributor to the facilitation of test-list performance in the present situation. This result appears to conflict with the one described earlier, which Storms (1958) obtained. However, it should be recalled that his situation differed from the present one in that it involved only a single mediating term in contrast to the present two term mediating link. Perhaps, the potency of the 'recency' effect to which he attributes his results varies inversely with the length of mediating chain. If this is the case, the present contradiction would be resolved easily.

In short, the results of Experiment I and II seem to provide fairly conclusive evidence that mediation in the Russell and Storms (1955) situation can be explained in terms of the facilitation of the associative phase of test-list acquisition via specific unidirectional associative chains linking the respective A and D items of the test-list pairs. Moreover, this inter-list response relationship is associated with previously acquired language habits reflected in free-association norms.

N. E. McGehee and R. W. Schulz

Summary

Two experiments were conducted to determine, among other things, how language habits inferred from free-association norms might mediate the learning of verbal paired associates in the Russell and Storms' (1955) situation. Their general procedure was replicated except that independent random groups and homogeneous lists as well as Ss of both sexes were used. The interlist relationship between the stimulus syllables and response words of the first and test lists were appropriately varied to define the various conditions under which the 216 Ss of the present experiments learned the 10-item lists on a memory drum at a 2:2-sec rate.

From the results it was concluded that: (a) The response-recall phase of test-list acquisition is not facilitated in the mediated condition. (b) Mediated interference can be produced with the Russell and Storms' (1955) materials. (c) Under the mediated condition, the associative phase of test-list acquisition is facilitated via the specific associative chains linking the stimulus and response units of the respective pairs. (d) The free-association norms are 'critical' in defining these associative chains. (e) Russell and Storms' (1955) results are reproducible and of considerable generality even though the facilitation produced by mediation does not result in absolute positive transfer.

References
NORCROSS, K. J., and SPIKER, C. C. (1958), 'Effects of mediated associations on transfer in paired-associate learning', *Journal of Experimental Psychology*, vol. 55, pp. 129–33.
RUSSELL, W. A., and STORMS, L. H. (1955), 'Implicit verbal chaining in paired-associate learning', *Journal of Experimental Psychology*, vol. 49, pp. 287–93.
STORMS, L. H. (1958), 'Apparent backward association: A situational effect', *Journal of Experimental Psychology*, vol. 55, pp. 390–95.
UNDERWOOD, B. J., RUNQUIST, W. N., and SCHULZ, R. W. (1959), 'Response learning in paired-associate lists as a function of intralist similarity', *Journal of Experimental Psychology*, vol. 58, pp. 70–78.
UNDERWOOD, B. J., and SCHULZ, R. W. (1960), *Meaningfulness and Verbal Learning*, Lippincott.

24 L. R. Goulet and L. Postman

An Experimental Evaluation of the Pseudomediation
Hypothesis

L. R. Goulet and L. Postman, 'An experimental evaluation of the pseudomediation hypothesis', *Psychonomic Science*, vol. 4 (1966), pp. 163–4.

The chaining paradigm of mediation and the corresponding paradigm
of pseudomediation were compared. Significant facilitation attributable
to associative chaining was obtained in the mediation paradigm whereas
the pseudomediation effect previously reported by Mandler and Earhard failed to appear. The adequacy of pseudomediation as an explanation of the apparent effects of associative chaining is questioned.

Present Status of Pseudomediation

A study by Mandler and Earhard (1964) suggested that the media
tion effect observed in the three-stage paradigm of associative
chaining may be an artifact resulting from the difference in th
amount of test-stage interference between the experimenta
condition (A–B, B–C, A–C) and the control condition (A–E
D–C, A–C). This interpretation is based on the assumption tha
the first-list associations are unlearned during the acquisition o
the second list in the experimental but not in the control cond
tion. As a consequence, the acquisition of A–C in the test stage
subject to less interference from A–B under the experimental tha
the control treatment. To test this hypothesis, Mandler an
Earhard used a design in which the first two stages of training we
the same as in the conventional paradigm but mediation was pr
cluded in the third stage by the use of entirely new respon
terms, i.e. A–B, B–C, A–E for the experimental condition a
A–B, D–C, A–E for the control condition. As expected, t'
experimental group showed negative transfer in the second sta
but was superior to the control group in the third stage. (T
difference between the two groups was significant for trials to t
criteria of one and two perfect recitations, but not for the numb
of correct responses on the first six trials.) The superior p

formance of the experimental group in the test stage was described as 'pseudomediation'. It was concluded that pseudomediation was probably responsible for the apparent facilitation produced by associative chains established in the laboratory.

Further experiments and theoretical discussions stimulated by the study of Mandler and Earhard have given rise to three questions: (a) Is the pseudomediation effect reproducible? An experiment by Jenkins and Foss (1965) yielded only marginal evidence for pseudomediation, whereas Schulz, Weaver, and Ginsberg (1965) failed to replicate the effect altogether. In both these cases, however, the procedure differed from that of Mandler and Earhard. In the experiment of Jenkins and Foss a test of first-list recall was interpolated between the second and third stages; Schulz et al. used different materials and multiple-choice learning in the second and third stages. A need for further replication is indicated, especially in view of the rather unusual finding of transfer effects which are maximal late rather than early in test-list learning. (b) Does the interpolation of B–C in fact result in the unlearning of A–B, as the hypothesis of pseudomediation assumes? Since it is the backward first-list association B–A which must be assumed to be in competition with B–C, such an effect is to be expected only if unlearning is bidirectional. The available evidence on this question is equivocal. Goulet (1966) and Jenkins and Foss (1965) failed to find lower recall of A–B after interpolation of B–C than of D–C. On the other hand, Earhard and Mandler (1965) obtained the expected difference on a test of associative matching. The discrepancy can be reconciled only on the assumption that the greater loss of associations in the experimental than in the control condition is fully offset by an opposed difference in response availability. (c) If pseudomediation does occur, is the amount of facilitation large enough to provide an adequate explanation of the conventional mediation effect? This last question defines the central interpretative problem raised by the findings of Mandler and Earhard. In a direct comparison of the two paradigms Schulz, Weaver, and Ginsberg (1965) obtained a substantial amount of mediation but no pseudomediation. As already noted, however, there were important procedural differences between the latter and the original study. The use of a multiple-choice method of learning is interpreted by Earhard and

Mandler (1965) as reducing task complexity and memory load so that mediational effects rather than interference have an opportunity to influence performance.

The present study addresses itself to the first and third of the above questions, i.e. the reproducibility of the pseudomediation effect and its adequacy as an explanation of the results obtained in conventional tests of mediation. A direct comparison was made between the paradigms of mediation and pseudomediation under conditions closely comparable to those of the study of Mandler and Earhard.

Method

The mediation and pseudomediation paradigms of associative chaining were used. In the mediation treatment the sequence of lists for the experimental condition (M–E) was A–B, B–C, A–C and for the control condition (M–C) it was A–D, B–C, A–C. For the corresponding pseudomediation conditions (PM–E and PM–C) the sequences were A–B, B–E, A–C and A–D, B–E, A–C respectively. Thus, the same test list was used for all groups, and within each paradigm the conditions of transfer were manipulated by appropriate variations in the first list. The use of a common second list within each paradigm makes it possible (a) to determine the amount of negative transfer in second-list learning, and (b) to assess the effects on test-list learning of prior familiarization with the response terms.

Lists of six paired associates were constructed from the pool of low-frequency words used by Mandler and Earhard (with substitution of *hutch* and *parle* for *prawn* and *llano*). There were three different pairings of the stimulus and response terms in each list which were used equally often. The lists were presented at a 2:2-sec rate, with a 4-sec intertrial interval. There were four different orders of presentation. The intervals between lists were approximately one min. All lists were learned by the anticipation method to a criterion of two successive perfect recitations.

The Ss were undergraduate students at the University of California who were not necessarily naïve to rote learning experiments. There were eighteen Ss per group. Assignment to conditions was in blocks of four, with one S per block from each condition.

Results and Discussion

The mean numbers of trials to a criterion of one perfect recitation on the first list were 11·3, 11·7, 11·8, and 12·0 for Conditions M–E, M–C, PM–E, and PM–C, respectively. The corresponding scores for a criterion of two perfect recitations were 15·2, 15·2, 15·3, and 15·7. For both measures $F < 1$.

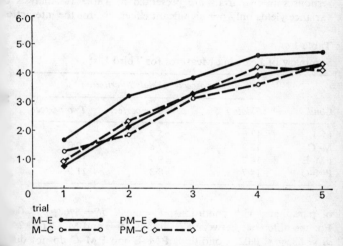

trial

M–E ●——●   PM–E ◆——◆
M–C ○——○   PM–C ◇——◇

Figure 1 Performance on the first five trials of the third stage

There is clear evidence for negative transfer in the experimental conditions during second-list learning. The mean numbers of correct responses on the first five trials, on which all Ss were presented, were as follows: M–E – 10·7, M–C – 15·6, PM–E – 7, PM–C – 14·2. The difference between the experimental and control conditions is highly significant, $F = 18·48$, $df = 1/68$, $< 0·001$. There is no interaction of paradigms with conditions, < 1. With the groups listed in the same order as above, the mean numbers of trials to a criterion of one perfect recitation are 10·4, 7·0, 11·2, and 8·4, and to a criterion of two perfect recitations 14·1, 9·8, 14·0, and 10·2. For both criterion measures, the difference between the experimental and control conditions

remains highly significant, $F = 8.86$, $df = 1/68$ ($p < 0.005$), and
12.32 ($p < 0.001$), respectively. In both cases the F for interaction
is less than 1.00.

Figure 1 shows the acquisition curves for the first five trials o*
the third stage (with all Ss represented). Condition M–E is clearly
superior to the remaining three conditions; the variations amon*
the latter are relatively small. The total numbers of correc*
responses in five trials are presented in Table 1. Analysis o*
variance yields only one significant effect, viz. for the interactio*

Table 1
Summary of Learning Measures for Third List

	Mean No. correct	Trials to criterion	
Cond.	Trials 1–5	One perfect	Two perfect
M–E	17·8	5·9	9·5
M–C	13·9	7·8	10·0
PM–E	14·2	9·7	12·6
PM–C	14·7	8·3	11·9

of paradigms with conditions, $F = 3.98$, $df = 1/68$, $p < 0$·*
For the difference between Conditions M–E and M–C, $t = 2$·*
$df = 68$, $p < 0.02$. Conditions PM–E and PM–C do not di*
reliably, $t = 0.89$, $df = 68$. The small difference that is pres*
favors Condition PM–C. As Table 1 shows, the rank order of
conditions is maintained on the criterion scores. Howev*
analysis of variance of the criterion measures does not y*
statistically reliable effects.

Reference to Figure 1 shows that on the first trial performa*
in Condition M–C is slightly better than in Condition PM*
whereas on the second trial the difference is in the oppo*
direction. This interaction is significant, $F = 4.77$, $df = 1$*
$p < 0.05$. Consequently, the slope of the learning curve is so*
what steeper for PM–C than for M–C. Prior familiarization *
the response terms gives an advantage to Condition M–C; or*
other hand, the relationship between the second and third *
conforms to the A–B, C–B paradigm for M–C, and to the *

–D paradigm for PM–C. The former may be expected to yield negative associative transfer relative to the latter. The advantage of response familiarization appears to be offset by the negative transfer effects after the first trial. The equality of the two control conditions rules out the possibility that response familiarization contributes appreciably to the superiority of condition M–E over condition PM–E.

These results fully agree with those of Schulz *et al.* in showing a significant amount of mediation and the absence of a pseudo-mediation effect. The reasons for the discrepancy between the findings of Mandler and Earhard and those of the present study are not apparent. Subtle differences in procedure or subject ability may be responsible. In any event, pseudomediation does not appear to be a strong effect which is readily reproducible. More important, however, clear evidence for mediation was obtained under conditions in which the pseudomediation effect failed to appear. The cumulative evidence available to-date makes it increasingly unlikely that chaining is an artifact attributable to pseudomediation.

References

EARHARD, B., and MANDLER, G. (1965), 'Pseudomediation: A reply and more data', *Psychonomic Science*, vol. 3, pp. 137–8.

GOULET, L. R. (1966), 'Retroaction and the "fate" of the mediator in three-stage mediation', *Journal of Verbal Learning and Verbal Behavior*, vol. 6, pp. 172–6.

JENKINS, J. J., and FOSS, D. J. (1965), 'An experimental analysis of pseudomediation', *Psychonomic Science*, vol. 2, pp. 99–100.

MANDLER, G., and EARHARD, B. (1964), 'Pseudomediation: Is chaining an artifact?', *Psychonomic Science*., vol. 1, pp. 247–8.

SCHULZ, R. W., WEAVER, G. E., and GINSBERG, S. (1965), 'Mediation with pseudomediation controlled: Chaining is not an artifact!', *Psychonomic Science*, vol. 2, pp. 169–70.

In the remaining readings we shall be concerned with the study of memory. A sharp conceptual separation between learning and memory is, of course, impossible: performance on successive learning trials depends on the subject's ability to store and to recall material after varying periods of time. Consider, for example, a typical learning experiment in which a list of paired associates is presented to a subject for study and he is then tested on each pair immediately after the end of the study trial. Unless the first pair that is tested was also the last pair presented, there must necessarily be a delay between study and test for each pair in the list. Moreover, since the pairs are typically presented in different orders on the study and the test trials, the delay will not be the same for all pairs. The delay intervals are not empty but are filled with both 'input events' (studying other pairs) and 'output events' (being tested on other pairs). Both input and output events are potential sources of interference (Tulving and Arbuckle, 1963). Only those pairs which resist forgetting during the filled delay interval after the original presentation will be given correctly on the test trial. As practice continues, the number of such pairs increases. The rises in the learning curve reflect the progressively higher levels of retention between study and test.

While learning and retention are in this sense inextricably related, the distinction between them is useful for purposes of experimental manipulation and analysis. In the typical learning experiment there is a succession of input–output cycles, and the investigator's interest is directed towards the changes in performance over cycles. Evidence for learning is obtained when there is an increase in the number of correct responses from one input to the next. In an experiment on memory, training is terminated at some specified point (after attainment of a criterion of performance or after a fixed number of trials), and then reten tion tests are given after varying intervals of delay. The delay intervals may or may not be filled with the presentation or recal of new materials. If the intervals are long, there is usually no additional treatment after the end of practice, and subjects ar dismissed from the laboratory with instructions to return at th appropriate time. If the intervals are relatively short, they ar usually filled. If the experimental design does not call for th interpolation of practice or test trials, an attempt is typicall made to prevent rehearsal by having subjects perform an ap parently neutral task. Forgetting is said to occur when there is drop in recall between the end of practice and the delayed tes

A Reference Experiment

The specific topic of discussion in this section is short-ter memory (STM). Much of the current activity in this field w stimulated by the appearance of the study by Peterson a Peterson (Reading 25). This study exemplifies well several fe tures which have become characteristic of research on STI (a) The amount of material to be recalled falls within the range the span of immediate memory and thus is considerably less th in list learning. In the Petersons' experiments the test items w single consonant syllables. (b) A single presentation of material is given: the interest is in the course of immedi memory after the initial perception of the item. However, quency of presentations was manipulated both in this and subsequent studies (Hellyer, 1962). (c) The retention intervals brief, rarely exceeding 30 seconds, again because of the focus the course of immediate memory. (d) An activity designed prevent rehearsal, in this case backward counting, fills the re tion intervals. (e) Each subject is tested on a number of differe items, and the results are usually averaged over blocks of suc sive tests. (For a discussion of some of the difficulties inheren the use of multiple tests see Keppel, 1965.) The most stri feature of the results obtained under these conditions is the r rate of forgetting for single items. While the retention losse subsequent studies have not always been as drastic as th

eported by the Petersons, the basic findings have been confirmed
y numerous other investigators. No attempt will be made here to
onsider the large body of experimental findings obtained in
xtensions and variations of the Petersons' original situation.
.ttention will be given instead to some of the theoretical issues
hich have come to the fore as a result of the upsurge of interest
 STM.

heoretical Issues

he demonstration of rapid retention losses over short intervals
 time has given impetus to the advocacy of dual-process models
hich postulate separate storage systems for STM and for long-
rm memory (LTM). Some of the major implications of such a
nception have been discussed by Melton (1963). One line of
perimental investigation has been to determine whether dif-
ent phenomena and functional relations are associated with
 two assumed memory systems. Perhaps of more critical
portance, however, is the question of whether different theo-
ical explanations will be required to account for STM and
'M phenomena. This general issue has by no means been
olved. One source of difficulty is that there are no clear-cut
erational criteria for distinguishing between the observed facts
STM and LTM. Nevertheless, there is sufficient agreement on
 approximate range of phenomena which can be subsumed
er the heading of STM to warrant consideration of two alter-
ive theories which have been put forward to account for short-
n forgetting, viz. decay theory and interference theory.

ay theory

ecay theory, as described by Brown (Reading 26), asserts that
etting is a consequence of the passage of time; there is a
gressive deterioration of the memory trace as a function of
. It follows that as long as a subject is effectively prevented
 rehearsal during the retention interval, the level of recall
 a given period of delay should be independent of the acti-
 that fills the interval. Thus, Brown predicted that in his
nd experiment consonant pairs should be forgotten to the
 degree regardless of whether pairs of numbers (dissimilar

items) or other consonant pairs (similar items) were presente
during the retention interval. That result was obtained, althoug
the difference was in the direction expected by interferenc
theory. From the latter point of view the absence of a reliab
difference between the two conditions is not critical, howeve
because the *dimension* of similarity was not fully explored. T
make the argument conclusive, a condition is needed in which th
interval activity is maximally similar (with respect to duplicatic
of elements) to the material being recalled. An experiment l
Wickelgren (1965) is relevant here. In this study, the retentic
interval was filled with items which were either acoustica'
similar or dissimilar to the test materials. Recall was found to
poorer when the similar material was used in the interval activi'
More generally, it has been extremely difficult to devise criti
tests of the decay hypothesis because the retention intervals a
usually filled with some activity designed to prevent rehears
Such interpolated activities are potential sources of interferen
no matter how dissimilar the materials are to the items wh
have to be recalled. Consequently, the sharp operational sepa
tion of decay from interference processes faces serious metl
dological obstacles.

Interference theory

According to interference theory, short-term forgetting is
result of interference from materials which either precede
follow the items to be recalled. Consider, for example, the ra
forgetting of single syllables in the Petersons' experiment. '
decay theorist would attribute these losses to the autonom
decay of the traces of the individual syllables during the reten
intervals. By contrast, any one of three sources of interfere
may be invoked to account for the observed forgetting functi
(a) interference from the retention-interval activity (backw
number-counting), i.e. retroactive inhibition produced by
interpolation of formally dissimilar materials; (b) interfere
from previously presented syllables, i.e. proactive inhibition;
(c) interference from conflicting language habits, i.e. e
experimental proactive inhibition. In Reading 27 Keppel
Underwood suggest that proactive interference from previc
presented syllables is largely responsible for the rapid forge

eported by Peterson and Peterson. Their argument ran as follows: First, it was noted that each subject in the Petersons' experiment was tested eight different times after each of the six retention intervals, for a total of forty-eight retention tests. It was then assumed that the presentation of a new syllable would result in the unlearning of the syllables which had been introduced previously. It was further assumed that these 'old' syllables would recover in strength during the retention interval to produce confusion (response competition) at the time that the subject was attempting to recall the most recent syllable. Since this recovery (and competition) would be expected to increase with the length of the retention interval, the forgetting curve reported by the Petersons could be explained. One implication of this interpretation is that the amount of forgetting should be a direct function of the number of prior syllables. That is, relatively early in the experiment, after only a small number of syllables had been presented, forgetting should not be as great as it would be later in the experiment, when the number of prior syllables would be considerably greater. An analysis of the Petersons' experiment actually provided some support for this expectation (see Reading 23, Figure 1). In addition, Keppel and Underwood reported an experiment in which the number of prior syllables which could become sources of proactive interference was varied from 0 to 5. In this study, they found increasing amounts of forgetting as the number of prior syllables increased. Both of these findings strongly suggest that most, if not all, of the forgetting observed in this type of experiment is the result of proactive inhibition.

Decay theorists have not been discouraged by these results, however, but have offered a different explanation of the proactive effects reported by Keppel and Underwood. Conrad (1967), for example, has suggested that the probability of a correct recall is dependent not only upon the trace strength of the 'new' syllable, but also upon the strengths of the 'old' syllables. Suppose, for instance, that the rate of decay of the new syllable actually remains the same throughout the experiment and that forgetting is not complete until the passage of several minutes or so. As the number of prior tests increases, there is a corresponding increase in the number of weak traces which are present at the time of recall. Thus, as the trace of the most recent syllable fades over the

retention interval, the subject will find it increasingly difficult t
distinguish it from the traces of the old syllables. It should b
noted that both the decay and the interference explanation
assume that the subject's ability to discriminate between old an
new syllables declines as the experimental session continue
According to decay theory, the rate of decay of the successiv
traces remains constant, but there is an increase in the number
old traces which are potential sources of confusion during t
recall of the item presented last. The interference hypothesis,
the other hand, is that the loss of differentiation comes abo
because of the recovery in strength of the old items during t
retention interval. The resolution of this controversy will depe
on the formulation of experimental problems which permit
decision between opposing predictions derived from the tw
theoretical positions.

The limited-capacity hypothesis

The final reading in Part Four, by Murdock, focuses attention
a basic characteristic of short-term memory – the sharp limitat
on the amount of material that can be processed and recall
The phenomenon of the immediate memory span points dire
to a system of limited capacity. The span is measured in term
the number of discrete units (e.g. letters or digits) which car
reproduced in correct serial order after a single exposure. I
characteristically of the order of seven units; when that numb
exceeded, recall is likely to be incomplete and additional ex
sures are required to produce perfect performance. As M
(1956) showed in a classical paper, the length of the immed
memory span is limited by the number of discrete functi
units and is independent of the amount of information per
It is possible, therefore, to increase the amount of informatic
the span by expanding the informational content of the f
tional units. An earlier study of STM by Murdock (1961)
interest in relation to this analysis. Using the Petersons'
nique, Murdock found essentially identical retention curve
single trigrams and for clusters of three monosyllabic word
both cases the material to be recalled consisted of grou
three familiar units – letters and words, respectively. The ra
forgetting appeared to be invariant with the number of

onal units or 'chunks'. This result is consistent with the view
at STM is limited by the rate at which information can be
:ocessed.

The experimental report reproduced below shows that the
nount of short-term recall remains nearly invariant with pre-
ntation time, i.e. variations in the number of presentations and
 the rate of presentation constitute equivalent ways of mani-
lating effective study time. The findings here parallel those
tained in studies of paired-associate and serial learning and
d to the generality of the total-time principle discussed in an
rlier section. If, as Murdock suggests, the invariance reflects a
nitation on the rate of processing information, a common basic
aracteristic of STM and LTM has been identified.

ferences

NRAD, R. (1967), 'Interference or decay over short retention
ntervals?', *Journal of Verbal Learning and Verbal Behavior*, vol. 6, pp.
9–54.

LLYER, S. (1962), 'Frequency of stimulus presentation and short-term
ecrement in recall', *Journal of Experimental Psychology*, vol. 64, p.
50.

PPEL, G. (1965), 'Problems of method in the study of short-term
emory', *Psychological Bulletin*, vol. 63, pp. 1–13.

LTON, A. W. (1963), 'Implications of short-term memory for a
eneral theory of memory', *Journal of Verbal Learning and Verbal
ehavior*, vol. 2, pp. 1–21.

LER, G. A. (1956), 'The magical number seven, plus or minus two:
ome limits on our capacity for processing information', *Psychological
eview*, vol. 63, pp. 81–97.

RDOCK, B. B., Jr. (1961), 'The retention of individual items',
urnal of Experimental Psychology*, vol. 62, pp. 618–25.

VING, E., and ARBUCKLE, T. Y. (1963), 'Sources of intratrial
terference in immediate recall of paired associates', *Journal of
rbal Learning and Verbal Behavior*, vol. 1, pp. 321–34.

KELGREN, W. A. (1965), 'Acoustic similarity and retroactive
erference in short-term memory', *Journal of Verbal Learning and
rbal Behavior*, vol. 4, pp. 53–61.

Short-term Retention of Individual Verbal Items

L. R. Peterson and M. J. Peterson, 'Short-term retention of individual verbal items', *Journal of Experimental Psychology*, vol. 58 (1959), pp. 193–8.

is apparent that the acquisition of verbal habits depends on the effects of a given occasion being carried over into later repetitions of the situation. Nevertheless, textbooks separate acquisition and retention into distinct categories. The limitation of discussions of retention to long-term characteristics is necessary in large part the scarcity of data on the course of retention over intervals of the order of magnitude of the time elapsing between successive repetitions in an acquisition study. The presence of a retentive action within the acquisition process was postulated by Hull (1940) in his use of the stimulus trace to explain serial phenomena. Again, Underwood (1949) has suggested that forgetting occurs during the acquisition process. But these theoretical considerations have not led to empirical investigation. Hull (1952) quantified the stimulus trace on data concerned with the CS–CS interval in eyelid conditioning and it is not obvious that the construct so quantified can be readily transferred to verbal learning. One objection is that a verbal stimulus produces a strong predictable response prior to the experimental session and this is not true of the originally neutral stimulus in eyelid conditioning. Two studies have shown that the effects of verbal stimulation decrease over intervals measured in seconds. Pillsbury and Sylvester (1940) found marked decrement with a list of items tested for recall 10 sec after a single presentation. However, it is unlikely that this traditional presentation of a list and later testing for recall of the list will be useful in studying intervals near or shorter than the time necessary to present the list. Of more interest is a recent study by Brown (1958) in which among other conditions a single pair of consonants was tested after a 5-sec interval. Decrement was found at the one recall interval, but no

systematic study of the course of retention over a variety
intervals was attempted.

Experiment I

The present investigation tests recall for individual items aft
several short intervals. An item is presented and tested witho
related items intervening. The initial study examines the course
retention after one brief presentation of the item.

Method

Subjects. The Ss were twenty-four students from introducto
psychology courses at Indiana University. Participation in expe
ments was a course requirement.

Materials. The verbal items tested for recall were forty-ei
consonant syllables with Witmer association value no grea
than 33 per cent (Hilgard, 1951). Other materials were for
eight three-digit numbers obtained from a table of rand
numbers. One of these was given to S after each presentat
under instructions to count backward from the number. It v
considered that continuous verbal activity during the time
tween presentation and signal for recall was desirable in orde
minimize rehearsal behavior. The materials were selected tc
categorically dissimilar and hence involve a minimum of in
ference.

Procedure. The S was seated at a table with E seated facing in
same direction on S's right. A black plywood screen shielde
from S. On the table in front of S were two small lights mou
on a black box. The general procedure was for E to spell a
sonant syllable and immediately speak a three-digit number.
S then counted backward by three or four from this num
On flashing of a signal light S attempted to recall the conso
syllable. The E spoke in rhythm with a metronome clic
twice per second and S was instructed to do likewise. The ti
of these events is diagrammed in Figure 1. As E spoke the
digit, he pressed a button activating a Hunter interval time
the end of a preset interval the timer activated a red light ar

electric clock. The light was the signal for recall. The clock ran until *E* heard *S* speak three letters, when *E* stopped the clock by depressing a key. This time between onset of the light and completion of a response will be referred to as a latency. It is to be distinguished from the interval from completion of the syllable by *E* to onset of the light, which will be referred to as the recall interval.

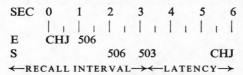

Figure 1 Sequence of events for a recall interval of 3 sec

The instructions read to *S* were as follows: 'Please sit against the back of your chair so that you are comfortable. You will not be shocked during this experiment. In front of you is a little black box. The top or green light is on now. This green light means that we are ready to begin a trial. I will speak some letters and then a number. You are to repeat the number immediately after I say it and begin counting backwards by 3s (4s) from that number in time with the ticking that you hear. I might say, A B C 309. Then you say, 309, 306, 303, etc., until the bottom or red light comes on. When you see this red light come on, stop counting immediately and say the letters that were given at the beginning of the trial. Remember to keep your eyes on the black box at all times. There will be a short rest period and then the green light will come on again and we will start a new trial.' The *E* summarized what he had already said and then gave *S* two practice trials. During this practice *S* was corrected if he hesitated before starting to count, or if he failed to stop counting on signal, or if he in any other way deviated from the instructions.

Each *S* was tested eight times at each of the recall intervals, 3, 6, 12, 15, and 18 sec. A given consonant syllable was used only once with each *S*. Each syllable occurred equally often over the group at each recall interval. A specific recall interval was represented once in each successive block of six presentations. The *S* counted backward by three on half of the trials and by four on the remaining trials. No two successive items contained letters in common. The time between signal for recall and the start of the next presentation was 15 sec.

Results and discussion

Responses occurring any time during the 15-sec interval following signal for recall were recorded. In Figure 2 are plotted the proportions of correct recalls as cumulative functions of latency for

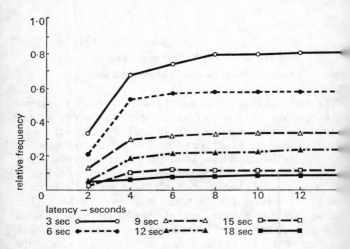

Figure 2 Correct recalls as cumulative functions of latency

each of the recall intervals. Sign tests were used to evaluate differences among the curves (Walker and Lev, 1953). At each latency differences among the 3-, 6-, 9-, and 18-sec recall interval curves are significant at the 0·05 level. For latencies of 6 sec and longer these differences are all significant at the 0·01 level. Note that the number correct with latency less than 2 sec does not constitute a majority of the total correct. These responses would not seem appropriately described as identification of the gradually weakening trace of a stimulus. There is a suggestion of an oscillatory characteristic in the events determining them.

The feasibility of an interpretation by a statistical model

xplored by fitting to the data the exponential curve of Figure 3.
The empirical points plotted here are proportions of correct
sponses with latencies shorter than 2·83 sec. Partition of the
orrect responses on the basis of latency is required by considera-
ons developed in detail by Estes (1950). A given probability of
sponse applies to an interval of time equal in length to the
verage time required for the response under consideration to

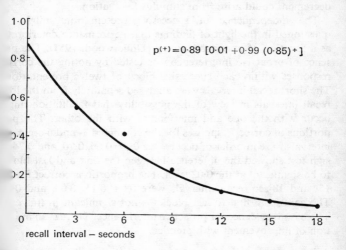

$$p^{(+)} = 0.89 \, [0.01 + 0.99 \, (0.85)^+]$$

re 3 Correct recalls with latencies below 2·83 sec as a function of
l interval

ur. The mean latency of correct responses in the present
riment was 2·83 sec. Differences among the proportions of
ect responses with latencies shorter than 2·83 sec were evalu-
by sign tests. The difference between the 3- and 18-sec
itions was found to be significant at the 0·01 level. All
rences among the 3-, 6-, 9-, 12-, and 18-sec conditions were
ficant at the 0·05 level.
e general equation of which the expression for the curve of
re 3 is a specific instance is derived from the stimulus fluctua-
model developed by Estes (1955). In applying the model to
resent experiment it is assumed that the verbal stimulus

produces a response in S which is conditioned to a set of ele
ments contiguous with the response. The elements thus cor
ditioned are a sample of a larger population of elements into whic
the conditioned elements disperse as time passes. The proportio
of conditioned elements in the sample determining S's behavic
thus decreases and with it the probability of the response. Sin
the fitted curve appears to do justice to the data, the observe
decrement could arise from stimulus fluctuation.

The independence of successive presentations might
questioned in the light of findings that performance deteriorat
as a function of previous learning (Underwood, 1957). The pr
sence of proactive interference was tested by noting the corre
responses within each successive block of twelve presentatio
The short recall intervals were analysed separately from the lo
recall intervals in view of the possibility that facilitation mig
occur with the one and interference with the other. The pr
portions of correct responses for the combined 3- and 6-sec rec
intervals were in order of occurrence 0·57, 0·66, 0·70, and 0·74
sign test showed the difference between the first and last blo
to be significant at the 0·02 level. The proportions correct for
15- and 18-sec recall intervals were 0·08, 0·15, 0·09, and 0
The gain from first to last blocks is not significant in this ca
There is no evidence for proactive interference. There is an ind
tion of improvement with practice.

Experiment II

The findings in Experiment I are compatible with the proposi
that the after-effects of a single, brief, verbal stimulation ca
interpreted as those of a trial of learning. It would be predi
from such an interpretation that probability of recall at a g
recall interval should increase as a function of repetitions of
stimulation. Forgetting should proceed at differential rates
items with differing numbers of repetitions. Although this se
to be a reasonable prediction, there are those who would pr
otherwise. Brown (1958), for instance, questions whether re
tions, as such, strengthen the 'memory trace'. He suggests
the effect of repetitions of a stimulus, or rehearsal, may be m
to postpone the onset of decay of the trace. If time is meas

from the moment that the last stimulation ceased, then the forgetting curves should coincide in all cases, no matter how many occurrences of the stimulation have preceded the final occurrence. The second experiment was designed to obtain empirical evidence relevant to this problem.

Method

The Ss were forty-eight students from the source previously described. Half of the Ss were instructed to repeat the stimulus aloud in time with the metronome until stopped by E giving them a number from which S counted backward. The remaining Ss were not given instructions concerning use of the interval between S's presentation of the stimulus and his speaking the number from which to count backward. Both the 'vocal' group and the 'silent' group had equated intervals of time during which rehearsal inevitably occurred in the one case and could occur in the other case. Differences in frequency of recalls between the groups would indicate a failure of the uninstructed Ss to rehearse. The zero point marking the beginning of the recall interval for the silent group was set at the point at which E spoke the number from which S counted backward. This was also true for the vocal group.

The length of the rehearsal period was varied for Ss of both groups over three conditions. On a third of the presentations S was not given time for any repetitions. This condition was thus comparable to Experiment I, save that the only recall intervals used were 3, 9, and 18 sec. On another third of the presentations 1 sec elapsed during which S could repeat the stimulus. On the other third of the presentations 3 sec elapsed, or sufficient time for three repetitions. Consonant syllables were varied as to the rehearsal interval in which they were used, so that each syllable occurred equally often in each condition over the group. However, a given syllable was never presented more than once to a S. The Ss were assigned in order of appearance to a randomized list of conditions. Six practice presentations were given during which corrections were made of departures from instructions. Other details follow the procedures of Experiment I.

Results and discussion

Table 1 shows the proportion of items recalled correctly. In th
vocal group recall improved with repetition at each of the reca
intervals tested. Conditions in the silent group were not con
sistently ordered. For purposes of statistical analysis the reca
intervals were combined within each group. A sign test betwee
numbers correct in the 0- and 3-repetition conditions of the voc

Table 1
Proportions of Items Correctly Recalled in Experiment II

Group	Repetition time (sec)	Recall interval (sec)		
		3	9	18
Vocal	3	0·80	0·48	0·34
	1	0·68	0·34	0·21
	0	0·60	0·25	0·14
Silent	3	0·70	0·39	0·30
	1	0·74	0·35	0·22
	0	0·72	0·38	0·15

group showed the difference to be significant at the 0·01 le
The difference between the corresponding conditions of the sil
group was not significant at the 0·05 level. Only under conditi
where repetition of the stimulus was controlled by instructi
did retention improve.

The obtained differences among the zero conditions
Experiment II and the 3-, 9-, and 18-sec recall intervals
Experiment I require some comment, since procedures v
essentially the same. Since these are between-S comparis
some differences would be predicted because of sampling v
ability. But another factor is probably involved. There v
forty-eight presentations in Experiment I and only thirty-si
Experiment II. Since recall was found to improve over succes
blocks of trials, a superiority in recall for Ss of Experiment
reasonable. In the case of differences between the vocal and s
groups of Experiment II a statistical test is permissible, fo
were assigned randomly to the two groups. Wilcoxon's (1949'

or unpaired replicates, as well as a *t* test, was used. Neither howed significance at the 0·05 level.

The 1- and 3-repetition conditions of the vocal group afforded n opportunity to obtain a measure of what recall would be at the ero interval in time. It was noted whether a syllable had been orrectly repeated by *S*. Proportions correctly repeated were 90 for the 1-repetition condition and 0·88 for the 3-repetition

able 2

ependent Probabilities of a Letter Being Correctly Recalled the Vocal Group when the Preceding Letter was Correct

epetition time c)	Recall interval (sec)		
	3	9	18
	0·96	0·85	0·72
	0·90	0·72	0·57
	0·86	0·64	0·56

ndition. The chief source of error lay in the confusion of the ters 'm' and 'n'. This source of error is not confounded with repetition variable, for it is *S* who repeats and thus per- tes his error. Further, individual items were balanced over three conditions. There is no suggestion of any difference in ponding among the repetition conditions at the beginning of recall interval. These differences developed during the time *S* was engaged in counting backward. A differential rate of getting seems indisputable.

he factors underlying the improvement in retention with etition were investigated by means of an analysis of the status lements within the individual items. The individual consonant able, like the nonsense syllable, may be regarded as presenting ith a serial learning task. Through repetitions unrelated com- ents may develop serial dependencies until in the manner of iliar words they have become single units. The improved ntion might then be attributed to increases in these serial ndencies. The analysis proceeded by ascertaining the de- lent probabilities that letters would be correct given the event that the previous letter was correct. These dependent probabilties are listed in Table 2. It is clear that with increasing repetitior the serial dependencies increase. Again combining recall interval. a sign test between the zero condition and the three repetitic condition is significant at the 0·01 level.

Learning is seen to take place within the items. But this findir does not eliminate the possibility that another kind of learning proceeding concurrently. If only the correct occurrences of tl first letters of syllables are considered, changes in retention apa from the serial dependencies can be assessed. The proportions first letters recalled correctly for the 0-, 1-, and 3-repetiti conditions were 0·60, 0·65, and 0·72, respectively. A sign te between the 0- and 3-repetition conditions was significant at t 0·05 level. It may tentatively be concluded that learning of second kind took place.

The course of short-term verbal retention is seen to be relat to learning processes. It would not appear to be strictly accur to refer to retention after a brief presentation as a stimulus tra Rather, it would seem appropriate to refer to it as the result c trial of learning. However, in spite of possible objections to Hu terminology the present investigation supports his general pc tion that a short-term retentive factor is important for the anal of verbal learning. The details of the role of retention in the ac sition process remain to be worked out.

Summary

The investigation differed from traditional verbal reten studies in concerning itself with individual items instead of l Forgetting over intervals measured in seconds was found. course of retention after a single presentation was related statistical model. Forgetting was found to progress at differe rates dependent on the amount of controlled rehearsal of stimulus. A portion of the improvement in recall with re tions was assigned to serial learning within the item, but a se kind of learning was also found. It was concluded that short- retention is an important, though neglected, aspect of acquisition process.

References

BROWN, J. (1958), 'Some tests of the decay theory of immediate memory', *Quarterly Journal of Experimental Psychology*, vol. 10, pp. 12–21.

ESTES, W. K. (1950), 'Toward a statistical theory of learning', *Psychological Review*, vol. 57, pp. 94–107.

ESTES, W. K. (1955), 'Statistical theory of spontaneous recovery and regression', *Psychological Review*, vol. 62, pp. 145–54.

HILGARD, E. R. (1951), 'Methods and procedures in the study of learning', in S. S. Stevens, ed., *Handbook of Experimental Psychology*, Wiley.

HULL, C. L., HOVLAND, C. I., ROSS, R. T., HALL, M., PERKINS, D. T., and FITCH, F. B. (1940), *Mathematico-Deductive Theory of Rote Learning: A Study in Scientific Methodology*, Yale University Press.

HULL, C. L. (1952), *A Behavior System*, Yale University Press.

PILLSBURY, W. B., and SYLVESTER, A. (1940), 'Retroactive and proactive inhibition in immediate memory', *Journal of Experimental Psychology*, vol. 27, pp. 532–45.

UNDERWOOD, B. J., (1949), *Experimental Psychology*, Appleton–Century–Crofts.

UNDERWOOD, B. J., (1957), 'Interference and forgetting', *Psychological Review*, vol. 64, pp. 49–60.

WALKER, H., and LEV, J. (1953), *Statistical Inference*, Holt.

WILCOXON, F. (1949), *Some Rapid Approximate Statistical Procedures*, American Cyanamid Co.

26 J. Brown

Some Tests of the Decay Theory of Immediate Memory

J. Brown, 'Some tests of the decay theory of immediate memory',
Quarterly Journal of Experimental Psychology, vol. 10 (1958), pp. 12–21.

The hypothesis of decay of the memory trace as a cause of forgetting
has been unpopular. The reasons for this unpopularity are criticized
and a theory of the memory span, based on this hypothesis, is put forward. Three experiments which test the hypothesis are described. In
each, two kinds of stimuli are presented to the subject, viz. 'required'
stimuli, which he attempts to remember, and 'additional' stimuli, to
which he merely makes responses. The first experiment will show that
even when the number of required stimuli is well below the memory
span, forgetting occurs if the presentation of additional stimuli delay
recall for several seconds. The second shows that the effect of the additional stimuli depends only slightly on their similarity to the required
stimuli: it also shows that their effect is negligible when they precede
instead of follow, the required stimuli. The third shows that the effect
of additional stimuli interpolated before recall remains considerable
even when there is an interval of several seconds between presentation
of required and additional stimuli.

Introduction

The experiments reported below concern memory over a period of
a few seconds, when only a single presentation of the material has
been given. It is convenient to describe such memory as 'immediate'. The experiments form part of a series described in a
unpublished Ph.D. dissertation (Brown, 1955): two of the series
have already been published (Brown, 1954, 1956).

Immediate memory usually operates under conditions very
different from those provided in conventional immediate memory
tests. Typically, it is necessary to retain information while
continuing to carry out other activities. In a lecture delivered
Cambridge in 1950, Sir Frederic Bartlett suggested that few

getting may be extremely rapid under these circumstances. The series of experiments began as an attempt to put this suggestion to an experimental test, with highly positive results. However, the three experiments described below, while they illustrate rapid loss of information in immediate memory when other activity intervenes before recall, were designed to test a particular theory of immediate memory. The basic hypothesis of this theory is that when something is perceived, a memory trace is established which decays rapidly during the initial phase of its career. (By memory trace is meant only the neural substrate of retention, whatever this may be.) Some decay of the trace is assumed to be compatible with reliable recall – just as partial fading of print may be compatible with perfect legibility. But recall will cease to be reliable if decay of the trace proceeds beyond a critical level.

Two fundamental problems of immediate memory are (1) the origin and nature of the immediate memory span, and (2) why we forget when this span is exceeded. One solution to these problems is to postulate a special mechanism for short-term retention. The memory span can then be regarded as the capacity of this special mechanism. When the span is exceeded, forgetting will occur because retention becomes dependent on a mechanism which is less efficient. The hypothesis of rapid decay of the memory trace, however, also provides a possible solution to these problems and one which has the merit of simplicity. The hypothesis leads to a theory of the memory span which in outline runs as follows: when a sequence of items is presented, the interval between the perception of each item and the attempt to recall that item will depend on the length of the sequence. If the sequence exceeds a certain length, decay of the memory traces of some of the items will proceed too far for accurate recall of the sequence to be possible. This length is the memory span. Thus the trace-decay hypothesis can explain both the origin of the span and why forgetting occurs when the span is exceeded.

The hypothesis that decay of the memory trace is an important cause of forgetting has been unpopular. However, theories of forgetting have developed almost entirely in relation to forgetting over relatively long periods. Where forgetting over very short periods has been specifically considered, there has been greater readiness to postulate a decay process. Thus the 'stimulus trace' which plays an important role in Hull's explanations of serial learning phenomena (Hull, 1940) is assumed to decay rapidly. Decay of the trace has also been invoked from time to time to explain negative time errors in psychophysical judgement (e.g. Pratt, 1933). The two main reasons for the unpopularity of the decay theory are the existence of distortions in remembering and the importance of the similarity factor in PI and RI (pro- and retro-active inhibition). These facts have seemed to some to imply a more dynamic theory of forgetting than is provided by decay of a static trace (notably to Bartlett, 1932, and to Koffka, 1935). To others they have seemed to show that a competition-in-recall theory of forgetting is adequate (e.g. McGeoch, 1942 and Underwood, 1957). But it is possible to argue that distortions in remembering are due to the constructive and inferential character of recall, made necessary by decay of the memory trace (Brown, 1956). In like manner, competition-in-recall may itself be a manifestation of such decay, a point which seems to have been overlooked and which merits discussion.

Competition-in-recall may mean one of two things. It may mean that a competing response inhibits recall of the required response. In this case, the competition theory is a genuine theory of forgetting and belongs to that class of theories according to which, for some reason, not dependent on the state of the trace itself, the trace fails to lead to effective recall. Alternatively, it may mean that both responses tend to be elicited and that the organism is unable to distinguish which of the two responses is correct. It is important to recognize that such failure of discrimination, i.e. confusion between responses, cannot be regarded as a primary cause of forgetting. Failure of discrimination presupposes forgetting of that which determines which of the responses is correct. It is thus a possible *effect* of forgetting, however caused, but is not itself a primary cause of forgetting. No experiments which have demonstrated the importance of the similarity factor on RI and PI have invariably used an interfering material which could be confused with the required material; very often, for example, both materials have consisted of nonsense syllables. Properly considered, therefore, the results of such experiments do *not* constitute evidence against the decay of the trace of forgetting.

Experiment I

On the hypothesis of decay of the memory trace, recall will become unreliable if decay proceeds too far, i.e. if the retention interval exceeds a certain length. This will apply whether or not the amount the subject attempts to retain lies within the memory span. One way to test the hypothesis of decay of the trace, therefore, is to see whether if recall is delayed for several seconds forgetting occurs even when the amount of material is well within the memory span. However, if the subject is left free to rehearse the material during the delay, no forgetting is to be expected. For rehearsal is itself a form of recall, albeit implicit, and is likely to counteract the effect of decay, either directly, or through the establishment of a new trace. Thus, in order to test the hypothesis, it is necessary to require the subject to perform an additional activity during the delay period so that rehearsal is prevented. And it must be arranged that this activity involves a high information rate, if prevention of rehearsal is to be really effective. In the following experiment, between 1 and 4 pairs of stimuli were presented for the subject to remember and there was an interval of just under 5 sec before recall. Under one condition, the subject was required to make immediate responses to 5 pairs of additional stimuli during this interval in order to prevent rehearsal; under a second condition, the interval was empty.

Method

Condition I. On each trial two sets of stimuli were presented in immediate succession. The subject was instructed to read out the stimuli of both sets during presentation and to attempt to remember the stimuli of the first set. The first set will therefore be called the required or 'M' stimuli and the second set the additional or 'X' stimuli. The required stimuli consisted of between one and four pairs of consonants (excluding the consonant Y), which were randomly selected except that no consonant was repeated in the stimuli for any one trial. The additional stimuli consisted of five pairs of number digits copied directly from tables of random numbers. Both sets of stimuli were recorded on a paper strip, the required stimuli in black and the additional stimuli in red. This strip was passed behind a screen in which there was a viewing window so that the stimuli appeared pair by pair (for details of apparatus, see Brown, 1954). The sequence of events on each trial was as follows. The experimenter said 'ready' and a warning line appeared in the window. Then, after 0·5 sec, the pairs of stimuli followed at intervals of 0·78 sec (all the M pairs were presented before the X pairs). As soon as presentation was over, the subject attempted to write down the required stimuli. Each consonant was scored correct if, and only if, it was reproduced in the correct position in the sequence.

Condition II. This was the control condition and differed in that the additional stimuli were omitted, i.e. there was still an interval (4·7 sec) before recall, but it was unfilled.

Six stimulus strips were prepared, three for each condition. Each strip carried stimuli for three trials with one pair of M stimuli, followed by three trials with two pairs, three with three pairs and three with four pairs (but trials with only one pair were omitted under Condition II). Ten university students were tested and each was first given a practice strip. Condition I and Condition II strips were given alternately. Half the subjects started with Condition I and half with Condition II.

Two of the original ten subjects made an unacceptable number of errors in reading out the stimuli during presentation. Accordingly, two substitutes were tested instead. With the other subjects reading errors were rare. Reading errors were also rare in the other two experiments.

Results

Table 1 shows the scores for the subject as a group under the two conditions. In Figure 1, these scores are shown as percentage

Table 1
Pooled Recall Scores

| | Number of pairs required stimuli | | | |
	1	*2*	*3*	*4*
Condition I	176	244	221	181
Condition II	—	358	505	471
Maximum possible	180	360	540	720

The most striking feature of the results is that only a single pair of stimuli were retained without error when the additional stimuli intervened before recall. The dotted line in Figure 1 represents the effect of this activity as percentage RI. It will be seen that the effect increases with the number of pairs of required stimuli. Table 2 shows that percentage recall for the last pair of required stimuli was much higher when there was only one pair of required stimuli than when there were four pairs: the difference is significant for each subject individually on a χ^2 test ($p < 0.05$).

Discussion

The results confirm what was expected on the hypothesis of decay of the memory trace: a delay of several seconds before recall would produce considerable forgetting, if rehearsal was prevented, even when the number of stimuli was within the memory span, as shown by a control condition.

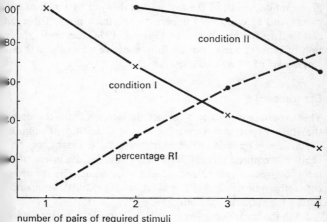

number of pairs of required stimuli

Figure 1

Figure 1 shows that the effect of preventing rehearsal varied with the number of required stimuli. This can be partly attributed to the increase in the mean interval between presentation of stimuli and the start of the recall period which occurs as their

number increases (since the stimuli are presented successively)
But this is not the whole explanation. Table 2 shows that reca
of the last pair of required stimuli, for which the interval wa
constant, was not independent of whether there were previou
pairs. Several factors may contribute to this result. Firstly, sinc

Table 2

Recall of Last Pair

Number of required pairs	Subjects								
	1	2	3	4	5	6	7	8	9
1	18	18	18	18	15	18	18	18	17
4	11	10	14	4	0	10	7	9	9

Note: Each entry is the number of pairs recalled out of 18.

the subject attempts recall of the stimuli in the order of th
presentation, recall of the last pair is delayed by recall of earl
pairs. And as one might expect on the trace decay theory, t
can lead to further forgetting (Brown, 1954). Secondly, prev
tion of rehearsal may not be fully effective when there is onl
single pair of stimuli to rehearse.

Experiment II

This experiment tests two further deductions from the deca
the trace hypothesis about the effect of additional stimuli
which the subject is asked merely to make responses, on
recall of required stimuli. The first concerns the effect of s
larity between required and additional stimuli. The second
cerns the effect of additional stimuli presented immedia
before the required stimuli.

1. On the trace-decay hypothesis, the similarity factor shoul
important only in so far as it leads to confusion in recall. Thi
already been argued in the Introduction. On certain other the
of forgetting, the similarity factor can be a crucial one.
example, according to Koffka (Koffka, 1935), similarity d
mines the extent to which perceptions interfere with pre-exi
traces and to which traces interfere with one another.

2. Stimuli presented immediately before the required stimuli should have little effect on recall on the trace decay hypothesis, since they cannot prevent rehearsal of the required stimuli during retention. Again on other theories of forgetting, interference is possible or even likely. For if incidental learning of the additional stimuli occurs, the traces so established may interact with the traces subsequently established by the required stimuli or may lead to blocking of recall. Even on the decay hypothesis however, such incidental learning may have a slight effect. For it may lead to confusion of the additional and required stimuli in recall. Accordingly, in the experiment, the effect of additional stimuli which precede the required stimuli is studied, both where such confusion is possible (i.e. both sets of stimuli belong to the same class) and where it is not possible (i.e. one set consists of digits and the other of consonants).

Previous work: Several experiments have concerned the similarity factor in immediate memory. Robinson (1927) found, as we might expect, that recall increased with the degree of percentage identity between the two halves of a list. Harden (1929) and Young and Supa (1941) found that, if one half of the list consisted of consonants and the other of digits, recall was higher than when the whole list consisted of items of the same kind. This result is held to show that intra-serial RI and PI in immediate memory are a function of the similarity factor. But it is a result which seems readily explicable in terms of reduced intra-serial confusion when the two halves differ. Thus eight consonants, for example, can be arranged in 40,320 ways; whereas four consonants followed by 4 digits can be arranged in only 576 ways. It is therefore quite compatible with the trace-decay hypothesis. An experiment by Pillsbury and Sylvester (1940) – to which little attention has been paid – makes questionable any assumption that RI in immediate memory is a function of similarity to a marked extent. They studied the effect of different activities interpolated during a 10-sec retention interval. Comparison between the effects of these activities is a little difficult, since there was no control of the rates at which they were performed. Nevertheless, it is noteworthy that all activities produced considerable RI, irrespective of whether there was much similarity between original and interpolated materials.

Method

Only differences from the method of Experiment I will be described. The required, M, stimuli consisted of four pairs of consonants. The additional, X, stimuli consisted of either three pairs of consonants or of three pairs of digits: these two types of X will be referred to as Xs and Xd respectively (i.e. similar to or different from M). No consonant or digit was repeated in the stimuli for any one trial. The additional stimuli were presented either immediately before or immediately after the required stimuli. Thus there were four experimental conditions which will be labelled Xs (before), Xd (before), Xs (after), Xd (after). In addition there was a control condition under which no additional stimuli were presented. The pairs of stimuli were presented at intervals of 1·33 sec. This relatively slow rate was chosen so that subjects would not have any tendency to make mistakes in reading out M stimuli when they had been immediately preceded by X stimuli. The interval between the start of each trial and the presentation of M and the interval between the presentation of and the start of the recall period were both 5·33 sec under all conditions. Five paper strips were prepared: each carried eight trials under one of the five conditions. After a practice strip, with samples of all conditions, each subject was given the strips in different order. Each strip was taken equally often at each stage of the experiment. The fifteen subjects were university students

Table 3

Percentage Recall Scores

Control	Xs (before)	Xs (after)	Xd (before)	Xd (after)
67·3	58·6	25·6	65·5	30·6

Results

Table 3 shows percentage recall of the required stimuli by subjects as a group under the various conditions. An analysis variance of individual scores was performed, after transforming each score, s, to $\sin^{-1} s$ in order to improve the stability of error variance. The variance attributable to conditions was hi significant ($p < 0.001$). The residual variance of this analysis was then used to calculate 't' for each of the comparisons (in transformed scores) shown in Table 4. From Tables 3 and 4 it will be seen that (i) both Xs (after) and Xd (after) produced very large amounts of interference, (ii) Xs (after) produced slightly but significantly ($p < 0.05$) more interference than Xd (after), (iii) Xs (before) produced slight interference ($p < 0.01$) but Xd (before) did not.

Table 4

Comparison	t *(with 56 df)	Significance
Control with Xs (before)	3·39	$p < 0.01$
Control with Xd (before)	<1·0	not significant
Xd (after) with Xs (after)	2·03	$p < 0.05$

* Derived from analysis of variance. See text.

The extent to which subjects inadvertently gave additional stimuli in their recall attempts, when both sets of stimuli consisted of consonants, is of interest. No consonant was repeated in the stimuli for each trial and the letter Y was not used. On each trial, of the twenty possible consonants, eight were used for stimuli, six for X stimuli and six were not used on each trial. Thus on a chance basis, intrusions from Xs should form about half the total number of intrusions. With Xs (after), 122 out of a total of 234 intrusions, i.e. a little over one half, were Xs stimuli. This is not significantly more than chance expectation on a χ^2 test, which provides an approximate test of significance. But with Xs (before), seventy-six out of a total of 194 intrusions, i.e. *less* than one half, were Xs stimuli. This is significantly less than chance expectation on a χ^2 test ($p < 0.01$).

Discussion

The deductions from the trace-decay hypothesis appear to be confirmed. When the additional stimuli intervened before recall, their similarity to the required stimuli was of minor importance in determining the amount of interference produced. When they preceded the required stimuli, the interference was slight, and occurred only when the two sets of stimuli could be confused in recall. Several points require discussion, however.

The effects of consonants and digits as additional stimuli may differ intrinsically, irrespective of their similarity to the required stimuli. This could distort the apparent importance of the similarity factor. Another experiment of the series (Brown, 1955) which is primarily concerned with a different problem – shows, in conjunction with the results of the present experiment, that there is in fact little difference in the intrinsic effects of the two kinds of stimuli. It is therefore safe to accept the conclusion that the similarity factor is of minor importance (at any rate for the type of similarity studied).

On the trace-decay hypothesis, it was expected that any effect of similarity would be attributable to confusion in recall. In conformity with this expectation, intrusions from these stimuli were a little higher than would be expected on a chance basis when similar stimuli intervened before recall. But when similar stimuli preceded the required stimuli, intrusions were significantly *less* than would be expected on a chance basis, although slight interference was produced by these stimuli. This is certainly puzzling. A possible explanation is that, if the unwanted stimuli intrude in the process of recall, this will tend to delay recall of required stimuli, even when the subject recognizes them as intrusions and does not include them in his overt recall attempt. This would impair recall, on the trace-decay hypothesis, and lead to fewer intrusions than would be expected on a chance basis since no consonant was used twice in the stimuli for any one trial.

Experiment III

If an interval is introduced between the required stimuli and additional stimuli which intervene before recall, the subject is likely to rehearse the stimuli during this interval. Everyday experience – of trying to remember telephone numbers, for example – suggests that the effect of such rehearsal may be to counteract decay of the trace rather than to strengthen it more, since continuing rehearsal tends to be necessary to prevent forgetting. If this is so, an interval between the required and additional stimuli should not drastically reduce the interference produced by the latter on the trace-decay hypothesis. On a theory which ascribes the effect of intervening stimuli to interference with the traces of the required stimuli, however, this interval might prove to be very critical, for there is much evidence to suggest that the lability of the memory trace – at least to gross cerebral disturbance – is highest immediately after learning and declines rapidly with its age. Thus a blow on the head often produces a short-term retrograde amnesia and the various forms of shock therapy have the same effect. Some of the most interesting evidence comes from experiments on the effect of electro-convulsive shock on learning. Duncan (1949), for example, studied the effect of different time intervals between learning trials and the administration of shock for rats learning a simple avoidance response. There was little evidence of learning if the interval was under 20 sec and little interference with learning if it exceeded 60 sec.

It is of interest that Müller and Pilzecker (1900), who introduced the misleading expression 'retroactive inhibition' (*ruck-virkende Hemmung*), believed that an activity interpolated during retention interferes with a process of consolidation in the memory trace. Consolidation was believed to depend on a sort of after-discharge of the neural elements involved in learning (it is not, therefore, to be identified with rehearsal, which consists of successive voluntary recall). The idea of a perseverating neural activity following learning, which consolidates a (presumably) structural trace, is not unlike the dual trace mechanism of Hebb (1949) and others.

Method

Again only differences from the method of Experiment I will be described. The required, M, stimuli consisted of three pairs of consonants and the additional, X, stimuli of three pairs of digits. The pairs were presented at intervals of 0·78 sec. However, the interval between the last M pair and the first X pair was varied and was either 0·78, 2·34, or 4·68 sec; these will be referred to as intervals I_1, I_2 and I_3 respectively. The total length of the retention interval was held constant at 7 sec. A practice strip was prepared and three test strips. Each test strip carried stimuli for three I_1, three I_2 and three I_3 trials. The orders of I_1, I_2 and I_3 in the different strips formed a Latin square. After the practice strip, different subjects took the different strips in different orders. At the start of each trial, the subject was told the position of the X stimuli. Twelve university students were tested.

Table 5
Interval in Seconds

0·78 (I₁)	2·34 (I₂)	4·68 (I₃)
41	54	59

(percentage recall scores)

Results

Table 5 shows mean percentage recall scores for the group fo different sizes of the interval between the required and additiona stimuli. As in the previous experiment, individual scores wer subjected to analysis of variance. The variance attributable t variation of the interval was highly significant ($p < 0.001$). Th analysis also showed that the effect of increasing the size of th interval was nonlinear ($p < 0.05$). It will be seen from Table that as the interval increased from 0·78 to 4·68 sec recall rose fro 41 to 59 per cent. It will also be seen that the increase in the inte val from 0·78 to 2·34 sec was relatively more important than th increase from 2·34 to 4·68. Another experiment of the seri under comparable conditions gave similar results. Nearly subjects spontaneously reported 'going over' the letters duri the longer two intervals. Some subjects also reported searchi for interpretations of the letters such as 'National Debt' for N

Discussion

Recall was 59 per cent when the interval between the requir and additional stimuli was about 4 sec and about 41 per ce when the interval was less than 1 sec. With similar subjects, rec was 94 per cent in Experiment I when there were no additio stimuli, but conditions were otherwise almost identical. T even when the interval was about 4 sec, the additional stim must still have produced considerable interference to keep re as low as 59 per cent. The conclusion is that increase in the inter from less than 1 sec to about 4 sec only moderately reduces the interference produced by the additional stimuli. This reduction can plausibly be attributed to the effect of rehearsal during the interval, without postulating any additional effect such as diminished interference with traces. A rough check – based on asking subjects to rehearse aloud – suggests that two or three complete rehearsals of the required stimuli are possible during an interval of 4 sec. It is not impossible that the moderate strengthening of learning which did occur was due, not to rehearsal as such, but to finding interpretations of the letters, in the manner spontaneously reported by some subjects (e.g. 'National Debt' for ND). If so, this raises the interesting problem of why immediate rehearsal has no permanent effect on learning.

General Discussion

The results of the individual experiments have already been discussed. They fit well with the hypothesis of rapid decay of the memory trace when it is first established. It is not claimed that they are incompatible with alternative theories of forgetting. The merit of the decay hypothesis lies in its simplicity and its ability to explain the results without arbitrary auxiliary hypotheses. Results of other recent experiments can also be readily explained on the hypothesis. Brown (1954) found that the delay produced by recalling earlier members of a sequence impairs recall of later members. Conrad (1957) has reported that, if the rate of recall of the sequence as a whole is reduced, recall is likewise impaired. Broadbent (1956, 1957) presents results on a two-channel intake of information which can be interpreted, as he points out, as an effect of trace-decay, although in this case a subsidiary hypothesis is also required (1957, p. 6).

Any theory about forgetting in immediate memory, if it is to be acceptable, must take account of the memory span. A theory of the memory span, based on the hypothesis of trace-decay, was outlined in the introduction. However, the main problem is not the mere existence of a limit to the amount which can be fully recalled following a single presentation: it is the fact that this limit is on a number of disconnected items or 'chunks' (Miller, 1956) rather than on information content. Can the trace-decay hypothesis provide a solution to this problem? This will now be considered.

Partial decay of the memory trace of an item is assumed to be compatible with reliable recall because the trace may adequately specify the item, even when it has lost some of its initial features in other words, because of initial 'redundancy' in the trace. The extent of this redundancy should be inversely related to the information content of the item (cf. a chalk mark remains legible after more smudging if it can only be 'A' or 'B' than if it can be 'A' or 'B' or 'C' or 'D'). This means that the critical interval after which recall becomes unreliable, will be longer for items of low information content than for items of high information content. Consequently one might expect the span to vary directly with the information content of the items. But this does not take account of the fact that the items have to be recalled in a sequence. If the redundancy of those aspects of the traces which mediate retention of the order of the items is low, it is primarily the information content of the order which will determine the size of the span. This could explain why the span is a relatively fixed number of items irrespective of the information content of the items, since the order information depends only on the number of items, provided the items are all different and the order random (the order information in such a sequence of n items $\log_2 n!$ 'bits'). One way to test this hypothesis would be to see whether the size of the span becomes much larger if the subject is not required to recall the order of the items. But unless he recalls the items in order of presentation, the retention interval will be disproportionately long for some items. Moreover, recall in the order of presentation may well aid recall of what the items are. A better test, therefore, would be to see whether the span is greatly increased if the order information is reduced or eliminated. It is significant and probably not just accidental that the span is high for words in a meaningful passage, since here the constraints of language partly predetermine the order of the words and hence greatly reduce the order information.

References

BARTLETT, F. C. (1932), *Remembering*, Cambridge.

BROADBENT, D. E. (1956), 'Successive responses to simultaneous stimuli', *Quarterly Journal of Experimental Psychology*, vol. 8, pp. 145–52.

BROADBENT, D. E. (1957), 'Immediate memory and simultaneous stimuli', *Quarterly Journal of Experimental Psychology*, vol. 9, pp. 1–11.

BROWN, J. (1954), 'The nature of set to learn and of intra-material interference in immediate memory', *Quarterly Journal of Experimental Psychology*, vol. 6, pp. 141–8.

BROWN, J. (1955), *Unpublished Ph.D. thesis, Cambridge*.

BROWN, J. (1956), 'Distortions in immediate memory', *Quarterly Journal of Experimental Psychology*, vol. 8, pp. 134–9.

CONRAD, R. (1957), 'Decay theory of immediate memory', *Nature*, vol. 179, p. 4564.

DUNCAN, C. P. (1949), 'The retroactive effect of electroshock on learning', *Journal of Comparative and Physiological Psychology*, vol. 42, pp. 32–44.

HARDEN, L. M. (1929), 'The quantitative study of the similarity factor in retroactive inhibition', *Journal of General Psychology*, vol. 2, pp. 421–30.

HEBB, D. O. (1949), *The Organization of Behaviour*, New York.

HULL, C. L. *et al.* (1940), *Mathematico-Deductive Theory of Rote Learning*, New Haven.

KOFFKA, K. (1935), *Principles of Gestalt Psychology*, New York.

MCGEOCH, J. A. (1942), *The Psychology of Human Learning*, New York.

MILLER, G. A. (1956), 'The magical number seven, plus or minus two', *Psychological Review*, vol. 63, pp. 81–97.

MÜLLER, G. E., and PILZECKER, A. (1900), 'Experimentelle Beiträge zur Lehre vom Gedächtnis', *Zeitschrift für Psychologie mit Zeitschrift für angewandte Psychologie Ergb.*, vol. 1, pp. 1–288. (Quoted in McGeoch, 1942.)

PILLSBURY, W. B., and SYLVESTER, A. (1940), 'Retroactive and proactive inhibition in immediate memory', *Journal of Experimental Psychology*, vol. 27, pp. 532–45.

PRATT, C. C. (1933), 'Time errors in the method of single stimuli', *Journal of Experimental Psychology*, vol. 16, pp. 798–814.

ROBINSON, E. S. (1927), 'The similarity factor in retroaction', *American Journal of Psychology*, vol. 39, pp. 297–312.

UNDERWOOD, B. J. (1957), 'Interference and forgetting', *Psychological Review*, vol. 64, pp. 49–60.

YUNG, C. W., and SUPA, M. (1941), 'Mnemic inhibition as a factor in the limitation of the memory span', *American Journal of Psychology*, vol. 54, pp. 546–52.

27 G. Keppel and B. J. Underwood

Proactive Inhibition in Short-Term Retention of Single Items

Abridged from G. Keppel and B. J. Underwood, 'Proactive inhibition in short-term retention of single items', *Journal of Verbal Learning and Verbal Behavior*, vol. 1 (1962), pp. 153–61.

In 1959 Peterson and Peterson developed a technique whereby a single verbal item was presented to S for a learning trial o approximately 0·5-sec duration, with retention being measure over intervals of up to 18 sec. These procedures produced a ver systematic relationship between length of retention interval an percentage of items correct at recall, with 78 per cent correct afte 3 sec, and 8 per cent after 18 sec. Thus, forgetting of the singl item is nearly complete after 18 sec. The reliability of this for getting curve is demonstrated by the fact that Murdock (196 has repeated the Peterson–Peterson experiment and obtaine nearly identical results.

The present experiments were designed to obtain data whic would aid in interpreting theoretically the extraordinarily rap forgetting of the single items which has been observed in th above experiments. The nature of the interpretative problem a how it arises, requires some background discussion.

The first distinction which must be made is between short-ter retention procedures and long-term retention procedures. T short-term studies, as exemplified by Peterson and Peterso involve retention of *single* items over very short intervals, sa 60 sec or less. The long-term retention studies involve retenti of *lists* of items over much longer intervals, such as 20 m although usually hours or days are employed. Clearly no dich tomy is possible between the two types of studies based on leng of retention interval, but in actual practice a working distincti between the two exists. We may identify the short-term studies measuring short-term memory (STM) and the long-term stud as measuring long-term memory (LTM) with the understand

hat the present usage also involves memory for singly presented
 items versus memory for lists of items.

The critical issue is whether or not LTM and STM will
require fundamentally different interpretative principles. The
resolution of this issue rests primarily on determining the role
which proactive inhibition (PI) plays in STM. Interference
theories of LTM use PI as a cornerstone paradigm (e.g. Postman,
1961); associations learned prior to the learning of associations
for which retention is being tested may interfere with recall.
However, a secondary fact reported by Peterson and Peterson
1959) and by Peterson (1963) is that little or no evidence is found
for PI in STM. In addition, since little or no retroactive inhibition (RI) is believed to be produced by the activity used to prevent rehearsal in the studies of STM, it would appear that an
interference theory, based on PI and RI, is quite incapable of
handling the extraordinarily rapid forgetting observed in the
studies of STM. Thus, we are faced with a potential theoretical
schism, with one set of propositions being used for LTM and
another possibly wholly different set for STM. In the interests of
theoretical continuity, such a schism should be avoided if possible.

As noted above, the critical issue involved is the role which PI
plays in STM. If PI is operative in STM, the variables which
govern magnitude of PI in LTM should also have counterparts
in the laws of STM. Some of these more critical variables will
now be discussed.

Number of Interfering Associations

In LTM the greater the number of previously acquired associations the greater the PI (Underwood, 1945; 1957). It is the
reported failure to reproduce this law in studies of STM that has
led to the conclusion that there is little, if any, PI in STM.
Actually, the procedure used in these studies of STM would
seem to be ideal for obtaining PI. For example, in the Peterson–
Peterson study, a counterbalancing technique was used in which
S served eight times at each of six retention intervals. Thus,
S at the termination of his conditions had been presented
forty-eight different items. The items presented late in the session

should be subject to a greater number of potentially interfering associations than would those items presented early in the session Yet there appears to be little difference in the retention of items presented early in the session and those presented late in the session (but see later discussion).

Degree of Learning

In LTM the higher the degree of learning of the list to be recalled the better the recall when the PI paradigm is used (Postman and Riley, 1959). This is not to say that the absolute PI is less with higher than with lower degrees of learning (when evaluated against a control group) of the list to be recalled, for according to Postman and Riley this relationship is complex. But, given a high degree of learning of a list, its recall will be higher than will the recall of a list with a low degree of learning when the proactive interference is constant on both lists. This fact has been used by Melton (1963) indirectly to suggest that PI is indeterminate in the available studies of STM. His reasoning is that as S proceeds through a series of conditions the learning-to-learn will serve to increase the degree of learning of items presented. This higher degree of learning, in turn, will counteract a decrement in retention which should occur as a function of the increasing number of potentially interfering associations which have been established as practice proceeds.

There is evidence that learning-to-learn does occur in STM studies (Peterson and Peterson, 1959). That it does occur requires a distinction between learning and retention in STM, a distinction which has not, in fact, been carefully maintained in studies to date. Normally, we may use an immediate test (say after 1 sec) as a measure of degree of learning. Retention longer intervals are assessed against the scores on the immediate test to determine the retention function. However, when percentage correct for immediate retention is essentially 100 per cent there is no way to derive a meaningful retention function. For a manner of speaking, the true degree of learning may be more than 100 per cent. Thus, if STM of common words is to compared with that of consonant syllables, and if the immediate test for words shows 100 per cent correct recall and that syllables 85 per cent, comparison of the retention of the two materials at longer intervals may be both a function of underestimated differences in degree of learning and of differences in material. Latency measures at recall might be used as subsidiary indices of forgetting which occurs when the percentage correct remains near 100 per cent for retention intervals of increasing length, but the moment recall falls substantially below 100 per cent we have subject selection (those who do not get an item correct are not included in the measures) which may distort the mean of the natural distribution of latencies based on all Ss.

Length of Retention Interval

The logic of the PI situation demands an increase in PI as a function of the length of the retention interval (Underwood, 1948). So far as is known, no completely satisfactory test of this relationship has been made for LTM. Theoretically the increase in PI with increase in length of the retention interval may be accounted for by the recovery of extinguished interfering associations. Several studies strongly suggest such recovery (e.g. Briggs, 1954).

Interaction of Variables

If the facts and theory of PI in LTM hold for STM, certain interactions among the above variables will be expected. Most critical among these is the interaction between the number of potentially interfering associations and the length of the retention interval. Theoretically it is assumed that the longer the retention interval the greater the recovery of interfering associations. If there are few or none such associations little or no decrement will be observed as a function of length of retention interval (i.e. forgetting will be very slow). If there are many potential associations which could interfere proactively, the longer the retention interval the greater the forgetting, since the longer the interval the greater the number of interfering associations which will have recovered.

We may now focus on the fact that PI is said not to be involved in the rapid forgetting in STM. In the Peterson–Peterson study Ss were tested on forty-eight successive items following two

practice items. It has been suggested that PI reaches some maxi
mum level rather quickly as a function of the number of previou
items and that a constant amount of PI may occur thereafter
Thus, two practice items may 'throw in' the maximum amoun
of PI and additional items may have no further decrement:
effects (Postman, 1962; Melton, 1963). While it seems apparer
that there must be a limit to the number of previous items whic
will contribute to interference in STM, it does not seem reasor
able that all potential interfering associations would be estal
lished with only two items – the two practice items. It seems mo
reasonable to look at the Peterson–Peterson data from anoth
point of view. If it is assumed that there is a practice effect
learning successive items, degree of learning for each successi
item will be higher and higher. By principles of PI in LTM, t
recall should also be higher and higher if amount of inte
ference remains constant. But, of course, interference does n
remain constant; more and more potentially interfering associ
tions are acquired as testing continues. As noted earlier in t
discussion, the question is how the positive effects of increas
degree of learning with successive stages of practice balance c
against the increased interference which accompanies the higl
degree of learning. Some indication of the direction the answ
may take is available in the Peterson–Peterson data.

These investigators divided the forty-eight experimental ite
into successive blocks of twelve items each so that block:
through 4 may reflect increasing degrees of learning of the ite
to be recalled and, simultaneously, increasing numbers of pot
tially interfering items. The percentage correct at recall by blo
was determined separately for two short intervals (3 and 6 s
and for two long intervals (15 and 18 sec). The results are p
sented in Figure 1. For the short retention intervals there i
consistent increase in recall from block 1 to block 4, the
ference between the recall for the two extreme blocks b
significant at the 0·02 confidence level. Peterson and Peter
identified this as a practice effect. Since there is no reasor
believe that the practice effect occurs in the recall process it n
mean that the degree of learning attained in the constant expo
period increases as trials proceed. For the longer reten
interval there is no increase in recall. If only practice effects

involved, this curve should rise in exactly the same manner as the
curve for shorter intervals. That it does not may indicate an increase in amount of PI as trials proceed. Thus, Figure 1 gives indirect evidence for the critical interaction discussed earlier; that

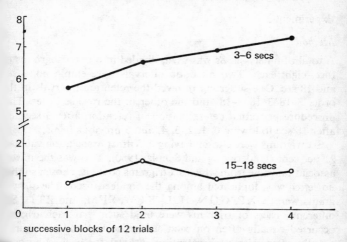

Figure 1 Retention of single consonant syllables over short (3–6 sec)
and long (15–18 sec) retention intervals as a function of number of
preceding items. From Peterson and Peterson (1959)

the interaction between amount of interference and length of
the retention interval. With short retention intervals the practice
effects more than compensate for increased interference; with
long retention intervals the interference is of sufficient magnitude
to mask the practice effects.

The evidence for the interaction between number of previous
items and length of retention interval as inferred from Figure 1 is
not entirely satisfactory. Not only is the magnitude of the interaction small, but the failure to find a change in retention over
blocks for the longer retention intervals must be interpreted as
due to a balance between practice and interference effects. We
believe it is possible to devise situations which will destroy this
balance and thus give more direct evidence for the role of PI.
Furthermore, studies are needed in which STM is examined for

*S*s without prior practice so that the rate of onset of PI as a function of 0, 1, 2, 3, etc., previous items is observed. The present experiments were designed to study these two issues.[1] [. . .]

Experiment 3

Method

A total of ninety-six *S*s was used, divided into two subgroups of forty-eight each. Two retention intervals were employed, 3 sec and 18 sec. One subgroup received the retention intervals in the order 3–18–3–18–3–18, and the other in the reverse order. The procedure permitted determination of retention after 3 sec and after 18 sec following 0, 1, 2, 3, 4, and 5 previous items.

Six trigrams were chosen having a Witmer association value of 21 per cent (Underwood and Schulz, 1960). This was the lowest association value from which six trigrams could be chosen so that no letter was duplicated among the eighteen used. The six trigrams were: CXP, GQN, HJL, KBW, SFM, and ZTD. Six different orders of trigrams were used such that each trigram occurred equally often on each successive test and, of course, equally often with each retention interval for each subgroup. None of the *S*s used had served previously in laboratory experiments on verbal learning. Each trigram was printed with lettering set on a 3 × 5-in card, the letters being ½ in. high. Following the presentation of a card for 2 sec, *E* spoke a number as the card was removed and *S* counted backward by three. Practice in number counting was given prior to the presentation of the first trigram.

---

1. *Editors' note*: Experiments 1 and 2 will not be presented .In these experiments, *S*s were tested for their retention of single trigrams after either 3 or 18 sec. Each *S* was tested once after each interval. Trigrams (KJF, MHZ, and CXJ) were presented auditorily (cf. Peterson and Peterson, 1959) in Experiment 1 and visually (2-sec exposure) in Experiment 2. Since each *S* was tested once after each interval, it was possible to determine the probability of recall for the three retention intervals after 0, 1, and 2 prior trigrams. Experiment 3 used a similar design, but extended the testing to six successive trigrams. Since the bulk of the authors' argument is based upon the results of Experiment 3, this study will be presented in detail.

Results

The proportions of correct responses for both interval patterns are combined in Figure 2. In this figure the six successive tests are given along the abscissa, with one curve representing retention after 3 sec and the other retention after 18 sec. The trend of proactive interference which was initiated by the three tests in Experiment 2 [not included here] is extended and clarified by Figure 2.

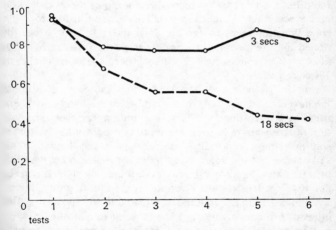

Figure 2 Retention as a function of number of prior syllables and length of retention interval. Experiment III

It may be noted first that the recall on the very first item presented to Ss does not differ for the 3-sec and the 18-sec retention intervals. However, with each successive test the differences increase, thus demonstrating the interaction between tests (number of prior interfering associations) and length of retention interval. Severe PI builds up over 18 sec with successive tests but this does not happen over 3 sec. For T-1 through T-6, the zs for the difference between proportions for 3 and 18 sec are: , 1·17, 2·17, 2·17, 4·51, and 4·23.

ignificant forgetting is shown for the 3-sec interval between and T-4 ($z = 2.33$). The rise between T-4 and T-5 is not significant statistically but may indicate that practice effects are more than counteracting interference effects produced by prior tests (see later).

The question as to whether a steady state of a constant amount of PI is being approached in the 18-sec curve is not clearly answered by Figure 2. The question can be more easily answered by replotting Figure 2 to separate the two independent groups. That is, the 3-sec curve in Figure 2 is based on two different groups of Ss, one having the 3–18–3–18–3–18 order of intervals the other the reverse. We may, therefore, plot the 3- and 18-sec curves separately for each group. This is done in Figure 3. The solid lines represent the group given the 3–18, etc., order, the dotted lines representing the group given the reverse order. The filled circles represent the 3-sec retention, the open circles the 18-sec retention.

For the 18-sec curves, the 3–18 group shows no evidence of leveling off and the 18–3 group shows only slight evidence of negative acceleration. In short, it would appear that extrapolation of these curves beyond the six tests used would give further continued larger and larger decrements in recall over 18 sec. That this is not so apparent in Figure 2 appears to be due to the fact that this figure combines two groups of slightly different ability levels. It also should be noted that for both groups there a rise in retention between the second and third tests for the 3-sec interval. Although neither rise is significant statistically, the trend may be reliable in view of the Peterson–Peterson data shown Figure 1 where performance does systematically improve as function of successive tests for short retention intervals.

Discussion

The results of the present experiments give strong support to presumption that short-term retention of single items and long-term retention of lists of items are subject to the same laws proactive inhibition.

No data on letter intrusions occurring for tests beyond have been given. The reason for this is simply that by the nature the designs used it is impossible to isolate variables which may involved in producing intrusions. In the present studies, t between successive recalls differ; degree of learning of items given previously differ for different intervals; whether or not a previously presented item was correct or incorrect at recall should influence overt intrusions on subsequent items. If systematic laws concerning evocation of letter intrusions are to be derived, experiments must be explicitly designed for the purpose. For these reasons we have not presented intrusion data.

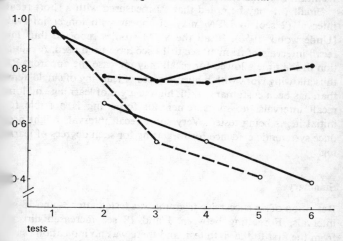

Figure 3 Retention as a function of number of prior syllables and length of retention interval (solid circles, 3 secs; open circles, 18 secs) Ss having intervals in the order 3–18–3–18–3–18 (solid lines) and in reverse order (dotted lines). Experiment III

f the conclusion of the present experiments are sound, that is, conclusion that the laws of proaction are the same for STM for LTM, some economy in time may be gained by working further laws of PI on STM rather than on LTM. For example, interitem similarity (e.g. letter duplication) should clearly uence STM. But there is reason to believe that this relation- may be complex. Specifically, in the present results it was ed that many intrusions consisted of a letter from a previous replacing a letter at recall which occupied the same serial tion, e.g. the middle letter. This suggests the operation of an , A–C interference paradigm in which A is the common serial position. Such intrusions also represent the evidence needed to support the notion of spontaneous recovery of extinguished or partially extinguished associations over short intervals. If, however, serial position does constitute a common stimulus from item to item, identical letters in the same position for different items may produce a positive effect – i.e. proactive facilitation may result.

Finally, it may be noted that PI measured with a short recall interval (2 sec) in LTM may disappear with longer intervals (Underwood, 1950). In all the STM studies reported thus far recall intervals of from 10 sec to 14 sec have been used. A reduction in the time allowed for recall may increase the apparent PI, thus allowing work with higher degrees of learning of single item than has been customary. With high degrees of learning and long recall intervals, no measurement of forgetting is possible for initial items being tested. Very short recall intervals might produce systematic evidence for forgetting for such degrees of learning.

Summary

Retention of six successive trigrams was tested after 3- and 18-sec intervals. Forgetting between 3 and 18 sec increased directly from the first to the sixth test, and there was no indication that a constant amount of proactive interference had been reached. The results were interpreted to mean that proactive inhibition in short-term memory of single items follows the same laws as proactive inhibition in long-term memory of lists.

References

BRIGGS, G. E. (1954), 'Acquisition, extinction and recovery functions in retroactive inhibition', *Journal of Experimental Psychology*, vol. 47, pp. 285–93.

MELTON, A. W. (1963), 'Discussion of Professor Peterson's paper', in C. N. Cofer, ed., *Problems and Processes in Verbal Behavior and Learning*, McGraw-Hill.

MURDOCK, B. B., Jr. (1961), 'The retention of individual items', *Journal of Experimental Psychology*, vol. 62, pp. 618–25.

PETERSON, L. R. (1963), 'Immediate memory: Data and theory', in C. N. Cofer, ed., *Problems and Processes in Verbal Behavior and Learning*, McGraw-Hill.

PETERSON, L. R., and PETERSON, M. J. (1959), 'Short-term retention of individual verbal items', *Journal of Experimental Psychology*, vol. 58, pp. 193–8.

POSTMAN, L. (1961), 'The present status of interference theory', in C. N. Cofer, ed., *Verbal Learning and Verbal Behavior*, McGraw-Hill.

POSTMAN, L. (1962), 'Short-term memory and incidental learning', *Paper read at ONR conference*, Ann Arbor, Michigan, February.

POSTMAN, L., and RILEY, D. A. (1959), 'Degree of learning and interserial interference in retention', *University of California Publication on Psychology*, vol. 8, pp. 271–396.

UNDERWOOD, B. J. (1945), 'The effect of successive interpolations on retroactive and proactive inhibition', *Psychological Monographs*, vol. 59, no. 3.

UNDERWOOD, B. J. (1948), 'Retroactive and proactive inhibition after five and forty-eight hours', *Journal of Experimental Psychology*, vol. 38, pp. 29–38.

UNDERWOOD, B. J. (1950), 'Proactive inhibition with increased recall time', *American Journal of Psychology*, vol. 63, pp. 594–9.

UNDERWOOD, B. J. (1957), 'Interference and forgetting', *Psychological Review*, vol. 64, pp. 49–60.

UNDERWOOD, B. J., and SCHULZ, R. W. (1960), *Meaningfulness and Verbal Learning*, Lippincott.

28 B. B. Murdock

A Test of the 'Limited Capacity' Hypothesis

B. B. Murdock, 'A test of the "limited capacity" hypothesis', *Journal of Experimental Psychology*, vol. 69 (1965), pp. 237–40.

If as suggested recently an individual does have a limited capacity fo recall in STM, then simultaneous variation in number of presentation and rate of presentation (with total presentation time constant) shoul result in equal recall. To test this hypothesis, Ss were given one pr sentation of six pairs at a rate of 4 sec/pair, two presentations 2 sec/pair, or four presentations at 1 sec/pair, then tested for recall the B member of one of the six A–B pairs. Recall probabilities for the 1 and 3rd condition were indistinguishable, while the 2nd condition w superior only at the shorter retention intervals. Considering this an other evidence, it was concluded that the limited capacity hypothes may be a useful 1st approximation.

Recently it was suggested (Murdock, 1964) that, in STM, i dividuals may have a limited capacity for immediate reca Further, it was suggested that the limitation may be on the ra of processing information. If so, then one should be able to tra off number of presentations and presentation rate if total prese ation time is held constant. For instance, if each pair in a list paired associates is presented for a total of 4 sec, the list can presented once at a presentation rate of 4 sec/pair, twice at a r of 2 sec/pair, or four times, at a rate of 1 sec/pair (symboli 1–4, 2–2, and 4–1, respectively). The hypothesis would pre equal recall under these three conditions; the present experim is a test of this hypothesis.

Method

To facilitate comparison with other studies the procedure essentially that used previously (e.g. Murdock, 1963a, 1963b). A–B pairs were composed of common English words paire random, and each list consisted of six pairs. After 1–4, 2–2, or one of the six pairs was tested by presenting A as the cue for recall of B. Each of the six serial positions was tested equally often under the three experimental conditions. Thus, one replication required eighteen lists. In all there were thirteen replications; group testing was used, and all Ss ($N = 20$) were tested on all 234 lists. The four test sessions required were held at the same time (11.00 a.m.) on four consecutive Tuesdays.

The same filmstrips that had been used previously (Experiment III, Murdock, 1963b) were used here. For the two conditions that required repetition (i.e. 2–2 and 4–1), after the last pair in the list had been shown for the requisite time, the stripfilm was rolled back to the first pair in the list. The roll-back took no appreciable time and was just a rapid blur on the screen. This procedure was repeated twice more for the 4–1 condition. Thus, with repetition the same serial order of the pairs was preserved, and for all practical purposes there was no intertrial interval. Actually, this lack of an intertrial interval is one of the two procedural differences between the 2–2 condition of the present experiment and the two-repetition condition of a previous study (Experiment III, Murdock, 1963a). The other difference is that, in the present experiment, Ss were given information before each trial as to whether the presentation rate would be 'fast', 'slow', or 'average'.

Naturally, the critical pair was in no way distinguished prior to the recall test. The recall period was 15 sec, and a 5-sec ready period preceded each list. The order of presentation of the eighteen conditions within each replication was randomized. With group testing the specific A–B pairs could not be counterbalanced across the eighteen conditions; however, with a total of 234 different word pairs randomly distributed, it seemed unlikely that any systematic differences in item difficulty could occur to bias the results. The Ss were students of both sexes from the introductory psychology course who were fulfilling a course requirement.

Results

The best over-all measure of performance is the area under the serial-position curve (i.e. the sum of the p values for the six different serial positions). For the 2–2 condition the value was 3·12; the comparable value for the two-repetition condition of the previous experiment (Murdock, 1963a) was 3·47. The elimination of the 2-sec. intertrial interval reduced the total presentation time by 8 per cent; the fact that the recall performance was reduced by 10 per cent does not seem disproportionate.

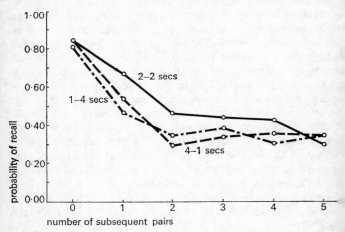

Figure 1 Probability of recall as a function of number of subsequent pa[irs]

The main results of the present experiment are shown in Figu[re] 1, where probability of recall is plotted as a function of number [of] subsequent pairs for each of the three conditions separately. It [is] apparent that the results for 1–4 and 4–1 are almost indistinguis[h]able; however, the p values for 2–2 are somewhat higher at t[he] shorter retention intervals (in particular, one and two subseque[nt] pairs).

The above conclusions are substantiated by analyses of va[ri]ance of number of correct recalls. Number of subsequent pa[irs] experimental conditions, and their interaction were all signific[ant] at well beyond the 0·001 level. Duncan's multiple-range [test] showed that, at the 0·01 level, 2–2 was better than either 1–4 [or] 4–1 but the latter two did not differ significantly. Separ[ate] analyses of variance at each of the six retention intervals sho[wed] that the experimental conditions were significant only for one and two subsequent pairs; at both these retention intervals $p < 0.001$. Finally, it has been suggested (Murdock, 1963a) that, after two subsequent pairs, the retention curve is essentially asymptotic. Therefore, the three longest retention intervals (i.e. three, four, and five subsequent pairs) were analysed separately; an analysis of variance showed that the effects of neither subsequent pairs nor experimental conditions were statistically significant (in both cases, $p > 0.05$).

Table 1

Proportion of Omissions, Extralist Intrusions, and Intralist A and B Intrusions for Each Experimental Condition

	1–4	2–2	4–1
Omissions	0·558	0·487	0·407
Extralist intrusions	0·200	0·179	0·127
Intralist A intrusions	0·079	0·085	0·113
Intralist B intrusions	0·163	0·250	0·353

As stated above, the area under the serial-position curve was 2 for the 2–2 condition. The comparable values for 1–4 and for 1 were 2·62 and 2·70, respectively. Thus, in terms of overall performance, the latter two conditions were about 15 per cent poorer than the 2–2 condition. However, as indicated by the statistical analysis, most of the difference appeared to be concentrated at one and two subsequent pairs.

There was a total of 2496 non-correct responses, and an analysis of errors is shown in Table 1. This table shows the proportion of omissions (failure to respond), extralist intrusions (any word not in the list), and intralist intrusions (any incorrect word from the list) broken down into A and B items. As number of presentations increased from one to four, both omissions and extralist intrusions decreased but intralist intrusions (both A and increased. Perhaps the most important point to note about the error analysis is that, for all four categories, the trend was monotonic; in no case was there a maximum or a minimum for the 2–2 condition.

To test for practice effects the first three replications were compared with the second three replications. An analysis of variances of the number of correct recalls showed that neither replications (i.e. 1–3 versus 4–6) nor the interaction of replications by conditions (i.e. 1–4, 2–2, 4–1) had a statistically significant effect on recall (in both cases $p > 0.05$). An inspection of the data gave no indication that learning to learn and proactive inhibition were counteracting each other. Performance at serial position 6 (probably the best measure of degree of original learning) did not appear to improve over these first six replications; neither did performance at serial positions 1–3 deteriorate over this period. However, such changes may have occurred within the first replication itself (see Murdock, 1964).

Finally, as the number of presentations increased from one to four, the opportunity for serial learning of the six pairs increased. (The same serial order was used with repetition.) One measure of such serial learning is the 'adjacent/penultimate' (A/P) ratio. In previous studies we have found that about two-thirds of the intralist intrusions are either from adjacent serial positions (i.e. immediately before or immediately after the critical pair) or from the penultimate pair in the list (i.e. serial position 5). With serial learning of the pairs the former could be expected to increase relative to the latter (see Slamecka, 1964) and, in one study (Experiment III, Murdock, 1963a), this ratio was 1·08, 1·38, and 1·61 for one, two, and three presentations, respectively. In the present study the A/P ratio was 1·48, 1·41, and 1·63 for one, two, and four presentations, respectively. Thus, it would seem as relatively little serial learning occurred; presumably the fast presentation rate worked against the factor of repetition.

Discussion

In general the 'limited capacity' hypothesis would seem to be confirmed. For the longer retention intervals (i.e. 3–5 subsequent pairs) the three conditions did not differ significantly, and at the shorter retention intervals (i.e. 1–2 subsequent pairs) 1–4 and 4–1 did not differ significantly. Also, the trend of omissions, extralist intrusions, and intralist A and B intrusions was monotonic; thus this measure of retention failed to show any evidence of cu linearity across conditions. The one disquieting feature was the superiority of 2–2 at the shorter retention intervals. However, there is some evidence already that there are two components to the STM paired-associate retention curve (Murdock, 1963a), yet even here the differences that did exist were only of the order of 5 per cent.

Recent studies by Bugelski (1962) and by Bugelski and Rickwood (1963) are particularly relevant to the present findings. In the former study a list of paired associates was learned to criterion at one of five different presentation rates. While the number of trials to criterion increased with presentation rate, the total exposure time for the five groups was essentially the same. In the latter study the trials were self-paced, yet the total learning time was nearly within the range established in the first study. Obviously, these results are just what would be expected by a hypothesis of limited capacity. Additional support comes from Nodine (1963) who reported that, '. . . an eightfold increase in exposure durations . . . produced slightly less than an eightfold increase in total correct responses' (p. 105).

There is some evidence, then, that with paired associates a constant amount of material can be learned or retained given a constant amount of time. The same time constancy seems to operate in free recall (Cohen, 1963; Murdock, 1960; Waugh, 1962, 1963): If the limitation is on the rate of processing information, then these studies in verbal learning would agree well with studies of choice reaction time (Leonard, 1961). All things considered, it would seem that the limited capacity hypothesis may be a useful first approximation.

References

BUGELSKI, B. R. (1962), 'Presentation time, total time, and mediation in paired-associate learning', Journal of Experimental Psychology, vol. 63, p. 409–12.

BUGELSKI, B. R., and RICKWOOD, J. (1963), 'Presentation time, total time, and mediation in paired-associate learning: Self-pacing', Journal of Experimental Psychology, vol. 65, pp. 616–17.

COHEN, B. H. (1963), 'An investigation of recoding in free recall', Journal of Experimental Psychology, vol. 65, pp. 368–76.

LEONARD, J. A. (1961), 'Choice reaction time experiments and information theory', in Colin Cherry, ed., Fourth London Symposium Information Theory, Butterworth.

Short-term Memory

MURDOCK, B. B., Jr. (1960), 'The immediate retention of unrelated words', *Journal of Experimental Psychology*, vol. 60, pp. 222–34.

MURDOCK, B. B., Jr. (1963a), 'Short-term memory and paired-associate learning', *Journal of Verbal Learning and Verbal Behavior*, vol. 2, pp. 320–28.

MURDOCK, B. B., Jr. (1963b), 'Short-term retention of single paired associates', *Journal of Experimental Psychology*, vol. 65, pp. 433–43.

MURDOCK, B. B., Jr. (1964), 'Proactive inhibition in short-term memory', *Journal of Experimental Psychology*, vol. 68, pp. 184–9.

NODINE, C. F. (1963), 'Stimulus durations and stimulus characteristics in paired-associate learning', *Journal of Experimental Psychology*, vol. 66, pp. 100–106.

SLAMECKA, N. J. (1964), 'An inquiry into the doctrine of remote associations', *Psychological Review*, vol. 71, pp. 61–76.

WAUGH, N. C. (1962), 'The effect of intralist repetition on free recall', *Journal of Verbal Learning and Verbal Behavior*, vol. 1, pp. 95–99.

WAUGH, N. C. (1963), 'Immediate memory as a function of repetition', *Journal of Verbal Learning and Verbal Behavior*, vol. 2, pp. 107–12.

Part Five **Interference**

In a classical paper McGeoch (1932) stated the basic postulate of an interference theory of forgetting in the following words: 'Retroactive inhibition, or interference from interpolated activities, is one of the major necessary conditions of forgetting. . . . Without the presence of inhibiting interpolated events forgetting would not in most cases appear. . . . Forgetting is, then, not a passive matter but a result of an active interference from interpolated events' (p. 364). He supported this assertion by a rapidly growing body of evidence showing that the amount of forgetting was determined not by the length of the time interval between learning and recall but by the nature of the activities during the retention interval. Since that time another equally important, or perhaps more important, source of interference has been recognized, viz. activities which precede the events which must be recalled – proactive inhibition. The addition of proactive inhibition extends, but does not basically alter, the principle that active habit interference is the cause of forgetting.

The distinction between retroactive inhibition (RI) and proactive inhibition (PI) is made most conveniently in terms of the experimental designs which are used to produce these two kinds of interference in the laboratory. Both designs call for the comparison of an experimental group with a control group. The experimental group learns two lists in succession; the control group learns a single list. The critical difference between the two designs lies in the temporal location of the list to be recalled. In the RI design, recall is measured for the list learned first. The difference in first-list recall between the experimental and the control group defines the amount of RI. In the PI design on the other hand, recall is taken for the second list; the experimental-control difference in second-list recall is the measure of PI. In the interest of simplicity the operations for the measurement of RI and PI have been stated with reference to a two-list situation. The same logic applies when there are more than one interfering lists. RI is attributed to the effects of interpolated learning, and PI to those of prior learning.

Transfer and Interference

Interference in recall is closely tied to negative transfer in acquisition, both in terms of experimental operations and hypothetical mechanisms. This relation is exhibited readily for the classical paradigm of negative transfer, A–B, A–D, in which different unrelated responses are attached to the identical stimuli in successive lists. Under these conditions there is typically negative transfer in the acquisition of A–D, RI of the recall of A–B, and PI of the recall of A–D. The fact that negative transfer and interference at recall could be shown to be complementary effects of the same experimental operations led to the hypothesis that the mechanisms responsible for these effects are complementary as well. Thus, McGeoch (1942) attributed RI in the recall of the first list to competition from second-list responses, just as negative transfer in acquisition was the result of competition from the earlier habits. According to this view, the two sets of responses (B and D) learned in succession both remain potentially available to the subject at the time of recall. They are, however, in competition with each other, and as a consequence first-list responses are blocked or momentarily displaced by stronger second-list responses. Much of this competition was assumed to be covert since overt intrusions of the correct associations are infrequent and certainly cannot account for the total amount of retention loss. This interpretation came known as the independence hypothesis because of the assumption that the two sets of associations remain independent and intact.

Two-Factor Theory

The fact that there is little correlation between overt response competition and the amount of RI, casts doubt on the independence hypothesis and the proposition that response competition is the only mechanism responsible for retroactive interference. In a classical paper Melton and Irwin (1940) proposed that the experimental facts could be subsumed more readily under a two-factor theory. Response competition at recall was retained as one of the factors, but to it was added as a second factor the unlearning of the first-list associations during interpolated practice. As formulated by Melton and Irwin, the two-factor theory holds that the unlearning of first-list associations is a process which is akin to the extinction of conditioned responses. That is, during the acquisition of A–D the old response B is elicited, fails to be reinforced and thus is weakened. Consequently the old associations A–B are less available at the time of recall than they had been at the end of original learning. Since second-list responses are not subject to unlearning, the theory implies that PI is entirely a matter of response competition. With two factors combining to produce RI, but only one of these contributing to PI, the former type of interference should be greater than the latter. This prediction was confirmed (Melton and von Lackum, 1941).

Experimental tests of the two-factor theory have sought to obtain independent evidence for each of the two assumed components of interference. To the extent that overt intrusions of responses from the interfering list do occur, there is apparent evidence for response competition, although it must be recognized that such intrusions may be a consequence rather than a cause of forgetting (Conrad, 1960). To obtain critical evidence for unlearning, it was necessary to devise a test of recall which could be assumed to be immune to the effects of response competition. A method of measuring retention designed to meet this requirement was introduced by Barnes and Underwood (1959). The procedure devised by these investigators is a test of modified free recall (MFR). Having learned A–B and A–D, the subject is presented with the common stimulus terms (A) and is given unlimited time to recall the responses from both lists (B and D) in the order in which they occur to him. Competition is assumed to be minimized because the subject is not paced; if two responses are available but in competition, there is time to give both of them. There is, moreover, no requirement to differentiate between first-list and second-list responses since both are called for; thus, responses will not be withheld because of errors in the identification of their list membership. The results of Barnes and Underwood and those of numerous subsequent investigations show that there is, indeed, a substantial reduction in the availability of first-list responses following interpolated learning.

Reading 29 by McGovern examines the question of what is unlearned as a result of interpolated practice. The author hypothesized that first-list recall depends on the integrity of three kinds of associations, viz. forward associations between stimuli and responses, backward associations between these terms, and contextual associations. The latter refer to connexions between the environmental situation and the prescribed responses. Each type of association will be unlearned whenever an A–B, A–D relation obtains for that association in the successive lists. In order to validate her analysis, McGovern used two methods of measuring first-list retention: one of these was a form of the MFR test which required recall of the response terms whereas the other was a test of associative matching in which performance depended only on the subject's ability to identify the correct stimulus–response pairings. It was assumed that recall on the MFR test would be reduced by the unlearning of all three types of associations whereas performance in the matching task would be influenced only by the unlearning of forward and backward associations. The data fully bore out these expectations. A more general implication of the findings which is worthy of emphasis is that the phenomena of interference, like those of transfer, are subject to analysis into the effects of component sub-processes.

It is still very much an open question whether unlearning is a process analogous to the extinction of conditioned responses. There are some experimental findings consistent with the hypothesis that unlearning is produced by the unreinforced evocation of first-list responses during second-list learning (e.g. Postman, Keppel and Stark, 1965). However, the available evidence is largely indirect and by no means conclusive (see Keppel, 19 for a review of relevant studies). One important implication of the extinction analogy is that unlearned associations should show spontaneous recovery over time, i.e. there should be increases in first-list recall as the interval between interpolated learning and test is lengthened. Such recovery has been observed under certain circumstances but it is not clear that the rises in recall necessarily reflect gains in associative strength. There are indications that the apparent recovery may reflect a dissipation of the subject's set to favour the most recent responses in recall (Postman, Stark and Fraser, 1968). While direct tests of the reversibility of unlearning have so far not yielded conclusive results, the theoretical construct of spontaneous recovery continues to play an important role in interference theory because of its use in the explanation of PI phenomena. This problem will be considered next.

Proactive Inhibition

As indicated earlier, PI refers to a decrement in the recall of the most recently learned materials, which is attributable to interference from prior learning activities. According to two-factor theory, competition between appropriate and inappropriate responses at recall is the sole factor responsible for PI. The massive retention losses produced by cumulative PI are exhibited early in Reading 30. This paper is a landmark in the analysis of forgetting and drastically changed the interpretation of many of the experimental findings reported in the earlier literature. It was customary for a long time to use experienced subjects in laboratory studies of learning and retention. The rate of forgetting for materials learned in the laboratory was characteristically found to be exceedingly rapid. Underwood's analysis shows that this rapid rate of loss was largely determined by proactive interference from previous experimental tasks. A naïve subject who learns a single list of materials in the laboratory and recalls it 24 hours later will show approximately 20 per cent forgetting. By way of contrast it may be noted that Ebbinghaus, who learned a very large number of lists in the course of his experiments in which he was the only subject, reported a loss of 66 per cent after hours. Underwood's analysis of a large number of different experiments firmly establishes the conclusion that PI increases steadily as a function of the number of prior lists learned in the laboratory.

The magnitude of PI is influenced by variables other than the number of prior lists. The amount of PI grows larger as the number of trials on the interfering list increases (although this relation may hold only over a limited range) and as the degree of learning of the test list decreases. As already noted, the similarity relations effective in transfer generally hold for interference as well. A major determinant of PI is the length of the retention interval. By definition, PI must increase from zero on a retention test immediately after the end of learning to some maximum value after a sufficient period of delay. Theoretically the lengthening of the retention interval allows the recovery of interfering associations which had been unlearned during the acquisition of the test list. Moreover, the subject will be increasingly unable to distinguish between the sets of appropriate and inappropriate responses as the retention interval increases. Both of these factors, recovery of prior habits and loss of list differentiation, are assumed to influence response competition at the time of recall.

Extra-Experimental Interference

For many years the RI design was used as the experimental analogue of the conditions of forgetting which are obtained outside of the laboratory. That is, it was assumed that most, if not all, the forgetting of a single list learned in the laboratory was produced by the interpolation of linguistic activity during the retention interval. Underwood's (1957) demonstration that PI has been an uncontrolled factor contributing to the amount of forgetting observed in previous experiments has two important implications for interference theory: (a) the amount of forgetting that would need to be explained by the theory is not as great as earlier studies had indicated and (b) extra-experimental interference should be largely proactive in nature. A direct outgrowth of this initial analysis was a formalized statement by Underwood and Postman (1960) of a generalized interference theory of forgetting. This theory is summarized by Postman in Reading 31. Briefly, the theory envisages two major sources of extra-experimental interference, letter-sequence and unit-sequence inter ference, as being responsible for the forgetting of a single list of materials learned by a naïve subject in the laboratory. Both sources of interference stem from linguistic habits which are acquired over a subject's lifetime. Specifically, letter-sequence interference is assumed to become effective when the learning materials consist of infrequent letter combinations, while unit-sequence interference comes into play when the list comprises sequences of well-integrated units (i.e. words). In this latter case, the source of the interference is the presence, in the subject's linguistic repertoire, of other sequences which involve the same words as those being learned. For both types of interference, the mechanism is basically the same as the one proposed to account for the increase in PI with time, viz. spontaneous recovery and loss of differentiation. Thus, during learning the linguistic interference will eventually be overcome, but is assumed to recover over the retention interval to compete with the correct responses at recall.

There have been numerous experimental tests of this theory of forgetting. Except for one or two cases, the outcome of these tests has been clear; forgetting is not related to variations in assumed unit-sequence or letter-sequence interference (see Keppel, 1968, for a summary of these experiments). These findings have led to a search for the shortcomings of the theory which may be responsible for the empirical failures. Underwood and Ekstrand (1966), for example, questioned the basic assumption that the typical PI design provides an adequate experimental analogue of linguistic interference. They pointed to two important differences between linguistic habits and experimentally acquired associations which may account for the breakdown of the theory: linguistic habits are considerably stronger and are acquired in much more widely spaced 'trials' than are the associations normally established in the laboratory. Underwood and Ekstrand then carried out an experiment in which they attempted to simulate these two properties of linguistic associations and found an almost complete elimination of PI when the first list was learned by distributed practice (24 hours between successive blocks of trials). This finding suggests that linguistic habits do not different-ly influence forgetting because they have been acquired by distributed practice. If this argument is accepted, we can under-stand the negative evidence which has been reported. It is still incumbent upon the interference theorist, however, to explain in interference terms the forgetting of the unpractised subject.

Another possibility is that the theory failed to take into consideration the potential role of linguistic habits in facilitating retention (Postman, 1963). For example, increases in word frequency, which were assumed to enhance unit-sequence interference, may also facilitate response recall; these two opposed influences might account for the failures to find differential forgetting as a function of word frequency. Clear evidence for the co-variation of unit-sequence facilitation and interference was reported in a later experiment (Postman, 1967) in which serial lists of associatively related and unrelated words were learned and recalled one week later. On the first recall trial the related word lists were superior to the unrelated ones, a finding which was attributed to a facilitation of response recall. The effect of unit-sequence interference was observed on the next trial after differences in response recall were presumably greatly reduced. These results imply, then, that the actual outcome of the retention test will depend upon the net effect of the positive and negative factors which are brought into operation by the manipulation of pre-experimental associative probabilities.

While the shortcomings of existing formulations are beginning to be understood, it is fair to say that the principles of RI and PI established in the laboratory have thus far failed to generate a model of the forgetting process which can be shown to have general validity. The ultimate usefulness of interference theory will depend upon the success with which future investigations are able to identify, measure, and manipulate the sources of interference outside the laboratory which are responsible for the forgetting of verbal materials.

References

BARNES, J. M., and UNDERWOOD, B. J. (1959), '"Fate" of first-list associations in transfer theory', *Journal of Experimental Psychology*, vol. 58, pp. 97–105.

CONRAD, R. (1960), 'Serial order intrusions in immediate memory', *British Journal of Psychology*, vol. 51, pp. 45–8.

KEPPEL, G. (1968), 'Retroactive and proactive inhibition', in T. R. Dixon and D. L. Horton, eds., *Verbal Behavior and General Behavior Theory*, Prentice-Hall.

KEPPEL, G., and UNDERWOOD, B. J. (1962), 'Proactive inhibition in short-term retention of single items', *Journal of Verbal Learning and Verbal Behavior*, vol. 1, pp. 153–61.

McGEOCH, J. A. (1932), 'Forgetting and the law of disuse', *Psychological Review*, vol. 39, pp. 352–70.

McGEOCH, J. A. (1942), *The Psychology of Human Learning*, Longmans Green.

MELTON, A. W., and IRWIN, J. McQ. (1940), 'The influence of degree of interpolated learning on retroactive inhibition and the overt transfer of specific responses', *American Journal of Psychology*, vol. 53, pp. 173–203.

MELTON, A. W., and VON LACKUM, W. J. (1941), 'Retroactive and proactive inhibition in retention: evidence for a two-factor theory of retroactive inhibition', *American Journal of Psychology*, vol. 54, pp. 157–73.

POSTMAN, L. (1963), 'Does interference theory predict too much forgetting?', *Journal of Verbal Learning and Verbal Behavior*, vol. 2, pp. 40–48.

POSTMAN, L. (1967), 'The effect of interitem associative strength on the acquisition and retention of serial lists', *Journal of Verbal Learning and Verbal Behavior*, vol. 6, pp. 721–8.

POSTMAN, L., KEPPEL, G., and STARK, K. (1965), 'Unlearning as a function of the relationship between successive response classes', *Journal of Experimental Psychology*, vol. 69, pp. 111–18.

POSTMAN, L., STARK, K., and FRASER, J. (1968), 'Temporal changes in interference', *Journal of Verbal Learning and Verbal Behavior*, vol. 7, pp. 672–94.

UNDERWOOD, B. J., and EKSTRAND, B. R. (1966), 'An analysis of some shortcomings in the interference theory of forgetting', *Psychological Review*, vol. 73, pp. 540–49.

UNDERWOOD, B. J., and POSTMAN, L. (1960), 'Extra-experimental sources of interference in forgetting', *Psychological Review*, vol. 67, pp. 73–95.

29 J. B. McGovern

Extinction of Associations in Four Transfer Paradigms

Abridged from J. B. McGovern, 'Extinction of associations in four transfer paradigms', *Psychological Monographs*, vol. 78 (1964), no. 16. [*Editors' note:* owing to the inclusion of Martin's paper, 'Transfer of verbal paired associates' (Reading 22), portions of the following article have been revised in order to conserve space. It is recommended that the reader study both papers concurrently.[1]]

This study deals with transfer theory and its implications for immediate recall. More specifically, it is an attempt to extend the implications of a recent set of experimental results (Barnes and Underwood, 1959) to a number of transfer situations. One of the conclusions arrived at in the Barnes–Underwood study was that the decrement in the recall of first-list responses in the A–B, A–C[1] negative transfer paradigm was the result of an extinction of first-list associations during second-list learning. This was suggested by the fact that after twenty trials on the second list (A–C), only about 50 per cent of the first-list responses (A–B) were recalled. Since subjects were asked to give both first- and second-list responses on an unpaced free-recall test, this loss was attributed to extinction or unlearning rather than to a competition between the two response terms.

Underwood, Runquist and Schulz (1959) have proposed that the learning of paired associates consists of at least two stages, the response-learning stage in which the response terms are learned as recallable units, and the associative-learning stage in which the responses are attached to the appropriate stimuli. In the present study it will be assumed that the associative stage consists of the formation of specific forward associations (S–R or A–B) as well as specific backward associations (R–S or B–A) and that the

Conventional notation is employed here. A pair of letters (e.g. A–B) stands for the stimuli (A) and responses (B) in a paired-associate list. Two pairs (e.g. A–B, A–C) identify two lists and the relationships between them. Thus the A–B, A–C paradigm is one in which the subject learns in succession two lists in which stimuli are identical (A), but responses differ (B in list 1; C in list 2).

response-learning stage is essentially a form of associative learning in which the important stimuli are context stimuli, that is
stimuli emanating from the room – the experimental equipment
etc. Thus, three types of associations are assumed to be learnee
during acquisition. Furthermore, it is assumed that each of th
three associations is extinguished whenever an A–B, A–C transfe
paradigm (new responses to old stimuli) is formed for these asso
ciations between lists. These latter assumptions were tested in thi
study by comparing the relative losses, for four different transfe
paradigms, of the first list as indexed by two methods of recal
modified free recall and associative-matching.

In the free-recall test, subjects were asked to recall the first-li
responses and to pair them, when possible, with the corre
stimulus terms. It is assumed that response recall is depende
upon the intactness of the contextual association, while the co
rect pairing of these responses depends upon the integrity of th
forward and backward associations. On the associative-matchi
test, subjects were provided with the correct responses and th
specifically asked to pair them. In this case, correct associative r
call is assumed to require intact forward and backward ass
ciations, while being uninfluenced by the contextual associatic
Thus, if an analysis of interlist relationships indicates the extin
ion of the contextual association, this should be reflected
(a) a decrement in the total number of words recalled on the fr
recall test, (b) no additional loss when free recall is scored for
number of responses correctly paired, and (c) no loss in assoc
tive matching. If, on the other hand, there is extinction of forwa
or backward associations, there should be (a) no loss in the to
number of words given in free recall, but a loss shown in (b) as
ciatively scored free recall as well as in (c) associative matchi
An analysis of the extinctive relationships in four transfer pa
digms will now be presented.

A–B, C–D. In this paradigm the stimuli and responses in the
lists are both different. Thus, there are no A–B, A–C relati
ships present for either forward or backward associations. Th
is, however, an extinctive arrangement for the contextual a
ciation. That is, the learning of two different sets of response
this paradigm establishes an A–B, A–C relationship where

410

timuli (A) involved are environmental stimuli. According to this
easoning, the A–B, A–C relationship involving environmental
timuli should be abolished when interpolated learning (IL)
ccurs in a different experimental situation. Consequently, re-
roactive inhibition (RI) should be reduced if IL takes place in an
nvironmental situation different from that in which original
arning (OL) and recall take place. At least two studies (Bilodeau
nd Schlosberg, 1951; Greenspoon and Ranyard, 1957) have
btained results which support this prediction. RI was signifi-
ntly reduced if IL took place in a different experimental room
s compared to a condition in which OL and IL took place in the
me experimental room. These results correspond to inter-
etations emphasizing the importance of context stimuli in the
ntrol of paired-associate learning. Since the only first-list asso-
ation which is unlearned in the A–B, C–D paradigm is the
ntextual association, the retention tests should show equal RI
r both measures (paired and total recall) on the free-recall test
d no RI on the associative-matching test.

-B, A–C. In this paradigm the stimuli are the same in the two
ts, but the responses differ. Since different responses appear in
e two lists, an extinctive arrangement is present for the context-
l association as there was for the A–B, C–D paradigm. In
dition, however, an A–B, A–C relationship also exists for the
R associations. Thus, there are two types of associations which
uld be extinguished in this paradigm. This will be reflected in
following outcome of the two retention tests: greater RI for
red recall than total recall on the free-recall test (S–R and
ntextual extinction affecting the former, with contextual
inction affecting the latter) and RI on the matching test (S–R
nction).

B, C–B. For this paradigm the stimuli in the two lists are
erent, while the response terms are the same. In this case,
her of the factors which are present for the A–B, A–C para-
n is involved in the A–B, C–B arrangement, since an
nctive relationship is not formed for either the S–R or con-
ual associations. There is, however, an A–B, A–C relationship
ch may be established for the backward (R–S) association.

411

Interference

Specifically, during OL, subjects form backward (B–A) as well as forward (A–B) associations. In IL the new forward association (C–B) does not involve the extinctive relationship, but the backward association (B–C) does, viz. B–A, B–C. Thus, to the extent that R–S associations are important in recall, the A–B, C–B paradigm contains the potential for producing RI. However, since the contextual association is not extinguished in this paradigm (the transfer relationship is A–B, A–B), there should be no RI for the total recall score on the free-recall test, but some RI present when attention is directed to the number of correct pairings on both the free-recall and associative-matching tests.

A–B, A–Br. In this final paradigm the same stimulus and response terms are used in OL and IL, but the terms are re-paired in the second list. If we consider the S–R association in this paradigm, there is an extinctive relationship since a 'new' response must be learned to an 'old' stimulus. Similarly, an A–B, A–C arrangement is present for the R–S association. On the other hand, the response terms are the same in the two lists so that the contextual association cannot be extinguished. Thus, there should be exactly the same outcome on the two tests as for the A–B, C–B paradigm, except that in the case of the A–B, A–Br paradigm the extinction of the S–R association will contribute additionally to the associative disruption reflected by the two tests.

Method

The subjects learned two lists of paired associates of one of the following relations: A–B, A–C; A–B, A–Br; A–B, C–B; A–C–D. The two lists were learned during one experimental session with a 1-minute rest interval between them. The lists were typed on white vellum tape and presented, employing the anticipation method, at a 2:2-second rate on a Hull-type memory drum. The intertrial interval was 4·0 seconds. The criterion of learning the first list was one errorless trial. The second list was presented for fifteen anticipation trials. Following practice on list 2, half the subjects were given a written free-recall test (MFR) in which they were given first-list stimuli and asked to write down first responses after receiving fifteen anticipation trials on the second

412

ist. The other half of the subjects in each condition were also given a list of the responses learned in List 1 and were instructed to pair them with first-list stimuli. These subjects formed the *associative-matching* subgroups of the four transfer paradigms. The remaining subjects in each transfer condition formed the *free-recall* subgroups. The two conditions of recall in the four transfer paradigms form eight independent groups. The four transfer groups employed in the present experiment will be identified, hereafter, by their second lists. Thus, the group learning the two lists of an A–B, A–C paradigm will be identified as the A–C condition; the group learning two lists of an A–B, A–Br relation will be identified as the A–Br condition, etc.

In addition to these eight experimental groups, a control group was run as a check on the possibility that uncontrolled 'forgetting', rather than the unlearning or extinction introduced by second-list learning, was responsible for any obtained decrement in recall of first-list responses in the transfer conditions. These subjects spent 9 minutes on an unrelated task, 9 minutes being the amount of time taken by the experimental subjects for practice on list 2. All subjects received a free-association task following recall.

Subjects and design

The 216 elementary psychology students who served as subjects were assigned to one of the nine conditions described above by the following procedure. The nine conditions were arranged in independent orders. The subjects were then assigned in succession to a condition within one of these six blocks as they appeared at the laboratory. Four subjects were assigned to each condition within each block. Thus there were twenty-four subjects in each experimental condition. Twelve subjects were dropped and replaced when they admitted to attempting rehearsal of 1 during the learning of list 2.

Materials

The first list of paired associates was identical for all nine conditions. The stimuli in all lists consisted of nonsense syllables with per cent – 73 per cent Glaze association value (Stevens, 1951, p. . Intralist similarity of stimuli was kept at a minimum. A

given consonant was used but once in the eight syllables of a
given list, and three of the five vowels were used twice. In conditions where different stimuli were used in the first and second lists
i.e. in the A–B, C–D and A–B, C–B paradigms, interlist stimulus
similarity was kept at a minimum; none of the stimuli in the
second list started with a consonant used as the initial letter of
any stimulus in the first list. In the A–B, C–B and A–B, A–B
paradigms, the two stimuli associated with a given response had
no letters in common. Responses in all lists consisted of common
adjectives. Intralist and interlist response similarity were also
minimized where appropriate. First-list responses (Joyful, Evil
Great, Fatigued, Calm, Frightened, Unfilled, Filthy) were
obtained empirically in a 'free-association' task. [See original
article for details – *editor*.] Second-list responses which were not
identical to first-list responses were chosen for their apparent lack
of meaningful similarity to first-list responses from Haagen
(1949) lists of two-syllable adjectives.

Four orders of presentation of list pairs were used to prevent
serial learning of the responses. The starting order of the first
list for each group was completely counterbalanced throughout
the nine experimental conditions.

Procedure

Standard paired-associate learning instructions were read to the
subjects at the beginning of the experimental session. Brief
instructions for second-list learning were read to the subjects in
the 1-minute interval between list 1 and list 2. The subjects were
stopped after fifteen anticipation trials on list 2, given a mimeographed list of stimulus terms, and instructed to write the first-
list responses they had learned opposite the appropriate stimuli.
The instructions emphasized that the subject should guess when
he was unsure of a particular association. The stimuli on the
mimeographed sheet were presented in the order which the subject would have received them on the trial following the criterion
trial in first-list learning. This method of presenting first-list
stimuli in recall was expected to maximize recall. As was noted
above, half of the subjects in each transfer condition received an
index card with the set of words used as first-list responses printed
on it. These subjects formed the associative-matching subgroup

of the transfer conditions. The remaining subjects in each paradigm formed the free-recall subgroups. In all cases, the subjects were given a 2-minute period in which to write.

Results

Equivalence of groups

The mean number of trials to criterion for the nine groups was 9·52, with a range in means from 8·29 to 10·67. Since the groups did not differ on this measure, $F < 1·00$, it would appear that the random assignment of subjects to groups was effective in equating groups in learning ability.

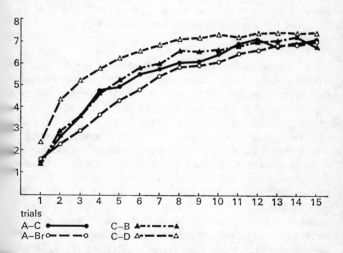

trials

A–C ●———●   C–B ▲–·–·–▲
A–Br ○– – –○   C–D △– – –△

Figure 1 Mean number of correct responses in second-list learning plotted over fifteen trials as a function of transfer conditions

Transfer effects

Performance over the fifteen second-list trials for the four transfer paradigms is shown in Figure 1. (The free-recall and associative-matching subgroups of each paradigm have been combined.) An inspection of Figure 1 indicates that the ordering of the transfer

415

groups remains relatively constant throughout the fifteen trials o
IL. Statistical analysis showed these differences to be significan
($F = 13.09$, $df = 3/184$, $p < 0.01$). Moreover, the rank orderin;
of the groups corresponds to that found in previous studie
employing these paradigms (see Twedt and Underwood, 1959) i
that the A–Br, A–C, and C–B transfer conditions all show nega
tive transfer effects when compared to the C–D conditio
($ps < 0.01$). Of course, since the transfer lists were different fc
the four paradigms, it is necessary to determine whether thes
lists were of equivalent difficulty before any meaningful state
ment can be made concerning these transfer effects. This wa
accomplished in a second experiment which showed that th
lists did not differ significantly in difficulty ($F < 1.00$). Thus, th
differences among the four transfer groups reflected in Figure
represent differences in specific transfer effects.

Methods used in scoring recall of first-list responses

Recall was scored in two different ways for each subject in t
free-recall subgroups. The first method was the most stringent
that only those first-list adjectives paired with the appropri;
stimuli were counted as correct. In the second, or liberal, scori
method, all first-list adjectives recalled by the subject were sco
as correct regardless of placement. The stringent method d
cribed above was the only meaningful method for scoring re
in the associative-matching subgroups since subjects in these s
groups were given a list of first-list adjectives to pair with first-
stimuli. The maximum possible recall score for any scor
method was 8.00.

The stringent and liberal methods of scoring recall in the fi
recall subgroups and the stringent scoring method in the a:
ciative-matching subgroups make three separate analyses
recall possible. The median test (Walker and Lev, 1953) has b
used in these analyses because inspection of the recall sc
revealed negatively skewed distributions for some of the gr
involved in each analysis as well as heterogeneous varian
Where chi-square values obtained in the median tests
approached significance, t-tests were also performed on the
in an attempt to compensate for the lack of power associ
with nonparametric tests.

Associative matching

The mean recall scores for the matching groups and the free-recall groups are presented in Table 1. As noted earlier, the recall scores of the matching groups should supply information concerning the weakening of first-list associative connexions independent of any extinction effects in the response-recall phase. This is because the technique assures perfect response recall in all groups and should eliminate the negative effects of having to learn and retain two different sets of responses in the A–C and C–D paradigms.

Table 1

Mean Number of Responses Recalled from List 1 for Each Transfer Paradigm as Scored by Two Methods

Method	Paradigm				
	A–C	A–Br	C–B	C–D	Control
	Associative-matching subgroups				
Contingent	6·54	5·58	6·87	7·83	—
	Free-recall subgroups				
Contingent	4·79	4·75	6·42	6·54	7·71
General	5·00	6·96	7·71	6·62	7·71

The over-all median test performed on the four associative-matching groups produced a significant chi-square ($p < 0.01$). Before turning to individual comparisons, it should be noted that the C–D group may serve as the control for determining whether or not extinction of S–R and/or R–S associative connexions has occurred in the three other transfer paradigms. Theoretically, there is no opportunity for the disruption of first-list forward and backward associations in the C–D paradigm; hence, mean recall of the C–D subgroup in the present analysis should be perfect, 8·00. Inspection of the recall scores in the C–D condition indicates that twenty-two subjects had recall scores of 8, and two subjects had recall scores of 6, producing a mean recall of 7·83. Thus, theory would appear to be supported, and the C–D condition may be used as a control for the other three transfer groups.

Interference

With response recall assured, there should be only one negative factor operating in the A–C condition, the weakening of S–R associations, an effect which may be assessed by a comparison of the performance of the A–C group with that of the C–D group. The significant difference in this comparison ($p < 0.01$) indicates the presence of this factor and verifies the interpretation presented in the introduction. In a like fashion, the significant chi square value ($p < 0.01$) obtained for the C–B condition indicates the extinction of R–S associations in the C–B paradigm. Both of the negative factors involving first-list associative connections were assumed to operate in the A–Br condition. The fact that recall is lower in the A–Br group than in the A–C group suggests the additional presence of R–S extinction, assuming that the A–C group provides a reasonable estimate of S–R extinction in the A–Br group independent of R–S extinction. Similarly, the difference between the A–Br and C–B groups supports the contention that there is also S–R extinction in the A–Br paradigm. Thus, these comparisons provide convincing evidence for the operation of two extinction processes in the A–Br condition. In fact, the decrement in recall attributed to the extinction of S–R associative connections, as estimated in the A–C condition, and the decrement in recall attributed to the extinction of R–S associations, as estimated by the C–B condition, are sufficient to account for the decrement observed in the A–Br condition, when they are combined in an additive fashion.

Free recall: stringent scoring

The results provided by the stringent scoring method in the free recall subgroups are summarized in the second row of Table 1. A comparison of the two sets of stringent scores (rows 1 and 2) shows that supplying the subjects with first-list responses (row 2) increased mean recall in all transfer groups. Statistical tests indicate that this increase was significant, however, only in the case of the C–D and A–C paradigms. This finding would suggest, then, that learning two different sets of responses in the A–C and C–D conditions has a detrimental effect on recall and that this effect is eliminated in the associative-matching conditions when the subjects are supplied with the set of responses learned in the first list.

J. B. McGovern

This interpretation must be viewed with caution because these
ncreases in recall may be due in part, at least, to increased oppor-
unities for guessing when first-list responses are supplied. No
iethod of assessing the role played by guessing in these two
roups has been provided for in this experiment. On the other
and, while the significant increase in recall in the A–C and C–D
onditions is not conclusive in the present analysis, this increase
consistent with other analyses which point more conclusively
ward extinction in the response-recall phase of paired-associate
arning. The increases in recall in the A–Br and C–B conditions
e slight and may be attributed statistically to random error.

ee recall: liberal scoring

ie liberal method of scoring in the free-recall subgroups pro-
des further information concerning extinction in the response-
all phase in the A–C and C–D paradigms. In this method of
oring, a response is counted as correct if it is merely recalled.
ie over-all median test produced a significant chi-square (p
0·01). Inspection of mean recall in Table 1 (row 3) indicates a
s in recall for all transfer conditions except the C–B condition
en comparisons are made with the control group. The indivi-
al median tests indicate that this decrement in response recall
significant only for the A–C and C–D paradigms. Thus, a
eral loss in response recall is significant only for those two
adigms for which it was hypothesized as playing an important
e. In addition, response recall in the A–C and C–D paradigms
s significantly lower than in the A–Br and C–B conditions for
ch no response-recall extinction was hypothesized. These
ings support the results obtained by comparing free recall as
ed by the stringent method with associative matching in the
eding section.

t first glance, it might appear that the extinction produced by
learning of a new set of responses in the second list occurs to a
ter extent in the A–C than in the C–D paradigm ($p < 0·01$).
does not mean, however, that greater extinction effects in
response-recall phase are produced in the A–C condition.
ough the associative connexions between environmental
uli and first-list responses are weakened in the C–D condi-
first-list S–R associative connexions presumably have been

419

unaffected. Thus, recall of a given first-list response may b
mediated by its first-list S–R associative connexion even thoug
its associative connexions with environmental stimuli have bee
weakened. In the A–C condition, on the other hand, evidenc
summarized in previous analyses indicates that S–R associativ
connexions have been weakened as well. Thus, in the A–C para
digm, a given response may have lost both its associative co
nection with environmental stimuli and with its first-list stimulu
and, without either of these two connexions, cannot be recalle
Hence, the significant difference in recall in the A–C and C–
conditions when scored by the liberal method is more likely d
to the weakening of S–R associations in the A–C condition tha
to greater extinction effects in the response-recall phase of t
A–C condition.

Inspection of Table 1 shows that for the A–C and C–D fre
recall groups there is little difference in mean recall produced
the two scoring methods. Similar results were obtained for
A–C condition in the Barnes–Underwood (1959) study. This
sult was interpreted in that study as indicating that if a subj
recalled a response, he could also identify it correctly as
stimulus. It should be noted that subjects in their experime
were urged to pair any recalled responses with appropriate stin
and never told to guess if they were not certain of the stimuli w
which the recalled responses were associated. This might lead
the speculation that perhaps the subject could have corre
paired *all* first-list responses with first-list stimuli in recall if fi
list responses were supplied. Results obtained with the A
condition in associative matching and summarized in a preced
section indicated that this was not the case.

Comparisons of recall in the A–Br and C–B conditions with
control group indicated that no significant loss in response re
occurred in the A–Br and C–B conditions. This was as it sh
be since, theoretically, there is no opportunity for extinctio
response recall in these two paradigms. Similarly, a compar
of liberally scored free recall for the A–Br and C–B condit
should reveal no significant difference between these two gr
in response recall. However, a statistical comparison indicat
significant difference in response recall ($t = 2 \cdot 40$, $df =$
$p < 0 \cdot 05$). There is no ready explanation for this differenc

nay be that the extinction of both S–R and R–S associative onnexions in the A–Br condition confused the subjects to such n extent that they hesitated to guess even though instructed to do o.

Discussion

heoretically, three factors were identified in the introduction as •volved in the production of RI in the immediate written free •call of four transfer paradigms. The results of the present study ave been interpreted only in terms of their implications for the istence of the three negative factors hypothesized as responsible r RI in immediate recall. This does not mean that the author •shes to imply that these are the only factors which are involved RI or that they necessarily constitute the most parsimonious •planation of the results. The results, however, may be interpre d as favorable evidence for the operation of such extinction e factors. The evidence indicates that when an A–B, A–C ationship exists between sets of associative connexions, an •inction of the first set of associative connexions learned occurs a consequence of having learned the second set.

)ne or more of these three processes was identified as a possible •rce of RI in written free recall for each of the four transfer •adigms studied in the present experiment. Consequently, RI • predicted for free recall as scored by the stringent method in •h of the four transfer paradigms. This prediction was verified. •ddition, recall was significantly lower in those groups which •oretically had two negative factors operating during second •learning (the A–C and A–Br paradigms) than in those groups which only one negative factor was indicated (the C–B and) paradigms). Specific evidence for each of the three sources •I in immediate recall is summarized separately for each •sfer paradigm.

A–B, C–D paradigm

•ost perfect recall (mean recall of 7·83 versus perfect recall of • was obtained in the C–D condition when the subjects were •lied with the set of responses learned in the first list. In other •s, when the subject had first-list responses at his disposal in

recall, he could pair them properly with first-list stimuli. This
indicates that the extinction of first-list S–R and R–S association
does not play an important role in recall in the C–D paradigm
On the other hand, the significant decrement in recall found fo
the C–D condition in free recall scored in either of two way
indicates that the learning of two different sets of responses pro
duces extinction in the response–recall phase of paired-associa
learning.

The A–B, A–C paradigm

Two negative factors in recall were identified for the A–C par
digm: (a) extinction of first-list S–R associations and (b) extin
tion of contextual associations. The second factor has be
verified independently in the A–B, C–D paradigm as discussed
the preceding section.

Evidence for the extinction of first-list S–R associations w
found in recall as stringently scored in the free-recall and matc
ing subgroups of the A–C condition. An independent verificati
of first-list S–R extinction was obtained in the matching su
group of the A–C condition. Recall in this A–C subgroup v
significantly lower than in the appropriate control conditi
indicating that extinction of associative connexions betwe
first-list stimuli and responses is involved in the A–C paradi
Since the R–S or backward associative connexions involved
this paradigm presumably have zero transfer value, it may
inferred that the factor responsible for the loss of recall in
matching subgroup is the extinction of first-list S–R or forw
associative connexions.

The A–B, C–B paradigm

A significant decrement in recall was obtained in the C–B
dition as compared with the appropriate control in both
recall and associative matching as scored by the strin
method, indicating a weakening of first-list associative con
ions. Liberal scoring of the free-recall subgroup of the
condition indicates that extinction in the response–recall pl
per se, is not a factor in the C–B paradigm as might be expe
from the nature of the paradigm. Since S–R or forward ass
tions are assumed to have zero transfer value due to the mat

used in the present experiment, the presence of R I in the C–B paradigm may be attributed to the extinction or weakening of first-list R–S associations.

At this point, a question may be raised as to how backward associations might be important in recall. Two possibilities suggest themselves: First, backward associations may serve as a means of 'checking' responses recalled via first-list S–R associations. For example, in the C–B condition, a given first-list stimulus may elicit, via first-list S–R association, the response that was paired with it in first-list learning. The R–S or backward association formed during first-list learning may act as a check for any possible confusion of first-list stimuli and their appropriate first-list responses. Extinction of first-list R–S associations in the C–B condition removes this possible source of checking in recall. Second, first-list backward associations may mediate recall when first-list S–R associations have been weakened or extinguished. For example, in the A–C condition, a first-list stimulus and response might be correctly paired because the subject has available the R–S association which was formed between that response and that stimulus in first-list learning even though the backward or S–R association has been weakened or extinguished in second-list learning. Thus, backward associations may serve either or both of two functions in recall: (a) they may serve as a check on possible confusion in recall mediated by first-list S–R associations; (b) they may mediate the pairing of first-list stimuli and responses when first-list S–R associations have been extinguished or weakened.

A–B, A–Br paradigm

Two factors were postulated as producing recall decrement in the A–Br paradigm: (a) extinction of first-list S–R associative connexions and (b) extinction of first-list R–S associative connexions. This first factor has been verified independently in the matching group of the A–C condition, and the existence of the second factor has been supported by the associative-matching results in the C–B condition. These independent verifications of the two processes have been discussed above.

In addition, a comparison of matching subgroups indicated that recall in the A–Br condition was lower than recall in the A–C

condition and significantly lower than recall in the C–B condition
Moreover, the magnitude of the decrement found in associativ
matching for the A–Br condition is approximately equivalent t
the sum of the magnitudes of the decrements found in the A–C
and C–B conditions. It would appear, then, that as far as first
list associative factors are concerned, RI in immediate recall i
the A–Br paradigm can be accounted for in terms of the extinc
tion of first-list S–R and R–S associative connexions.

Conclusion

The results of the present study would seem to indicate th
paired-associate recall may be logically and empirically divide
into two phases or stages comparable to the two stages identifie
in paired-associate learning (Underwood *et al.*, 1959), namely,
response–recall phase and an association phase. Evidence has al
been obtained which indicates that a loss in recall may occur
one phase independently of loss in the other phase. Thus, a sig
ficant loss occurred in the response–recall phase of the C–D pa
digm, yet no loss in recall was found in the associative pha
when loss in the response-recall phase was eliminated. Similar
a significant decrement in the associative phase of recall w
determined for the C–B and A–Br paradigms, whereas the
sponse–recall phase remained unaffected. In addition, it wo
appear that loss in recall in the associative phase may be p
duced by either of two extinctionlike processes or a combinat
of these two processes; a weakening or extinction of first-list S
associative connexions and extinction of first-list R–S associat
connexions. In order to account for losses in response-recall,
extinction or weakening of associative connexions which w
formed between environmental stimuli and first-list respo
during first-list learning was hypothesized. Assuming th
explanations of recall decrement are valid ones, the results
seem to indicate that the presence of an A–B, A–C relation
between two sets of associative connexions is an 'extinctive' o
regardless of the type of association. That is, an A–B, A–C r
tionship appears to produce a loss in recall when the associat
involved are S–R or forward associations, R–S or backward a
ciations, and when the associations involved are between a sa

of environmental cues and list responses. Thus, the results of the present experiment support those obtained in the Barnes–Underwood study for the A–B, A–C paradigm and confirm the conclusions concerning extinction of first-list responses. The present study also indicates that this extinction can be separated into two phases for the A–B, A–C paradigm and extends the findings to three other transfer paradigms.

Summary

Three factors were identified as involved in the production of retroactive inhibition (RI) in immediate, written free recall for our transfer paradigms: (a) extinction of first-list S–R or forward associative connexions; (b) extinction of first-list R–S or backward associations; and (c) extinction in response recall, i.e. extinction of associative connexions formed between environmental or contextual stimuli and first-list responses. The first and third factors were hypothesized as operating in the A–B, A–C paradigm. The first and second factors were hypothesized as operating in the A–B, A–Br paradigm. The A–B, C–B and A–B, C–D paradigms were included for independent verification of factors b and c, respectively. Results verified the contribution of these factors to the RI produced in the four paradigms and supported an interpretation of paired-associate recall in terms of a response–recall phase and an association phase.

References

BARNES, J. M. (1960), '"Fate" revisited', Unpublished doctoral dissertation, Northwestern University.

BARNES, J. M., and UNDERWOOD, B. J. (1959), '"Fate" of first-list associations in transfer theory', Journal of Experimental Psychology, vol. 58, pp. 97–105.

BILODEAU, I. McD., and SCHLOSBERG, H. (1951), 'Similarity in stimulating conditions as a variable in retroactive inhibition', Journal of Experimental Psychology, vol. 41, pp. 199–204.

GREENSPOON, J., and RANYARD, R. (1957), 'Stimulus conditions and retroactive inhibition', Journal of Experimental Psychology, vol. 53, pp. 55–9.

HAAGEN, C. H. (1949), 'Synonymity, vividness, familiarity, and associative value ratings of 400 pairs of common adjectives', Journal of Experimental Psychology, vol. 27, pp. 453–63.

Interference

STEVENS, S. S. (ed.) (1951), *Handbook of Experimental Psychology*, Wiley.

TWEDT, H. M., and UNDERWOOD, B. J. (1959), 'Mixed vs. unmixed lists in transfer studies', *Journal of Experimental Psychology*, vol. 58, pp. 111–16.

UNDERWOOD, B. J., RUNQUIST, W. N., and SCHULZ, R. W. (1959), 'Response learning in paired-associate lists as a function of intralist similarity', *Journal of Experimental Psychology*, vol. 58, pp. 70–78.

WALKER, H. M., and LEV, J. (1953), *Statistical Inference*, Holt.

30 B. J. Underwood

Interference and Forgetting

B. J. Underwood, 'Interference and forgetting', *Psychological Review*, vol. 64 (1957), pp. 49-60.

know of no one who seriously maintains that interference among tasks is of no consequence in the production of forgetting. Whether forgetting is conceptualized at a strict psychological level or at a neural level (e.g. neural memory trace), some provision is made for interference to account for at least some of the measured forgetting. The many studies on retroactive inhibition are probably responsible for this general agreement that interference among tasks must produce a sizeable proportion of forgetting. By introducing an interpolated interfering task very marked decrements in recall can be produced in a few minutes in the laboratory. But there is a second generalization which has resulted from these studies, namely, that most forgetting must be a function of the learning of tasks which interfere with that which has already been learned (19). Thus, if a single task is learned in the laboratory and retention measured after a week, the loss has been attributed to the interference from activities learned outside the laboratory during the week. It is this generalization with which I am concerned in the initial portions of this paper.

Now, I cannot deny the data which show large amounts of forgetting produced by an interpolated list in a few minutes in the laboratory. Nor do I deny that this loss may be attributed to interference. But I will try to show that use of retroactive inhibition as a paradigm of forgetting (via interference) may be seriously questioned. To be more specific: if a subject learns a single task, such as a list of words, and retention of this task is measured after a day, a week, or a month, I will try to show that very little of the forgetting can be attributed to an interfering task learned outside the laboratory during the retention interval.

427

Before pursuing this further, I must make some general comments by way of preparation.

Whether we like it or not, the experimental study of forgetting has been largely dominated by the Ebbinghaus tradition, both in terms of methods and materials used. I do not think this is due to sheer perversity on the part of several generations of scientists interested in forgetting. It may be noted that much of our elementary knowledge can be obtained only by rote learning. To work with rote learning does not mean that we are thereby no concerning ourselves with phenomena that have no counterpart outside the laboratory. Furthermore, the investigation of these phenomena can be handled by methods which are acceptable to science. As is well known, there are periodic verbal revolts against the Ebbinghaus tradition (e.g. 2, 15, 22). But for some reason nothing much ever happens in the laboratory as a consequence of these revolts. I mention these matters neither by way of apology nor of justification for having done some research in rote learning but for two other reasons. First, it may very well be true, as some have suggested (e.g. 22), that studies of memory in the Ebbinghaus tradition are not getting at all of the important phenomena of memory. I think the same statement – that research has not got at all of the important processes – could be made about areas in psychology; so that the criticism (even if just) should not be indigenous to the study of memory. Science does not deal will with all natural events. Science deals with natural events only when ingenuity in developing methods and techniques measurement allow these events to be brought within the scope of science. If, therefore, the studies of memory which meet scientific acceptability do not tap all-important memorial processes, all I can say is that this is the state of the science in this area at the moment. Secondly, because the bulk of the systematic data on forgetting has been obtained on rote-learned tasks, I must of necessity use such data in discussing interference and forgetting.

Returning to the experimental situation, let me again put in concrete form the problem with which I first wish to deal. A subject learns a single task, such as a list of syllables, nouns, adjectives. After an interval of time, say, 24 hours, his retention of this list is measured. The explanatory problem is what responsible for the forgetting which commonly occurs over the 24 hours. As indicated earlier, the studies of retroactive inhibition led to the theoretical generalization that this forgetting was due largely to interference from other tasks learned during the 24-hour retention interval. McGeoch (20) came to this conclusion, his last such statement being made in 1942. I would, therefore, like to look at the data which were available to McGeoch and others interested in this matter. I must repeat that the kind of data with which I am concerned is the retention of a list without formal interpolated learning introduced. The interval of retention with which I am going to deal in this, and several subsequent analyses, is 24 hours.

First, of course, Ebbinghaus' data were available and in a sense served as the reference point for many subsequent investigations. In terms of percentage saved in relearning, Ebbinghaus showed about 65 per cent loss over 24 hours (7). In terms of recall after 24 hours, the following studies are representative of the amount forgotten: Youtz, 88 per cent loss (37); Luh, 82 per cent (18); Krueger, 74 per cent (16); Hovland, 78 per cent (11); Cheng, 65 per cent and 84 per cent (6); Lester, 65 per cent (17). Let us assume as a rough average of these studies that 75 per cent forgetting was measured over 24 hours. In all of these studies the list was learned to one perfect trial. The percentage values were derived by dividing the total number of items in the list into the number lost and changing to a percentage. Thus, on the average of these studies, if the subject learned a 12-item list and recalled three of these items after 24 hours, nine items (75 per cent) were forgotten.

The theory of interference as advanced by McGeoch, and so far as I know never seriously challenged, was that during the 24-hour interval subjects learned something outside the laboratory which interfered with the list learned in the laboratory. Most of the materials involved in the investigations cited above are nonsense syllables, and the subjects were college students. While realizing that I am viewing these results in the light of data which McGeoch and others did not have available, it seems to me to be an incredible stretch of an interference hypothesis to hold that this 75 per cent forgetting was caused by something which subjects learned outside the laboratory during the 24-hour interval. Even if we agree with some educators that much of what we teach our students in college is nonsense, it does not seem to be the kind of learning that would interfere with nonsense syllables.

If, however, this forgetting was not due to interference from tasks learned outside the laboratory during the retention interval, to what was it due? I shall try to show that most of this forgetting was indeed produced by interference – not from tasks learned outside the laboratory, but from tasks learned previously in the laboratory. Following this I will show that when interference from laboratory tasks is removed, the amount of forgetting which occurs is relatively quite small. It then becomes more plausible that this amount could be produced by interference from tasks learned outside the laboratory, although, as I shall also point out the interference very likely comes from prior, not interpolated learning.

In 1950 a study was published by Mrs Greenberg and myself (10) on retention as a function of stage of practice. The orientation for this study was crassly empirical; we simply wanted to know if subjects learn how to recall in the same sense that they learn how to learn. In the conditions with which I am concerned naïve subjects learned a list of ten paired adjectives to a criterion of eight out of ten correct on a single trial. Forty-eight hours later this list was recalled. On the following day, these same subjects learned a new list to the same criterion and recalled it after 48 hours. This continued for two additional lists, so that the subjects had learned and recalled four lists, but the learning and recall of each list was complete before another list was learned. There was low similarity among these lists as far as conventional symptoms of similarity are concerned. No words were repeated and no obvious similarities existed, except for the fact that they were all adjectives and a certain amount of similarity among prefixes, suffixes, and so on must inevitably occur. The recall of the four successive lists is shown in Figure 1.

As can be seen, the more lists that are learned, the poorer recall, from 69 per cent recall of the first list to 25 per cent recall of the fourth list. In examining errors at recall, we found sufficient number of intrusion responses from previous lists to let us to suggest that the increasing decrements in recall were function of proactive interference from previous lists. And, while we pointed out that these results had implications for the design of experiments on retention, the relevance to an interference theory of forgetting was not mentioned.

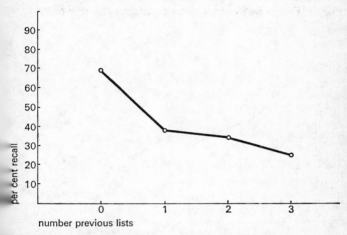

Figure 1 Recall of paired adjectives as a function of number of previous lists learned (10)

Dr E. J. Archer has made available to me certain data from an experiment which still is in progress and which deals with this issue. Subjects learned lists of twelve serial adjectives to one perfect trial and recalled them after 24 hours. The recall of a list always took place prior to learning the next list. The results for the successive lists are shown in Figure 2. Let me say again that there is no laboratory activity during the 24-hour interval; the subject learns a list, is dismissed from the laboratory, and returns after 24 hours to recall the list. The percentage of recall falls from per cent for the first list to 27 per cent for the ninth.

In summarizing the more classical data on retention above, I indicated that a rough estimate showed that after 24 hours 75 per cent forgetting took place, or recall was about 25 per cent correct. viewing these values in the light of Greenberg's and Archer's findings, the conclusion seemed inescapable that the classical

studies must have been dealing with subjects who had learned
many lists. That is to say, the subjects must have served in many
conditions by use of counterbalancing and repeated cycles. To
check on this I have made a search of the literature on the studies
of retention to see if systematic data could be compiled on this
matter. Preliminary work led me to establish certain criteria for

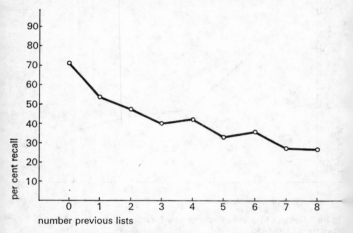

Figure 2 Recall of serial adjective lists as a function of number of
previous lists learned. Unpublished data, courtesy of Dr E. J. Archer

inclusion in the summary to be presented. First, because degree o
learning is such an important variable, I have included only thos
studies in which degree of learning was one perfect recitation o
the list. Second, I have included only studies in which retentio
was measured after 24 hours. Third, I have included only studie
in which recall measures were given. (Relearning measures ad
complexities with which I do not wish to deal in this paper
Fourth, the summary includes only material learned by relative
massed practice. Finally, if an investigator had two or mo
conditions which met these criteria, I averaged the values for pr
sentation in this paper. Except for these restrictions, I have us
all studies I found (with an exception to be noted later), althou
I do not pretend to have made an exhaustive search. From each
these studies I got two facts: first, the percentage recalled af

24 hours, and second, the average number of previous lists the subjects had learned before learning the list on which recall after 24 hours was taken. Thus, if a subject had served in five experimental conditions via counterbalancing, and had been given two practice lists, the average number of lists learned before learning the list for which I tabulated the recall was four. This does not take into account any previous experiments in rote learning in which the subject might have served.

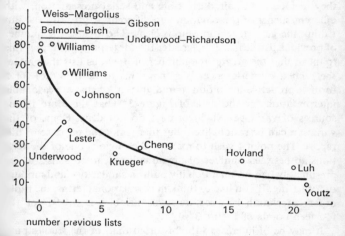

Figure 3 Recall as a function of number of previous lists learned as determined from a number of studies. From left to right: Weiss and Margolius (35), Gibson (9), Belmont and Birch (3), Underwood and Richardson (33), Williams (36), Underwood (27, 28, 29, 30), Lester (17), Johnson (14), Krueger (16), Cheng (6), Hovland (11), Luh (18), Youtz (37)

For each of these studies the two facts, average number of previous lists learned and percentage of recall, are related as in Figure 3. For example, consider the study by Youtz. This study is concerned with Jost's law, and had several degrees of learning, several lengths of retention interval, and the subjects served two cycles. Actually, there were fifteen experimental conditions and each subject was given each condition twice. Also, each subject learned six practice lists before starting the experimental conditions. Among the fifteen conditions was one in which the learning of the syllables was carried to one perfect recitation and recall was taken after 24 hours. It is this particular condition in which I am interested. On the average, this condition would have been given at the time when the subject had learned six practice lists and fifteen experimental lists, for a total of twenty-one previous lists.

The studies included in Figure 3 have several different kinds of materials, from geometric forms to nonsense syllables to nouns; they include both paired-associate and serial presentation, with different speeds of presentation and different lengths of lists. But I think the general relationship is clear. The greater the number of previous lists learned the greater the forgetting. I interpret this to mean that the greater the number of previous lists the greater the *proactive* interference. We know this to be true (26) for a formal proactive-inhibition paradigm; it seems a reasonable interpretation for the data of Figure 3. That there are minor sources of variance still involved I do not deny. Some of the variation can be rationalized, but that is not the purpose of this report. The point I wish to make is the obvious one of the relationship between number of previous lists learned – lists which presumably had no intentionally built-in similarity – and amount of forgetting. If you like to think in correlational terms, the rank order correlation between the two variables is −0·91 for the fourteen points of Figure 3.

It may be of interest to the historian that, of the studies published before 1942 which met the criteria I imposed, I did not find a single one in which subjects had not been given at least one practice task before starting experimental conditions, and in most cases the subjects had several practice lists and several experimental conditions. Gibson's study (9) was the first I found in which subjects served in only one condition and were not given practice tasks. I think it is apparent that the design proclivities of the 1920s and 1930s have been largely responsible for the exaggerated picture we have had of the rate of forgetting of rote learned materials. On the basis of studies performed during the 1920s and 1930s, I have given a rough estimate of forgetting being 75 per cent over 24 hours, recall being 25 per cent. On the basis of modern studies in which the subject has learned no previous lists – where there is no proactive inhibition from previous laboratory tasks – a rough estimate would be that forgetting is 25 per cent; recall is 75 per cent. The values are reversed. (If in the above and subsequent discussion my use of percentage values as if I were dealing with a cardinal or extensive scale is disturbing, I will say only that it makes the picture easier to grasp, and in my opinion no critical distortion results.)

Before taking the next major step, I would like to point out a few other observations which serve to support my general point that proactive inhibition from laboratory tasks has been the major cause of forgetting in the more classical studies. The first illustration I shall give exemplifies the point that when subjects have served in several conditions, forgetting after relatively short periods of time is greater than after 24 hours if the subject has served in only one condition. In the Youtz study to which I have already referred, other conditions were employed in which recall was taken after short intervals. After 20 minutes recall was 4 per cent, about what it is after 24 hours if the subject has not served in a series of conditions. After two hours recall was 2 per cent. In Ward's (34) well-known reminiscence experiment, subjects who on the average had learned ten previous lists showed recall of only 64 per cent after 20 minutes.

In the famous Jenkins–Dallenbach (13) study on retention following sleep and following waking, two subjects were used. One subject learned a total of sixty-one lists and the other sixty-two in addition to several practice lists. Roughly, then, if the order of the conditions was randomized, approximately thirty lists had been learned prior to the learning of a list for a given experimental condition. Recall after eight waking hours for one subject was 4 per cent and for the other 14 per cent. Even after sleeping for eight hours the recall was only 55 per cent and 58 per cent.

I have said that an interpolated list can produce severe forgetting. However, in one study (1), using the A–B, A–C paradigm for original and interpolated learning, but using subjects who had never served in any previous conditions, recall of the original list was 46 per cent after 48 hours, and in another comparable study (), 42 per cent. Thus, the loss is not nearly as great as in the classical studies I have cited where there was no interpolated learning in the laboratory.

My conclusion at this point is that, in terms of the gross analysis I have made, the amount of forgetting which might be attributed to interference from tasks learned outside the laboratory has been 'reduced' from 75 per cent to about 25 per cent. I shall proceed in the next section to see if we have grounds for reducing this estimate still more. In passing on to this section, however, let me say that the study of factors which influence proactive inhibition in these counterbalanced studies is a perfectly legitimate and important area of study. I mention this because in the subsequent discussion I am going to deal only with the case where a subject has learned a single list in the laboratory, and I do not want to leave the impression that we should now and forevermore drop the study of interference produced by previous laboratory tasks. Indeed, as will be seen shortly, it is my opinion that we should increase these studies for the simple reason that the proactive paradigm provides a more realistic one than does the retroactive paradigm.

When the subject learns and recalls a single list in the laboratory, I have given an estimate of 25 per cent as being the amount forgotten over 24 hours. When, as shown above, we calculate percentage forgotten of lists learned to one perfect trial, the assumption is that had the subjects been given an immediate recall trial, the list would have been perfectly recalled. This, of course, is simply not true. The major factor determining how much error is introduced by this criterion-percentage method is probably the difficulty of the task. In general, the overestimation of forgetting by the percentage method will be directly related to the difficulty of the task. Thus, the more slowly the learning approaches a given criterion, the greater the drop on the trial immediately after the criterion trial. Data from a study by Runquist (24), using eight paired adjectives (a comparatively easy task), shows that amount of forgetting is overestimated by about 10 per cent. In a study (32) using very difficult consonant syllables, the overestimation was approximately 20 per cent. To be conservative, assume that on the average the percentage method of reporting recall overestimates the amount forgotten by 10 per cent. If we subtract this from the 25 per cent assumed above, forgetting is now re-estimated as being 15 per cent over 24 hours. That is to say, an interference theory, or any other form of theory has to account for a very small amount of forgetting as compared with the amount traditionally cited.

What are the implications of so greatly 'reducing' the amount of forgetting? There are at least three implications which I feel are worth pointing out. First, if one wishes to hold to an interference theory of forgetting (as I do), it seems plausible to assert that this amount of forgetting could be produced from learning which has taken place outside of the laboratory. Furthermore, it seems likely that such interference must result primarily from proactive interference. This seems likely on a simple probability basis. A 20-year-old college student will more likely have learned something during his 20 years prior to coming to the laboratory that will interfere with his retention than he will during the 24 hours between the learning and retention test. However, the longer the retention interval the more important will retroactive interference become relative to proactive interferences.

The second implication is that these data may suggest greater homogeneity or continuity in memorial processes than hitherto supposed. Although no one has adequately solved the measurement problem of how to make comparisons of retention among conditioned responses, prose material, motor tasks, concept learning, and rote-learned tasks, the gross comparisons have indicated that rote-learned tasks were forgotten much more rapidly than these other tasks. But the rote-learning data used for comparison have been those derived with the classical design in which the forgetting over 24 hours is approximately 75 per cent. If we take the revised estimate of 15 per cent, the discrepancies among tasks become considerably less.

The third implication of the revised estimate of rate of forgetting is that the number of variables which appreciably influence rate of forgetting must be sharply limited. While this statement does not inevitably follow from the analyses I have made, the current evidence strongly supports the statement. I want to turn to the final section of this paper which will consist of a review of the influence of some of the variables which are or have been thought to be related to rate of forgetting. In considering these variables, it is well to keep in mind that a variable which produces only a small difference in forgetting is important if one is interested in accounting for the 15 per cent assumed now as the

437

loss over 24 hours. If appropriate for a given variable, I will indicate where it fits into an interference theory, although in no case will I endeavor to handle the details of such a theory.

Time

Passage of time between learning and recall is the critical defining variable for forgetting. Manipulation of this variable provides the basic data for which a theory must account. Previously, our conception of rate of forgetting as a function of time has been tied to the Ebbinghaus curve. If the analysis made earlier is correct, this curve does not give us the basic data we need. In short, we must start all over and derive a retention curve over time when the subjects have learned no previous materials in the laboratory. It is apparent that I expect the fall in this curve over time to be relatively small.

In conjunction with time as an independent variable, we must, in explanations of forgetting, consider why sleep retards the processes responsible for forgetting. My conception, which does not really explain anything, is that since forgetting is largely produced by proactive interference, the amount of time which a subject spends in sleep is simply to be subtracted from the total retention interval when predicting the amount to be forgotten. It is known that proactive interference increases with passage of time (5) sleep, I believe, brings to a standstill whatever these processes are which produce this increase.

Degree of Learning

We usually say that the better or stronger the learning the more, better the retention. Yet, we do not know whether or not the rate of forgetting differs for items of different strength. The experimental problem is a difficult one. What we need is to have a subject learn a single association and measure its decline in strength over time. But this is difficult to carry out with verbal material, since almost of necessity we must have the subject learn a series of associations, to make it a reasonable task. And, when a series of associations are learned, complications arise from interaction effects among associations of different strength.

Nevertheless, we may expect, on the basis of evidence from a wide variety of studies, that given a constant degree of similarity, the effective interference varies as some function of the strength of associations.

Distribution of Practice

It is a fact that distribution of practice during acquisition influences retention of verbal materials. The facts of the case seem to be as follows. If the subject has not learned previous lists in the laboratory, massed practice gives equal or better retention than does distributed practice. If, on the other hand, the subject has learned a number of previous lists, distributed practice will facilitate retention (32). We do not have the theoretical solution to these facts. The point I wish to make here is that whether or not distribution of learning inhibits or facilitates retention depends upon the amount of interference from previous learning. It is reasonable to expect, therefore, that the solution to the problem will come via principles handling interference in general. I might also say that a theoretical solution to this problem will also provide a solution for Jost's laws.

Similarity

Amount of interference from other tasks is closely tied to similarity. This similarity must be conceived of as similarity among materials as such and also situational similarity (4). When we turn to similarity within a task, the situation is not quite so clear. Empirically and theoretically (8) one would expect that intratask similarity would be a very relevant variable in forgetting. As discussed elsewhere (31), however, variation in intratask similarity most inevitably leads to variations in intertask similarity. We do know from a recent study (33) that with material of low meaningfulness forgetting is significantly greater with high intratask similarity than with low. While the difference in magnitude is only about 8 per cent, when we are trying to account for a total loss of 15 per cent, this amount becomes a major matter.

Meaningfulness

The belief has long been held that the more meaningful the material the better the retention – the less the forgetting. Osgood (21) has pointed out that if this is true it is difficult for an interference theory to handle. So far as I know, the only direct test of the influence of this variable is a recent study in which retention of syllables of 100 per cent association value was compared with that of zero association value (33). There was no difference in the recall of these syllables. Other less precise evidence would support this finding when comparisons are made among syllables, adjectives, and nouns, as plotted in Figure 3. However, there is some evidence that materials of very low meaningfulness are forgotten more rapidly than nonsense syllables of zero association value. Consonant syllables, both serial (32) and paired associates (unpublished), show about 50 per cent loss over 24 hours. The study using serial lists was the one mentioned earlier as knowingly omitted from Figure 3. These syllables, being extremely difficult to learn, allow a correction of about 20 per cent due to criterion overestimation, but even with this much correction the forgetting (30 per cent) is still appreciably more than the estimate we have made for other materials. To invoke the interference theory to account for this discrepancy means that we must demonstrate how interference from other activities could be greater for these consonant syllables than for nonsense syllables, nouns, adjectives, and other materials. Our best guess at the present time is that the sequences of letters in consonant syllables are contrary to other well-established language habits. That is to say, letter sequences which commonly occur in our language are largely different from those in consonant syllables. As a consequence, not only are these consonant syllables very difficult to learn, but forgetting is accelerated by proactive interference from previously well-learned letter sequences. If subsequent research cannot demonstrate such a source of interference, or if some other source is not specified, an interference theory for this case will be in some trouble.

Affectivity

Another task dimension which has received extensive attention is the affective tone of the material. I would also include here the studies attaching unpleasant experiences to some items experimentally and not to others, and measuring retention of these two sets of items. Freud is to a large extent responsible for these studies, but he cannot be held responsible for the malformed methodology which characterizes so many of them. What can one say by way of summarizing these studies? The only conclusion that I can reach is a statistical one, namely, that the occasional positive result found among the scores of studies is about as frequent as one would expect by sampling error, using the 5 per cent level of confidence. Until a reliable body of facts is established for this variable and associated variables, no theoretical evaluation is possible.

Other Variables

As I indicated earlier, I will not make an exhaustive survey of the variables which may influence rate of forgetting. I have limited myself to variables which have been rather extensively investigated, which have immediate relevance to the interference theory, or for which reliable relationships are available. Nevertheless, I would like to mention briefly some of these other variables. There is the matter of *warm-up* before recall; some investigators find that this reduces forgetting (12); others, under as nearly replicated conditions as is possible to obtain, do not (23). Some resolution must be found for these flat contradictions. It seems perfectly reasonable, however, that inadequate set or context differences would reduce recall. Indeed, an interference theory would predict this forgetting if the set or context stimuli are appreciably different from those prevailing at the time of learning. In our laboratory we try to reinstate the learning set by careful instructions, and we simply do not find decrements that might be attributed to inadequate set. For example, in a recent study (33) subjects were given a 24-hour recall of a serial list after learning to one perfect trial. I think we would expect that the first item in the list would suffer the greatest decrement due to inadequate set, yet this item showed only 0·7 per cent loss. But let it be clear that when we are attempting to account for the 15 per cent loss over 24 hours, we should not overlook any possible source for this loss.

Thus far I have not said anything about forgetting as a function of characteristics of the subject, that is, the personality or intellectual characteristics. As far as I have been able to determine, there is not a single valid study which shows that such variables have an appreciable influence on forgetting. Many studies have shown differences in learning as a function of these variables, but not differences in rate of forgetting. Surely there must be some such variables. We do know that if subjects are severely insulted, made to feel stupid, or generally led to believe that they have no justification for continued existence on the earth just before they are asked to recall, they will show losses (e.g. 25, 38), but even the influence of this kind of psychological beating is short lived. Somehow I have never felt that such findings need explanation by a theory used to explain the other facts of forgetting.

Concerning the causes of forgetting, let me sum up in a somewhat more dogmatic fashion than is probably justified. One of the assumptions of science is finite causality. Everything cannot influence everything else. To me, the most important implication of the work on forgetting during the last ten years is that this work has markedly *reduced* the number of variables related to forgetting. Correspondingly, I think the theoretical problem has become simpler. It is my belief that we can narrow down the cause of forgetting to interference from previously learned habits, from habits being currently learned, and from habits we have yet to learn. The amount of this interference is primarily a function of similarity and associative strength, the latter being important because it interacts with similarity.

Summary

This paper deals with issues in the forgetting of rote-learned materials. An analysis of the current evidence suggests that the classical Ebbinghaus curve of forgetting is primarily a function of interference from materials learned previously in the laboratory. When this source of interference is removed, forgetting decreases from about 75 per cent over 24 hours to about 25 per cent. This latter figure can be reduced by at least 10 per cent by other methodological considerations, leaving 15 per cent as an estimate of the forgetting over 24 hours. This estimate will vary somewhat as a function of intratask similarity, distributed practice, and with very low meaningful material. But the overall evidence suggests that similarity with other material and situational similarity are by far the most critical factors in forgetting. Such evidence is consonant with a general interference theory, although the details of such a theory were not presented here.

References
1. E. J. ARCHER and B. J. UNDERWOOD, 'Retroactive inhibition of verbal associations as a multiple function of temporal point of interpolation and degree of interpolated learning', *Journal of Experimental Psychology*, vol. 42 (1951), pp. 283–90.
2. F. C. BARTLETT, *Remembering: A Study in Experimental and Social Psychology*, Cambridge University Press, 1932.
3. L. BELMONT, and H. G. BIRCH, 'Re-individualizing the repression hypothesis', *Journal of Abnormal Social Psychology*, vol. 46 (1951), pp. 226–35.
4. I. McD. BILODEAU and H. SCHLOSBERG, 'Similarity in stimulating conditions as a variable in retroactive inhibition', *Journal of Experimental Psychology*, vol. 41 (1951), pp. 199–204.
5. G. E. BRIGGS, 'Acquisition, extinction, and recovery functions in retroactive inhibition', *Journal of Experimental Psychology*, vol. 47 (1954), pp. 285–93.
6. N. Y. CHENG, 'Retroactive effect and degree of similarity', *Journal of Experimental Psychology*, vol. 12 (1929), pp. 444–58.
7. H. EBBINGHAUS, *Memory: A Contribution to Experimental Psychology*, (Trans. by H. A. Ruger and C. E. Bussenius, Bureau of Publications, Teacher's College, Columbia University 1913.)
8. E. J. GIBSON, 'A systematic application of the concepts of generalization and differentiation to verbal learning', *Psychological Review*, vol. 47 (1940), pp. 196–229.
9. E. J. GIBSON, 'Intra-list generalization as a factor in verbal learning', *Journal of Experimental Psychology*, vol. 30 (1942), pp. 185–200.
10. R. GREENBERG and B. J. UNDERWOOD, 'Retention as a function of stage of practice', *Journal of Experimental Psychology*, vol. 40 (1950), pp. 452–7.
11. C. I. HOVLAND, 'Experimental studies in rote-learning theory. VI. Comparison of retention following learning to same criterion by massed and distributed practice', *Journal of Experimental Psychology*, vol. 26 (1940), pp. 568–87.

12. A. L. IRION, 'The relation of "set" to retention', *Psychological Review*, vol. 55 (1948), pp. 336–41.

13. J. G. JENKINS and K. M. DALLENBACH, 'Oblivescence during sleep and waking', *American Journal of Psychology*, vol. 35 (1924), pp. 605–12.

14. L. M. JOHNSON, 'The relative effect of a time interval upon learning and retention', *Journal of Experimental Psychology*, vol. 24 (1939), pp. 169–79.

15. G. KATONA, *Organizing and Memorizing: Studies in the Psychology of Learning and Teaching*, Columbia University Press, 1940.

16. W. C. F. KRUEGER, 'The effect of overlearning on retention', *Journal of Experimental Psychology*, vol. 12 (1929), pp. 71–8.

17. O. P. LESTER, 'Mental set in relation to retroactive inhibition', *Journal of Experimental Psychology*, vol. 15 (1932), pp. 681–99.

18. C. W. LUH, 'The conditions of retention', *Psychological Monographs*, vol. 31 (1922), no. 3.

19. J. A. MCGEOCH, 'Forgetting and the law of disuse', *Psychological Review*, vol. 39 (1932), pp. 352–70.

20. J. A. MCGEOCH, *The Psychology of Human Learning*, Longmans, Green, 1942.

21. C. E. OSGOOD, *Method and Theory in Experimental Psychology*, Oxford University Press, 1953.

22. D. RAPAPORT, 'Emotions and memory', *Psychological Review*, vol. 50 (1943), pp. 234–43.

23. M. R. ROCKWAY and C. P. DUNCAN, 'Pre-recall warming-up in verbal retention', *Journal of Experimental Psychology*, vol. 43 (1952), pp. 305–12.

24. W. RUNQUIST, 'Retention of verbal associations as a function of interference and strength', *Unpublished Doctoral Dissertation, Northwestern University*, 1956.

25. W. A. RUSSELL, 'Retention of verbal material as a function of motivating instructing and experimentally-induced failure', *Journal of Experimental Psychology*, vol. 43 (1952), pp. 207–16.

26. B. J. UNDERWOOD, 'The effect of successive interpolations on retroactive and proactive inhibition', *Psychological Monograph*, vol. 59 (1945), no. 3.

27. B. J. UNDERWOOD, 'Studies of distributed practice: VII. Learning and retention of serial nonsense lists as a function of intralist similarity', *Journal of Experimental Psychology*, vol. 44 (1952), pp. 80–87.

28. B. J. UNDERWOOD, 'Studies of distributed practice: VIII. Learning and retention of paired nonsense syllables as a function of intralist similarity', *Journal of Experimental Psychology*, vol. 45 (1953), pp. 133–42.

29. B. J. UNDERWOOD, 'Studies of distributed practice: IX. Learning and retention of paired adjectives as a function of intralist similarity', *Journal of Experimental Psychology*, vol. 45 (1953), pp. 143–9.

30. B. J. UNDERWOOD, 'Studies of distributed practice: X. The influence of intralist similarity on learning and retention of serial adjective lists', *Journal of Experimental Psychology*, vol. 45 (1953), pp. 253–9.

31. B. J. UNDERWOOD, 'Intralist similarity in verbal learning and retention', *Psychological Review*, vol. 3 (1954), pp. 160–66.

32. B. J. UNDERWOOD and J. RICHARDSON, 'Studies of distributed practice: XIII. Interlist interference and the retention of serial nonsense lists', *Journal of Experimental Psychology*, vol. 50 (1955), pp. 39–46.

33. B. J. UNDERWOOD and J. RICHARDSON, 'The influence of meaningfulness, intralist similarity, and serial position on retention', *Journal of Experimental Psychology*, vol. 52 (1956), pp. 119–26.

34. L. B. WARD, 'Reminiscence and rote learning', *Psychological Monograph*, vol. 49 (1937), no. 4.

35. W. WEISS and G. MARGOLIUS, 'The effect of context stimuli on learning and retention', *Journal of Experimental Psychology*, vol. 48 (1954), pp. 318–22.

36. M. WILLIAMS, 'The effects of experimentally induced needs upon retention', *Journal of Experimental Psychology*, vol. 40 (1950), pp. 139–51.

37. A. C. YOUTZ, 'An experimental evaluation of Jost's laws', *Psychological Monograph*, vol. 53 (1941), no. 1.

38. A. F. ZELLER, 'An experimental analogue of repression: III. The effect of induced failure and success on memory measured by recall', *Journal of Experimental Psychology*, vol. 42 (1951), pp. 32–8.

31 L. Postman

Extra-Experimental Sources of Interference

Abridged from L. Postman, 'The present status of interference theory', in C. N. Cofer, ed., *Verbal Learning and Verbal Behavior*, McGraw-Hill, 1961, pp. 166–70. [*Editors' note:* The following is a selection taken from a longer article entitled, 'The present status of interference theory'.]

Perhaps the single most important recent development in inter-ference theory is the increasing recognition of proactive inhibition as a mechanism of interference. The major value of this develop-ment lies in the fact that it has provided us with a new purchase on the analysis of long-term forgetting outside the laboratory. The arguments pointing to the significance of proaction were marshalled by Underwood in his important paper 'Interference and forgetting' (1957). The evidence presented by Underwood shows that in the large majority of experimental studies of long-term retention the amount of forgetting was greatly over-estimated because of the use of practiced subjects whose performance was depressed by considerable amounts of PI accumulated in the course of the experiments. Recent studies using naïve subjects have, indeed, shown substantially smaller losses than had been reported under comparable conditions (e.g. Underwood and Richardson, 1956; Postman and Rau, 1957). Since the amount forgotten by naïve subjects turns out to be relatively small, it becomes plausible to attribute the observed losses to interferences outside the laboratory. Underwood points out that most of the extra-experimental interference is likely to be proactive rather than retroactive since the opportunities for acquiring competing verbal habits are clearly greater prior to the experiment than during the relatively short time intervals typically used in investigations of retention.

A major theoretical and experimental problem which faces us is the application of the concepts of interference theory which were developed in formal studies of RI and PI, to the analysis of long-term forgetting outside the laboratory. The basic assumption is that forgetting outside the laboratory is a function of the same variables and represents the same processes as are observed in formal studies of interserial interference. Thus far, there is little empirical evidence in support of this assumption. A systematic attack on this problem calls for (a) a detailed specification of the implications of interference theory for the retention of different kinds of materials, including the expected growth of error tendencies, and (b) the development of experimental designs which permit critical tests of these implications.

The following extension of interference theory to the analysis of extra-experimental forgetting is based largely on a paper by Underwood and Postman (1960) which also reports an experiment in which some of the propositions derived from the theory were put to experimental test.

Gradients of Interference in Long-Term Retention

When a single list of verbal items is learned in the laboratory, retention losses measured after an interval of time are assumed to result from interference by verbal habits practiced before or after the experimental session. Although both proactive and retroactive inhibition undoubtedly occur, forgetting must be attributed primarily to interference from stable language habits with which the subject entered the experimental situation, i.e. to proactive inhibition. The assumed process of interference may be represented most conveniently in terms of the A–B, A–C paradigm, where A is a stimulus term in the experimental list, B is a response associated with A through linguistic usage, and C is the response to A prescribed in the experiment. Acquisition of the prescribed association requires the unlearning or extinction of the pre-experimental association, A–B, and its replacement by A–C. The evidence reviewed earlier [in the chapter] makes it reasonable to assume that the extinguished habit, A–B, will gradually recover as a function of time and compete with A–C at the time of recall. If A–B is a stable language habit, its pre-experimental strength was undoubtedly much greater than that imparted to A–C during the experiment. Thus, A–B will readily recover sufficient strength to compete effectively with A–C. Of course, if A–B is practiced after the end of the experiment, the process of recovery is speeded up and the probability of effective competition is increased.[1]

Experimental tests of this hypothesis require, first of all, the specification of the linguistic habits (A–B) with which the subject enters the experimental situation and which become sources of interference at recall. Two major sources of interference which contribute to the forgetting of rote series may be distinguished, viz. letter-sequence interference and unit-sequence interference.

Letter-sequence interference will occur to the extent that the sequences of letters prescribed in the experiment do not conform to those characteristic of the language. For any given sequence of letters making up a nonsense syllable, a consonant syllable, or a word, there are certain transitional probabilities in the language. During the acquisition of such items, letter-sequence habits characteristic of normal linguistic patterns must be temporarily broken in order for the prescribed sequence to be acquired. These habits recover in time and interfere with the retention of the arbitrary units. The higher the probability of occurrence of the prescribed sequence in the language, the smaller should be the amount of letter-sequence interference at recall. Thus, it is possible to specify a gradient of letter-sequence interference which drops progressively as the items to be learned approach the sequences which occur most frequently in the language. When the items to be learned are words with high frequencies of occurrence the amount of letter-sequence interference is assumed to have decreased to zero.

Sequential associations between units constitute another source of interference. The discrete responses which the subject is required to emit, e.g. nonsense syllables, consonant syllables, words, are the units with which we are concerned here. Linguistic usage establishes a hierarchy of associations between such units just as it does in the case of letter sequences. In the typical rote learning situation the A–B, A–C paradigm again applies; in the pre-experimental associations must be unlearned or extin-

1. It may be possible to construct lists for which the relationship between the subject's language habits and the associations prescribed in the experiment conforms to the A–B, A–B' paradigm. Under these conditions, retention losses would result from a confusion between mediators and mediated responses. The A–B, A–C case is, however, much more likely to apply to the retention of arbitrary rote series.

guished and the prescribed associations substituted for them. The extinguished associations recover over time and compete with the prescribed units at the time of recall. The amount of unit sequence interference will be expected to vary directly with the frequency of occurrence of the unit qua unit in the language. The more frequently a unit is used, the more likely it is to acquire strong associates which will compete with those prescribed in the experimental series. The gradient of unit-sequence interference thus increases as a function of the frequency of occurrence of the unit in the language. If the items to be learned are ranged along a continuum extending from the most improbable letter-sequences to the most frequent words, two intersecting gradients of interference can be plotted against this continuum. The gradient of letter-sequence interference is at its maximum at the low end of the continuum where the association between successive letters is weak, and declines as common linguistic units are approached. The gradient of unit-sequence interference first comes into play when the sequences of letters begin to constitute syllables or words with some probability of occurrence in the language, and increases thereafter, reaching its maximum for high-frequency words. If the arrangement of the items is thought to reflect the dimension of meaningfulness, maxima of interference are expected to occur for items at the low and high extremes of the dimension, the former attributable predominantly to letter-sequence interference and the latter to unit-sequence interference. Interference should be minimal for items falling toward the center of the continuum. Such items would represent frequent combinations of letters without being verbal units to which strong associations are likely to accrue in the course of daily usage.

Implications for Learning and Retention

The implications of the hypothesis for learning and retention will now be discussed in some detail. Turning to acquisition first, it is useful for purposes of this discussion to adopt an analytic distinction between two successive stages of learning, viz., an integrative and an associative stage (Underwood, Runquist, and Schulz, 1959). During the first stage the items in the list become available to the subject as responses. If the required units are not already in the subject's repertoire, they must be integrated during that stage, i.e. associations must be formed between the successive letters making up the sequence. During the second stage the responses are connected with the appropriate stimuli, e.g. the preceding items in a serial list or the prescribed stimulus terms in a list of paired associates. Although the two stages undoubtedly overlap, the distinction has proved useful for analytic purposes. It is clear that letter-sequence interference should slow down the integrative stage. It is difficult to make precise predictions concerning the effects of unit-sequence interference on the associative stage. It is a fact that speed of learning has been found to be positively correlated with m value, i.e. with the number of different associations evoked by the learning items (Noble, 1952; Noble and McNeely, 1957; Cieutat, Stockwell and Noble, 1958). The availability of multiple associations appears to facilitate the establishment of the prescribed linkages among the items in the list. Our analysis makes it plausible, on the other hand, that the extinction of pre-experimental associations should delay acquisition. Much will probably depend on the extent to which units are included in the list among which there are pre-experimental associations. Importations of units from outside the list during learning are typically few and far between; i.e. identification of list membership is rapid and accurate. The data obtained in our recent study (Postman, 1961) do, indeed, show that pre-experimental associations among the units within a list give rise to frequent and persistent intra-list errors. In any event, it is essential that account be taken of differences in associative strength at the end of learning in assessing the amount of forgetting for different kinds of materials. Appropriate corrections for differences in associative strength can be made by means of successive-probability analysis (Underwood, 1954) or by adding control groups whose retention is measured immediately after the end of learning.

For retention, the hypothesis predicts that losses due to letter-sequence interference should be accompanied by overt errors reflecting the subject's letter-sequence habits. Thus, letter-sequence interference necessarily makes the correct responses less available at recall. As for unit-sequence interference, recovery of pre-experimental associations may reduce the subject's ability reproduce the items in the prescribed order without necessarily reducing their availability as responses. In fact, as Deese (1959) has shown, strong interitem associations may, under certain conditions, facilitate retention when the items do not have to be reproduced in sequential order. In assessing unit-sequence interference, the effects on response availability and on the reproduction of serial order must, therefore, be distinguished. The problem here is reminiscent of that encountered in the discussion of unlearning [earlier in the chapter].

References

CIEUTAT, V. J., STOCKWELL, F. E., and NOBLE, C. E. (1958), 'The interaction of ability and amount of practice with stimulus and response meaningfulness (*m*, *m'*) in paired-associate learning', *Journal of Experimental Psychology*, vol. 56, pp. 193–202.

DEESE, J. (1959), 'Influence of inter-item associative strength upon immediate free recall', *Psychological Reports*, vol. 5, pp. 305–12.

NOBLE, C. E. (1952), 'The role of meaningfulness (*m*) in serial verbal learning', *Journal of Experimental Psychology*, vol. 43, pp. 437–46.

NOBLE, C. E., and MCNEELY, D. A. (1957), 'The role of meaningfulness (*m*) in paired-associate verbal learning', *Journal of Experimental Psychology*, vol. 53, pp. 16–22.

POSTMAN, L. (1961), 'Extra-experimental interference and the retention of words', *Journal of Experimental Psychology*, vol. 61, pp. 97–110.

POSTMAN, L., and RAU, L. (1957), 'Retention as a function of the method of measurement', *University of California Publications on Psychology*, vol. 8, pp. 217–70.

UNDERWOOD, B. J. (1954), 'Speed of learning and amount retained: A consideration of methodology', *Psychological Bulletin*, vol. 51, pp. 276–82.

UNDERWOOD, B. J. (1957), 'Interference and forgetting', *Psychologica Review*, vol. 64, pp. 49–60.

UNDERWOOD, B. J., and POSTMAN, L. (1960), 'Extraexperimental sources of interference in forgetting', *Psychological Review*, vol. 67, pp. 73–95.

UNDERWOOD, B. J., and RICHARDSON, J. (1956), 'The influence of meaningfulness, intralist similarity and serial position on retention', *Journal of Experimental Psychology*, vol. 52, pp. 119–26.

UNDERWOOD, B. J., RUNQUIST, W. N., and SCHULZ, R. W. (1959), Response learning in paired-associate lists as a function of intralist similarity', *Journal of Experimental Psychology*, vol. 58, pp. 70–78

Part Six **Measurement of Retention**

Part Six calls attention to some persistent methodological problems in the measurement of retention. It is apparent that the amount retained after a given interval of time will depend on both the degree of original learning and the method by which retention is measured. These facts bring to the fore the two particular methodological questions considered in the articles included here, viz. (a) the determination of an appropriate baseline for the evaluation of the amount of forgetting, and (b) the comparison of retention scores obtained by different methods of measurement.

Degree of Learning and Retention

The fact that there is a strong positive relation between degree of learning and amount retained has long been recognized. The more an individual has learned the higher his recall score is likely to be. This relation is readily demonstrated when degree of learning is manipulated systematically in a study of retention. A methodological problem arises, however, when one wishes to determine the effects on retention of a variable which is known to influence speed of acquisition. Such a variable may be characteristic of the task or of the subject. For instance, one may wish to compare retention for materials of high and low meaningfulness or for fast and slow learners. Given the operational distinction between learning and retention discussed in Part Four, it is essential that the terminal degree of learning be held constant in such comparisons. The question which is asked is whether the rate of forgetting after the termination of practice is influenced by the variable under investigation. Is material of high meaningfulness more susceptible to extra-experimental interference than material of low meaningfulness; do fast learners retain more than slow learners? Such questions can obviously not be answered if acquisition has been carried to different levels of mastery. In that case differences in the amount retained may reflect inequalities in the degree of original learning, the effect of the experimental variable on retention *per se*, or both.

Reading 32 by Underwood considers various methods which have been used in studies of retention to take account of differences in speed of acquisition. His survey shows that these attempts to eliminate potential sources of bias were not successful. For example, the problem of an appropriate baseline is not solved by measuring retention after the attainment of a fixed criterion. When acquisition is slow, the easiest items in the list are usually overlearned to a higher degree than when the terminal level of mastery is attained rapidly. On the other hand, the amount learned on the criterial trial may be assumed to be greater in the latter case; this conclusion becomes apparent when the slopes of the acquisition curves of fast and slow learners are considered. The critical point here is that each correct response or 'reinforcement' is likely to add a greater increment in associative strength when learning is fast than when it is slow. Any procedure for equating the terminal strengths of association must take account of this fact. The successive probability analysis described by Underwood is designed to do just that.

The basic objective of this analysis is to obtain for each item as precise an estimate as possible of the probability of a correct response if a test trial were added after the end of practice. The estimates are extrapolations from the functions describing the growth of associative strength. As is shown in Reading 32 the technique makes it possible to identify sets of items which have equal probabilities of being correct on the hypothetical next test trial even though they were acquired at different speeds. To satisfy the requirement of equal probabilities, difficult items must have had more reinforcements than easy ones, and a parallel situation obtains for items learned by slow and fast subjects respectively. Once the associative strengths at the end of practice have been thus equated, the retention losses for easy and hard items, and for fast and slow subjects, become directly comparable.

Contrary to what had been widely assumed, application of this method of analysis shows that the rates of forgetting for fast and slow subjects do not differ reliably. Previous findings showing superior retention by fast subjects must be attributed to a failure to equate the degree of original learning.

The analyses presented in Reading 32 were carried out on sets of items pooled from the protocols of a group of subjects. It is also possible to determine expected recall scores for individual subjects by adding the projected probabilities of all the items in the list. The differences between expected and obtained scores provide measures of retention loss. These loss scores can be subjected to the usual tests of statistical significance (Richardson and Underwood, 1957).

In a subsequent paper Underwood (1964) reviewed applications of probability analysis to a considerable range of experimental data and also described a useful modification of the original technique. The earlier version was developed for measures of retention taken after learning to a criterion of performance. The modified procedure is used when a fixed number of learning trials is given. When materials differ in difficulty, the numbers of trials can be adjusted so as to yield approximately equal probabilities of recall on the next trial. Thus, in order to equate the expected scores, fifteen trials might be given on a difficult list, and ten trials on an easy one. (The appropriate numbers of trials have first to be determined in a pilot study.) If the adjustment in the number of trials equalizes the expected scores, the retention losses become directly comparable. The projected probabilities obtained in this fashion have been found to have a high degree of validity as measured by correlations between predicted and obtained scores. When an immediate retention test is actually given, there are typically only minor discrepancies between the means of the expected values and of the observed measures of performance. The predictions of individual scores are less accurate when learning is to a criterion and the method described in the original paper is used. However, the average predicted and obtained scores agree well in both cases. In light of past experience with the method, the use of fixed numbers of learning trials, adjusted so as to yield equal projected probabilities under the conditions to be compared, is the preferred procedure.

Measurement of Retention

A precise assessment of the terminal degree of learning becomes especially important when the interpretation of small differences in retention is at issue. Underwood (1964) points out that as theories of forgetting become more explicit, the evaluation of relatively subtle effects is often critical. Thus, a failure to take account of variations in degree of learning may lead to incorrect theoretical inferences. The available evidence gives growing support for the conclusion that degree of original learning is a decisive determinant of the level of retention. Manipulation of a wide array of task variables, including meaningfulness and intralist similarity, has in most cases failed to produce significant effects on the rate of forgetting.

Comparison of Recall and Recognition

With the conditions of practice and the retention interval held constant, the observed amount of forgetting depends on the method of testing. This fact makes it clear that there is no one 'true' measure of memory. In a strictly operational sense there are as many kinds of memory as there are measures of retention. The general concept of memory is an inference from the congruence of the functional relations yielded by different measurement procedures.

Whenever the degree of retention is found to vary as a function of the method of testing, the question arises of what factors are responsible for the observed differences in performance. Do the various tests tap different aspects of memory; to what extent do the obtained scores diverge because of the differential sensitivity of the measuring instruments? Questions such as these have been asked in particular about the commonly observed difference between recall and recognition. The usual finding has been that after a given amount of practice, recognition is higher than recall (e.g. Luh, 1922; Postman and Rau, 1957). An important qualification must at once be added. The difficulty of a recognition test depends critically on the selection of the incorrect alternatives or distractors which the subject must reject in favour of the correct items: the greater the similarity between the correct and incorrect alternatives, the more difficult is the recognition test and the smaller will be the advantage of recognition over recall.

fact, a difference in the opposite direction may be obtained (see Bahrick and Bahrick, 1964). Nevertheless, when correct items and distractors are drawn from the same general pool, the most likely result is that recognition is significantly better than recall. The recall score is, of course, determined by the number of correct items reproduced. In the calculation of the recognition score, a correction for guessing is normally applied. For example, if there are n incorrect alternatives, the corrected recognition score is $R - \dfrac{W}{n}$, where R refers to right choices and W to wrong choices.

The logic of these measures, and hence the validity of the conventional comparisons between recognition and recall, is questioned in Reading 33 by Brown. The basic objection raised by Brown is that the usual correction for guessing is appropriate only on the assumption that retention is all-or-none: if a choice is incorrect, it is classified as a random guess. The all-or-none assumption should not, however, be made arbitrarily, but instead should be evaluated empirically. When a subject must choose among three alternatives, one correct and two incorrect, his first choice may be incorrect, but there may be a higher than chance probability that on a second attempt he will prefer the correct item to the remaining distractor. Thus, multiple-response data make it possible to determine precisely the probability that incorrect alternatives will be rejected. The measures obtained by this procedure are more sensitive indicants of recognition than the conventional scores corrected for guessing. Similar considerations apply to recall. If the range of permissible responses is limited and known to the subject, it becomes reasonable to conceive of recall as well as of recognition as contingent upon the rejection of distractors in favour of the correct item. Given a failure on a first attempt at recall, therefore, there may again be a higher than chance probability that the second attempt will be successful. As before, multiple-response data permit an estimate of the number of distractors rejected on each recall occasion.

Brown's experimental findings show that in his situations the all-or-none assumption holds neither for recognition nor for recall. The results of Bregman (1966) support this conclusion for recognition. While the differences between recognition and recall are of a smaller magnitude than in earlier studies, they nevertheless remain statistically significant. Brown is inclined to attribute this difference to subjects' failures to scan the appropriate alternatives in recall; such failures cannot occur in recognition since the alternatives are physically present. This interpretation is based on the assumption that both recognition and recall are outcomes of a scanning process in which a limited range of alternatives is considered prior to the overt reaction – the choice of one of the test items in one case and the reproduction of an item in the other. In a somewhat similar vein, Davis, Sutherland, and Judd (1961) argued that recognition will surpass recall to the extent that the range of alternatives to be considered is more restricted in the former than in the latter case. They predicted that the difference between the two measures should be eliminated if the number of alternatives to be considered was equated. This condition was realized when the set of permissible responses (two-digit numbers or bigrams) was delimited so as to provide the same number of potential distractors in recall as were present on the test of recognition. Under these circumstances, the differences between the two types of measures were neither substantial nor consistent so that the results appeared to be favourable to the hypothesis.

A recent study by Field and Lachman (1966) casts doubt on the assumption that the number of alternatives to be scanned is the critical factor responsible for the relative efficiency of recognition and recall. These investigators devised several procedures for determining what proportion of the specified alternatives were actually scanned by the subject at the time of recall. The results show clearly that only a part of the total set of permissible responses was in fact considered by the subject. This finding agrees with Brown's suggestion that scanning failures will occur at the time of recall. It is probably too early to say, however, whether scanning is indeed a basic underlying mechanism common to recognition and recall.

References

BAHRICK, H. P., and BAHRICK, P. O. (1964), 'A re-examination of the inter-relations among measures of retention', *Quarterly Journal of Experimental Psychology*, vol. 16, pp. 318–24.

BREGMAN, A. S. (1966), 'Is recognition memory all-or-none?' *Journal of Verbal Learning and Verbal Behavior*, vol. 5, pp. 1–6.

DAVIS, R., SUTHERLAND, N. S., and JUDD, B. R. (1961), 'Information content in recognition and recall', *Journal of Experimental Psychology*, vol. 61, pp. 422–9.

FIELD, W. H., and LACHMAN, R. (1966), 'Information transmission (*I*) in recognition and recall as a function of alternatives (*k*)', *Journal of Experimental Psychology*, vol. 72, pp. 785–91.

LUH, C. W. (1922), 'The conditions of retention', *Psychological Monographs*, vol. 31, no. 142.

POSTMAN, L., and RAU, L. (1957), 'Retention as a function of the method of measurement', *University of California, Publications in Psychology*, vol. 8, no. 3.

RICHARDSON, J., and UNDERWOOD, B. J. (1957), 'Comparing retention of verbal lists after different rates of acquisition', *Journal of General Psychology*, vol. 56, pp. 187–92.

UNDERWOOD, B. J. (1964), 'Degree of learning and the measurement of forgetting', *Journal of Verbal Learning and Verbal Behavior*, vol. 3, pp. 112–29.

32 B. J. Underwood

Speed of Learning and Amount Retained: a Consideration of Methodology

B. J. Underwood, 'Speed of learning and amount retained: a consideration of methodology', *Psychological Bulletin*, vol. 51 (1954), pp. 276–82.

A common generalization found in textbooks is that the fast learner retains more than the slow learner. McGeoch (6), apparently on the basis of Gillette's work (1) and on the basis of his general conception of learning and forgetting processes, wrote: 'This high positive relation between individual scores in learning and retention is to be expected, of course, from the fact that these are continuous processes' (6, p. 388). Although not explicitly stated in terms of rate of learning and forgetting of individuals, the present writer has also assumed the validity of the general principle that speed of learning and amount retained are directly related (8, p. 510). Kingsley (4, p. 469), Munn (7, p. 213), and Hilgard (2, p. 10) have also accepted the generalization.

The present paper has two purposes. First, we will show that the methods used to obtain the data from which this principle was derived are inappropriate. Secondly, we will show that when suitable methodology is applied to the problem, there is no difference in rate of forgetting of fast and slow learners.

Methods Used by Previous Investigators

The last extensive work on the problem of the relation between speed of learning and amount retained was Gillette's monograph (1) published in 1936. It is highly probable that this monograph is responsible for the general conclusions appearing in textbooks as noted above. In this monograph Gillette critically summarizes the methods and results of all previous investigations, going back as far as Ebbinghaus. Two methods of investigation had been used in these previous investigations. Gillette's criticisms of these methods may be noted briefly.

Method of equal amount learned

By this method all Ss learn a task to a given criterion of proficiency, and after a rest interval retention measurements are obtained. The most commonly used statistic is the correlation coefficient between a measure of time to learn to the standard criterion and the recall or relearning scores. Gillette points out that this technique favors retention of the slow learner since certain of the items or parts of the task will be much over-learned and therefore might be expected to enhance retention. This would tend to reduce differences in retention between fast and slow learners. Indeed, correlations near zero between time to learn and amount recalled are interpreted by Gillette as actually indicating the slow learners have forgotten more rapidly than fast learners. Nevertheless, Gillette rightfully rejects this method as a means of reaching a definitive conclusion on the issue.

Method of equal opportunity to learn

By this method all Ss are allowed the same amount of time to study the material before the retention interval. Again, Gillette notes that this method is quite inappropriate because the fast learners will learn more than the slow learners and therefore may be expected to have higher retention simply because they have learned more. In general, the studies she reviews show fairly high correlation between amount learned and amount retained, and her own data resulting from this technique likewise yield high correlations. Actually, of course, using this technique, fast Ss could show more rapid forgetting than slow Ss, and the high correlations would still obtain if there were wide differences in amount originally learned. This method, therefore, must be rejected as a means of investigating the problem.

Method of adjusted learning

Gillette's solution to the methodological problem was to use the adjusted-learning technique. By this technique items in a list are 'dropped out' after being learned to a minimum criterion (such as one correct anticipation). Thus, all items of a list are given the same number of 'reinforcements'. And, while slow learners would take more time to obtain these reinforcements than would fast learners, Gillette assumed that the strength of associations at the end of learning was the same for fast and for slow Ss.

Gillette's conclusion from her experiment using the method of adjusted learning is as follows: 'The slow learner when given sufficient time to learn the *same amount* as the fast learner, but not allowed to *overlearn* the material, is not able to retain as much as the fast learner' (1, p. 50). Her final conclusion, after using all three methods, was that there are very clear indications that the fast learner retains better than the slow learner.

Inadequacy of the Method of Adjusted Learning

The inadequacy of the method used by Gillette can best be understood if a brief résumé is given of certain calculations made on data which were available to us. As a result of a series of investigations on rote learning which we have published elsewhere in connexion with other problems (9, 10, 11, 12), we had a large amount of data which could be analysed in an attempt to obtain more information on the relationship between speed of learning and amount retained. These experiments involved both paired-associate and serial learning, and both nonsense syllables and adjectives. The lists were always learned to a criterion of one perfect recitation with recall and relearning occurring after 24 hr.

Using these data, we first obtained correlations between trials to learn and recall, and between trials to learn and relearn. Since our Ss all learned to the same criterion, the method is the one referred to above as the method of equal amount learned. In general conformance with previous findings summarized by Gillette, correlations between time to learn and amount recalled were all near zero. Correlations betweeen time to learn and time to relearn were high and positive. Viewed by this method, then, our results are quite in accord with previous findings.

Our next step was to analyse the data in such a fashion that we would in effect be using the adjusted-learning technique. We divided a group of Ss for a given experiment into two equal subgroups based on number of trials to learn, thus giving a group of slow learners and a group of fast learners. We then counted the number of correct anticipations made by each S for each item in learning a list to one perfect trial. Each correct anticipation we call a reinforcement simply because the greater the number of correct anticipations the more resistant is an item to forgetting. All items having the same number of reinforcements were pooled, using separate pools for slow and fast Ss. Thus, we might have 200 items which had been given five reinforcements while being learned by slow Ss and 225 items which had been given five reinforcements while being learned by fast Ss. The final step was to determine the percentage correct at recall for each frequency of reinforcement for fast and slow Ss. This is, in effect, comparable to Gillette's adjusted-learning technique.

Results of such comparisons between fast and slow Ss for several experiments showed consistently that for items equated for number of reinforcements during learning, retention was consistently superior for fast learners. This was true regardless of the actual number of reinforcements obtained during original learning. That is, fast Ss were superior in recall for items having only a few reinforcements and for items having many reinforcements. Thus, this analysis gave strong empirical confirmation to Gillette's findings.

The assumption on which acceptance of Gillette's method (and of our modification of it) rests is that the making of a correct anticipation (a reinforcement) by a slow S results in the same associative strength as a reinforcement for a fast S. If this assumption is not valid, comparisons of retention of fast and slow learners are as misleading by this method as by the other methods thus far discussed. For, if a reinforcement adds more strength to an association being acquired by a fast S than it does to one for a slow S, it means that degree of learning of the material is not equal before introduction of the retention interval. Comparisons of retention, therefore, are distorted in the same fashion as with the other two methods discussed above.

In order to make comparisons of retention of fast and slow learners, it is absolutely essential that the response strengths the items for fast and slow learners be equated at the end learning – at the start of the retention interval. The method adjusted learning and our variation on this method do not assume that this is the case. Indeed, it is a very reasonable hypothesis that the essential difference between fast and slow learners is that reinforcement *does* result in more associative strength for a fast than for a slow S. Thus, the better retention of fast Ss as found by Gillette and also by our method may be entirely a function of the unequal degree of learning before the retention interval was introduced.

Technique for Equating Degree of Learning for Fast and Slow Subjects

The solution to the problem results from what we call a successive probability analysis of learning. The data we will use to demonstrate the method come from five experiments on the learning and retention of paired nonsense syllable lists (10). Each experiment employed thirty-six Ss. We have divided these into two groups of eighteen each based on number of trials to learn. Each S learned and recalled three lists, the conditions for learning differing only in terms of intertrial interval. These intervals (4, 30 and 60 sec) produced no difference in learning, and they do not interact with S's ability level. Therefore, we may treat them as three equivalent learning tasks for each S. Since there were five experiments, and since we get eighteen fast Ss and eighteen slow Ss from each experiment, we have a total of ninety fast and ninety slow Ss, each having learned and recalled three lists. Effectively, then, we have 270 lists for each group, and since each list had ten pairs, we have 2700 items for each group.

The successive probability analysis consists of determining the growth of the associative function for each item. We first observed when an item was correctly anticipated initially. We then noted whether the response was anticipated correctly or incorrectly on the immediately following trial. When an item had been anticipated correctly twice (whether on successive trials or not), we noted whether it was correct or incorrect on the next trial. This continued until the item was analysed for the entire course of learning. As an illustration, suppose that an item was first given correctly on trial 6. On trial 7 it was also given correctly, on trial 8 incorrectly, trial 9 correctly, trial 10 correctly, with S also getting other items correct on trial 10. Our entries would be: after one reinforcement, it was correct on next trial; after two reinforcements it was incorrect on next trial; and after three reinforcements, correct.

Measurement of Retention

When such an analysis is made for each item for a large number of Ss, and when these data are pooled, we are in a position to make exact statements of the probability of getting an item correct on a succeeding trial when this item has been correctly anticipated on previous trials once, twice, three times, etc.

As can be seen, the labor involved in making this successive probability analysis is great. To reduce the labor somewhat we eliminated some items which were very easy to learn and hence had been given a great many reinforcements. Working first with data for slow Ss, we eliminated all items which had been correctly anticipated more than thirty-one times by S in learning a list. Out of the 2700 items, 289 were eliminated by this criterion. We then made a distribution of number of reinforcements given the 2700 items by the fast Ss. On the assumption that easy items for slow Ss would also be the easy items for fast Ss, we eliminated approximately 289 of the easiest items for the fast Ss. The actual number was 322 since we did not want to eliminate a portion of a category, as would have been necessary if we had eliminated exactly 289 items. For these fast Ss, the elimination of 322 items left only items which had been reinforced less than eighteen times.

The successive probability curves for fast and slow Ss are plotted in Figure 1. The number of observations decrease as the number of reinforcements increase. For the fast Ss a total of 18,379 observations are involved, with 2372 for the case of one reinforcement and fifty-four for the seventeen reinforcements. For the slow Ss 31,560 observations were totalled, with 2403 for one reinforcement and twenty-eight for thirty reinforcements. The amount of labor involved in compiling the data for the curves has some compensation in the smoothness of the functions.

From Figure 1 it is clear that a reinforcement on a given trial (or series of trials) does not result in equal probabilities that the response is correct on the next trial for fast and slow Ss. Following one reinforcement, for example, the probability is 0.62 for a fast S that the item will be correctly anticipated on the next trial. For the slow Ss the value is 0.50. Such differences occur throughout the entire range of reinforcements plotted. It is thus apparent that studies which have 'equated' fast and slow learners by equating number of reinforcements have not equated for associative strength. Therefore, our next step is to equate associative strength at the end of learning so that comparable retention measurements may be made for fast and slow Ss.

It can be seen from Figure 1 that the equation of associative strength could be made graphically. Thus, we see that six reinforcements for slow Ss result in about the same associative strength during learning as do three reinforcements for fast Ss. Other comparable values could be determined and two base lines

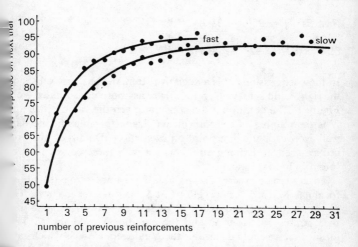

Figure 1 The relationship between number of reinforcements during learning and the probability of correct response on next trial for fast and slow learners

plotted, one for fast Ss and one for slow Ss, in such a fashion that associative strength at the end of learning is equal for the two groups at any point along the base lines. Such adjustments would allow us to say that if these Ss had been measured on an immediately succeeding trial following the end of learning, the associative strength for fast and slow Ss would have been the same. Knowing this, we can then make observations of recall with confidence that differences in retention are a function of differences in rates of forgetting of fast and slow Ss, and not a function of differences in response strength at the end of original learning.

Measurement of Retention

In general, the above procedure has been followed. The critical step, of course, is to equate response strengths along the base line for fast and slow Ss. To do this we first gave mathematical expression to the curves of Figure 1. After trying several types of curves, it was found that the exponential-type function gave the best fits. Essentially the formula is that of Hull (3, p. 119), with the exception that we have not forced the curves to pass through the origin. The two formulas are:

Fast Ss: $H = 95 \cdot 6 - 35 \cdot 20 e^{-0 \cdot 1031 N}$

Slow Ss: $H = 92 \cdot 5 - 40 \cdot 91 e^{-0 \cdot 0801 N}$

In these expressions H is associative strength. The first values on the right-hand side (95·6 and 92·5) are asymptotes estimated from Figure 1. The notation e is a constant given the value of 10, and N is the number of reinforcements. These formulas fit the data well except for the first point on each curve. Details of the procedure used in deriving and working with these curves may be found in Lewis (5, pp. 61–2).

To construct exactly comparable base lines using the above formulas we used the curve for fast Ss as a reference curve. The H values for each successive N for fast Ss were substituted in the formula for slow Ss and the equation solved for N. This means that we could determine the N value for slow Ss which gave the same H value for a given N value for fast Ss. Thus, for each value we have two N values, one for each group. The two values for successive H values are plotted on coordinated base lines in Figure 2. At any point along these base lines we know that the probability that a response will be correct on an immediately succeeding trial is the same for both groups. In Figure 2 the highest N value for fast Ss is 10, this being almost equivalent associative strength to N of 30 for slow Ss.

The final step is to plot the proportion of items recalled after 24 hr for each group for each level of associative strength. When this is done (Figure 2) we see that no consistent difference exists between the two curves. We conclude that when associative strength at the end of learning is equivalent for slow and fast, no difference in recall after 24 hr may be expected. This ho true for a wide range of associative strengths. Because forgetting is rather great in both groups, and because it does not vary between groups as a function of associative strength, we would not expect differences to emerge with longer retention intervals.

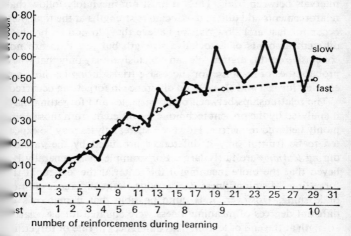

number of reinforcements during learning

Figure 2 Retention of fast and slow learners after 24 hours when associations are equated for strength at the end of learning

ther Implications

he results of the above analyses lead to a strong temptation to sert that the critical difference between fast and slow Ss is that e associative strength resulting from a reinforcement is less for w than for fast learners. In a descriptive sense this is true, as icated by Figure 1. However, in the theoretical sense some ervation is necessary. Between successive presentations of a en item during learning, a maximum of about 1·5 min elapsed. is interval might be as low as a few seconds depending upon location of the item in successive presentations of the list and n the intertrial interval used. It might be argued that if there o difference in forgetting between fast and slow Ss over 24 hr, s highly unlikely that there are differences in forgetting over se very short intervals between successive presentations of the e item during learning. Nevertheless, it is possible that a reinforcement for a fast and a slow S adds the same associative strength, but that in the context of learning a group of items (as contrasted with the relative rest over 24 hr) more forgetting might take place for an item for slow Ss than for fast Ss over these short intervals between trials. Thus, it must not inevitably follow that reinforcements add different associative strengths at the time they occur for fast and slow Ss; we believe they do add or produce different amounts of associative strength but our data are not conclusive on this matter. We can conclusively say only that when probabilities of response for successive trials during learning are equated for fast and slow Ss, no difference in forgetting occurred.

The relationships between other variables and forgetting may if analysed by the present technique, be different from those commonly believed to be true. However, such analyses may be expected to be fruitful only if differences produced by the variable during *learning* are fairly large. For example, it is generally believed that the more meaningful the material the less rapid the forgetting. Meaningfulness *does* produce large differences in rate of learning. However, it is quite possible that if materials of different degrees of meaningfulness were equated for associative strength at the end of learning, no differences in rate of forgetting would be demonstrable. It goes without saying that if such findings do occur we will need to shift our ideas when constructing theories of forgetting.

Summary

A review of previous methods used to study the relationship between rate of learning and rate of forgetting showed that none was adequate to the problem. In no case was it established that associative strength before the retention interval was equal for Ss learning at different rates.

A method for equating associative strength at the termination of learning was described and applied to data obtained in learning and recalling paired nonsense syllables. With such equality established it was shown that no difference in forgetting occurred over 24 hr; the recall of slow Ss was as good as that of fast Ss.

The method may be useful for studying the influence of other variables on retention.

References

1. A. L. GILLETTE, 'Learning and retention: a comparison of three experimental procedures', *Archives of Psychology*, vol. 28 (1936), no. 198.
2. E. R. HILGARD, *Introduction to Psychology*, Harcourt, Brace, 1953.
3. C. L. HULL, *Principles of Behavior*, D. Appleton-Century, 1943.
4. H. L. KINGSLEY, *The Nature and Conditions of Learning*, Prentice-Hall, 1946.
5. D. LEWIS, *Quantitative Methods in Psychology*, Gordon Bookshop, Iowa, 1948.
6. J. A. MCGEOCH, *The Psychology of Human Learning*, Longmans, Green, 1942.
7. N. L. MUNN, *Psychology*, 2nd edn, Houghton Mifflin, 1951.
8. B. J. UNDERWOOD, *Experimental Psychology*, Appleton-Century-Crofts, 1949.
9. B. J. UNDERWOOD, 'Studies of distributed practice: VII. Learning and retention of serial nonsense lists as a function of intralist similarity', *Journal of Experimental Psychology*, vol. 44 (1952), pp. 80–87.
10. B. J. UNDERWOOD, 'Studies of distributed practice: VIII. Learning and retention of paired nonsense syllables as a function of intralist similarity', *Journal of Experimental Psychology*, vol. 45 (1953), pp. 133–42.
11. B. J. UNDERWOOD, 'Studies of distributed practice: IX. Learning and retention of paired adjectives as a function of intralist similarity', *Journal of Experimental Psychology*, vol. 45 (1953), pp. 143–9.
12. B. J. UNDERWOOD, 'Studies of distributed practice: X. The influence of intralist similarity on learning and retention of serial adjectives', *Journal of Experimental Psychology*, vol. 45 (1953), pp. 253–9.

33 J. Brown

A Comparison of Recognition and Recall by a Multiple-Response Method

J. Brown, 'A comparison of recognition and recall by a multiple-response method', *Journal of Verbal Learning and Verbal Behavior*, vol. 4 (1965) pp. 401–8.

Recognition and recall were compared by estimating the average prob ability (R) of rejecting a wrong possibility in recall and recognitio tests. This method can only be applied if multiple-response data ar obtained. It is equivalent to the traditional guessing-correction metho if retention is all-or-none but not otherwise.

In Experiment I, lists of fifteen digits were played from magnetic tap At the end of each list, the same list was presented visually but wit four single digits missing. Retention of a missing digit was tested eith by two-choice recognition or by recall. Up to three attempts at recallin a missing digit were made.

In Experiment II, a list of twenty-one three-letter words were pr sented twice. Retention of successive words was then tested alternate by three-choice recognition and by recall. Up to three attempts at rec and up to two attempts at recognition were made. Unsuccessful rec was followed by a recognition test.

Estimating the value of R for recognition was straightforwa Estimating the value of R for recall involved making some assumpti concerning the probability of successful recall on attempts after third. The effects of various possible assumptions are considered. the preferred assumption, recognition was significantly superior to re in both experiments. It is shown that the traditional method of co paring recall and recognition exaggerates the difference between th

In Experiment II, the relation between confidence and the probabi of success when making a recall or recognition attempt was stud The association was found to be consistently high. In addition, probability of success on a second or third attempt at recall was m higher if there had been a rise in confidence from the previous atten These findings are held to be consistent with the hypothesis that inferiority of recall is due to a failure to scan the possibilities effectiv

For the purposes of this paper, a recognition test can be define one in which a choice must be made between physically pre alternatives and a recall test as one in which the alternatives are implicit but not physically present. Typically, a recognition test restricts the number of alternatives so that a lucky guess is more likely than in a recall test. Because of this, the traditional method of comparing recognition and recall has been to correct both scores for the effect of guessing. (In practice the probability of a correct guess in a recall test is often so low that a correction for guessing is not needed.) The correction is based on the assumption that retention is all-or-none, i.e. that each response in a recall or recognition test is either made on the basis of adequate retained information or represents what is effectively a random guess. If retention is not all-or-none, the usual analysis is invalid. Recently, Davis, Sutherland and Judd (1961) compared recognition and recall by estimating the information transmitted in recognition and recall tests. Their method is open to substantially the same criticism as the guessing-correction method. In order to estimate information transmitted, they were forced to assume that there was no retention of items not recalled or recognized, and that no information was conveyed by incorrect responses. This is close to assuming that retention is all-or-none. Their method is also open to a second criticism, namely that there is usually less opportunity to transmit information in a recognition test than in a recall test. For example, consider their recognition test in which fifteen correct items had to be selected from a list of thirty items and their recall test in which the fifteen correct items had to be selected from the full set of ninety possible items. Calculation shows that ·2 bits would be transmitted by perfect performance in the recognition test whereas 55·3 bits would be transmitted by perfect performance in the recall test. Comparison of the two tests in terms of information transmitted is therefore strongly weighted in favor of recall.

The need to assume all-or-none retention can be avoided if multiple-response data are obtained (Brown, 1965). Such data also reveal whether this assumption is correct (Brown, 1964). Consider a recall or recognition test consisting of one correct alternative and of n distractors, i.e. incorrect alternatives. Success at the first attempt implies that all n distractors have been rejected. Success at the second attempt implies that $(n - 1)$ distractors have been rejected, and so on. Thus multiple-response data reveal the number of distractors rejected on each occasion. From the number of distractors rejected on each occasion, the average proportion of distractors rejected can be calculated. This proportion provides an estimate of the average probability of rejecting a distractor and will be denoted by R. Tests involving differing numbers of alternatives can be compared directly in terms of R. A test with a large number of alternatives provides an estimate of R based on a large sample of the possible distractors, and a test with a small number of alternatives provides an estimate of R based on a small sample. The expected values of the two estimates are equal, provided there are no psychological differences between the two tests such as variation of scanning efficiency with the number of alternatives.

The following points should be noted: (a) A distractor i regarded as rejected if it is not selected before the correct alternative. No assumption is made concerning the reason for its rejection. A distractor may be rejected because it is discriminated to be incorrect, or because of a lucky guess, or even because it has no been considered. (b) The distractors for a test are defined by the permissible responses in the test. In a recall test, the distractor actually considered by the S before he makes each attempt a likely to be influenced by the response-hierarchy. (c) It is u necessary to assume that the distracting powers of different di tractors are equal, provided the distractors are randomly select from the ensemble of possible distractors. In the experiments be reported, the distractors used for each recognition test co stituted a random selection from the distractors used for t corresponding recall test. (d) Comparing tests in terms of R equivalent to the traditional guessing-correction method if rete tion is all-or-none, but not otherwise. (e) It is also equivalent t method used by Murdock (1963) for comparing recognition te provided his special assumptions concerning rejection of distr tors hold. (f) If attempts are made at random, the expected va of R is 0·5. This can be seen by considering the case of a tw choice test, in which the probability of success is also the p bability of rejecting the distractor.

The formula for R is:

$$R = \frac{1}{n} [nP_1 + (n-1)P_2 + (n-2)P_3 \ldots + P_n]$$

where n is the number of distractors and P_1, P_2, P_3 . . . P_n are the probabilities that 1, 2, 3 . . . n attempts are needed to select the correct alternative. In order for this formula to hold, an attempt is defined as the selection of an alternative for the first time. In the experiments to be reported, the values of n for the recall tests were 9, 11, and 17. It was, therefore, not practicable to obtain complete multiple-response data, i.e. to require the Ss to continue their attempts until the correct alternative was selected on all occasions. Instead, up to three attempts were permitted and the values of P from P_4 to P_n had to be inferred. In the initial analysis of the results, this was done by assuming that the improvement over chance shown at the third attempt would have declined linearly to unity at the $(n + 1)$th attempt, if attempts had been continued: at the $(n + 1)$th attempt, no improvement over chance is possible as all the n distractors have been eliminated. This will be called the linear-fall assumption. The effects of adopting other possible assumptions will be considered in the discussion.

Experiment I

This experiment compared recall and two-choice recognition of single digits.

Method

The task consisted in listening to lists of fifteen digits recorded on magnetic tape. At the end of each list, the same list was presented visually but with four of the digits missing. Retention of these missing digits was tested alternately by recall and recognition. The task will be seen to bear some resemblance to the 'missing scan' test (Buschke, 1963).

Lists were selected from random numbers with the single restriction that no digit was permitted to occur more than twice in immediate succession. Each list was recorded on the tape at a rate of 2/3 sec per digit. A test-slide was prepared for each list as follows. The fifteen digits were typed on a white card 5×0.75 in. The card was fixed to the back of a perspex slide 7×1 in so that the digits were visible through the perspex. The four critical digits were covered by narrow vertical strips of card inserted

475

between the card and the perspex. Each strip was blank on one side and on the other side bore the correct digit and a randomly selected incorrect digit: the numerically smaller digit was typed at the top. Two of the strips were inserted so that the digits on them were visible and two so that only the blank sides were seen. The digits tested by recognition and recall could thus be exchanged simply by turning round the strips. The missing digits either occupied positions 3, 6, 9, 12 in the list, or positions 4, 7, 10, 13, or positions 5, 8, 11, 14. The first missing digit was sometimes tested by recall and sometimes by recognition. There were, therefore, 3×2 types of test-slide. Two slides of each type were used with each S, i.e. he was tested on twelve slides/lists. The order in which the types of slide was given was semi-random and unknown to the S. This order varied for each successive batch of four Ss. For convenience, two sets of twelve lists were used. The first two Ss were tested on the lists of the first set and were treated identically except that when one S was tested by recall the other S was tested by recognition and vice versa. The second two Ss were tested on the lists of the second set. Before the next four Ss were tested, the positions tested on the individual slides were changed. This involved fresh random selection of recognition alternatives; the object of this procedure was to guard against the effects of response biases. In the analysis of results, the first eight Ss tested formed one subgroup, and the next eight Ss formed another subgroup, and so on.

The test-slides were exposed in an apparatus which consisted of four horizontal shutters. As each shutter was pushed back, an additional missing digit was exposed. The first shutter covered the digits on the slide up to and including the digit after the first missing digit. The second shutter covered the next four digits, the third shutter the four following digits and the last shutter covered the remaining digits.

The procedure was as follows. The S listened to one of the recorded lists. At the sound of the E switching off the tape recorder, he pushed back the first shutter. If the alternatives were shown for the missing digit, he stated his choice and the E replied 'yes' or 'no'. The S then pushed back the second shutter. If no alternatives were shown for the missing digit, the S made up to three attempts at recall. The E said 'yes' or 'no' after each recall-attempt. In third attempt was incorrect, the E said 'no' and then stated the correct digit. As soon as the S had made a correct attempt or had been told the digit, he pushed back the next shutter. Immediately after one list had been tested, the next list was played. For each S, the E had a combined key and record card on which S's responses were recorded as he made them. For checking, the whole of the experiment was recorded on a second tape recorder. The Ss were thirty-two graduate and undergraduate students of both sexes.

Table 1

Basic Results for Recall

Measure	Attempt		
	1	2	3
	205·0	109·0	82·0
	0·267	0·142	0·107
	0·267	0·194	0·181
	2·67	1·74	1·45

Note: f = frequency of needing 1, 2, or 3 attempts; P = probability of needing 1, 2, or 3 attempts; p = probability of success when making an attempt; z = p divided by the chance probability of success.

Results

The results for recall are shown in Table 1. The first row shows the frequency with which success was attained at the first, second, and third attempts. The second row shows the corresponding values of P, i.e. the probability of needing one, two, or three attempts. The third row (p) shows the probabilities of success *when making* each attempt. The chance values of these probabilities (the values expected if attempts are made at random) are 1/10, 1/9, and 1/8 for the first second and third attempts, respectively. The fourth row (z) shows each value of p divided by the corresponding chance value. The estimate of R from these data can be expressed in the following form: R = 0·476 + 0·484W where 0·476 is the contribution of P_1, P_2, and P_3, and 0·484W is the contribution of the unobserved values of P. The number 0·484 is simply $(1 - P_1 - P_2 - P_3)$ and W is a weight. On the linear-fall assumption, z declines linearly from the third attempt and reaches unity at the tenth attempt. On this assumption, $W = 0·382$ and $R = 0·662$. The value of R for recognition was 0·707. The significance of the difference between recall and recognition was tested as follows. First, separate estimates of W were derived from the results for each subgroup of eight Ss. (The frequencies of third attempts were too small for values of W to be estimated for individual Ss.) The difference between the R-values for recall and recognition was then computed for each of the four subgroups. The mean difference was found to be significant at the 0·05 level, $t(3) = 3·60$.

Experiment II

In this experiment, recall and three-choice recognition of words were compared. The multiple-response data obtained by allowing up to three attempts become inadequate if the number of possible distractors is large. In order to reduce the number of possible words two steps were taken. First, only consonant-vowel-consonant words were used. Second, the initial letter of the required word was provided when recall was tested.

The experiment also compared conditional recognition and conditional recall. If S failed three attempts at recalling a word he was then given a recognition test. Performance in this test could be compared with the performance expected if further attempts at recall had been made. It was predicted that the difference between recall and recognition would be greater for conditional recall and recognition.

Finally the relation between confidence and the probability of success when making a recall or recognition attempt was studied. Recall may be less efficient than recognition because of a scanning failure. If a recall attempt fails only because the correct word has not been scanned, then it will be selected if it is scanned on a subsequent attempt. On this hypothesis, success on the second or third attempt at recall is likely to be associated with a rise in confidence.

Method

A list of words was presented twice, after which retention of successive words was tested alternately by recall and recognition. After three failures to recall a word, retention of the word was tested by recognition (conditional recognition). Attempts at recall or recognition were written on an answer-slip containing five columns and three rows. Successive columns were used for successive attempts and each row represented a different level of confidence. The Ss were forty-eight graduate and undergraduate students of both sexes. A different list was used with each pair of Ss. One of the Ss of the pair was given a recognition test first, and the other a recall test first. Thus each word was tested once by recall and once by recognition.

The twenty-four lists each consisted of twenty-one words. Retention was not tested for the first three words (*yet, aim, vow*) nor of the last two words (ice, eat). The fourth and fifth words always began with the letters k and g, respectively. These were regarded as practice words for the recall and recognition procedures. The remaining fourteen words were divided into two groups, Words I and Words II. The seven words of Words I began with the letters j, l, m, n, t, w, and the seven words of Words II began with the letters b, c, f, h, p, r, s. Only CVC words were used for Words I and Words II and for the fourth and fifth words of the list. Each letter of Words I began between twelve and seventeen CVC words, and each letter of Words II began between eighteen and twenty-two CVC words, after certain atypical or poorly known CVC words had been excluded (*dun, mid, nab, nil, par, rex, sub, tic, and tun*). In order to facilitate the analysis of the results, certain words were not permitted as attempts at recall with each list. If a S produced a nonpermitted word, this was not counted as a recall attempt and he was asked to try again. The number of permitted words was twelve per letter for Words I, and eighteen per letter for Words II. Either Words I occupied positions 6, 7, 10, 11, 14, 15, 18 in the list and Words II occupied positions 8, 9, 12, 13, 16, 17, 19, or vice versa.

Lists were prepared in triplets. For the lists of a triplet, the permitted words were the same, the order of the letters was constant and the same recognition cards were used. The recognition card for a particular letter consisted of the three words beginning with that letter from the lists of the triplet and were typed across the card: positions 1, 2, and 3 on the card were correct about equally often for each list. Words for each list were selected randomly from the permitted words, with the restriction that no word appeared in more than one list until all the words with the same initial letter had been used. The permitted words (also selected randomly but without unnecessary repetition) were changed from triplet to triplet as was the order of the individual letters.

Each S was individually tested on only one list. Each word of the list was on a separate card and the series of cards was presented to the S by hand twice in immediate succession at a rate of about 2 sec per card. The S read each word aloud as it was presented and had received a prior instruction to attempt to learn the words. Next, instructions were given for the recall or recognition procedure, and the S was tested on the first (practice) word of the list. The definitions of 'high', 'low', and 'medium' confidence were 'fairly sure', 'just guessing', and 'in between high and low' respectively. Additional instructions were given as they became appropriate. Recall and recognition alternated for the sixteen words tested.

Results

Unconditional recall and recognition. The results are summarized in Table 2. The first five columns concern unconditional recall and recognition. For recall, the chance values of p_1, p_2, and p_3 are $1/12$, $1/11$, and $1/10$, respectively, for Words I; and $1/18$, $1/17$, and $1/16$, respectively, for Words II. For recognition, the chance values of p_1 and p_2 are $1/3$ and $1/2$, respectively, for both Words I and II. The value of z is obtained by dividing the observed value of p by the chance value. The overall value of R for recognition was 0.942 for Words I and 0.957 for Words II. The over-all value of R for recall can be expressed as $0.677 + 0.298W_1$ for Words I and as $0.581 + 0.405W_2$ for Words II. On the linear-fall assumption, W_1 is 0.500 and W_2 is 0.578. If this assumption is adopted, the value of R for recall is 0.826 for Words I and 0.816 for Words II. Both values are lower than the values for recognition.

With the value of W_1 derived from the over-all results, the values for Words I were calculated separately for each triplet of lists, i.e. for each subgroup of six Ss. The difference between the R-values for recall and recognition was significant at the 0·01 level, $t(7) = 4·60$. However, this analysis is not altogether satisfactory because it takes no account of the variance of the weight W_1. (It was not possible to estimate a value of W_1 separately for each group of Ss, which would have avoided the difficulty, be-

Table 2

Basic Results for Words I and Words II

| | | Attempt | | | | | | |
| | | Uncond. recall | | | Uncond. recog. | | Cond. recog. | |
Measure		1	2	3	1	2	1	2
Words I	f	87·0	16·0	15·0	153·0	10·0	28·0	5·0
	P	0·518	0·095	0·089	0·912	0·060	0·824	0·147
	p	0·518	0·198	0·231	0·912	0·667	0·824	0·834
	z	6·22	2·18	2·31	2·74	1·33	2·48	1·67
Words II	f	73·0	14·0	13·0	156·0	9·0	46·0	7·0
	P	0·435	0·083	0·077	0·930	0·054	0·793	0·121
	p	0·435	0·147	0·160	0·930	0·075	0·793	0·583
	z	7·82	2·50	2·56	2·79	1·50	2·38	1·17

Note: f = frequency of needing 1, 2, or 3 attempts; P = probability of needing 1, or 3 attempts; p = probability of success when making an attempt; z = p divided y the chance probability of success.

ause the frequencies of third attempts were too small.) Yet it is nlikely that the true value of W_1 is sufficiently high to make the fference between recall and recognition nonsignificant. This con- usion was reached as follows: The value of W_1 depends on the lue of p_3. A crude estimate of the *SE* of p_3 can be obtained by eating p_3 as a binomial proportion, which gives 0·052. Even if e true value of p_3 is $3 \times 0·052$ above the observed value, the fference remains significant at the 0·01 level.

The results for Words II were analysed in a similar way. Again e difference between recall and recognition was highly signifi- nt, $t(7) = 8·07$, $p < 0·001$. Again, although this test takes no count of the variance of the weight, the difference between recall d recognition is almost certainly real. Although the observed difference between recall and recognition was slightly greater for Words II than for Words I, it was not statistically significant ($t < 1$), i.e. the experiment failed to provide evidence that the number of possible words (on average about 50 per cent higher for Words II) affects the relation between recall and recognition.

Table 3

Association between Confidence and Probability (p) of Correct Choice and Mean Confidence (m)

	Attempt				
	Uncond. recall			Uncond. recog.	Cond. recog.
Measure	1	2	3	1	1
p_a	0·86 (144)	0·59 (17)	0·73(11)	0·97 (251)	0·94 (54)
p_b	0·31 (78)	0·20 (40)	0·27 (21)	0·85 (67)	0·72 (26)
p_c	0·12 (114)	0·10 (118)	0·09 (116)	0·50 (18)	0·42 (12)
m	0·54 (336)	0·42 (165)	0·29 (149)	0·85 (335)	0·72 (92)

Note: a = high confidence, b = medium confidence, c = low confidence. For calculating mean confidence, a = 2, b = 1, c = 0. The N for estimating each quantity is shown in parentheses.

Conditional recall and recognition. The last two columns of Table show the relevant results. On sixteen occasions out of fifty with Words I and on twelve occasions out of seventy with Words II one of the distractors in the recognition test was produced as one of the attempts at recall: the probabilities shown are based on the remaining occasions. The values of R for conditional recognition derived from the results shown are 0·897 for Words I and 0·8? for Words II. Values of R for conditional recall can be inferred on the same basis as the weights W_1 and W_2 and can be easily derived from these weights. On the linear-fall assumption, the values of R for conditional recall are 0·660 for Words I and 0·664 for Words II. In both cases the values for conditional recall are well below those for conditional recognition. Indeed the values of R for conditional recognition are above the values for unconditional recall. A further point of interest is that the discrepancy between recall nition and recall is greater for conditional than for unconditional recognition and recall, as predicted. It is difficult, however, to find satisfactory methods of testing the statistical significance of these findings.

Confidence. The results on confidence for Words I and Words II were combined. The association between changes in confidence and the probability of correct choice was as follows. On the forty-one occasions when there was a rise in confidence on either the second or third attempt (in relation to the confidence shown on the immediately previous attempt) the proportion of correct choices was 0·488. On the 281 occasions when there was no rise in confidence, the proportion of correct choices was only 0·135. Table 3 shows the association between confidence and the probability of correct choice. It will be seen that this association is consistently high. Of particular interest is the persistence of a fairly high association on the second and third attempts. The existence of this association between confidence and the probability of correct choice has implications for any future attempt to compare recall and recognition in information terms, since more information is transmitted when the S is able to distinguish between his correct and his erroneous responses. Table 3 also shows the mean confidence for successive attempts. Mean confidence was calculated by assigning values of 1·0, 0·5, and 0·0 when confidence was high, medium, and low, respectively. During recall, mean confidence declined with each successive attempt. Mean confidence rose sharply with the transition to conditional recognition: the rise was similar in magnitude for all fourteen initial letters of Words I and II and was therefore highly significant statistically.

Discussion

In both experiments, recognition was superior to recall, although reliable evidence for a difference was obtained only in Experiment II. In order to estimate the values of R for recall, it was assumed that the improvement over chance (z) declines linearly from the third attempt to unity when only one alternative remains. It is interesting to examine the effects of adopting other assumptions.

483

The linear-fall assumption will now be called Ass. I. Another possible assumption is that z remains constant from the third attempt onwards until the probability of success reaches unity (Ass. II). Adoption of Ass. II reduces the estimated difference between recognition and recall. This is shown in Table 4: each entry is the R-value for recall expressed as a percentage of the R-value for recognition. It is difficult to decide from the observed values of z (Tables 1 and 2) whether the extrapolation implied by Ass. I or by Ass. II is the more plausible. Assumption I was preferred because it seems more reasonable. For example, if z is 2·0 at the third attempt, then Ass. II implies that success is certain as soon as there are only two alternatives left, which is hardly plausible. A further possible assumption is that z falls abruptly to unity after the third attempt (Ass. III). Adoption of this assumption presumably leads to an underestimation of the R-value for recall (unless there is a bias against the correct alternation on some occasions; z might then fall below unity at some stage after the third attempt). On this assumption, the estimated difference between recall and recognition is increased (Table 4). Finally, an assumption contrary to the evidence is that z is unity after the first attempt, i.e. that retention is all-or-none (Ass. IV). In Experiment II, in which three-choice recognition was used, this assumption affects the assessment of recognition as well as of recall. Adoption of Ass. IV leads to an even larger apparent difference between recall and recognition than adoption of Ass. III. It has been included in Table 4 to show the pay-off given by the use of multiple-response data. When R-values are equal on Ass. IV, scores corrected for guessing by the traditional method will also be equal.

All entries in Table 4 are less than 100. This implies that which-ever assumption is adopted, unconditional recall was inferior to unconditional recognition and conditional recall was inferior to conditional recognition (disregarding the question of statistical significance). The effect of adopting different assumptions is less for unconditional than for conditional recall because there is a fixed contribution to the estimate of the R-value for unconditional recall from the observed values of P, but there is no fixed contribution to the estimate for conditional recall. The effect of adopting different assumptions is also greater for Words II than for Words I. For example, the difference between the R-values for recall

Ass. I and on Ass. IV was found to be 0·089 for Words I and 0·115 for Words II. This is because the number of alternatives was higher for Words II than for Words I, so that a larger proportion of the distribution of P for Words II depended on what assumption was adopted. In general, the extent to which a particular assumption exaggerates or underestimates retention tends to increase with the

Table 4

Relation between Recall and Recognition on Various Assumptions

Assumption	Uncond. recall and recog.			Cond. recall and recog.	
	Digits	Words I	Words II	Words I	Words II
I	93·6	87·7	85·3	73·6	77·8
II	95·8	89·3	87·0	83·3	83·6
III	90·2	83·5	78·2	55·8	58·5
IV	82·5	79·1	74·1	57·7	59·2

Note: Each entry is the R-value for recall expressed as a percentage of the R-value for recognition. Since R cannot fall below 0·5, the percentage cannot fall below 50 per cent.

number of alternatives in the test concerned. This explains why Ass. IV, which underestimates retention unless retention is all-or-none, exaggerates the difference between recall (involving many alternatives) and recognition (involving few alternatives).

Multiple-response data show that the difference between recall and recognition is not so great as the adoption of Ass. IV, and hence the use of the traditional guessing correction method, would indicate. Nevertheless there was a difference in favor of recognition both for digits (Experiment I) and for words (Experiment II), and the difference was statistically significant in both cases. A simple hypothesis to account for this superiority is that there is scanning-failure during attempts at recall. On this hypothesis, scanning-failure is assumed to occur on occasions when the probability of selecting the correct item would have been high if it had been scanned. Suggestive evidence in favor of this hypothesis was obtained in Experiment II. A correct choice on the second or third attempt was found to be associated with a rise in confidence. In addition, the association between confidence and the probability of correct choice was high on second and third attempts. There is, however, another possible interpretation of these findings. On his first attempt, for example, the S may be certain that the correct word is one of two. If he fails on his first attempt, his confidence will then rise and he will succeed on his second attempt. Further suggestive evidence for the hypothesis was the sharp rise in confidence when changing to recognition after three recall failures. Here again an alternative interpretation is possible. This is because the number of possible words falls to only three, when S passes from recall to recognition, so that some rise in confidence is expected with the concomitant increase in the probability of success.

Scanning-failure is more likely to occur with words than with digits. While this could account for the larger discrepancy between recall and recognition in Experiment II (words) than in Experiment I (digits), as shown in Table 4, the results of the two experiments are not really comparable in view of the differences in the conditions employed.

The finding (not evaluated statistically) that the difference between conditional recall and conditional recognition was greater than the difference between unconditional recall and unconditional recognition can be attributed to a process of selection. Those occasions on which three recall-failures have occurred will tend to be occasions on which recall is more difficult than recognition, if there are such occasions. This implies that conditional recall could be inferior to conditional recognition even though unconditional recall was equal to or superior to unconditional recognition, since there may be some occasions on which recognition would be superior and others on which recall would be superior. Comparing conditional recall and conditional recognition is a method of showing whether there are some occasions of the former type.

In this paper, the average probability of rejecting a distractor (R) has been used as an index of retention. The expected value of R cannot fall below 0·5. A better index of retention is therefore $(R - 0·5)/0·5$ and has been labelled the A-index (Brown, 1965). The raw R-value was used in preference to the A-index for sim

486

plicity. An interesting feature of the A-index is that, when retention is all-or-none, its expected value is the same as the expected value of the probability of a first-attempt success corrected for guessing.

References

BROWN, J. (1964), 'Two tests of all-or-none learning and retention', *Quarterly Journal of Experimental Psychology*, vol. 16, pp. 123–33.

BROWN, J. (1965), 'Multiple response evaluation of discrimination', *British Journal of Mathematical and Statistical Psychology*, vol. 18, pp. 125–37.

BUSCHKE, H. (1963), 'Relative retention in immediate memory determined by the missing scan method', *Nature*, vol. 200, pp. 1129–30.

DAVIS, R., SUTHERLAND, M. S., and JUDD, B. R. (1961), 'Information content in recognition and recall', *Journal of Experimental Psychology*, vol. 61, pp. 422–9.

MURDOCK, B. B., Jr. (1963), 'An analysis of the recognition process', in C. N. Cofer and B. S. Musgrave, ed., *Verbal Behavior and Learning: Problems and Processes*, McGraw-Hill, pp. 10–22.

Further Reading

J. A. ADAMS, *Human Memory*, McGraw-Hill, 1967.

F. C. BARTLETT, *Remembering*, Cambridge University Press, 1932.

E. A. BILODEAU, (ed.) *Acquisition of Skill*, Academic Press, 1966.

D. E. BROADBENT, *Perception and Communication*, Pergamon Press, 1958.

B. R. BUGELSKI, *The Psychology of Learning*, Holt, 1956.

C. N. COFER, (ed.) *Verbal Learning and Verbal Behavior*, McGraw-Hill, 1961.

C. N. COFER and B. S. MUSGRAVE, (eds.) *Verbal Behavior and Learning*, McGraw-Hill, 1963.

E. H. COOPER and A. J. PANTLE, 'The total-time hypothesis in verbal learning', *Psychological Bulletin*, vol. 68 (1967), pp. 221–34.

J. DEESE and S. H. HULSE, *The Psychology of Learning*, McGraw-Hill, 1967.

T. R. DIXON and D. L. HORTON, (eds.) *Verbal Behavior and General Behavior Theory*, Prentice-Hall, 1968.

B. EARHARD and G. MANDLER, 'Mediated associations: Paradigms, controls, and mechanisms', *Canadian Journal of Psychology*, vol. 19 (1965), pp. 346–78.

B. R. EKSTRAND, 'Backward associations', *Psychological Bulletin*, vol. 65 (1966), pp. 50–64.

J. F. HALL, *The Psychology of Learning*, Lippincott, 1966.

E. G. HILGARD and G. H. BOWER, Theories of Learning, 3rd edn, Appleton-Century-Crofts, 1966.

G. KEPPEL, 'Problems of method in the study of short-term memory', *Psychological Bulletin*, vol. 63 (1965), pp. 1–13.

G. A. KIMBLE, *Hilgard and Marquis' Conditioning and Learning*, Appleton-Century-Crofts, 1961.

J. A. MCGEOCH and A. L. IRION, *The Psychology of Human Learning*, Longmans, Green, 1952.

A. W. MELTON, (ed.) *Categories of Human Learning*, Academic Press, 1964.

G. A. MILLER, 'The magic number seven, plus or minus two: Some limits on our capacity for processing information', *Psychological Review*, vol. 63 (1956), pp. 81–97.

C. E. OSGOOD, *Method and Theory in Experimental Psychology*, Oxford University Press, 1953, Part III.

F. RESTLE, 'Significance of all-or-none learning', *Psychological Bulletin*, vol. 64 (1965), pp. 313–25.

S. ROSENBERG, (ed.) *Directions in Psycholinguistics*, Macmillan, 1965.

W. N. RUNQUIST, 'Verbal behavior', in J. B. Sidowski, ed., *Experimental Methods and Instrumentation in Psychology*, McGraw-Hill, 1966, pp. 487–540.

Further Reading

S. SAPORTA, (ed.) *Psycholinguistics*, Holt, Rinehard and Winston, 1961.

K. W. SPENCE and J. T. SPENCE, (eds.) *The Psychology of Learning and Motivation: Vol. I*, Academic Press, 1967.

E. TULVING, 'Subjective organization in free recall of "unrelated" words', *Psychological Review*, vol. 69 (1962), pp. 344–54.

B. J. UNDERWOOD, 'Degree of learning and the measurement of forgetting', *Journal of Verbal Learning and Verbal Behavior*, vol. 3 (1964), pp. 112–29.

B. J. UNDERWOOD, *Experimental Psychology*, Appleton-Century-Crofts, 2nd edn, 1966, ch. 11–13.

B. J. UNDERWOOD and R. W. SCHULZ, *Meaningfulness and Verbal Learning*, Lippincott, 1960.

W. P. WALLACE, 'Review of the historical, empirical, and theoretical status of the von Restorff phenomenon', *Psychological Bulletin*, vol. 63 (1965), pp. 410–24.

Acknowledgements

Permission to reproduce the readings in this volume is acknowledged from the following sources.

Reading 1 American Psychological Association and B. J. Underwood
Reading 2 American Psychological Association
Reading 3 *American Journal of Psychology*
Reading 4 American Psychological Association and A. L. Irion
Reading 5 American Psychological Association and J. E. Foley
Reading 6 American Psychological Association and B. J. Underwood
Reading 7 American Psychological Association, V. J. Cieutat, C. E. Noble and F. E. Stockwell
Reading 8 American Psychological Association and W. N. Runquist
Reading 9 American Psychological Association and R. L. Erickson
Reading 10 American Psychological Association
Reading 11 American Psychological Association and B. J. Underwood
Reading 12 American Psychological Association and B. R. Bugelski
Reading 13 Academic Press Inc. and A. Mechanic
Reading 14 *Psychological Reports* and J. Deese
Reading 15 *Psychological Reports* and W. A. Bousfield
Reading 16 University of Toronto Press and E. Tulving
Reading 17 University of Illinois Press
Reading 18 Academic Press Inc. and G. A. Miller
Reading 19 American Psychological Association and L. E. Thune
Reading 20 Academic Press Inc. and M. Schwartz
Reading 21 American Psychological Association and B. J. Underwood
Reading 22 American Psychological Association and E. Martin
Reading 23 American Psychological Association, N. E. McGehee and R. W. Schulz
Reading 24 *Psychonomic Science*
Reading 25 American Psychological Association and L. R. Peterson
Reading 26 *Quarterly Journal of Experimental Psychology* and J. Brown
Reading 27 Academic Press Inc. and B. J. Underwood
Reading 28 American Psychological Association and B. B. Murdock
Reading 29 American Psychological Association

Acknowledgements

Reading 30 American Psychological Association and
        B. J. Underwood
Reading 31 McGraw–Hill Book Company
Reading 32 American Psychological Association and
        B. J. Underwood
Reading 33 Academic Press Inc. and J. Brown.

Author Index

Subject Index

Penguin Modern Psychology

Other titles available in this series of Readings are:

Forthcoming titles to be published in 1969:

Penguin Science of Behaviour

This new series of short, original, unit texts will cover a very wide range of psychological inquiry. Many of the texts will be on central teaching topics, while others will deal with present theoretical and empirical work. The series is edited by Professor B. M. Foss. Each volume costs 6s.

Already available:

Assessment in Clinical Psychology C. E. Gathercole
The Beginnings of Modern Psychology W. M. O'Neil
Disorders of Memory and Learning George A. Talland
Pathology of Attention Andrew McGhie
Personal Relationship in Psychological Disorders Gordon R. Lowe
Psychometric Assessment of the Individual Child R. Douglass Savage
Teachers and Teaching A. Morrison and D. McIntyre

Forthcoming titles:

Feedback and Human Behaviour John Annett
On the Experience of Time Robert E. Ornstein
Selective Listening Neville Moray
Vigilance and Habituation Jane Mackworth